10/07

VIZ GRAPHIC NOVEL

THE RETURN OF LUM™
SWEET REVENGE

This volume contains THE RETURN OF LUM * URUSEI YATSURA #7 (second half), #8, and
THE RETURN OF LUM * URUSEI YATSURA PART TWO #1 through #5 in their entirety.

STORY AND ART BY
RUMIKO TAKAHASHI

English Adaptation/Gerard Jones & Mari Morimoto
Touch-Up Art & Lettering/Wayne Truman & Mary Kelleher
Cover Design/Viz Graphics
Editor/Annette Roman
Assistant Editor/Toshifumi Yoshida

Senior Editor/Trish Ledoux
Editor-in-Chief/Satoru Fujii
Publisher/Seiji Horibuchi
Director of Marketing/Dallas Middaugh
Assistant Sales Director/Denya Jur
Assistant Marketing Manager/Jaime Starling

Printed in Canada

Published by Viz Communications, Inc.
P.O. Box 77010 • San Francisco, CA 94107

10 9 8 7 6 5 4 3 2
First printing, December 1996
Second printing, February 2001

VIZ GRAPHIC NOVEL

THE RETURN OF LUM * URUSEI YATSURA™
SWEET REVENGE

STORY & ART BY
RUMIKO TAKAHASHI

CONTENTS

PART ONE
PRIVATE TUTOR

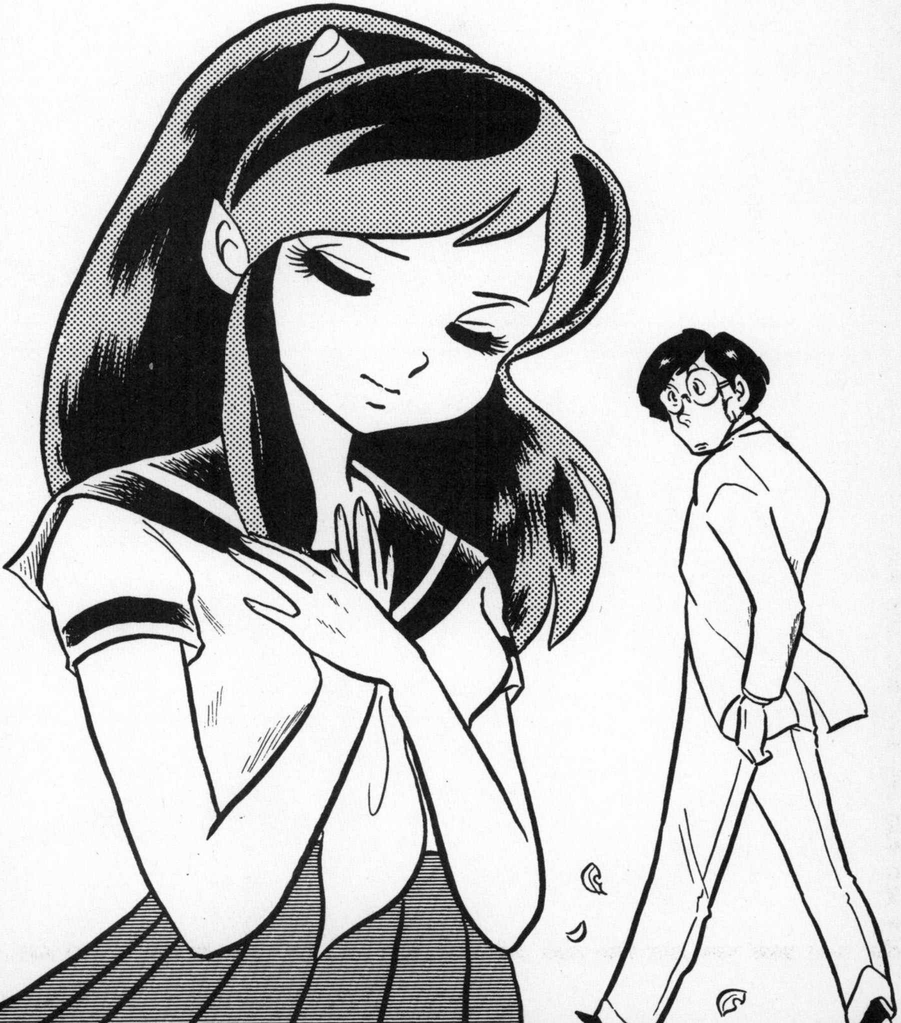

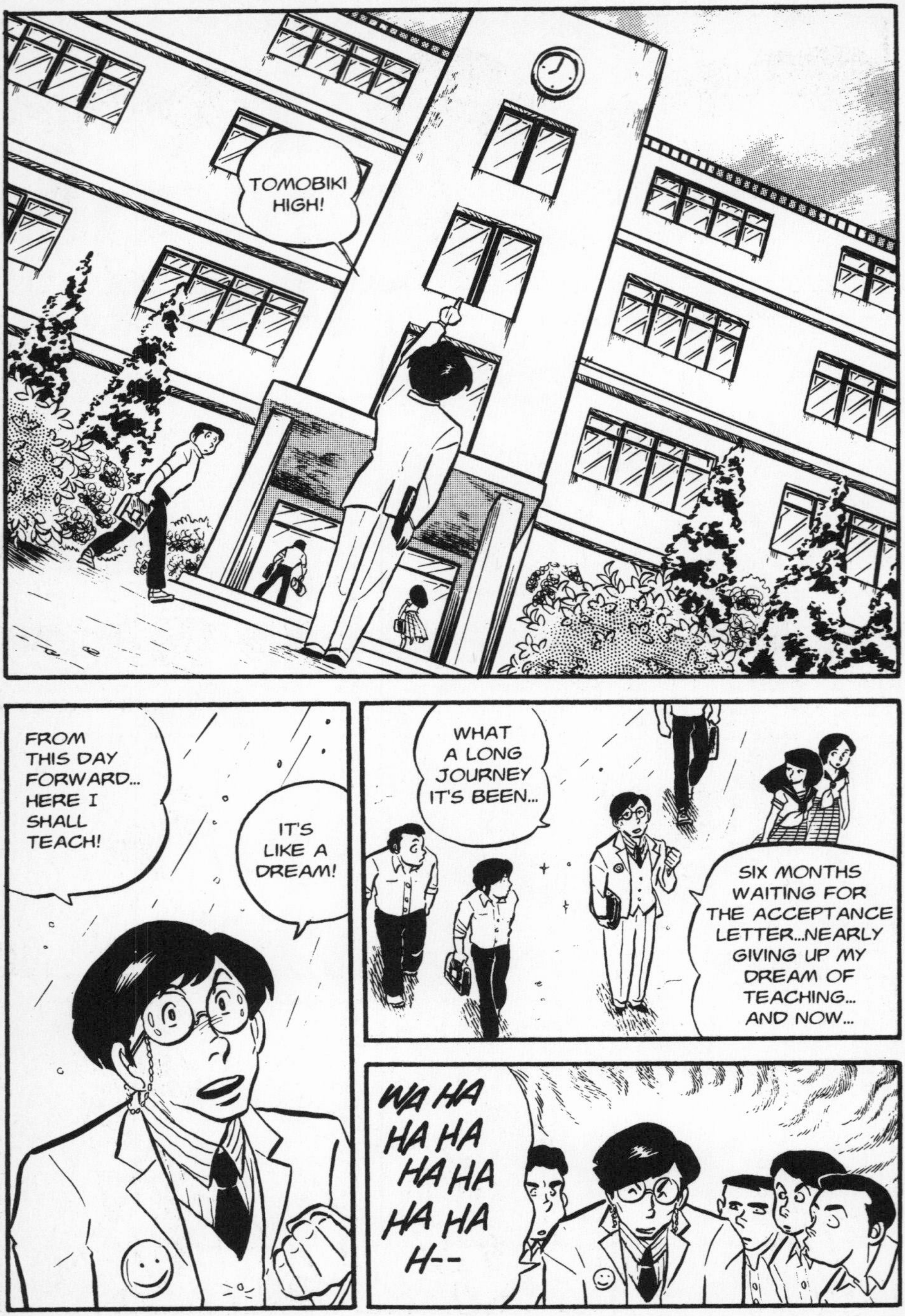
TOMOBIKI HIGH!
FROM THIS DAY FORWARD... HERE I SHALL TEACH!
IT'S LIKE A DREAM!
WHAT A LONG JOURNEY IT'S BEEN...
SIX MONTHS WAITING FOR THE ACCEPTANCE LETTER...NEARLY GIVING UP MY DREAM OF TEACHING... AND NOW...
WA HA HA HA HA HA HA HA H--

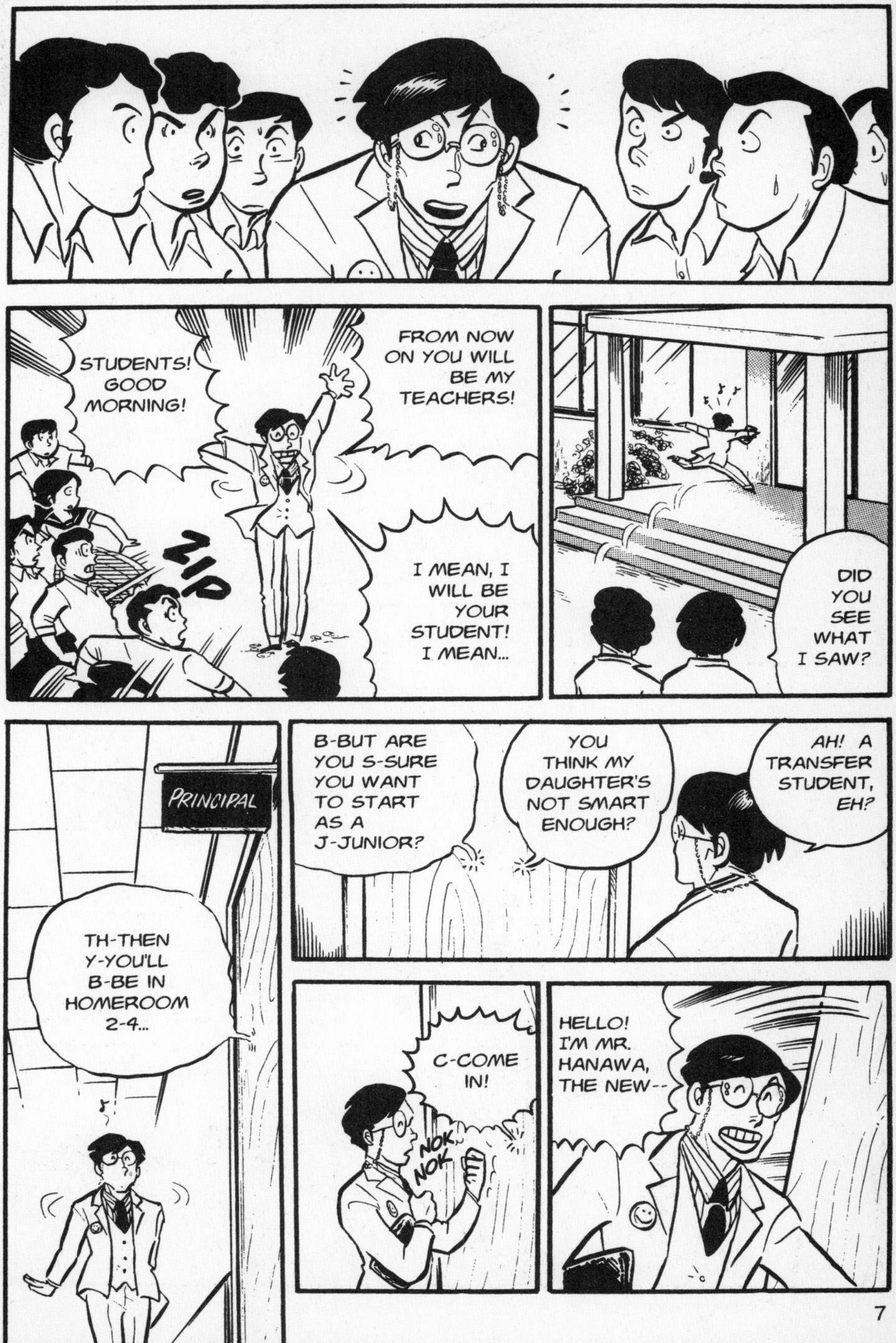
STUDENTS! GOOD MORNING!
FROM NOW ON YOU WILL BE MY TEACHERS!
ZIP
I MEAN, I WILL BE YOUR STUDENT! I MEAN...
DID YOU SEE WHAT I SAW?
PRINCIPAL
TH-THEN Y-YOU'LL B-BE IN HOMEROOM 2-4...
B-BUT ARE YOU S-SURE YOU WANT TO START AS A J-JUNIOR?
YOU THINK MY DAUGHTER'S NOT SMART ENOUGH?
AH! A TRANSFER STUDENT, EH?
C-COME IN!
NOK NOK
HELLO! I'M MR. HANAWA, THE NEW--

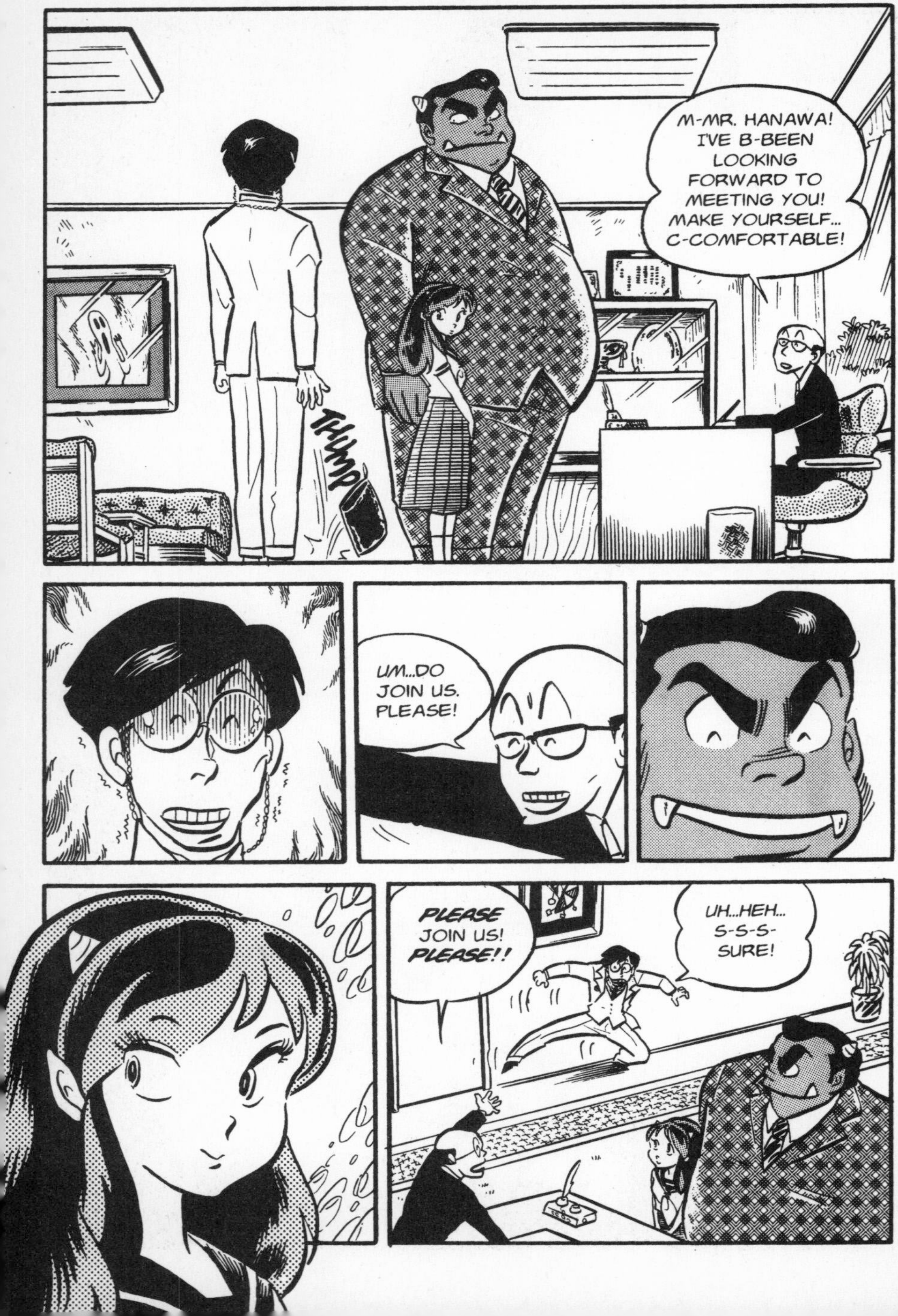
M-MR. HANAWA! I'VE B-BEEN LOOKING FORWARD TO MEETING YOU! MAKE YOURSELF... C-COMFORTABLE!
THUMP
UM...DO JOIN US. PLEASE!
PLEASE JOIN US! PLEASE!!
UH...HEH... S-S-S-SURE!

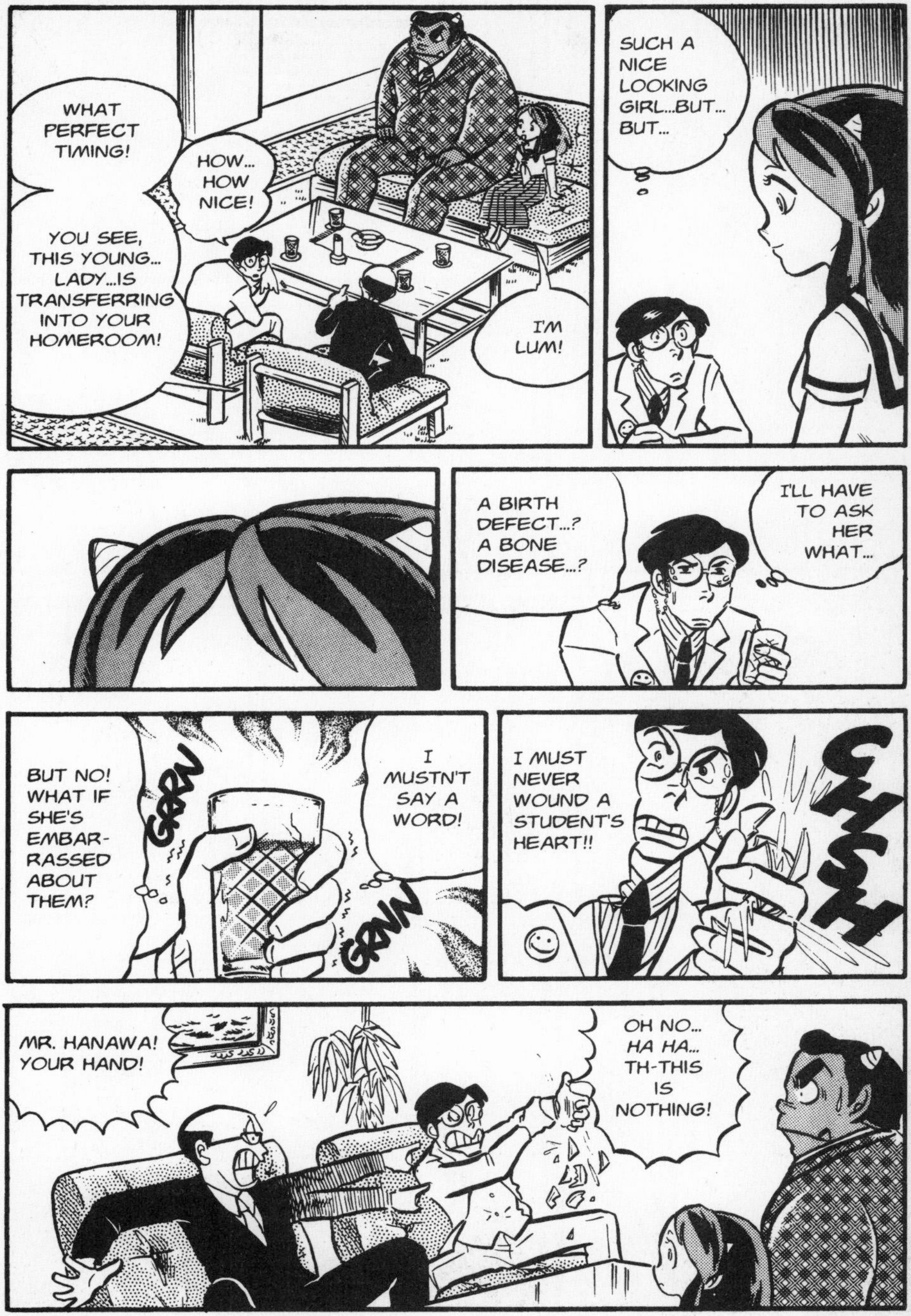
WHAT PERFECT TIMING!
YOU SEE, THIS YOUNG... LADY...IS TRANSFERRING INTO YOUR HOMEROOM!
HOW... HOW NICE!
I'M LUM!
SUCH A NICE LOOKING GIRL...BUT... BUT...
A BIRTH DEFECT...? A BONE DISEASE...?
I'LL HAVE TO ASK HER WHAT...
BUT NO! WHAT IF SHE'S EMBAR-RASSED ABOUT THEM?
GRRN
I MUSTN'T SAY A WORD!
GRNN
I MUST NEVER WOUND A STUDENT'S HEART!!
CHSH
MR. HANAWA! YOUR HAND!
OH NO... HA HA... TH-THIS IS NOTHING!

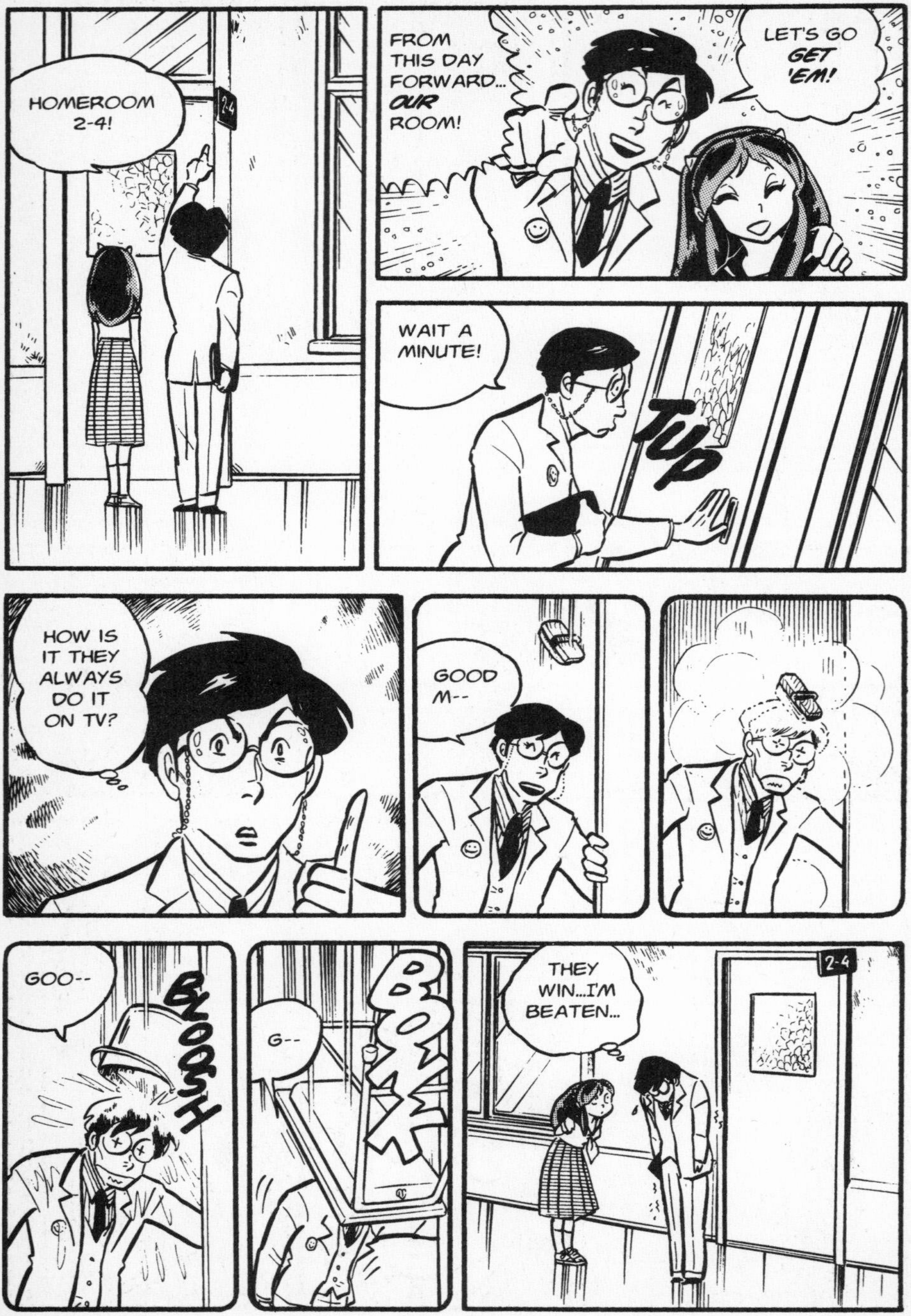
HOMEROOM 2-4!
2-4
FROM THIS DAY FORWARD... OUR ROOM!
LET'S GO GET 'EM!
WAIT A MINUTE!
TUP
HOW IS IT THEY ALWAYS DO IT ON TV?
GOOD M--
GOO--
BLOOSH
G--
BOOM
THEY WIN...I'M BEATEN...
2-4

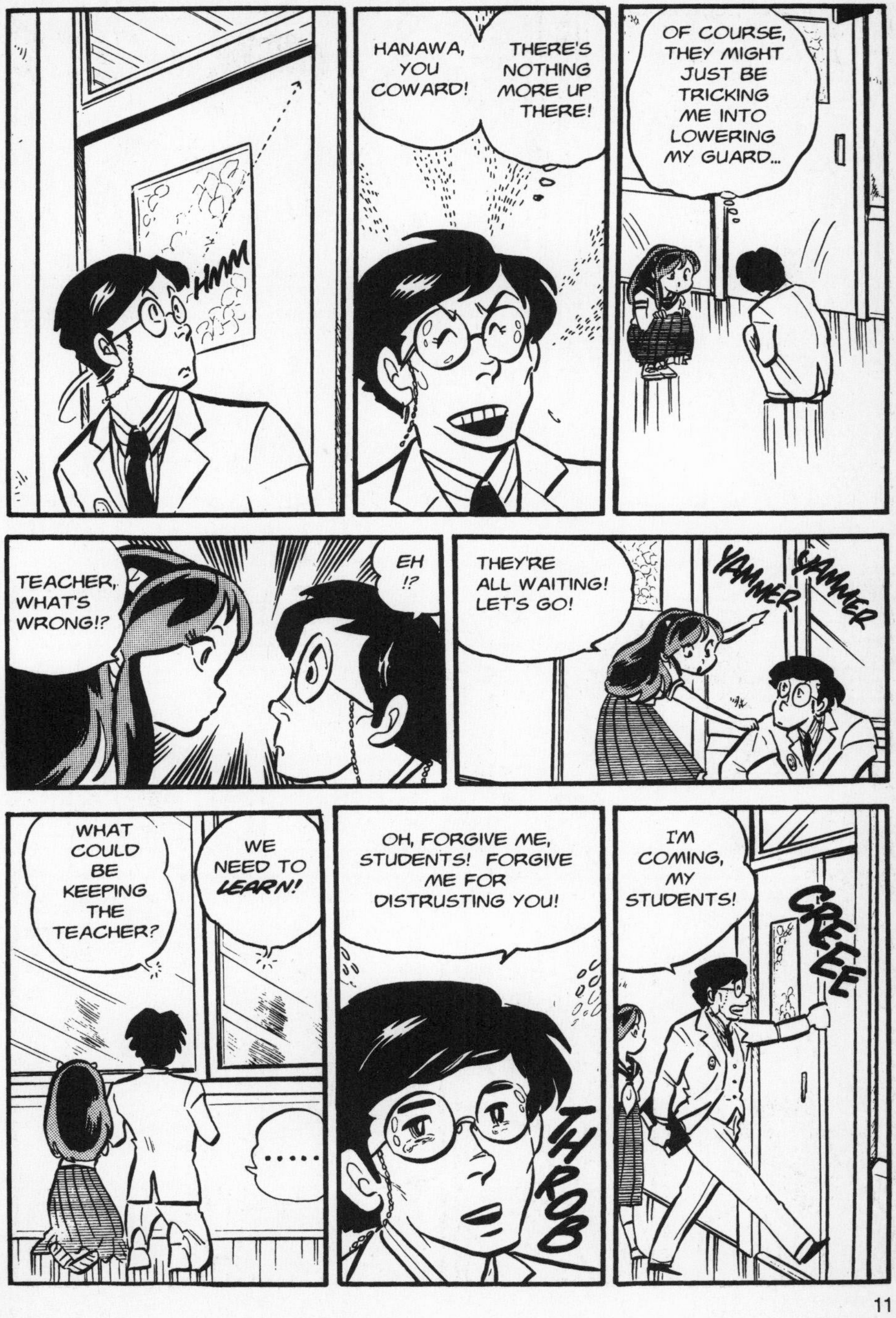
HMM
HANAWA, YOU COWARD!
THERE'S NOTHING MORE UP THERE!
OF COURSE, THEY MIGHT JUST BE TRICKING ME INTO LOWERING MY GUARD...
TEACHER, WHAT'S WRONG!?
EH !?
THEY'RE ALL WAITING! LET'S GO!
YAMMER
YAMMER
WHAT COULD BE KEEPING THE TEACHER?
WE NEED TO LEARN!
......
OH, FORGIVE ME, STUDENTS! FORGIVE ME FOR DISTRUSTING YOU!
THROB
I'M COMING, MY STUDENTS!
CREEE

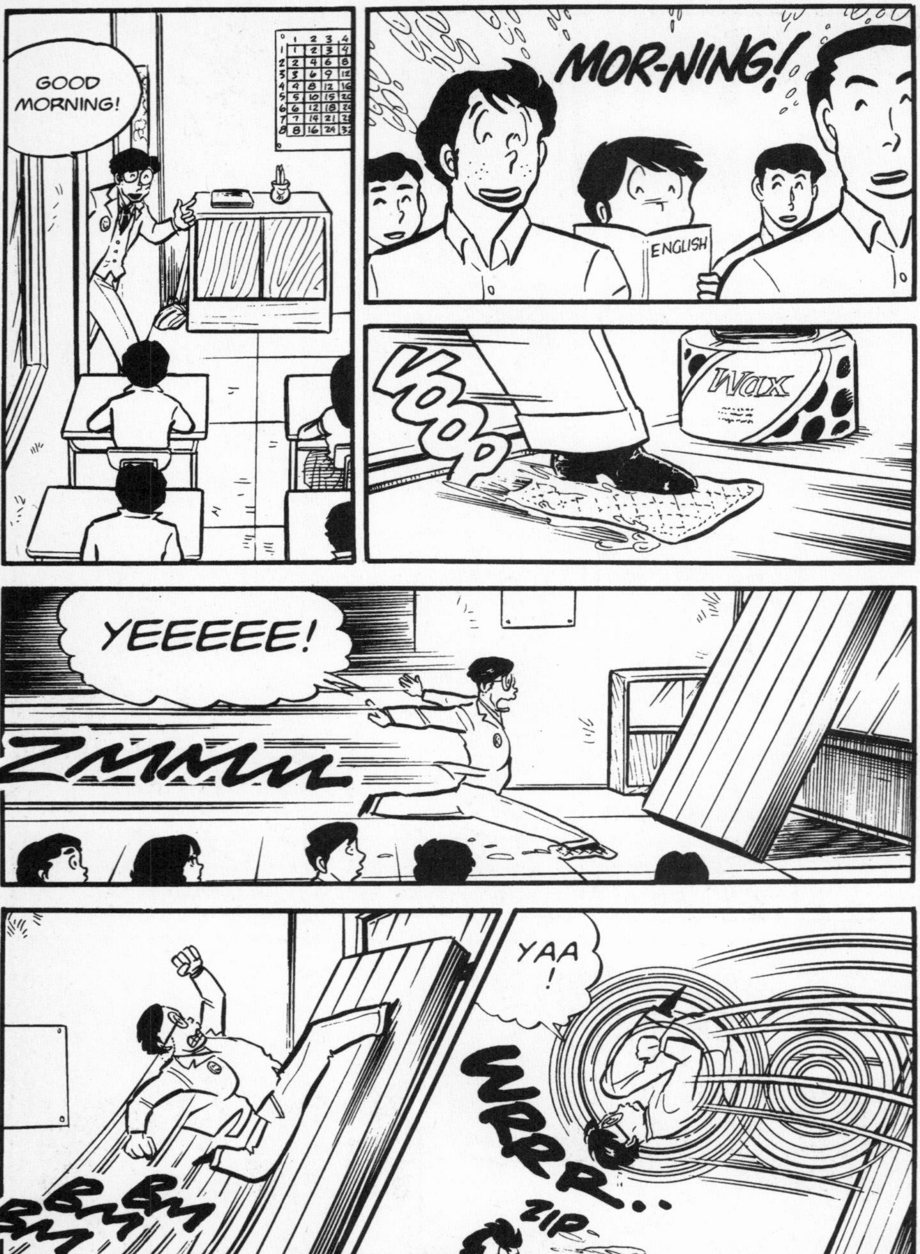
GOOD MORNING!
MOR-NING!
ENGLISH
Wax
VOOOP
YEEEEEE!
ZMMMM
YAA!
WRRR...
BM BM BM
ZIP

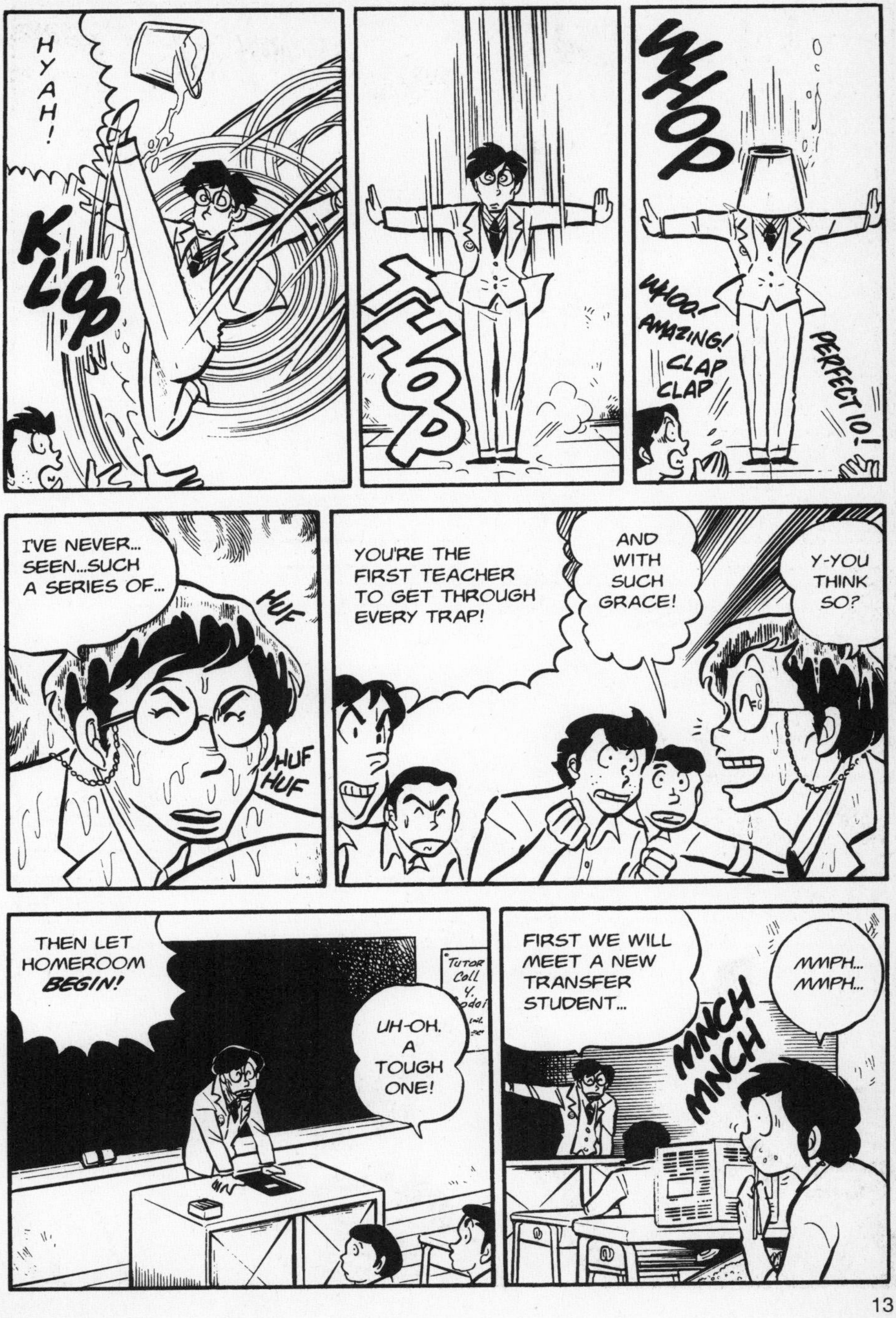
HYAH!
KLOP
THOP
WHOP
WHOA-
AMAZING!
CLAP
CLAP
PERFECT 10!
I'VE NEVER... SEEN...SUCH A SERIES OF...
HUF
HUF HUF
YOU'RE THE FIRST TEACHER TO GET THROUGH EVERY TRAP!
AND WITH SUCH GRACE!
Y-YOU THINK SO?
THEN LET HOMEROOM BEGIN!
UH-OH. A TOUGH ONE!
FIRST WE WILL MEET A NEW TRANSFER STUDENT...
MNCH MNCH
MMPH... MMPH...

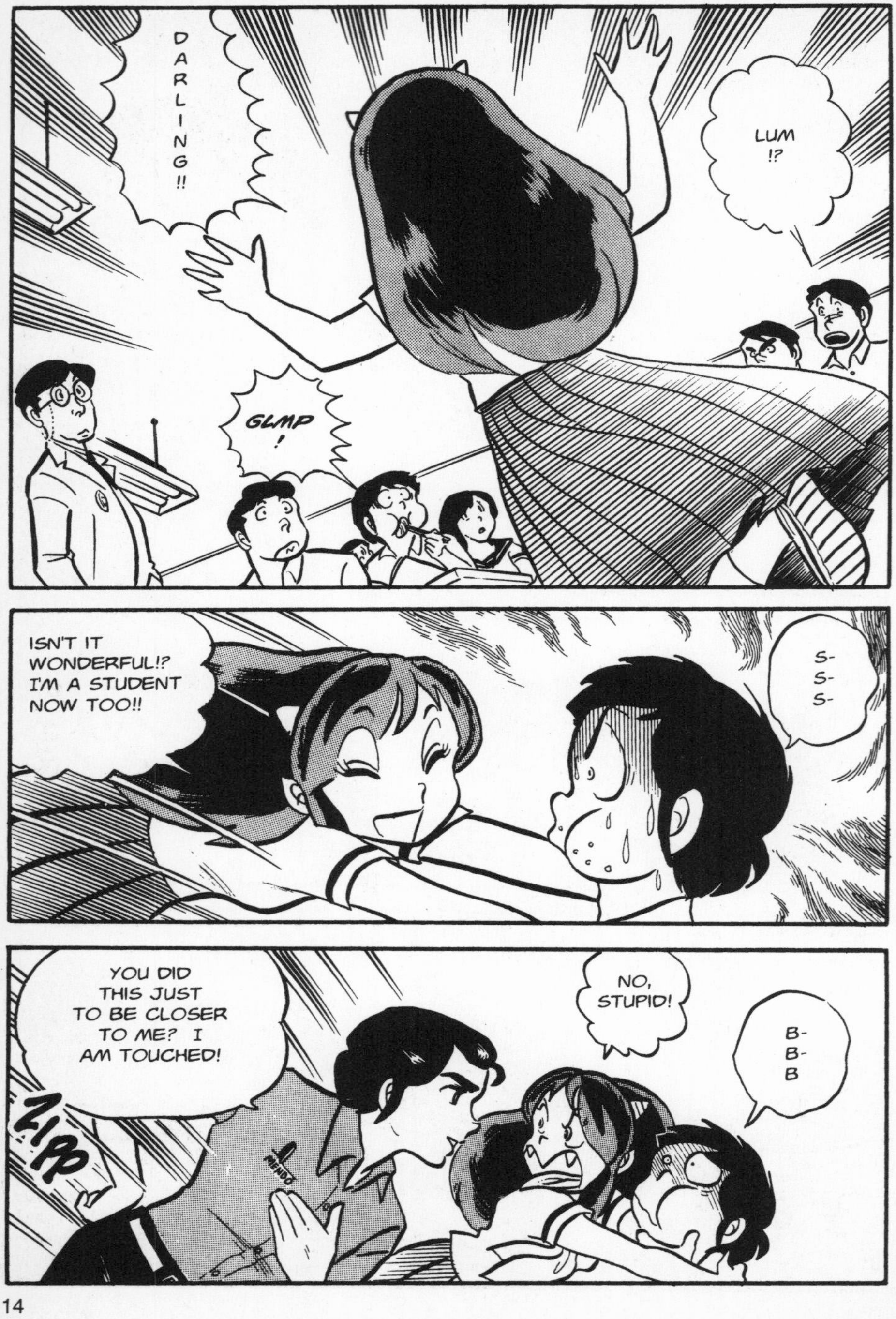
DARLING!!
LUM !?
GLMP !
ISN'T IT WONDERFUL!? I'M A STUDENT NOW TOO!!
S- S- S-
YOU DID THIS JUST TO BE CLOSER TO ME? I AM TOUCHED!
NO, STUPID!
ZIPP
B- B- B

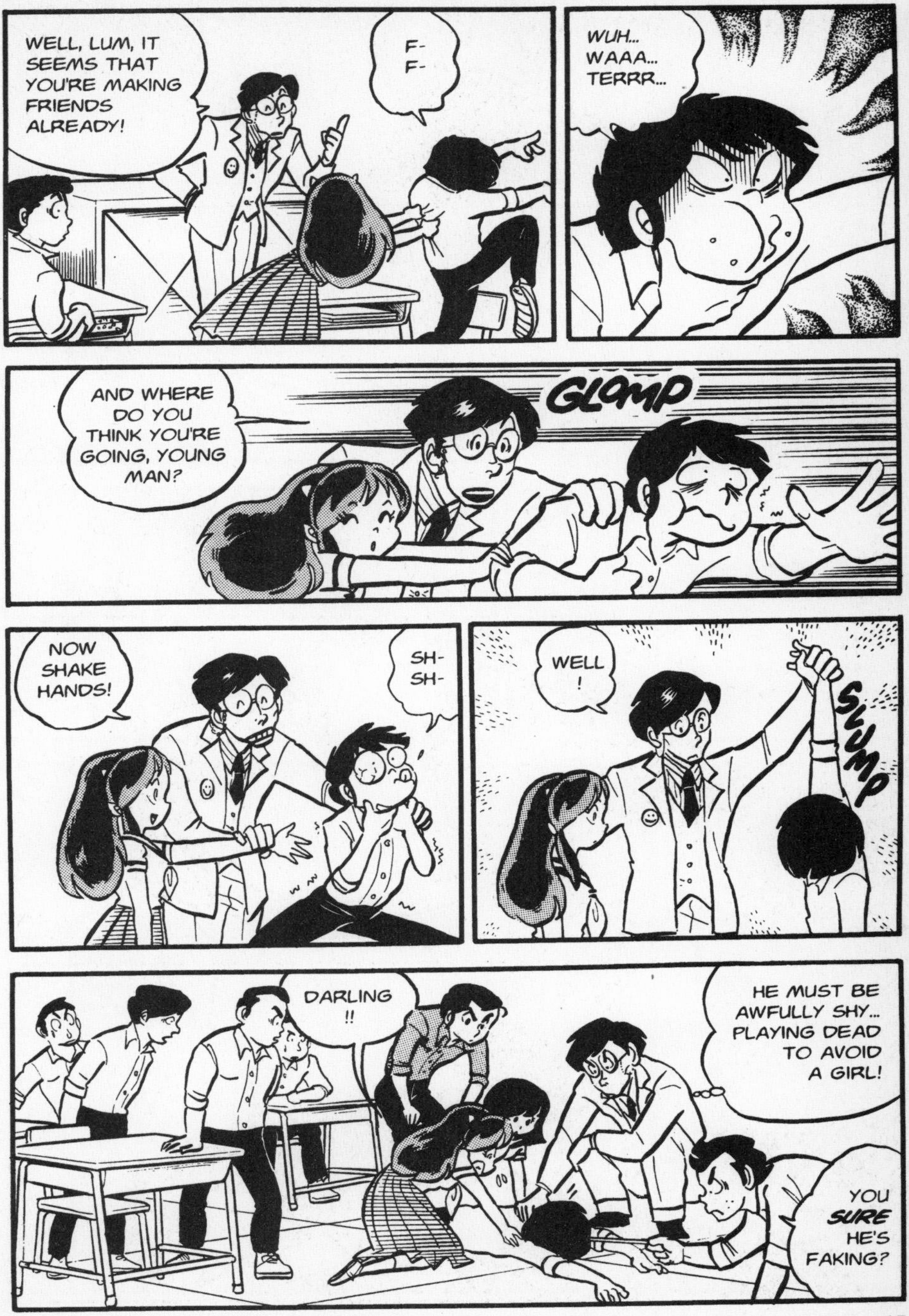
WELL, LUM, IT SEEMS THAT YOU'RE MAKING FRIENDS ALREADY!
F- F-
WUH... WAAA... TERRR...
AND WHERE DO YOU THINK YOU'RE GOING, YOUNG MAN?
GLOMP
NOW SHAKE HANDS!
SH- SH-
WELL !
SLUMP
DARLING !!
HE MUST BE AWFULLY SHY... PLAYING DEAD TO AVOID A GIRL!
YOU **SURE** HE'S FAKING?

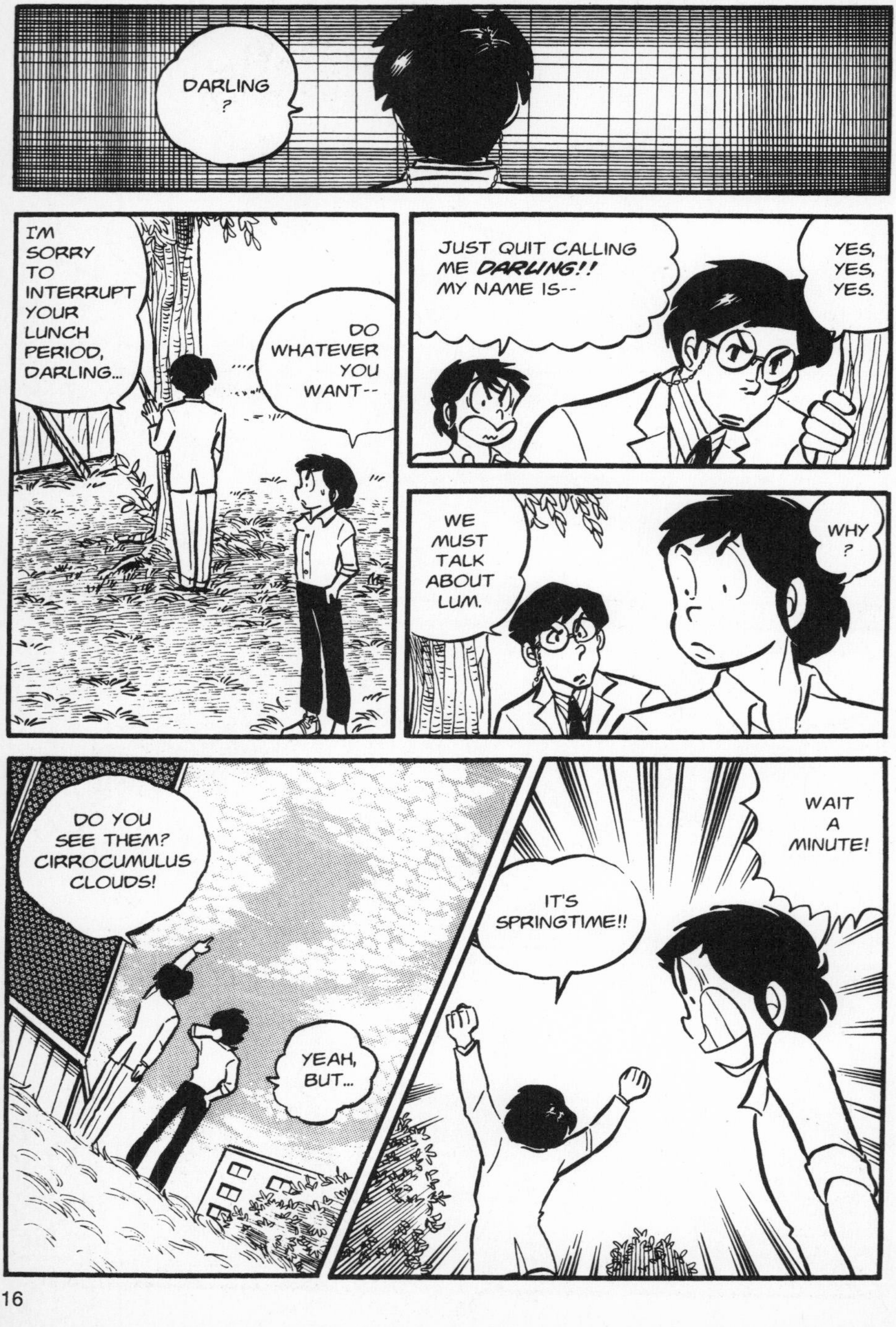
DARLING ?
I'M SORRY TO INTERRUPT YOUR LUNCH PERIOD, DARLING...
...
DO WHATEVER YOU WANT--
JUST QUIT CALLING ME DARLING!! MY NAME IS--
YES, YES, YES.
WE MUST TALK ABOUT LUM.
WHY ?
DO YOU SEE THEM? CIRROCUMULUS CLOUDS!
YEAH, BUT...
WAIT A MINUTE!
IT'S SPRINGTIME!!

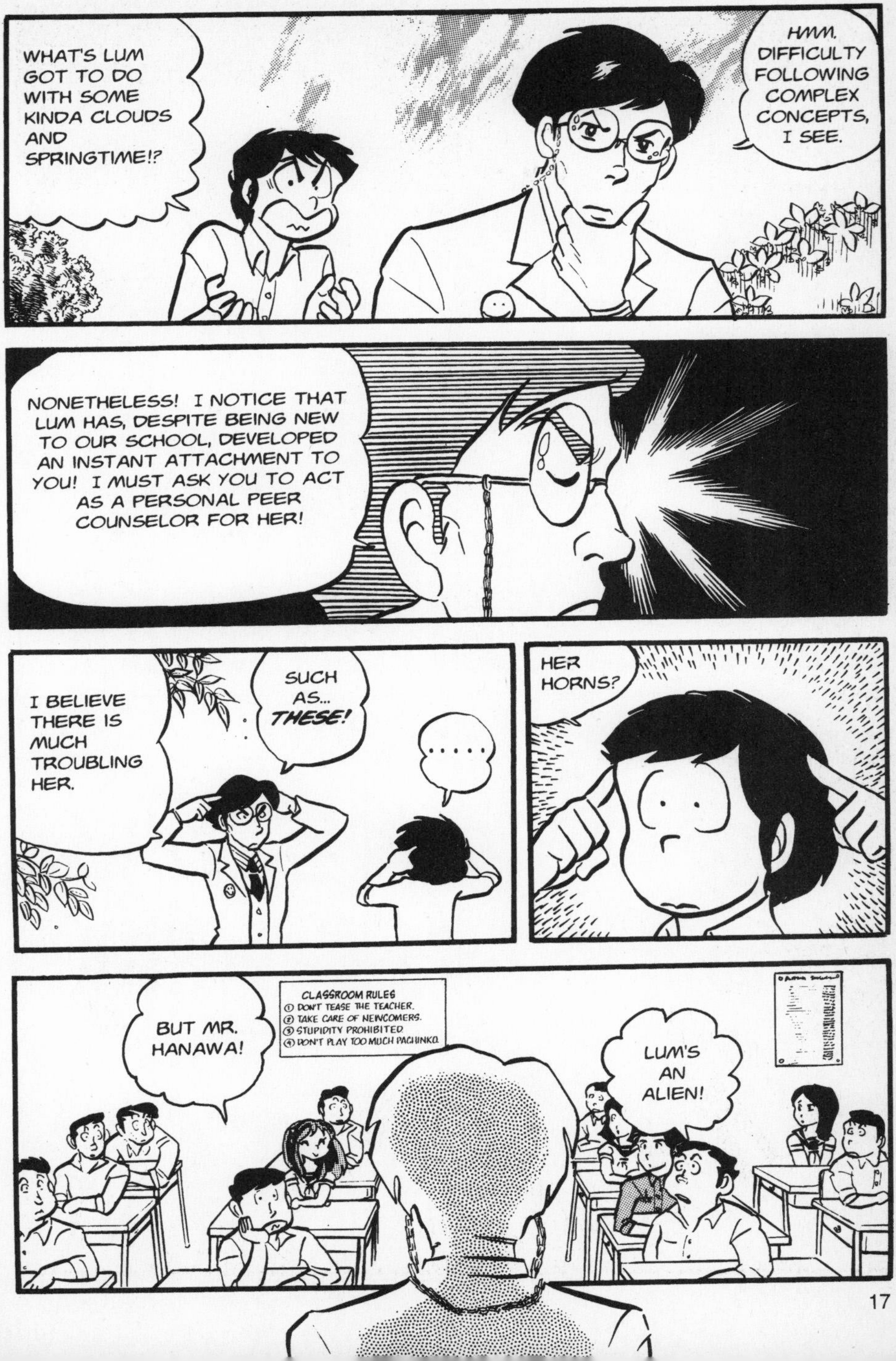
WHAT'S LUM GOT TO DO WITH SOME KINDA CLOUDS AND SPRINGTIME!?
HMM. DIFFICULTY FOLLOWING COMPLEX CONCEPTS, I SEE.
NONETHELESS! I NOTICE THAT LUM HAS, DESPITE BEING NEW TO OUR SCHOOL, DEVELOPED AN INSTANT ATTACHMENT TO YOU! I MUST ASK YOU TO ACT AS A PERSONAL PEER COUNSELOR FOR HER!
I BELIEVE THERE IS MUCH TROUBLING HER.
SUCH AS... THESE!
.....
HER HORNS?
BUT MR. HANAWA!
CLASSROOM RULES
① DON'T TEASE THE TEACHER.
② TAKE CARE OF NEWCOMERS.
③ STUPIDITY PROHIBITED.
④ DON'T PLAY TOO MUCH PACHINKO.
LUM'S AN ALIEN!

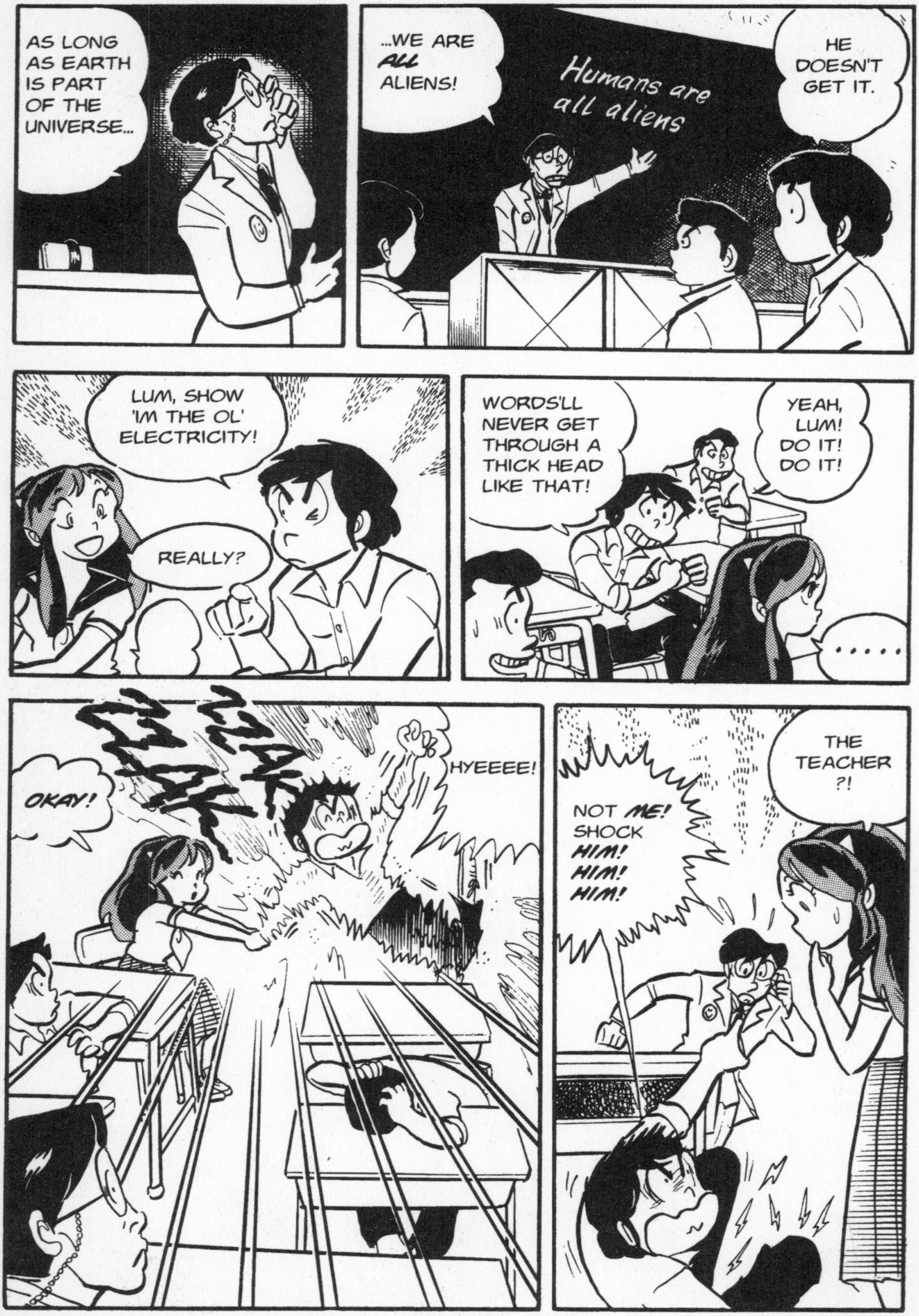
AS LONG AS EARTH IS PART OF THE UNIVERSE...
...WE ARE ALL ALIENS!
Humans are all aliens
HE DOESN'T GET IT.
LUM, SHOW 'IM THE OL' ELECTRICITY!
REALLY?
WORDS'LL NEVER GET THROUGH A THICK HEAD LIKE THAT!
YEAH, LUM! DO IT! DO IT!
.....
OKAY!
ZZAK
ZZAK
HYEEEE!
NOT ME! SHOCK HIM! HIM! HIM!
THE TEACHER ?!

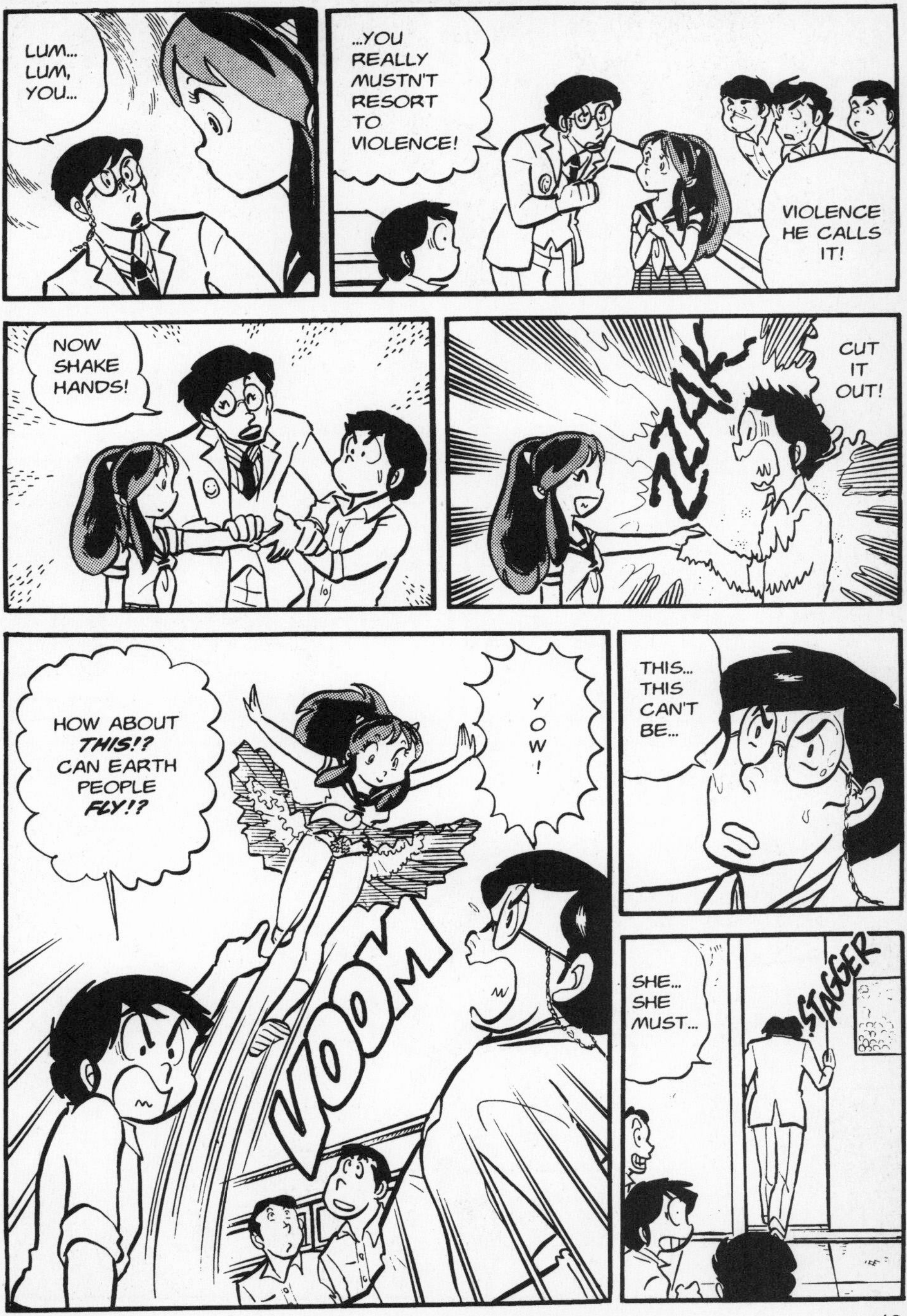
LUM... LUM, YOU...
...YOU REALLY MUSTN'T RESORT TO VIOLENCE!
VIOLENCE HE CALLS IT!
NOW SHAKE HANDS!
ZZAK
CUT IT OUT!
HOW ABOUT *THIS!?* CAN EARTH PEOPLE *FLY!?*
YOW!
VOOM
THIS... THIS CAN'T BE...
SHE... SHE MUST...
STAGGER

SIMMS LIBRARY
ALBUQUERQUE ACADEMY

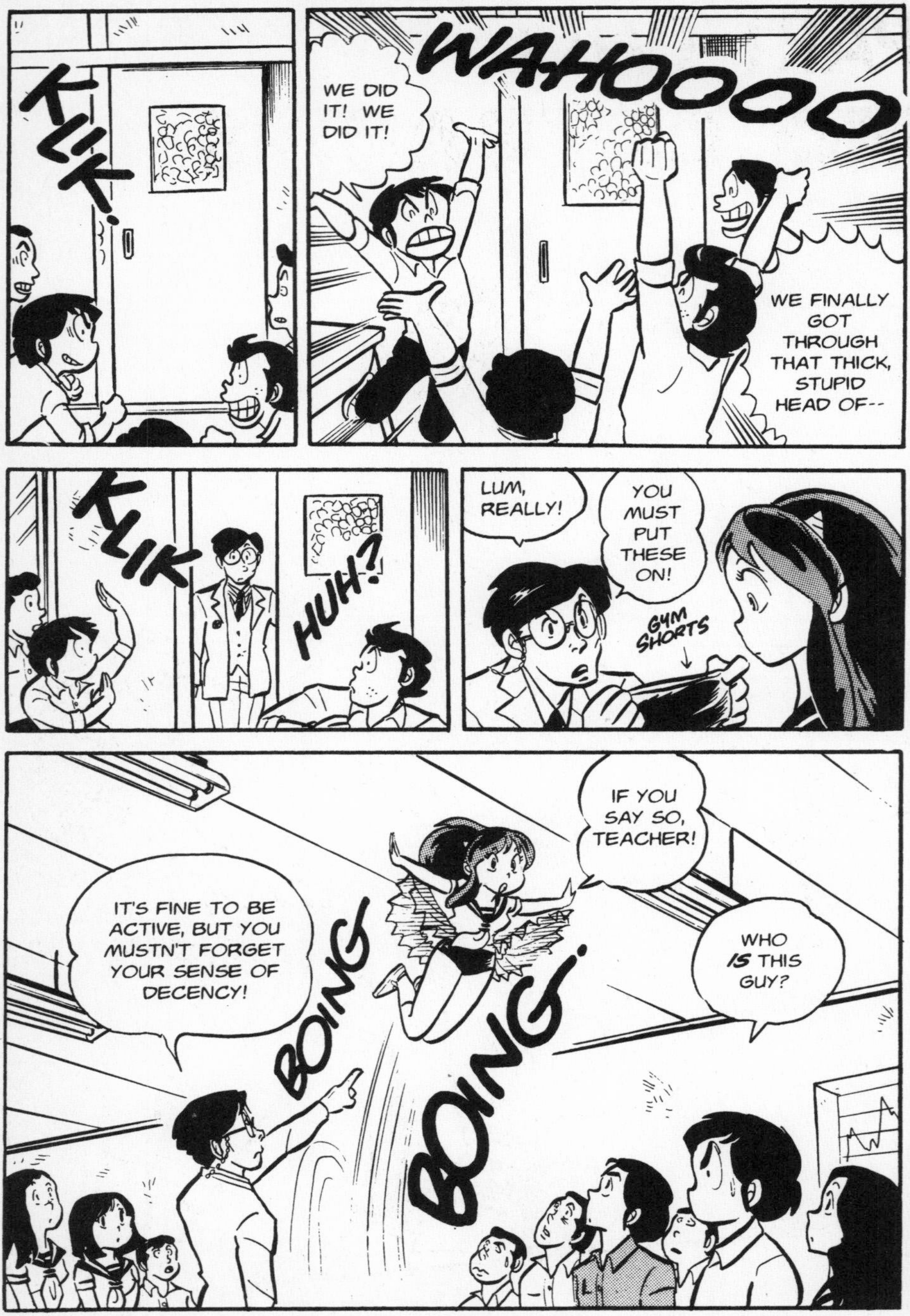

KLIK!
WE DID IT! WE DID IT!
WAHOOOOO
WE FINALLY GOT THROUGH THAT THICK, STUPID HEAD OF--
KLIK
HUH?
LUM, REALLY!
YOU MUST PUT THESE ON!
GYM SHORTS
IF YOU SAY SO, TEACHER!
IT'S FINE TO BE ACTIVE, BUT YOU MUSTN'T FORGET YOUR SENSE OF DECENCY!
BOING
BOING
BOING
WHO IS THIS GUY?

PART TWO
NO CRYBABIES

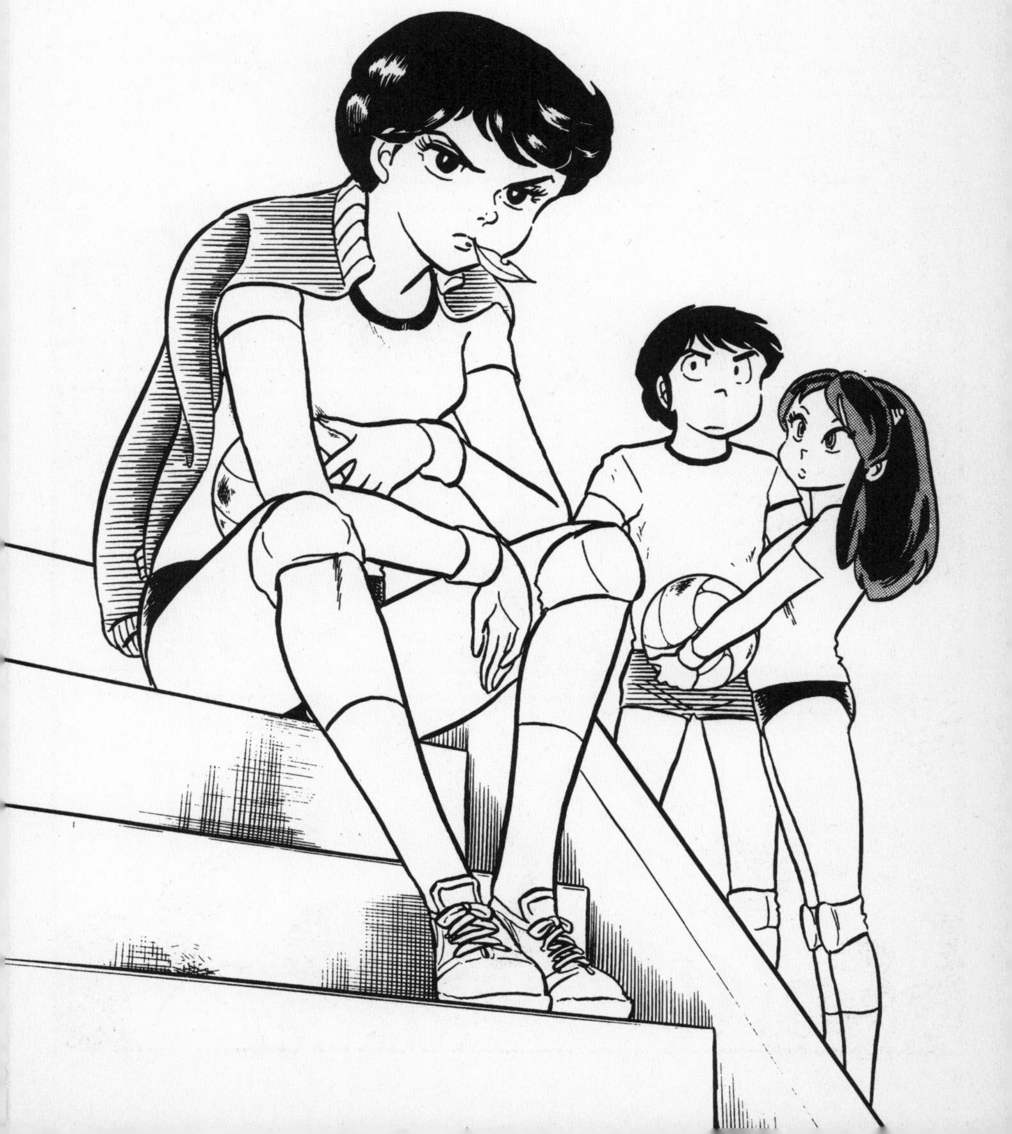

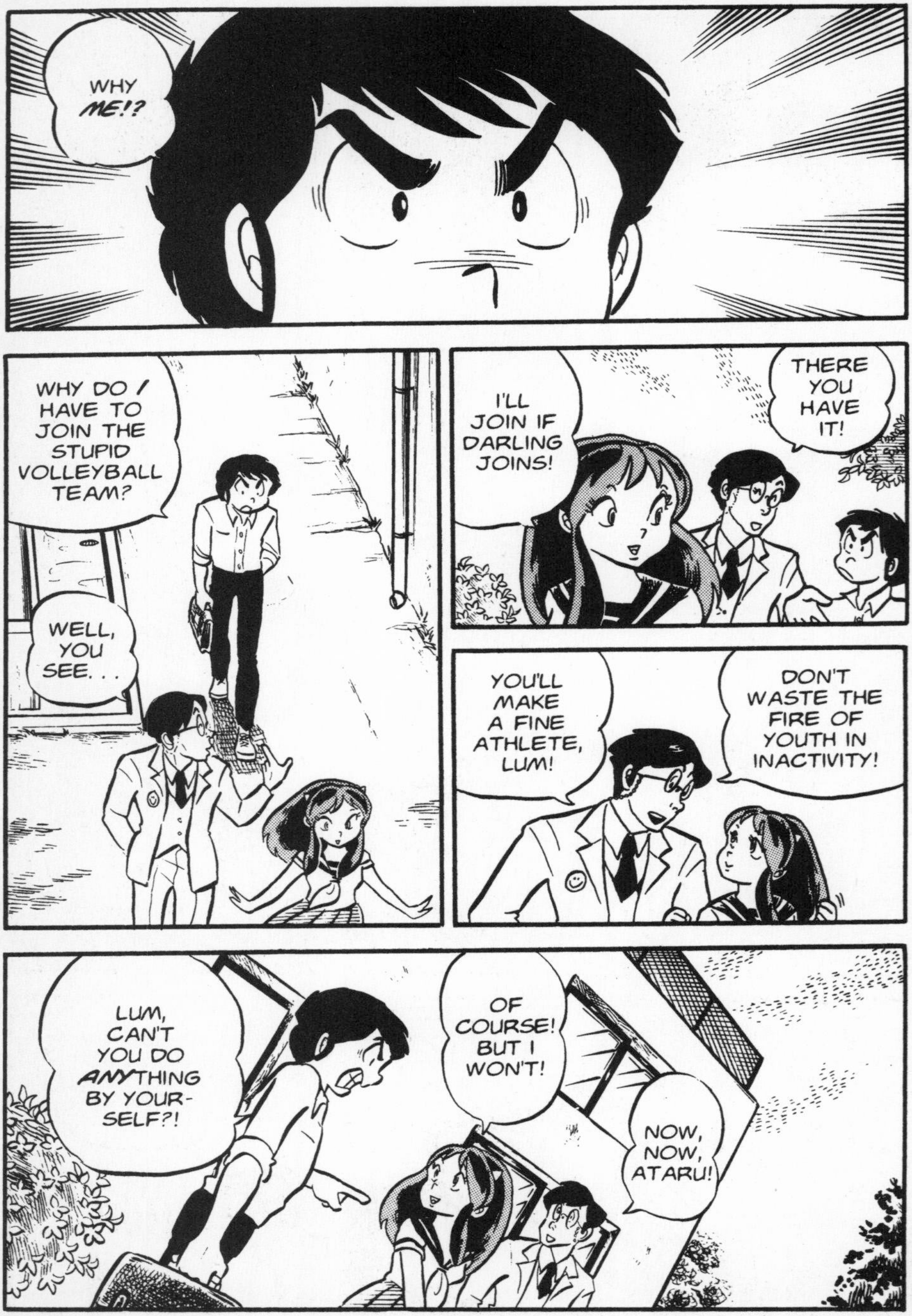
WHY *ME!?*
WHY DO *I* HAVE TO JOIN THE STUPID VOLLEYBALL TEAM?
WELL, YOU SEE. . .
I'LL JOIN IF DARLING JOINS!
THERE YOU HAVE IT!
YOU'LL MAKE A FINE ATHLETE, LUM!
DON'T WASTE THE FIRE OF YOUTH IN INACTIVITY!
LUM, CAN'T YOU DO *ANY*THING BY YOUR-SELF?!
OF COURSE! BUT I WON'T!
NOW, NOW, ATARU!

IT'S AUTUMN!

SO?

IT'S THE SEASON FOR SPORTS!

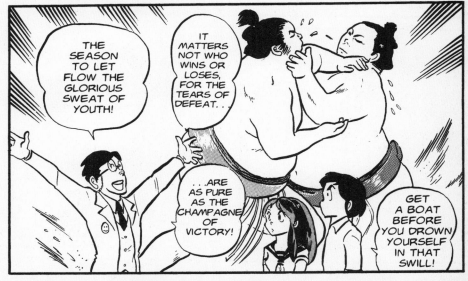

THE SEASON TO LET FLOW THE GLORIOUS SWEAT OF YOUTH!

IT MATTERS NOT WHO WINS OR LOSES, FOR THE TEARS OF DEFEAT...

...ARE AS PURE AS THE CHAMPAGNE OF VICTORY!

GET A BOAT BEFORE YOU DROWN YOURSELF IN THAT SWILL!

LOOK, HE'S GOT MY EARS SWIMMING FOR THEIR LIVES!

YOU MON-KEY!

LOOK! IT'S THE VOLLEYBALL TEAM!

HUP HUP

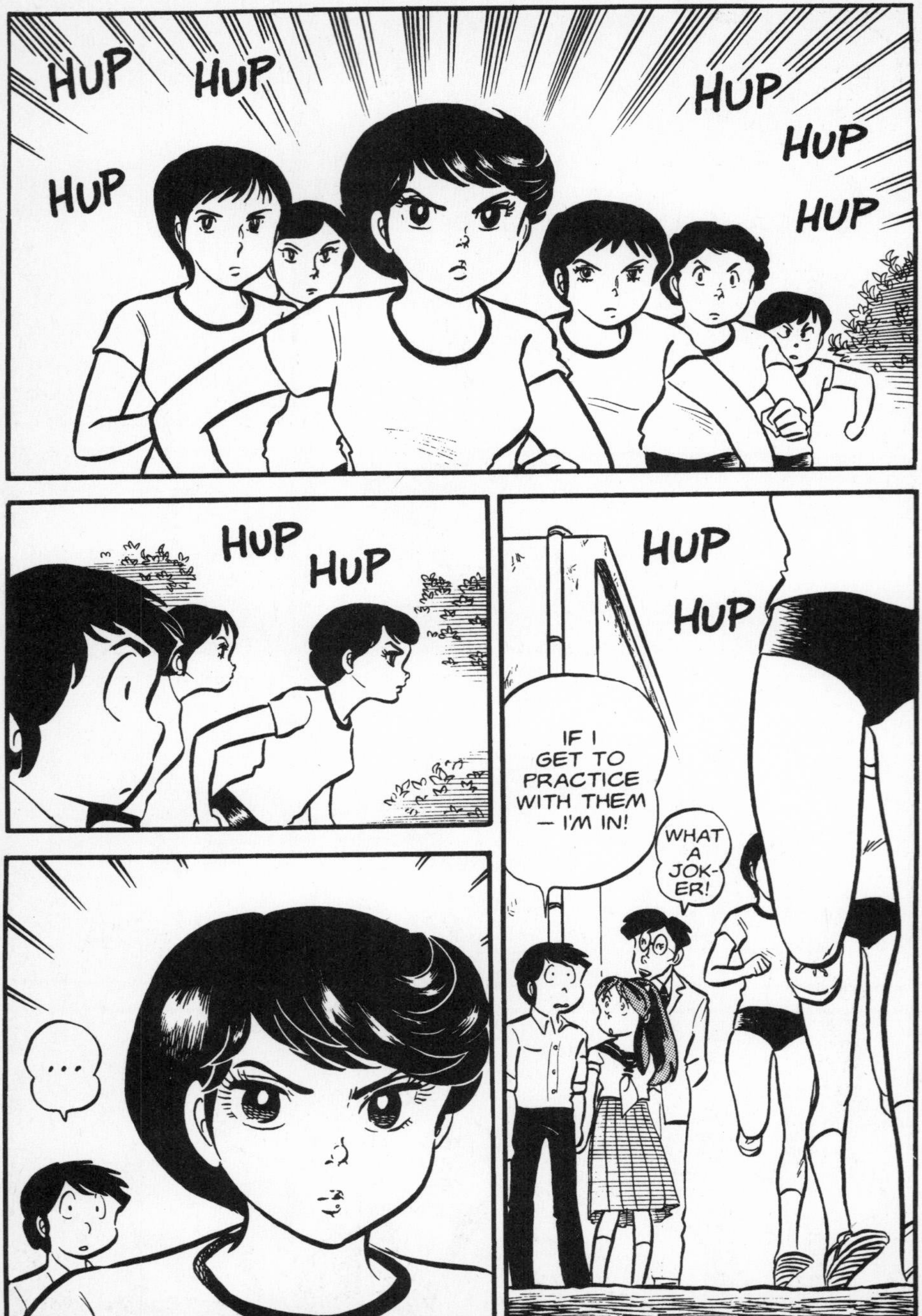
HUP
HUP
HUP
HUP
HUP
HUP
HUP
HUP
...
HUP
HUP
IF I GET TO PRACTICE WITH THEM — I'M IN!
WHAT A JOK-ER!

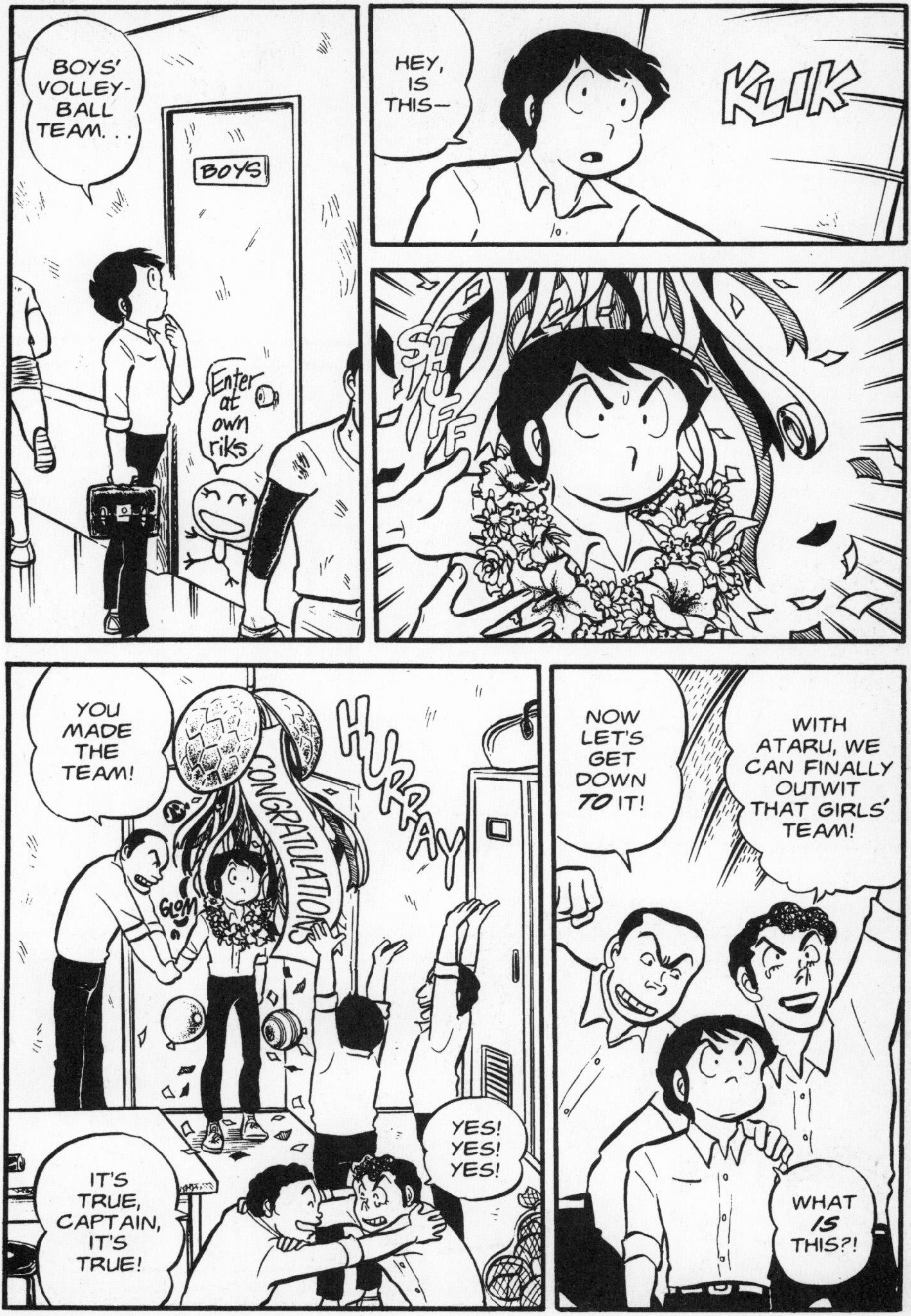

BOYS' VOLLEY-BALL TEAM. . .
BOYS
Enter at own riks
HEY, IS THIS—
KLIK
SHUFF
YOU MADE THE TEAM!
CONGRATULATIONS
HURRAY
GLOM
IT'S TRUE, CAPTAIN, IT'S TRUE!
YES! YES! YES!
NOW LET'S GET DOWN *TO* IT!
WITH ATARU, WE CAN FINALLY OUTWIT THAT GIRLS' TEAM!
WHAT *IS* THIS?!

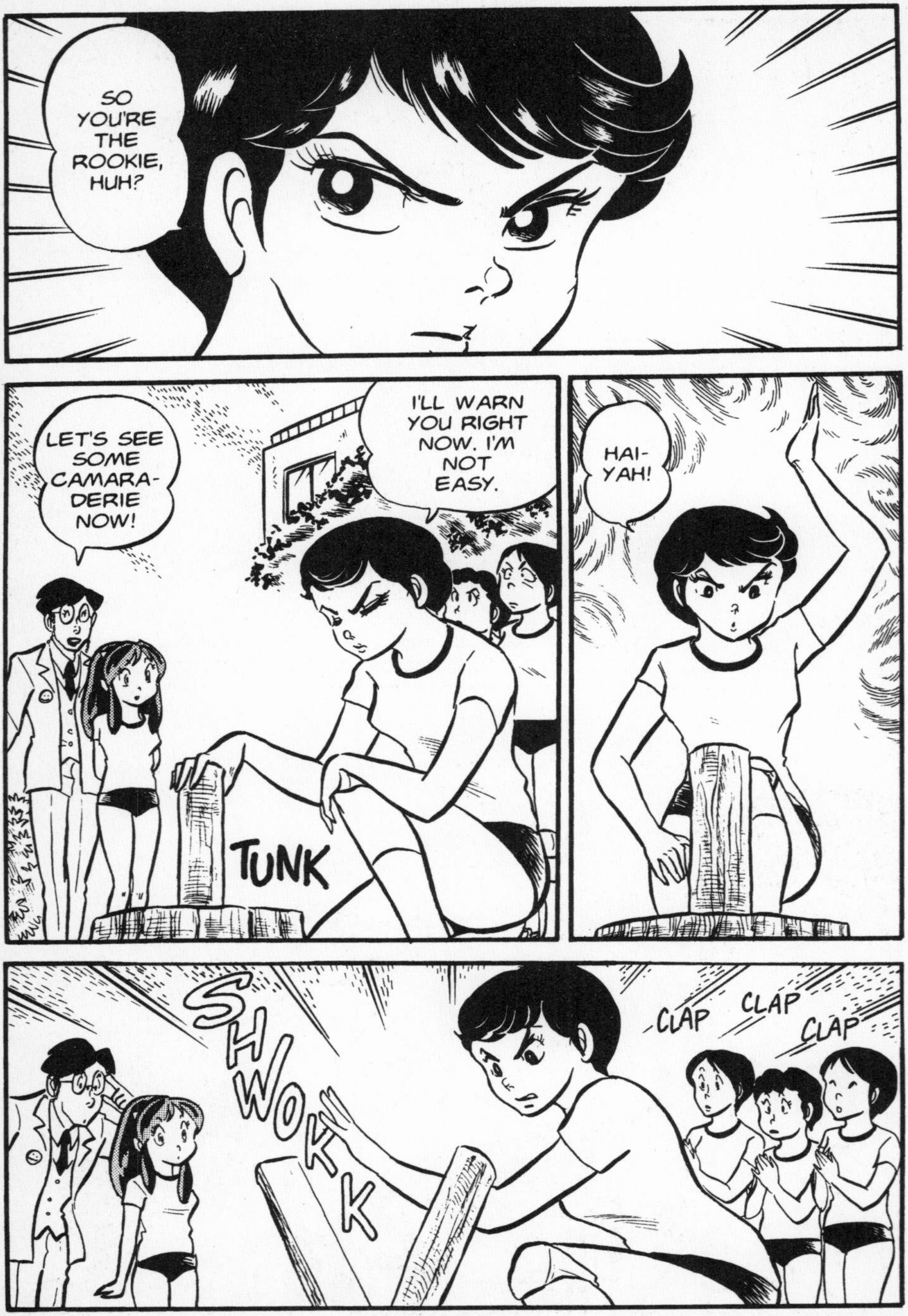
SO YOU'RE THE ROOKIE, HUH?
LET'S SEE SOME CAMARADERIE NOW!
I'LL WARN YOU RIGHT NOW. I'M NOT EASY.
TUNK
HAI-YAH!
SHWOKK
CLAP CLAP CLAP

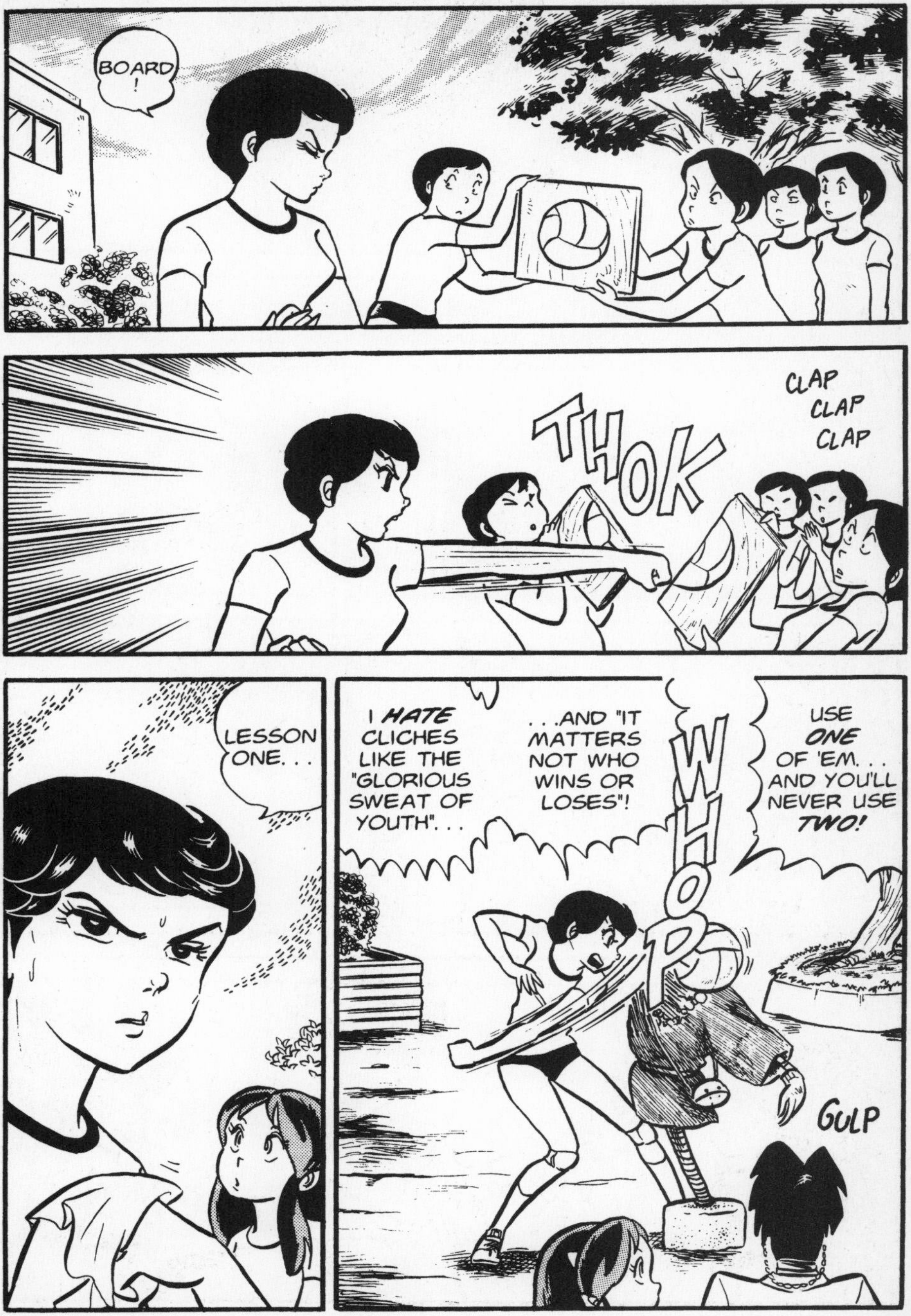

BOARD!
THOK
CLAP CLAP CLAP
LESSON ONE. . .
I HATE CLICHES LIKE THE "GLORIOUS SWEAT OF YOUTH". . .
. . .AND "IT MATTERS NOT WHO WINS OR LOSES"!
WHOP
USE ONE OF 'EM. . . AND YOU'LL NEVER USE TWO!
GULP

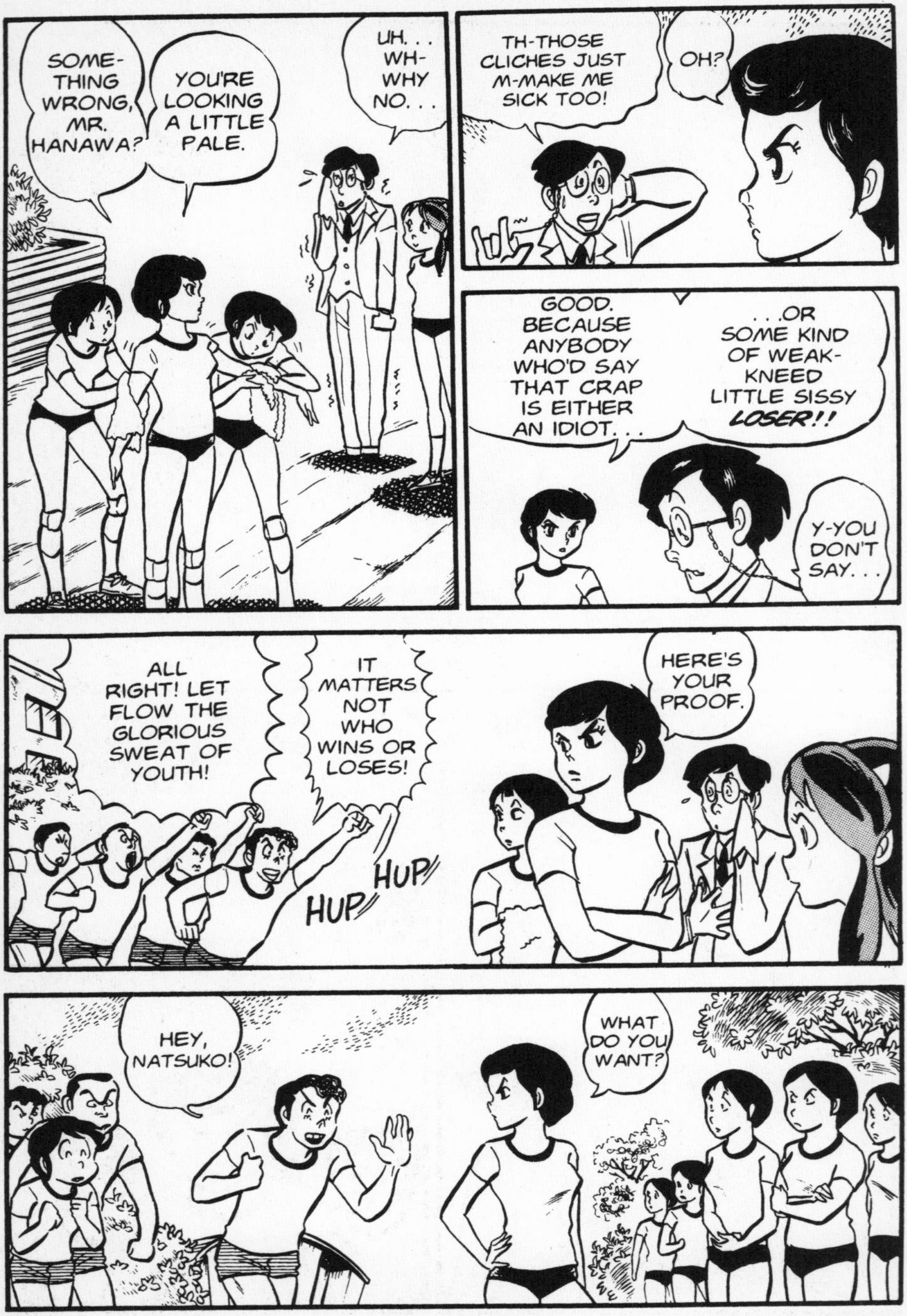
SOME-THING WRONG, MR. HANAWA?
YOU'RE LOOKING A LITTLE PALE.
UH. . . WH- WHY NO. . .
TH-THOSE CLICHES JUST M-MAKE ME SICK TOO!
OH?
GOOD. BECAUSE ANYBODY WHO'D SAY THAT CRAP IS EITHER AN IDIOT. . .
. . .OR SOME KIND OF WEAK-KNEED LITTLE SISSY LOSER!!
Y-YOU DON'T SAY. . .
ALL RIGHT! LET FLOW THE GLORIOUS SWEAT OF YOUTH!
IT MATTERS NOT WHO WINS OR LOSES!
HUP
HUP
HERE'S YOUR PROOF.
HEY, NATSUKO!
WHAT DO YOU WANT?

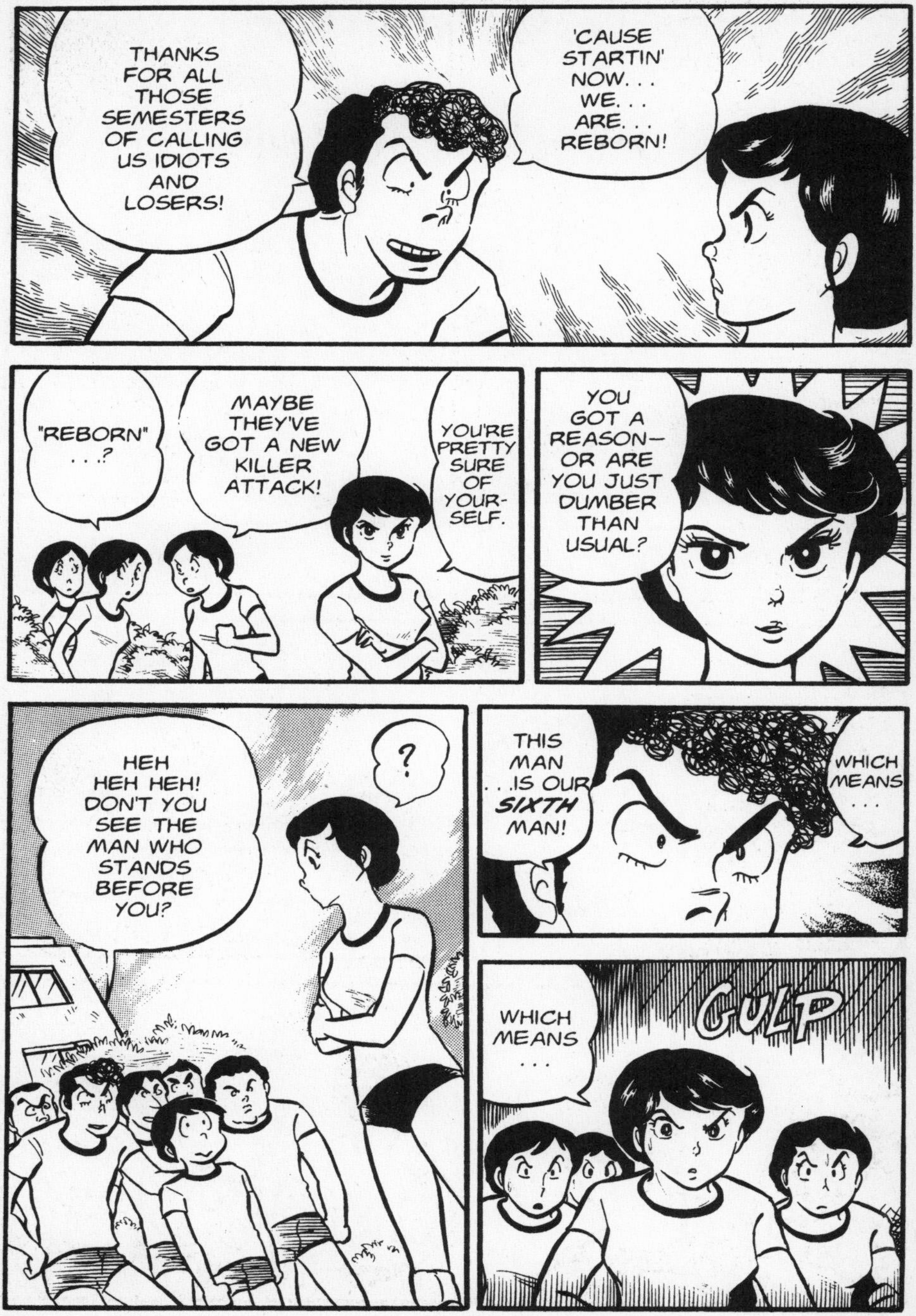
THANKS FOR ALL THOSE SEMESTERS OF CALLING US IDIOTS AND LOSERS!
'CAUSE STARTIN' NOW. . . WE. . . ARE. . . REBORN!
"REBORN" . . .?
MAYBE THEY'VE GOT A NEW KILLER ATTACK!
YOU'RE PRETTY SURE OF YOUR-SELF.
YOU GOT A REASON— OR ARE YOU JUST DUMBER THAN USUAL?
HEH HEH HEH! DON'T YOU SEE THE MAN WHO STANDS BEFORE YOU?
?
THIS MAN . . .IS OUR SIXTH MAN!
WHICH MEANS . . .
WHICH MEANS . . .
GULP

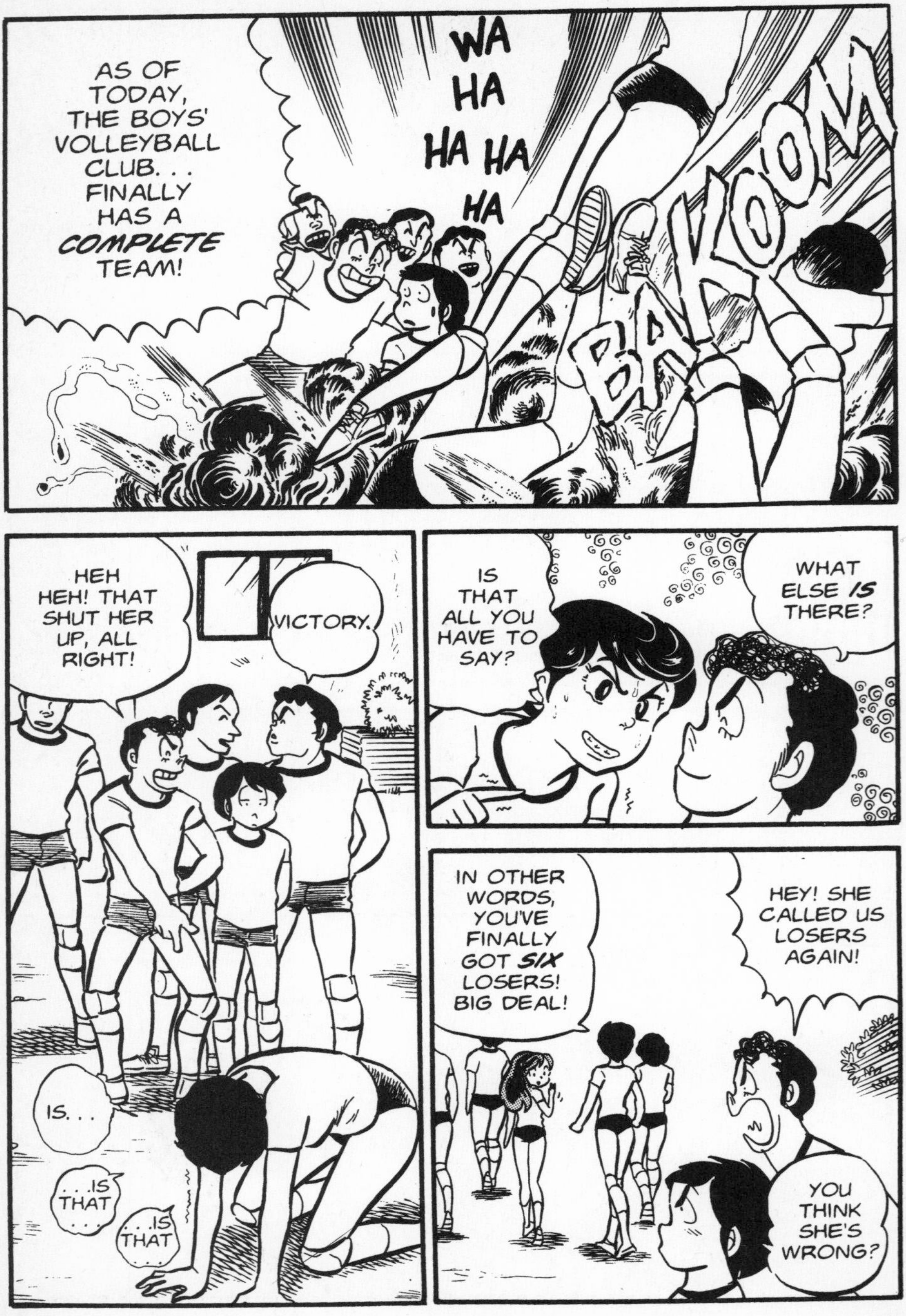
AS OF TODAY, THE BOYS' VOLLEYBALL CLUB. . . FINALLY HAS A *COMPLETE* TEAM!
WA HA HA HA HA
BAKOOM
HEH HEH! THAT SHUT HER UP, ALL RIGHT!
VICTORY.
IS. . .
. . .IS THAT . . .
. . .IS THAT . . .
IS THAT ALL YOU HAVE TO SAY?
WHAT ELSE *IS* THERE?
IN OTHER WORDS, YOU'VE FINALLY GOT *SIX* LOSERS! BIG DEAL!
HEY! SHE CALLED US LOSERS AGAIN!
YOU THINK SHE'S WRONG?

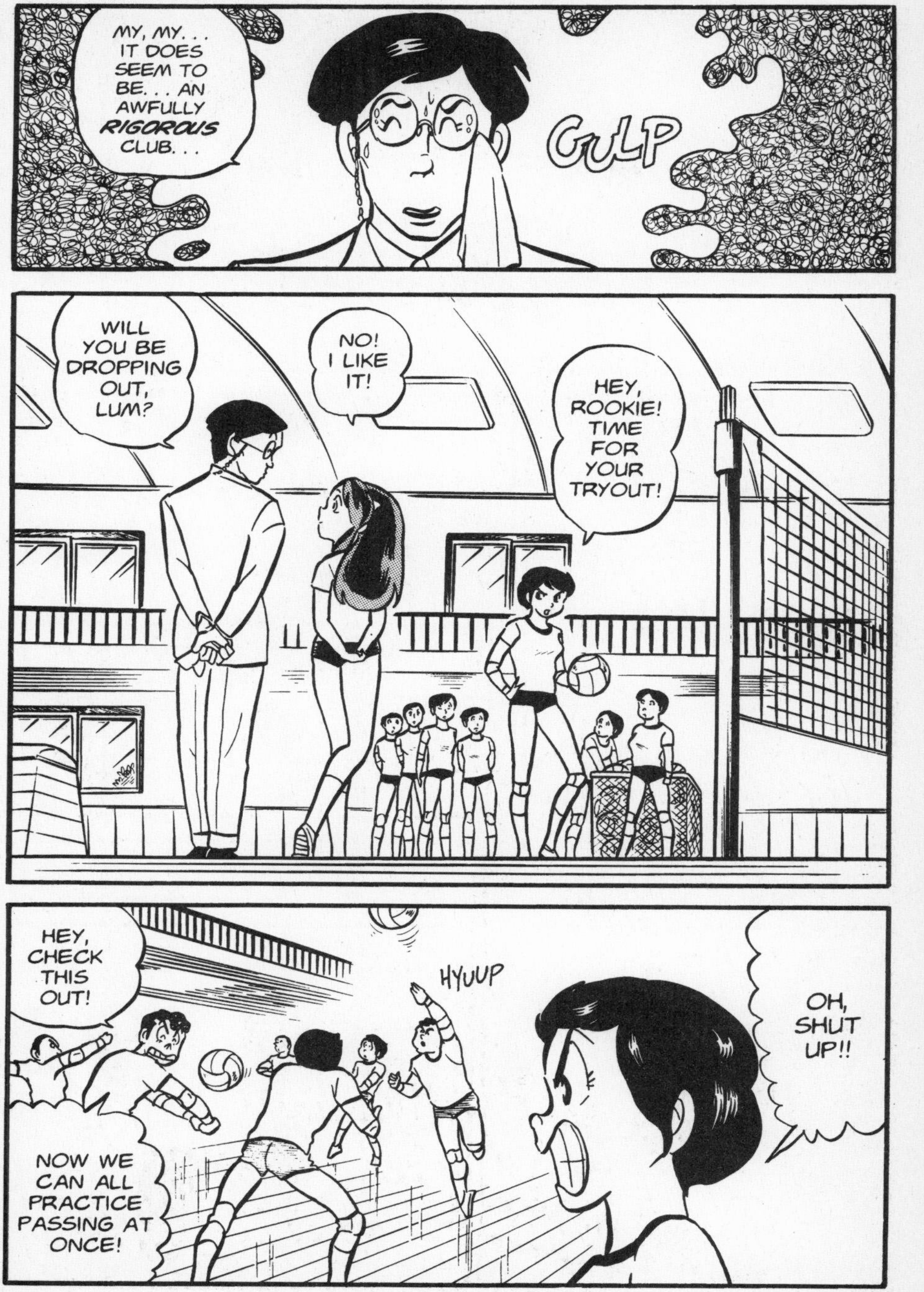
MY, MY... IT DOES SEEM TO BE... AN AWFULLY RIGOROUS CLUB...
GULP
WILL YOU BE DROPPING OUT, LUM?
NO! I LIKE IT!
HEY, ROOKIE! TIME FOR YOUR TRYOUT!
HEY, CHECK THIS OUT!
HYUUP
NOW WE CAN ALL PRACTICE PASSING AT ONCE!
OH, SHUT UP!!

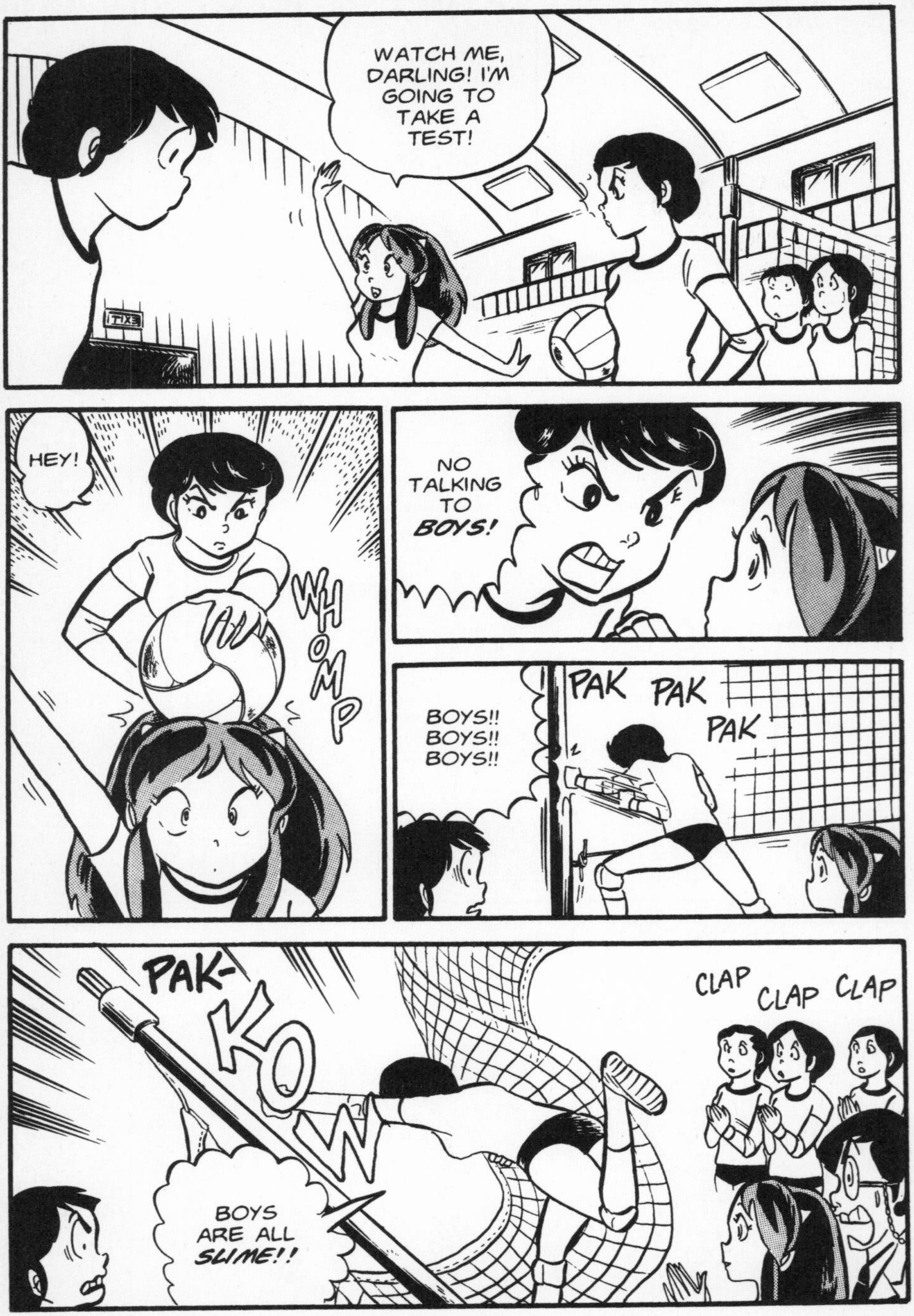

WATCH ME, DARLING! I'M GOING TO TAKE A TEST!
EXIT
HEY!
WHOMP
NO TALKING TO BOYS!
BOYS!! BOYS!! BOYS!!
PAK PAK PAK
PAK-KOW
CLAP CLAP CLAP
BOYS ARE ALL SLIME!!

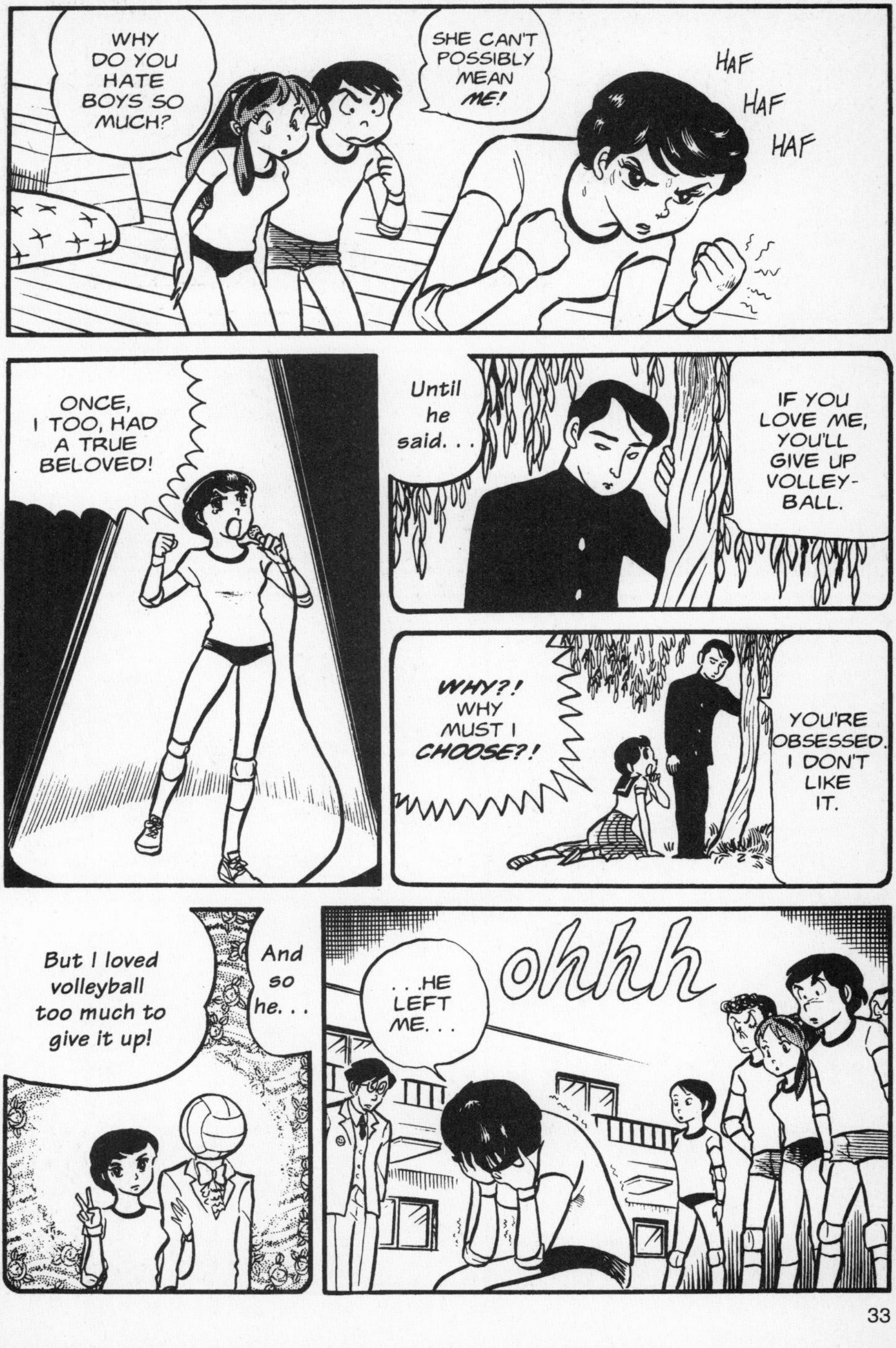
WHY DO YOU HATE BOYS SO MUCH?
SHE CAN'T POSSIBLY MEAN ME!
HAF HAF HAF
ONCE, I TOO, HAD A TRUE BELOVED!
Until he said. . .
IF YOU LOVE ME, YOU'LL GIVE UP VOLLEY-BALL.
WHY?! WHY MUST I CHOOSE?!
YOU'RE OBSESSED. I DON'T LIKE IT.
But I loved volleyball too much to give it up!
And so he. . .
. . .HE LEFT ME. . .
ohhh

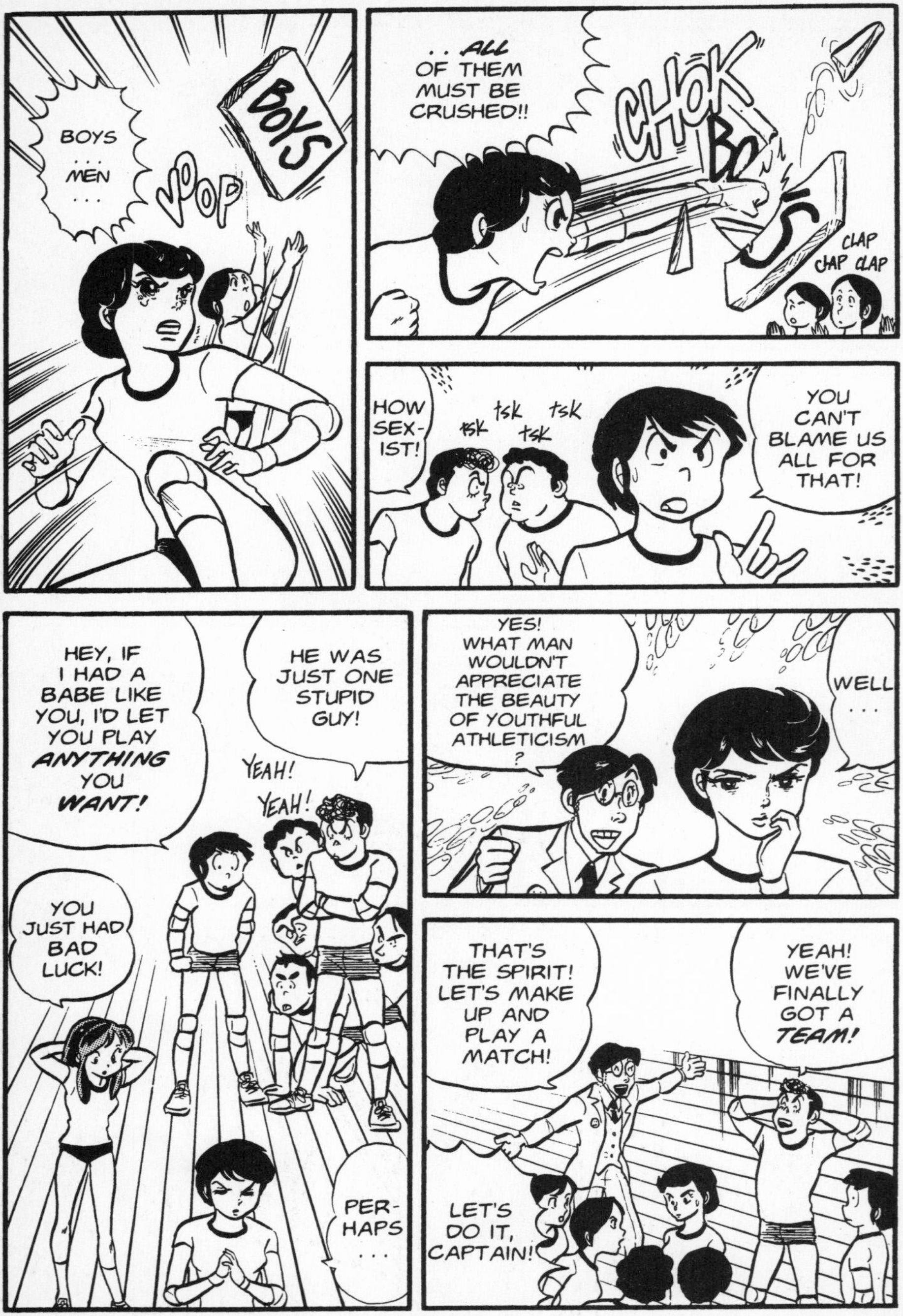
BOYS . . . MEN . . .
VOOP
BOYS
. . ALL OF THEM MUST BE CRUSHED!!
CHOK
CLAP CLAP CLAP
HOW SEX-IST!
tsk tsk tsk tsk
YOU CAN'T BLAME US ALL FOR THAT!
HEY, IF I HAD A BABE LIKE YOU, I'D LET YOU PLAY ANYTHING YOU WANT!
HE WAS JUST ONE STUPID GUY!
YEAH! YEAH!
YOU JUST HAD BAD LUCK!
PER-HAPS . . .
YES! WHAT MAN WOULDN'T APPRECIATE THE BEAUTY OF YOUTHFUL ATHLETICISM ?
WELL . . .
THAT'S THE SPIRIT! LET'S MAKE UP AND PLAY A MATCH!
YEAH! WE'VE FINALLY GOT A TEAM!
LET'S DO IT, CAPTAIN!

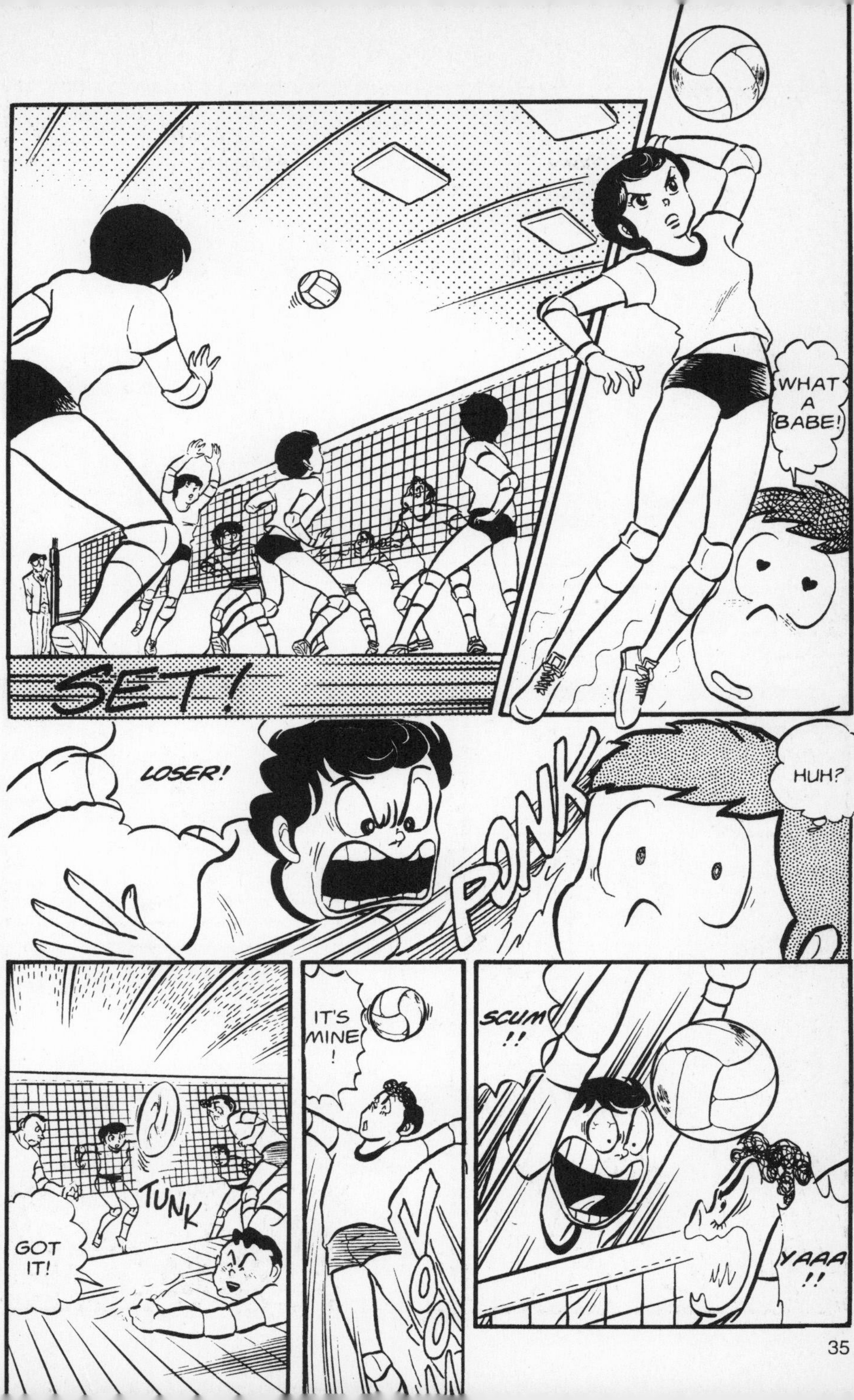
SET!
WHAT A BABE!
LOSER!
PONK
HUH?
TUNK
GOT IT!
IT'S MINE!
VOOM
SCUM!!
YAAA!!

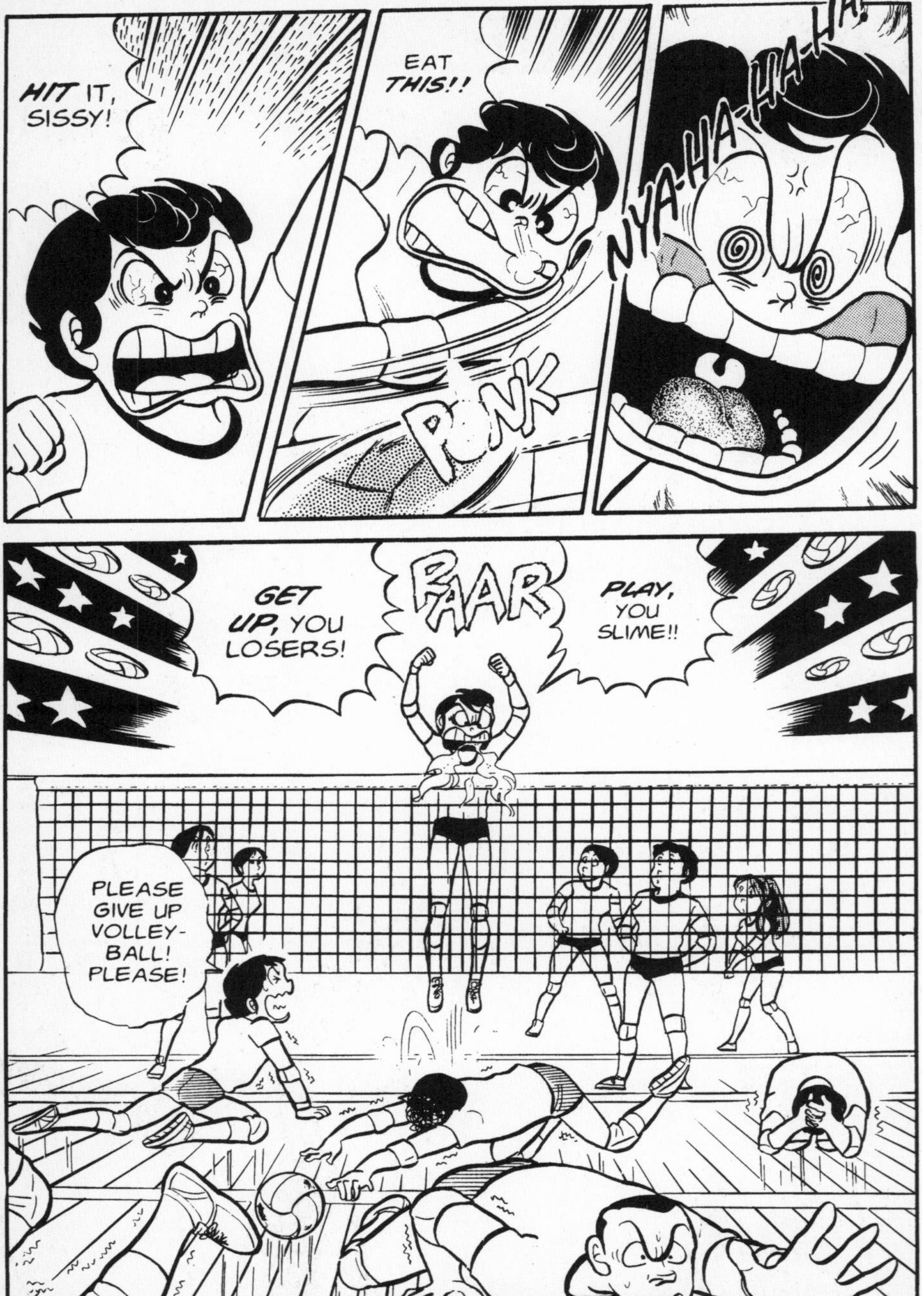
HIT IT, SISSY!
EAT THIS!!
PUNK
NYA-HA-HA-HA-HA!
GET UP, YOU LOSERS!
RAAR
PLAY, YOU SLIME!!
PLEASE GIVE UP VOLLEY-BALL! PLEASE!

PART THREE
NO LOVE ON THE COURT

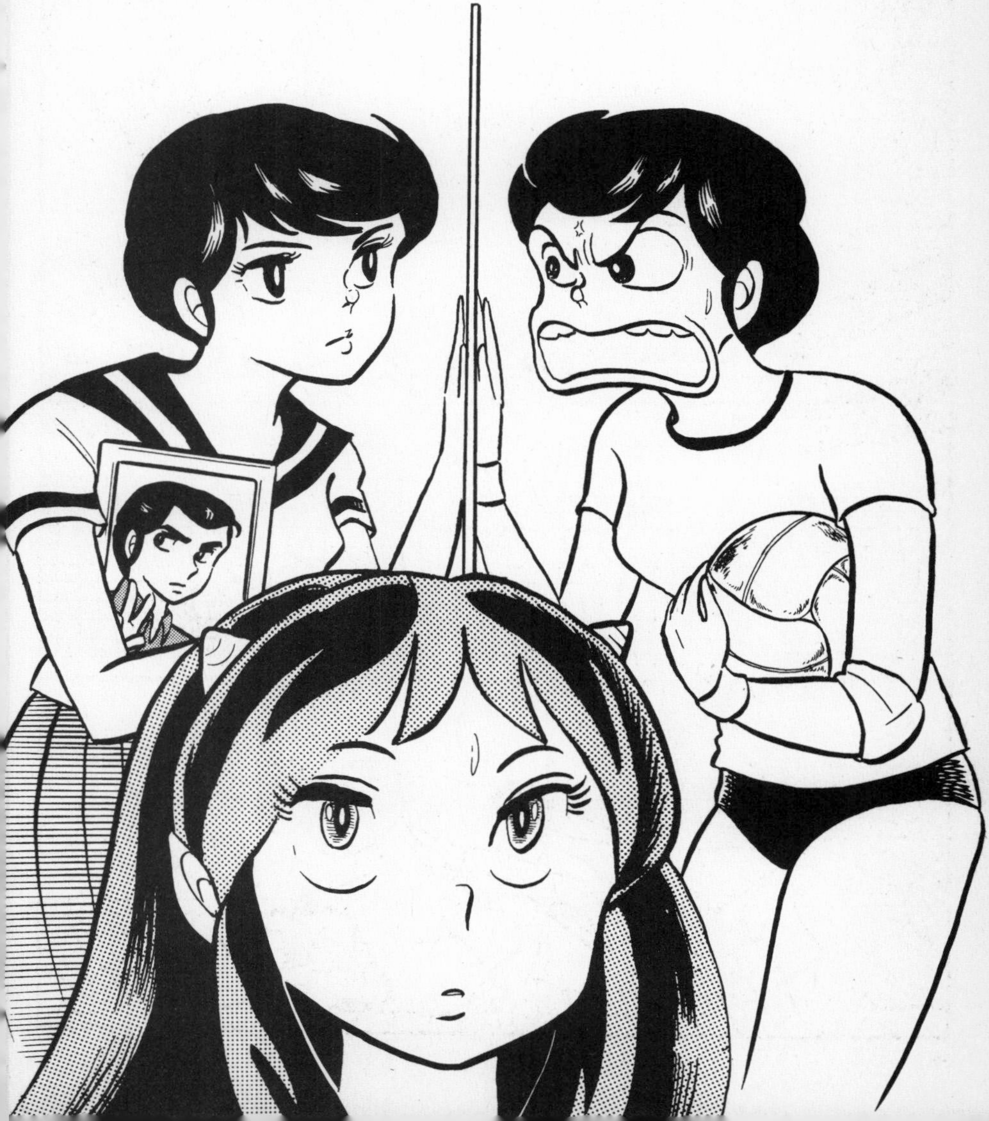

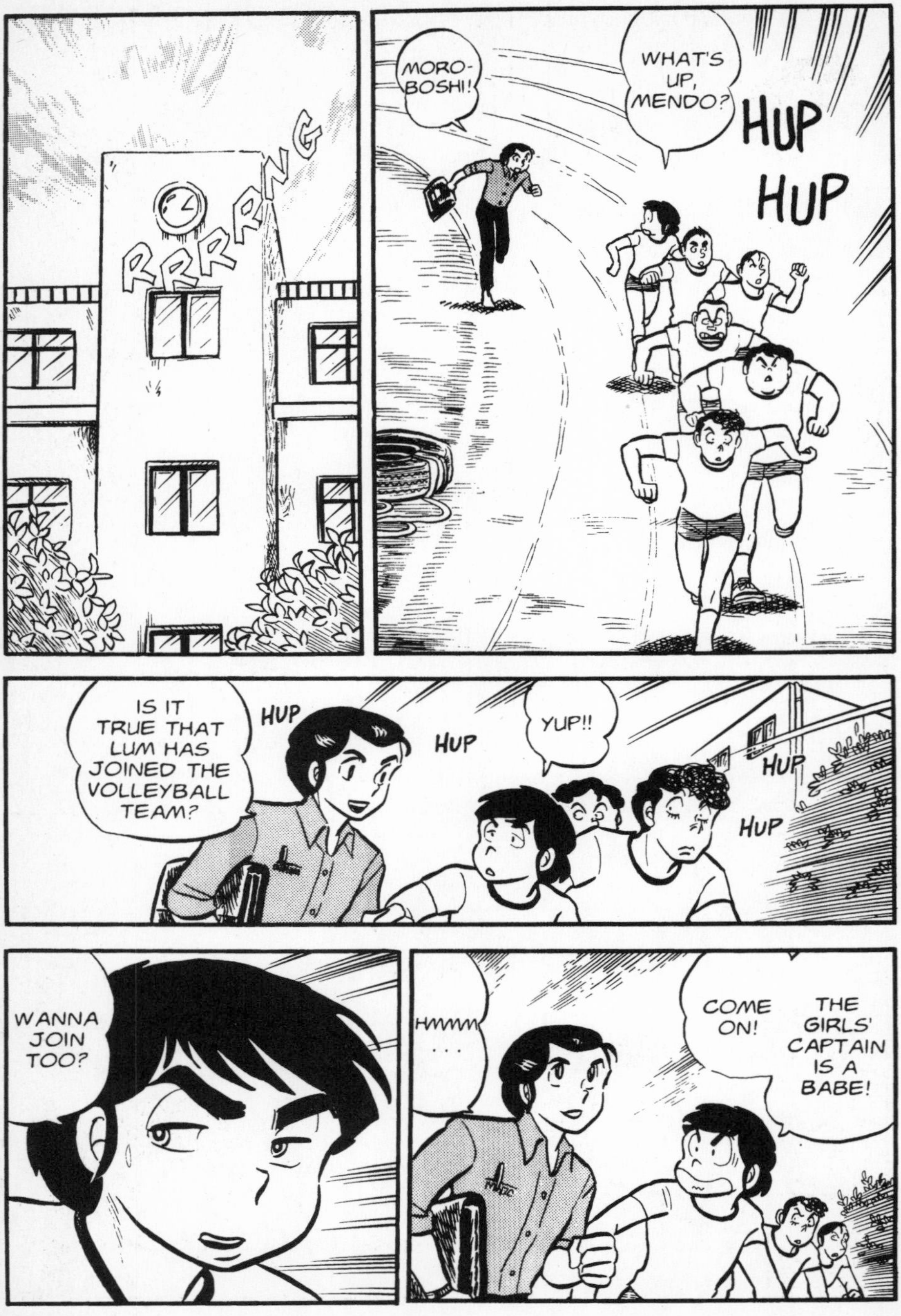
RRRRNG
MORO-BOSHI!
WHAT'S UP, MENDO?
HUP
HUP
IS IT TRUE THAT LUM HAS JOINED THE VOLLEYBALL TEAM?
HUP
HUP
YUP!!
HUP
HUP
WANNA JOIN TOO?
HMMM . . .
COME ON!
THE GIRLS' CAPTAIN IS A BABE!

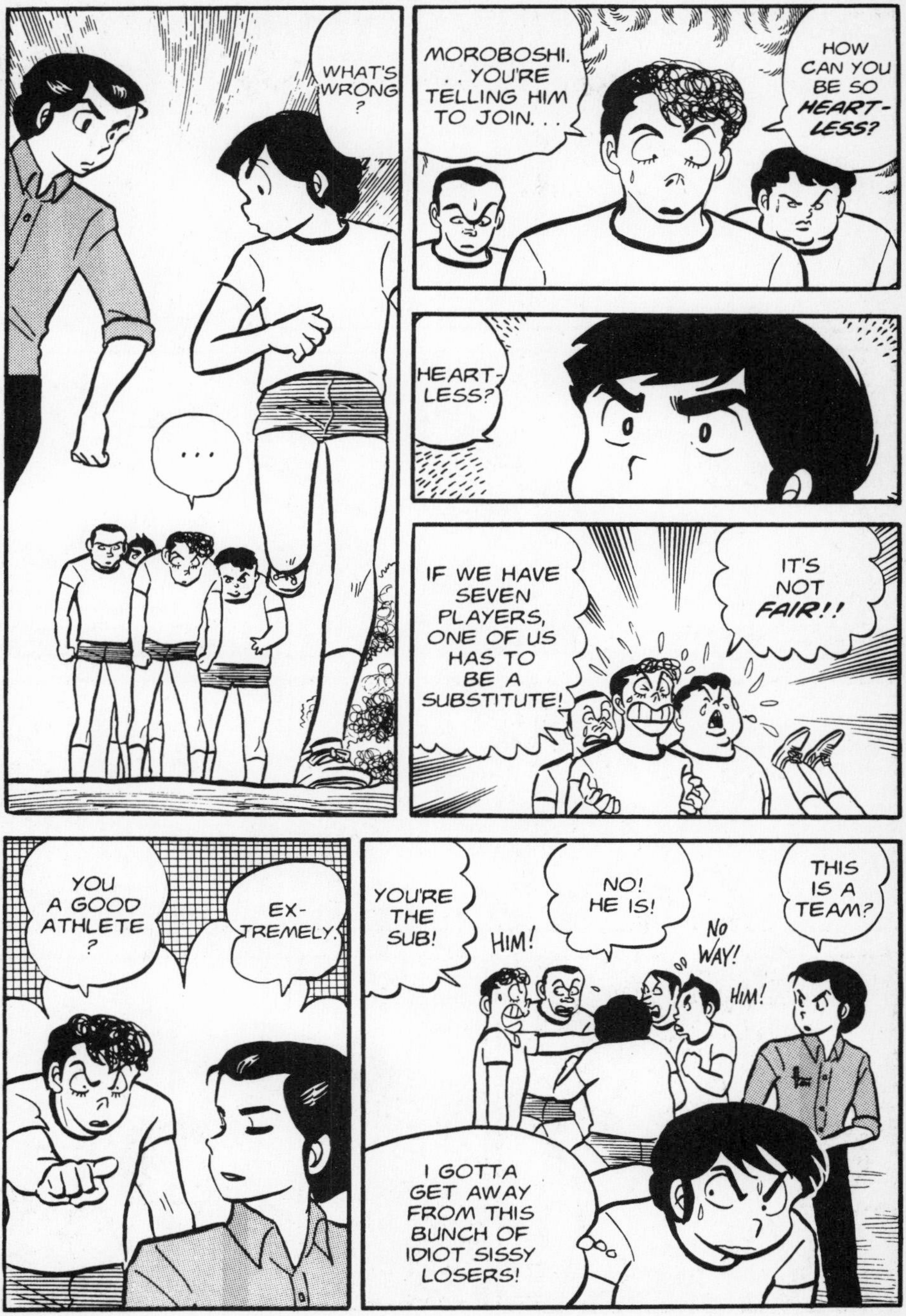
WHAT'S WRONG ?
. . .
MOROBOSHI. . . YOU'RE TELLING HIM TO JOIN. . .
HOW CAN YOU BE SO *HEARTLESS?*
HEARTLESS?
IF WE HAVE SEVEN PLAYERS, ONE OF US HAS TO BE A SUBSTITUTE!
IT'S NOT *FAIR!!*
YOU A GOOD ATHLETE ?
EXTREMELY.
YOU'RE THE SUB!
HIM!
NO! HE IS!
NO WAY!
HIM!
THIS IS A TEAM?
I GOTTA GET AWAY FROM THIS BUNCH OF IDIOT SISSY LOSERS!

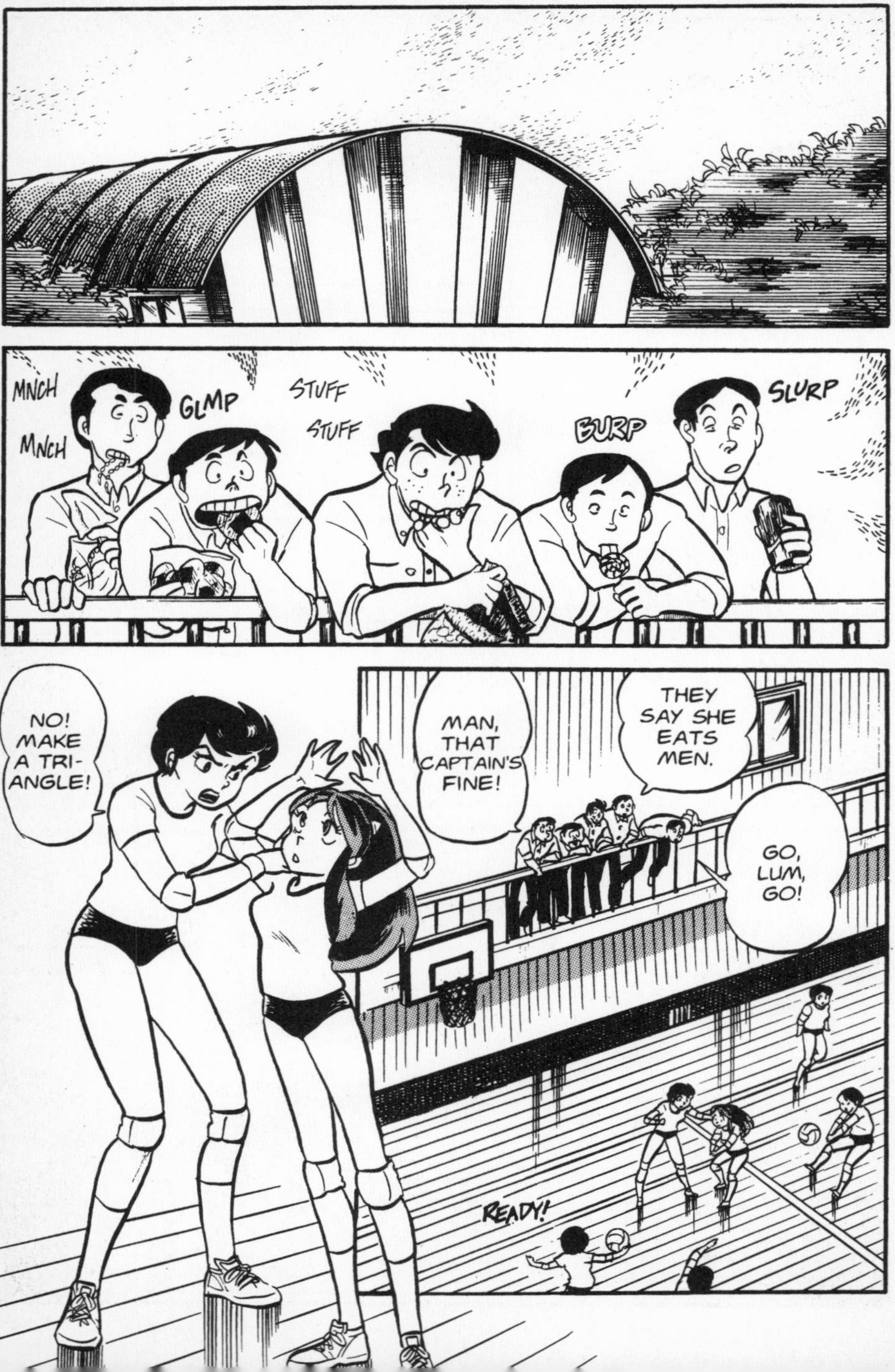
MNCH
MNCH
GLMP
STUFF
STUFF
BURP
SLURP
NO! MAKE A TRI-ANGLE!
MAN, THAT CAPTAIN'S FINE!
THEY SAY SHE EATS MEN.
GO, LUM, GO!
READY!

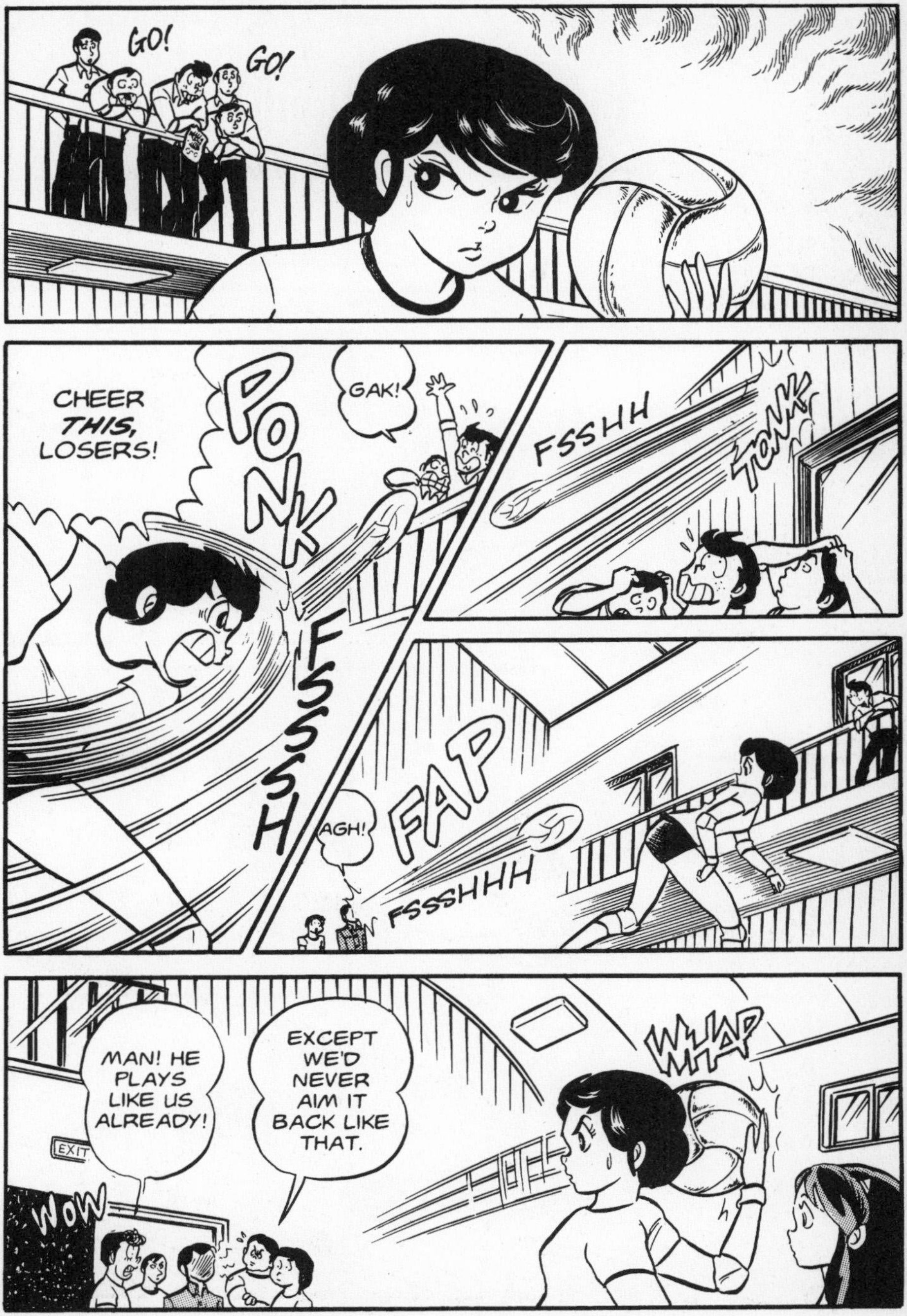
GO!
GO!
CHEER *THIS*, LOSERS!
PONK
GAK!
FSSSSH
FSSHH
TONK
AGH!
FAP
FSSSHHH
MAN! HE PLAYS LIKE US ALREADY!
EXCEPT WE'D NEVER AIM IT BACK LIKE THAT.
WHAP
EXIT
WOW

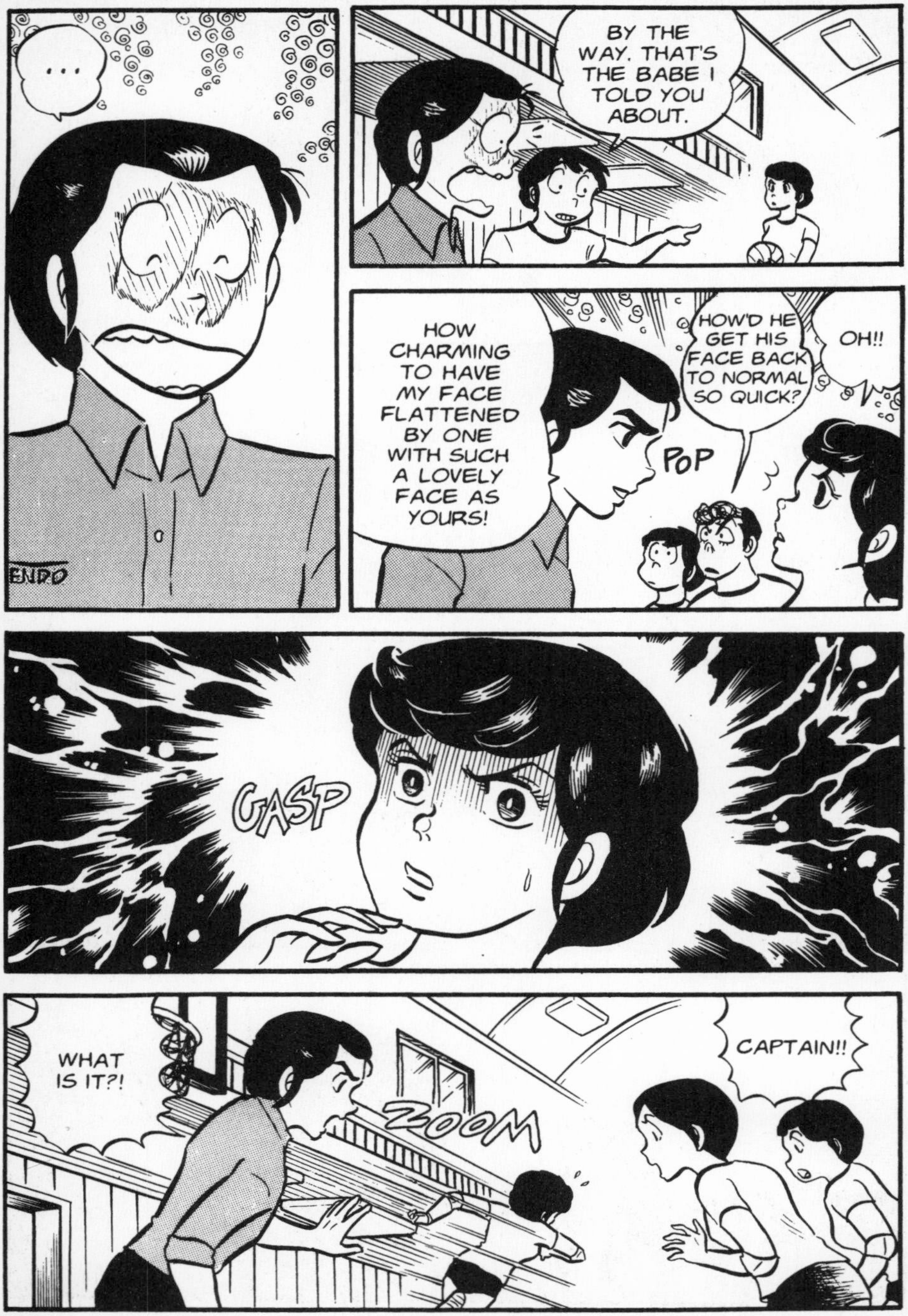
...
ENDO
BY THE WAY. THAT'S THE BABE I TOLD YOU ABOUT.
HOW CHARMING TO HAVE MY FACE FLATTENED BY ONE WITH SUCH A LOVELY FACE AS YOURS!
POP
HOW'D HE GET HIS FACE BACK TO NORMAL SO QUICK?
OH!!
GASP
WHAT IS IT?!
ZOOM
CAPTAIN!!

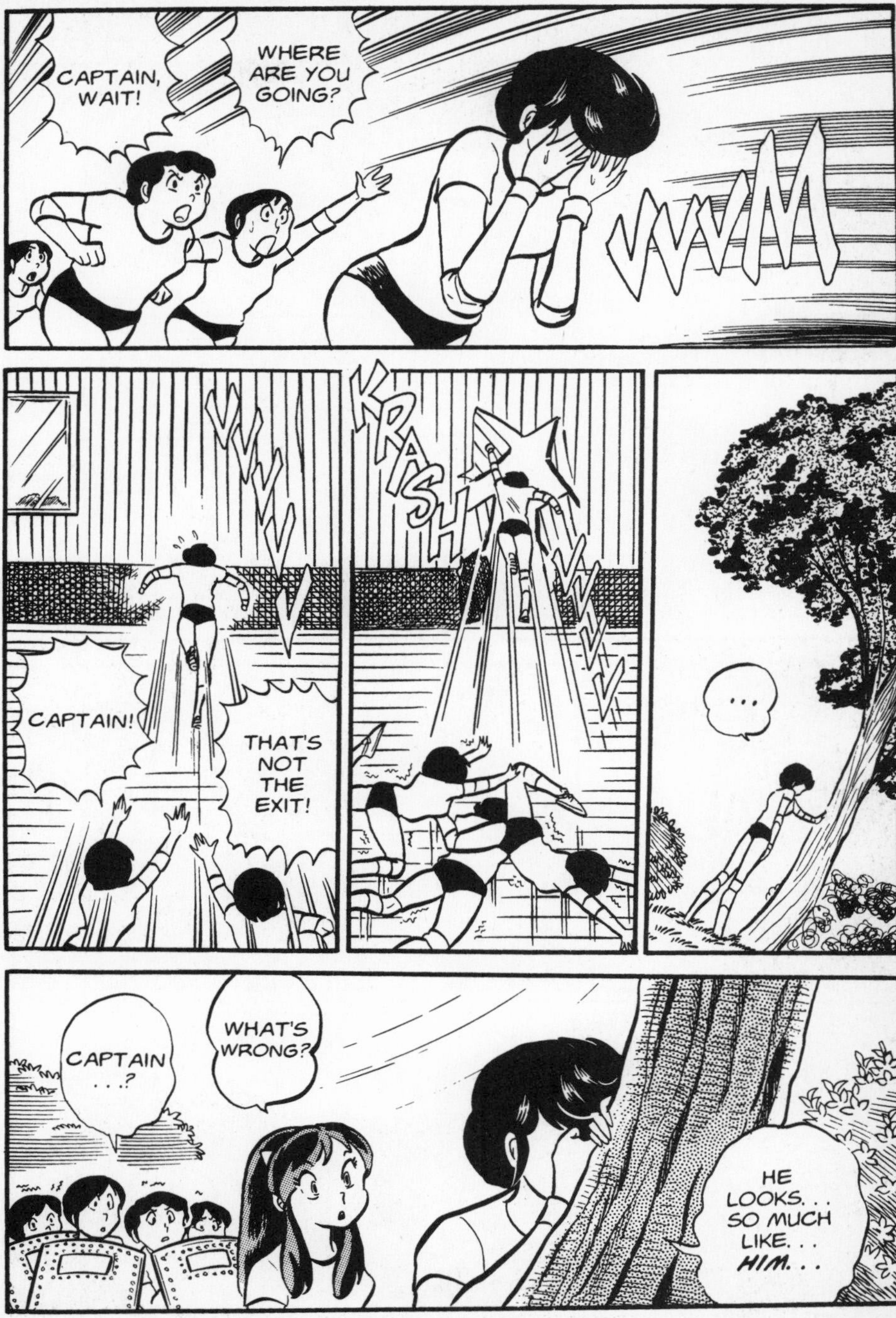
CAPTAIN, WAIT!
WHERE ARE YOU GOING?
VVVM
VVVV
CAPTAIN!
THAT'S NOT THE EXIT!
KRASH
VVVV
...
CAPTAIN ...?
WHAT'S WRONG?
HE LOOKS... SO MUCH LIKE... HIM...

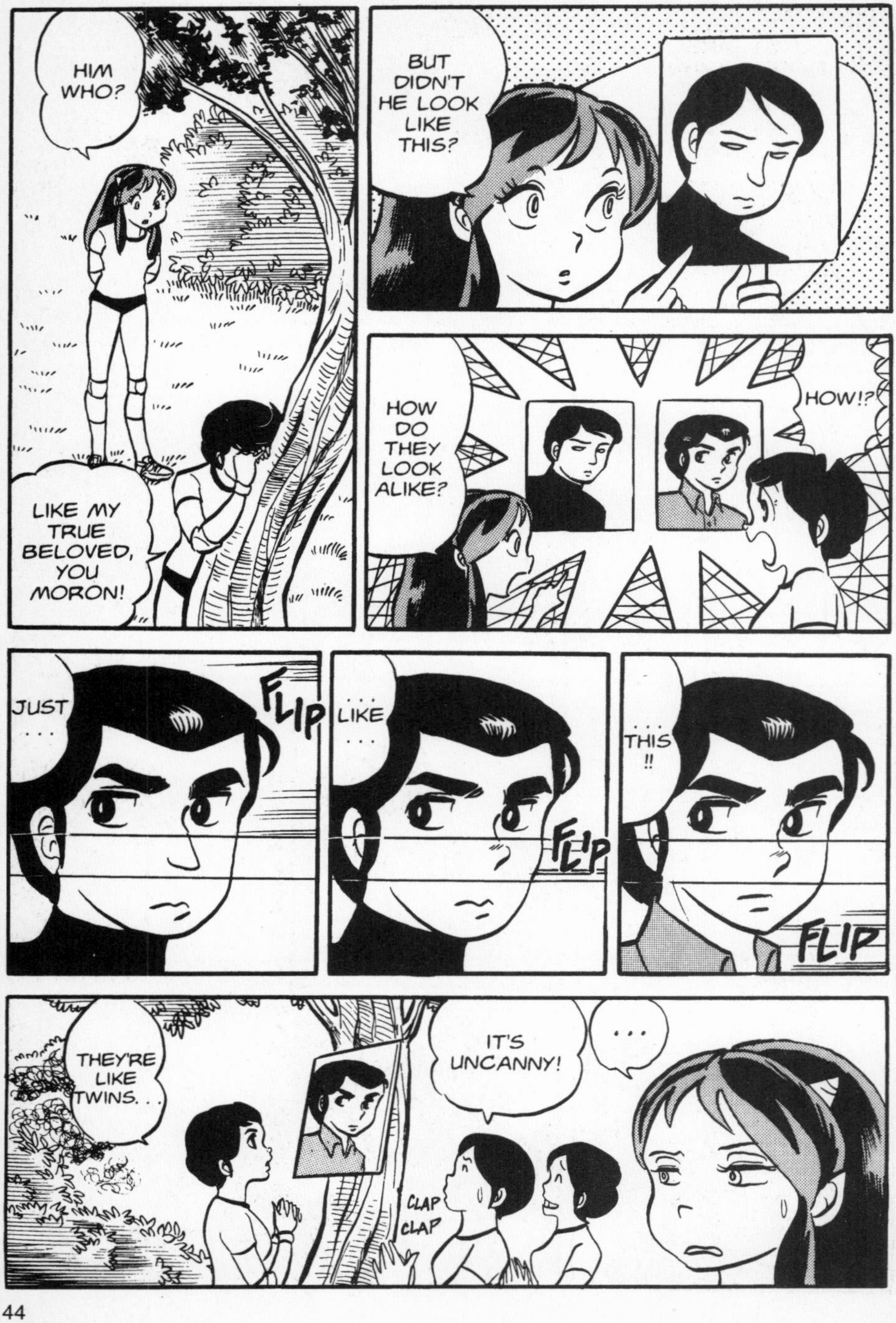
HIM WHO?
LIKE MY TRUE BELOVED, YOU MORON!
BUT DIDN'T HE LOOK LIKE THIS?
HOW DO THEY LOOK ALIKE?
HOW!?
JUST . . .
FLIP
. . . LIKE . . .
FLIP
. . . THIS !!
FLIP
THEY'RE LIKE TWINS. . .
IT'S UNCANNY!
. . .
CLAP CLAP

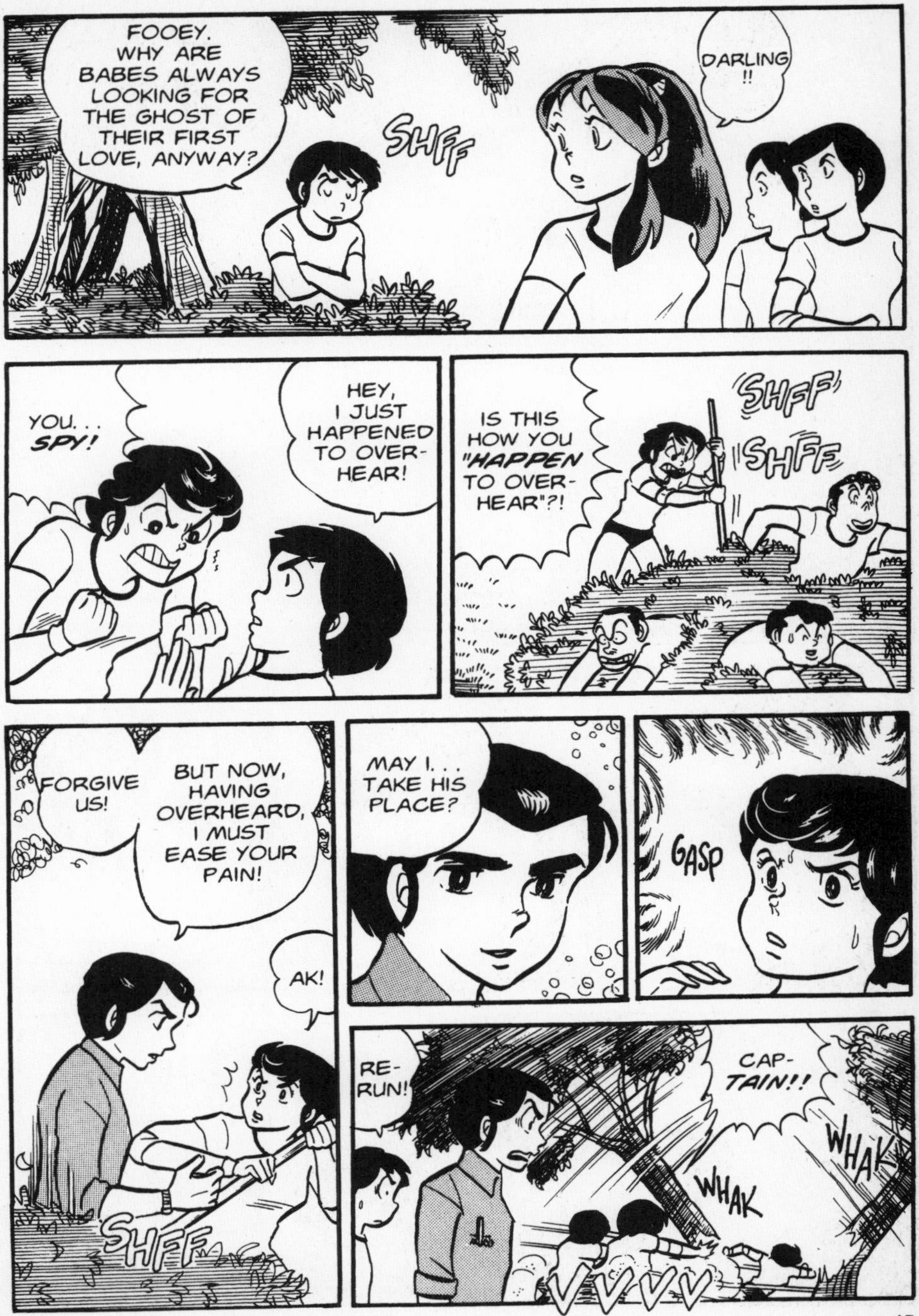
FOOEY. WHY ARE BABES ALWAYS LOOKING FOR THE GHOST OF THEIR FIRST LOVE, ANYWAY?
SHFF
DARLING !!
YOU. . . SPY!
HEY, I JUST HAPPENED TO OVER-HEAR!
IS THIS HOW YOU "HAPPEN TO OVER-HEAR"?!
SHFF
SHFF
FORGIVE US!
BUT NOW, HAVING OVERHEARD, I MUST EASE YOUR PAIN!
AK!
SHFF
MAY I. . . TAKE HIS PLACE?
GASP
RE-RUN!
CAP-TAIN!!
WHAK
WHAK

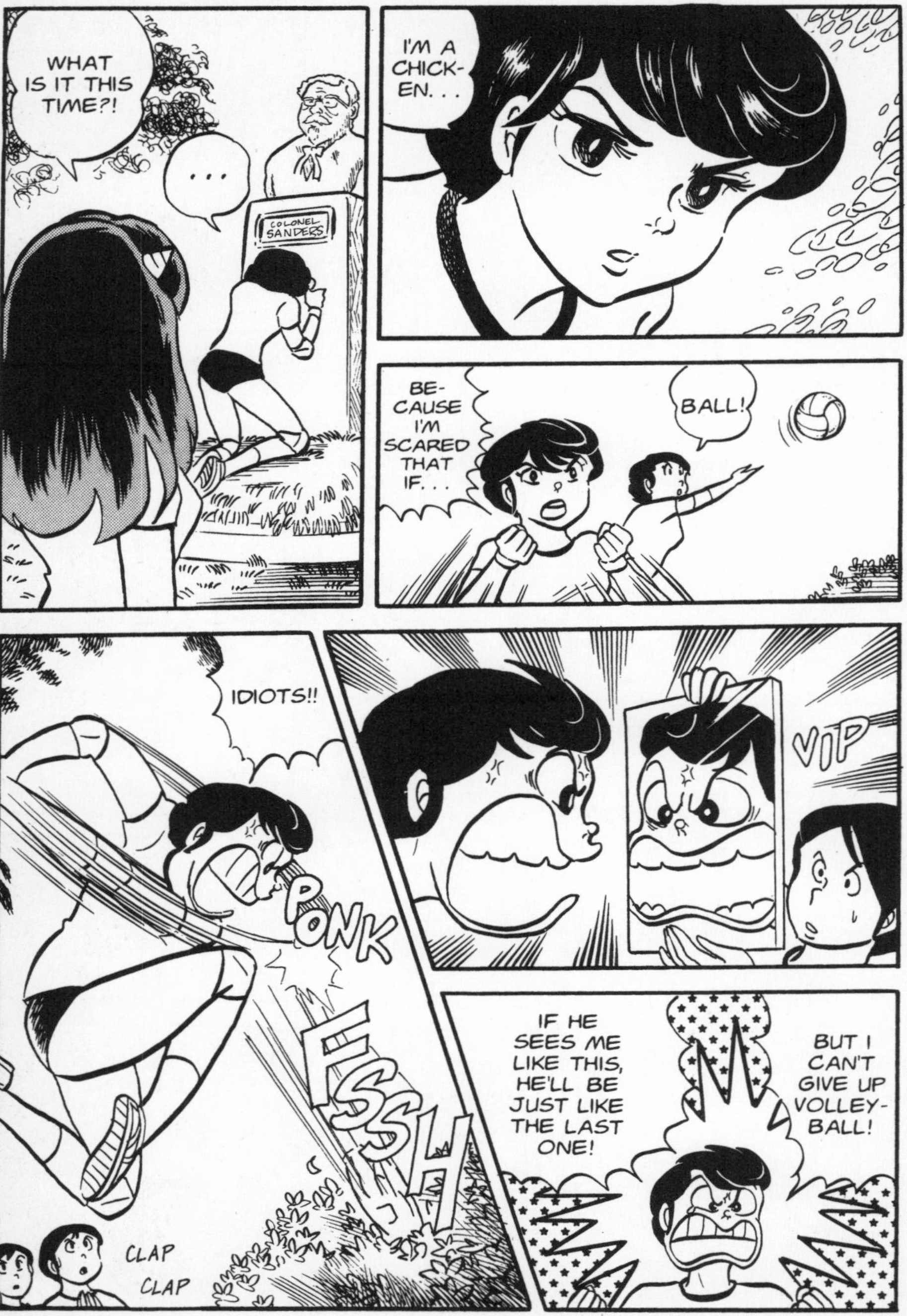

WHAT IS IT THIS TIME?!
. . .
COLONEL SANDERS
I'M A CHICK-EN. . .
BE-CAUSE I'M SCARED THAT IF. . .
BALL!
IDIOTS!!
PONK
FSSH
CLAP
CLAP
VIP
IF HE SEES ME LIKE THIS, HE'LL BE JUST LIKE THE LAST ONE!
BUT I CAN'T GIVE UP VOLLEY-BALL!

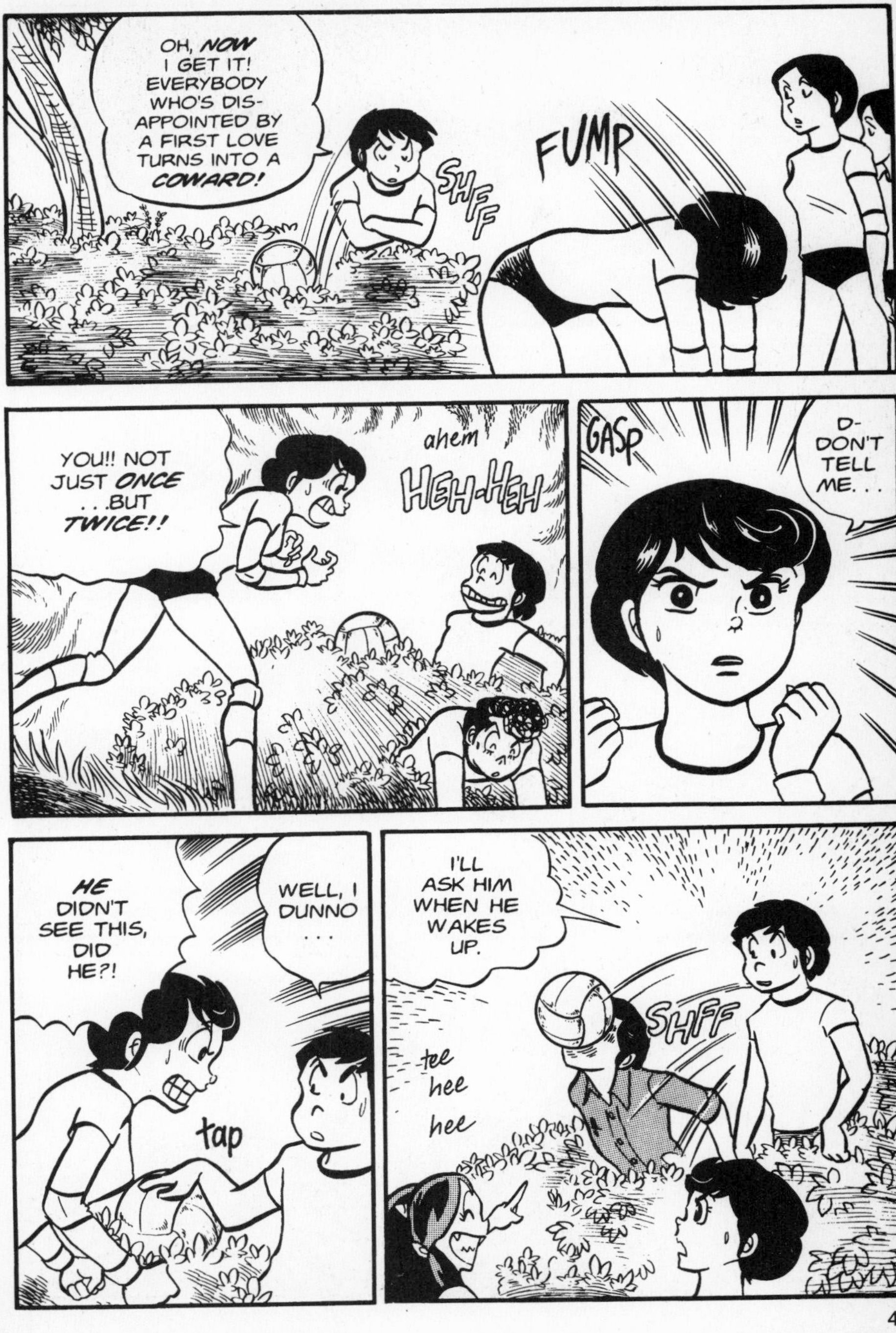
OH, NOW I GET IT! EVERYBODY WHO'S DIS-APPOINTED BY A FIRST LOVE TURNS INTO A COWARD!
SHFF
FUMP
YOU!! NOT JUST ONCE . . .BUT TWICE!!
ahem
HEH-HEH
GASP
D-DON'T TELL ME. . .
HE DIDN'T SEE THIS, DID HE?!
WELL, I DUNNO . . .
tap
I'LL ASK HIM WHEN HE WAKES UP.
SHFF
tee hee hee

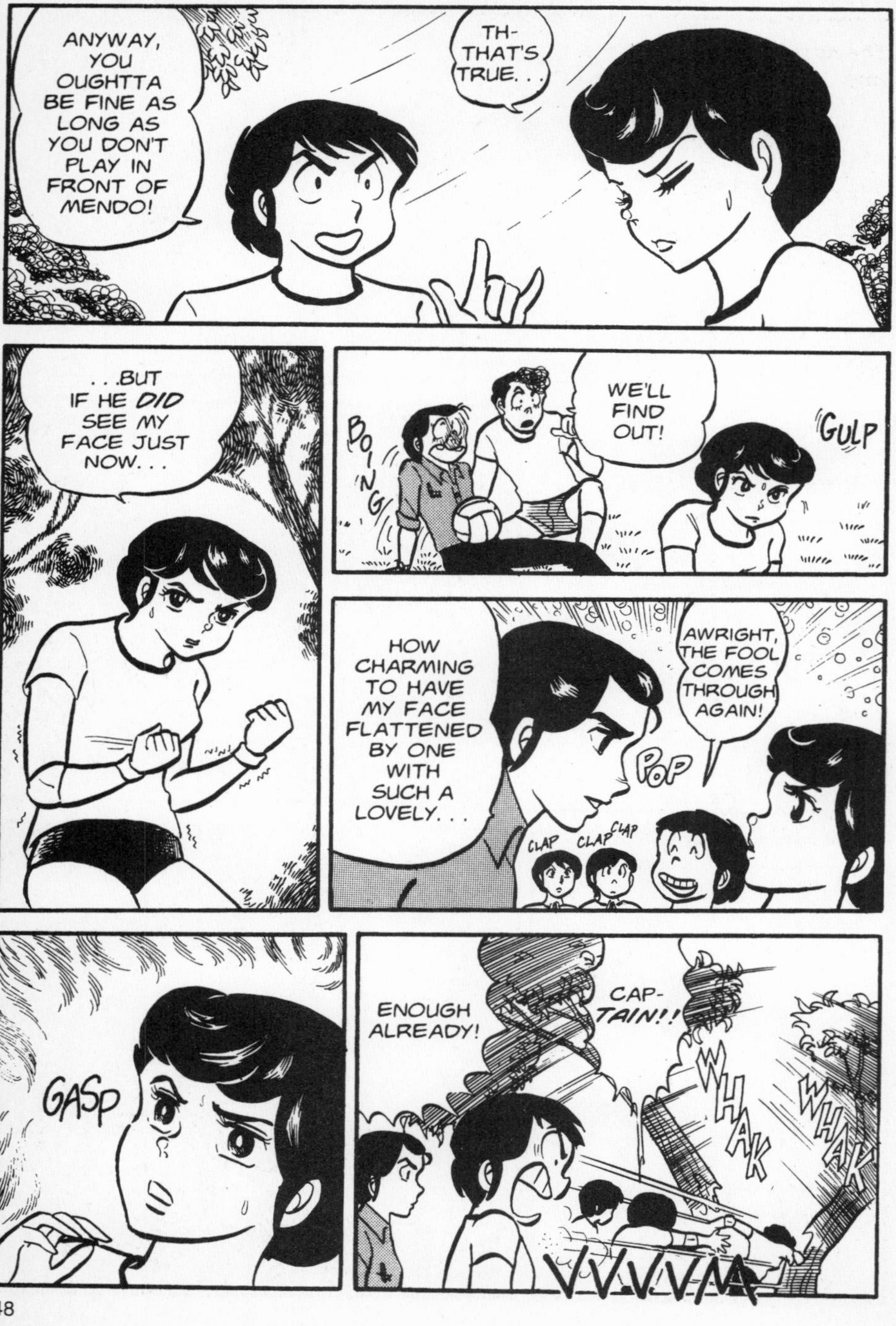
ANYWAY, YOU OUGHTTA BE FINE AS LONG AS YOU DON'T PLAY IN FRONT OF MENDO!
TH- THAT'S TRUE. . .
. . .BUT IF HE *DID* SEE MY FACE JUST NOW. . .
BOING
WE'LL FIND OUT!
GULP
HOW CHARMING TO HAVE MY FACE FLATTENED BY ONE WITH SUCH A LOVELY. . .
AWRIGHT, THE FOOL COMES THROUGH AGAIN!
POP
CLAP CLAP CLAP
GASP
ENOUGH ALREADY!
CAP-*TAIN!!*
WHAK
WHAK
VVVVM

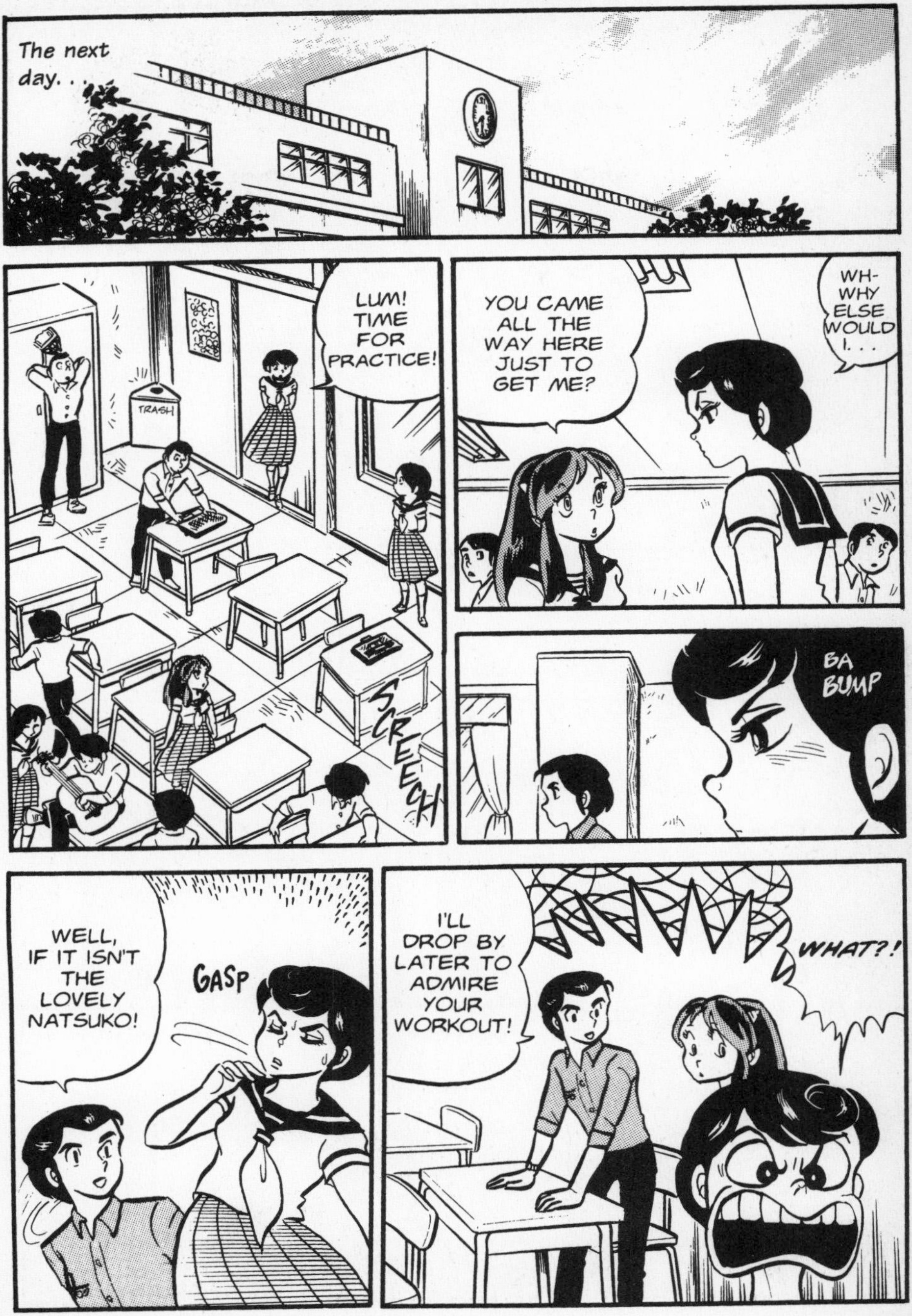

The next day. . .
LUM! TIME FOR PRACTICE!
TRASH
SCREECH
YOU CAME ALL THE WAY HERE JUST TO GET ME?
WH- WHY ELSE WOULD I. . .
BA BUMP
WELL, IF IT ISN'T THE LOVELY NATSUKO!
GASP
I'LL DROP BY LATER TO ADMIRE YOUR WORKOUT!
WHAT?!

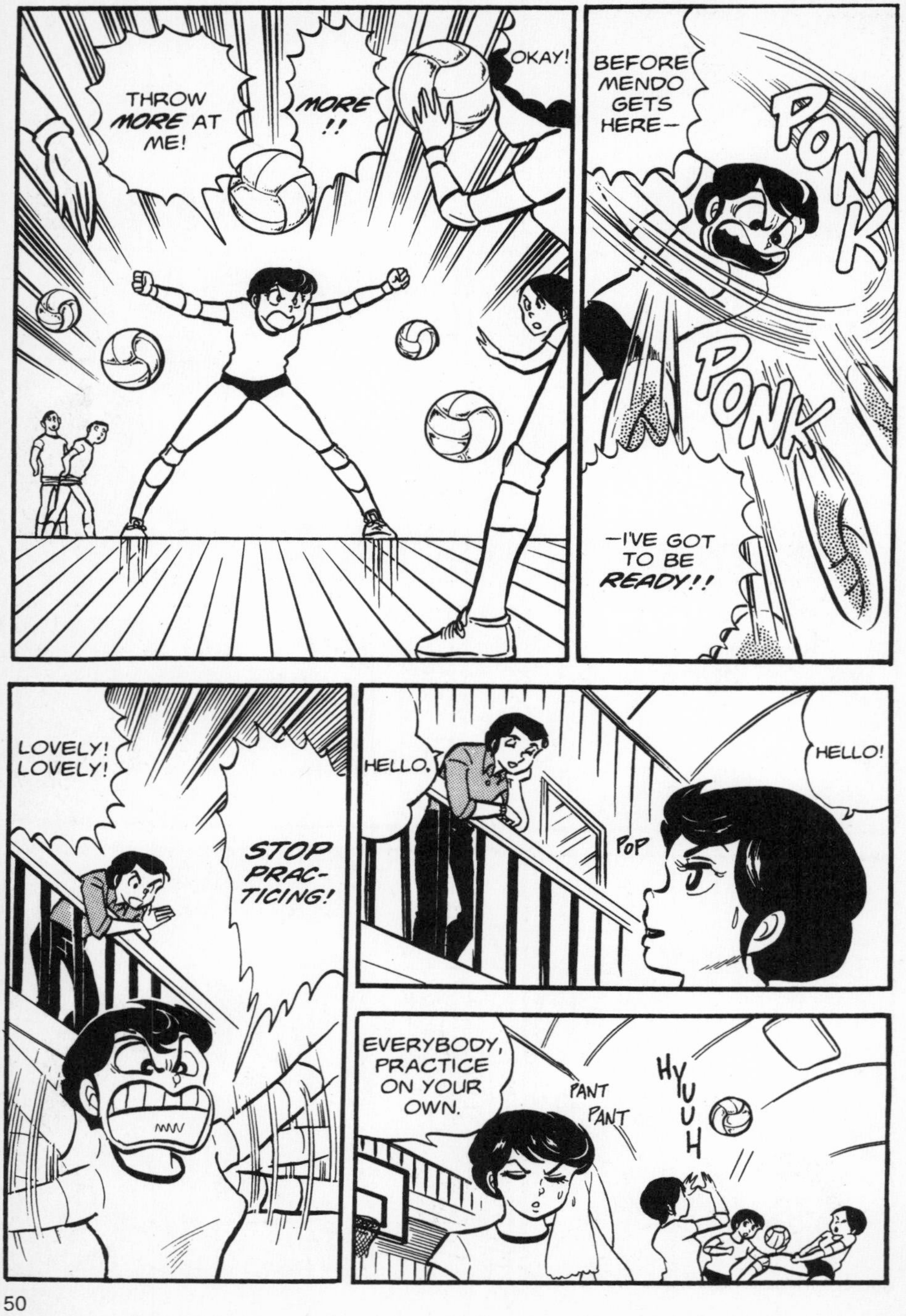
THROW MORE AT ME!
MORE !!
OKAY!
BEFORE MENDO GETS HERE—
PONK
PONK
—I'VE GOT TO BE READY!!
LOVELY! LOVELY!
STOP PRAC-TICING!
HELLO.
HELLO!
POP
EVERYBODY, PRACTICE ON YOUR OWN.
PANT PANT
HYUUH

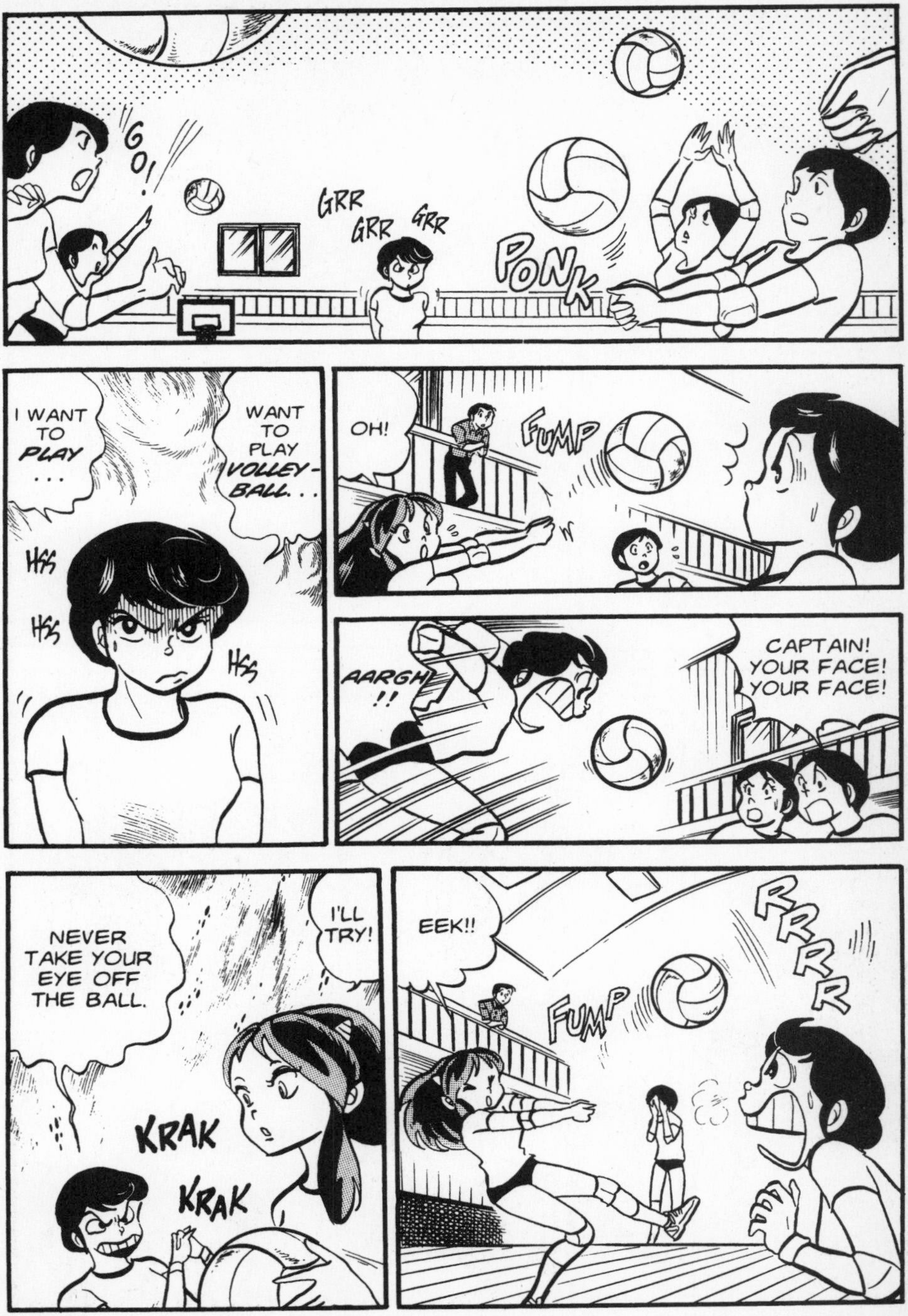
GO!
GRR
GRR
GRR
PONK
I WANT TO PLAY . . .
WANT TO PLAY VOLLEY-BALL. . .
HSS
HSS
HSS
OH!
FUMP
AARGH!!
CAPTAIN! YOUR FACE! YOUR FACE!
NEVER TAKE YOUR EYE OFF THE BALL.
I'LL TRY!
KRAK
KRAK
EEK!!
RRRR
FUMP

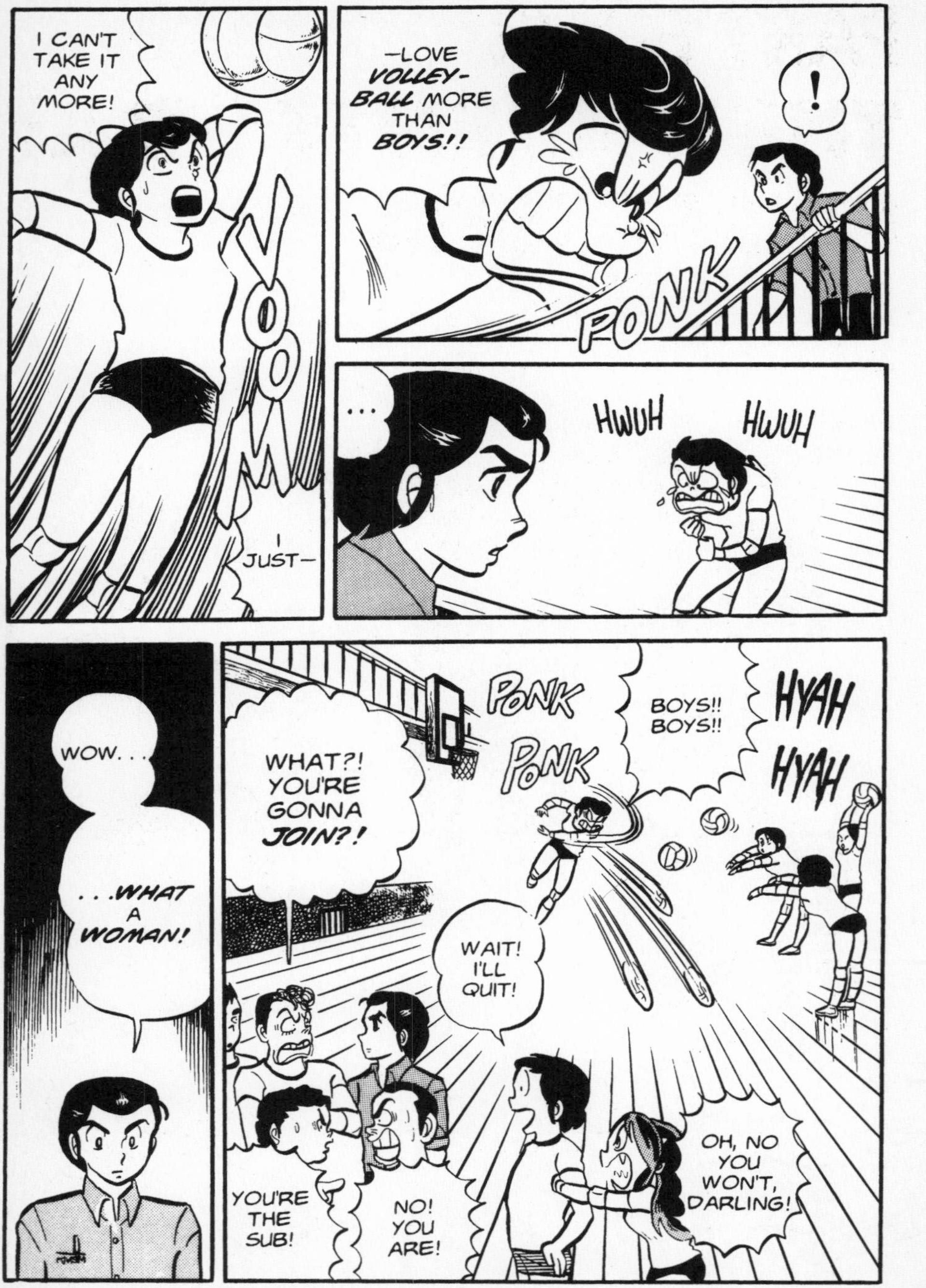
I CAN'T TAKE IT ANY MORE!
VOOM
I JUST—
—LOVE VOLLEY-BALL MORE THAN BOYS!!
!
PONK
...
HWUH
HWUH
WOW. . .
. . .WHAT A WOMAN!
PONK
PONK
WHAT?! YOU'RE GONNA JOIN?!
BOYS!! BOYS!!
HYAH
HYAH
WAIT! I'LL QUIT!
YOU'RE THE SUB!
NO! YOU ARE!
OH, NO YOU WON'T, DARLING!

PART FOUR
THE PARENTS' DAY FROM HELL

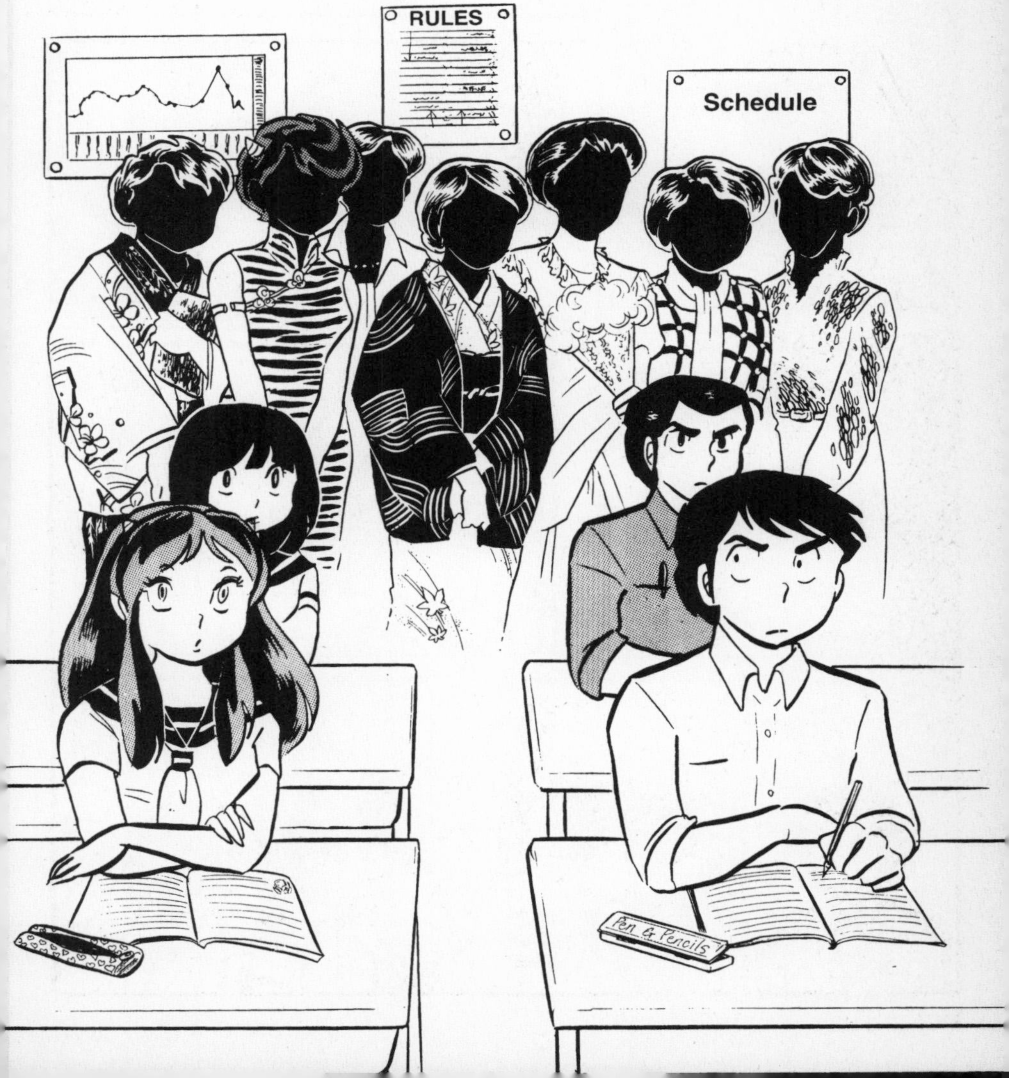
RULES
Schedule
Pen & Pencils

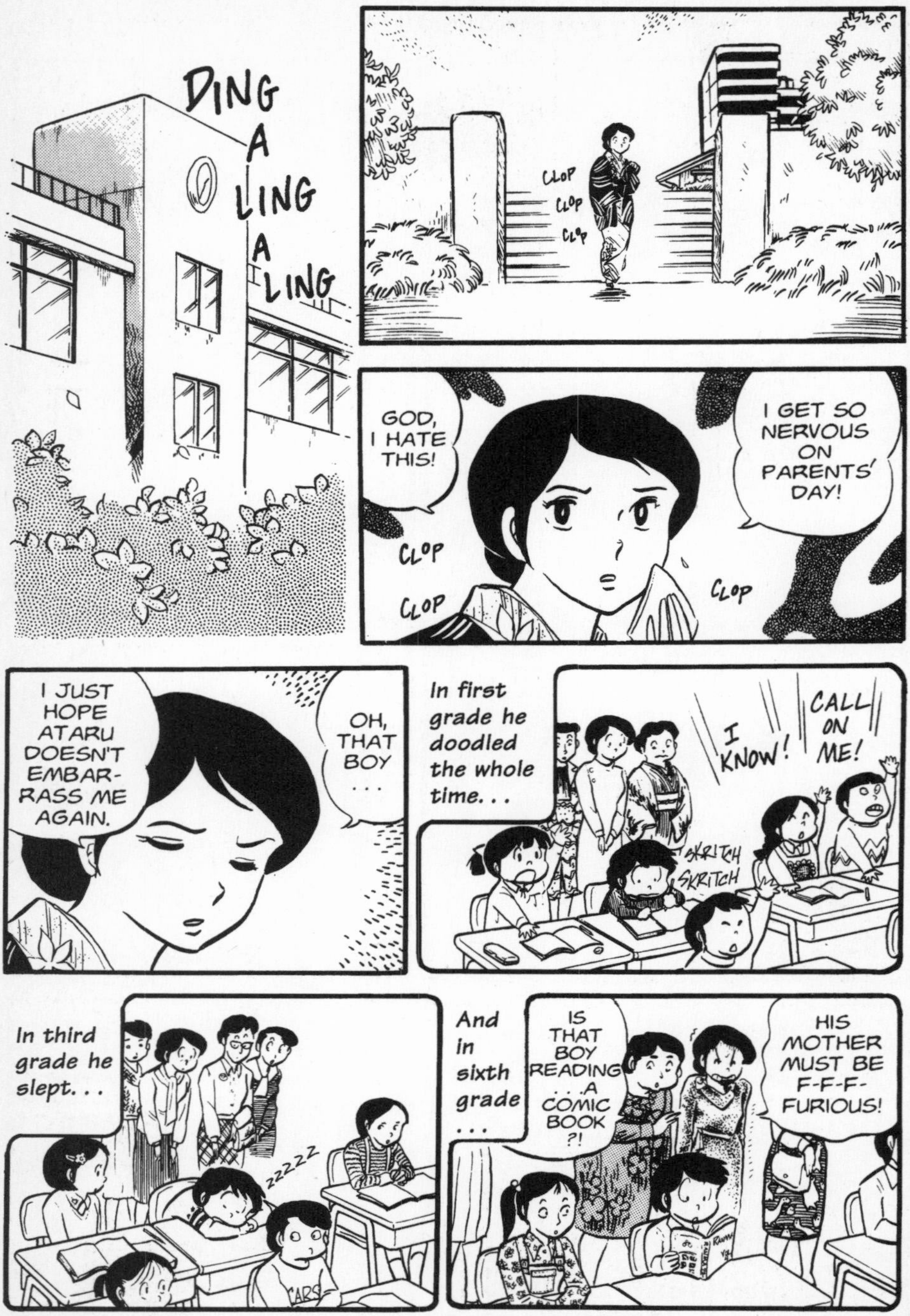
DING A LING A LING
CLOP CLOP CLOP
GOD, I HATE THIS!
I GET SO NERVOUS ON PARENTS' DAY!
CLOP CLOP CLOP
I JUST HOPE ATARU DOESN'T EMBAR-RASS ME AGAIN.
OH, THAT BOY . . .
In first grade he doodled the whole time. . .
I KNOW!
CALL ON ME!
SKRITCH SKRITCH
In third grade he slept. . .
ZZZZZ
And in sixth grade . . .
IS THAT BOY READING . . .A COMIC BOOK ?!
HIS MOTHER MUST BE F-F-F-FURIOUS!

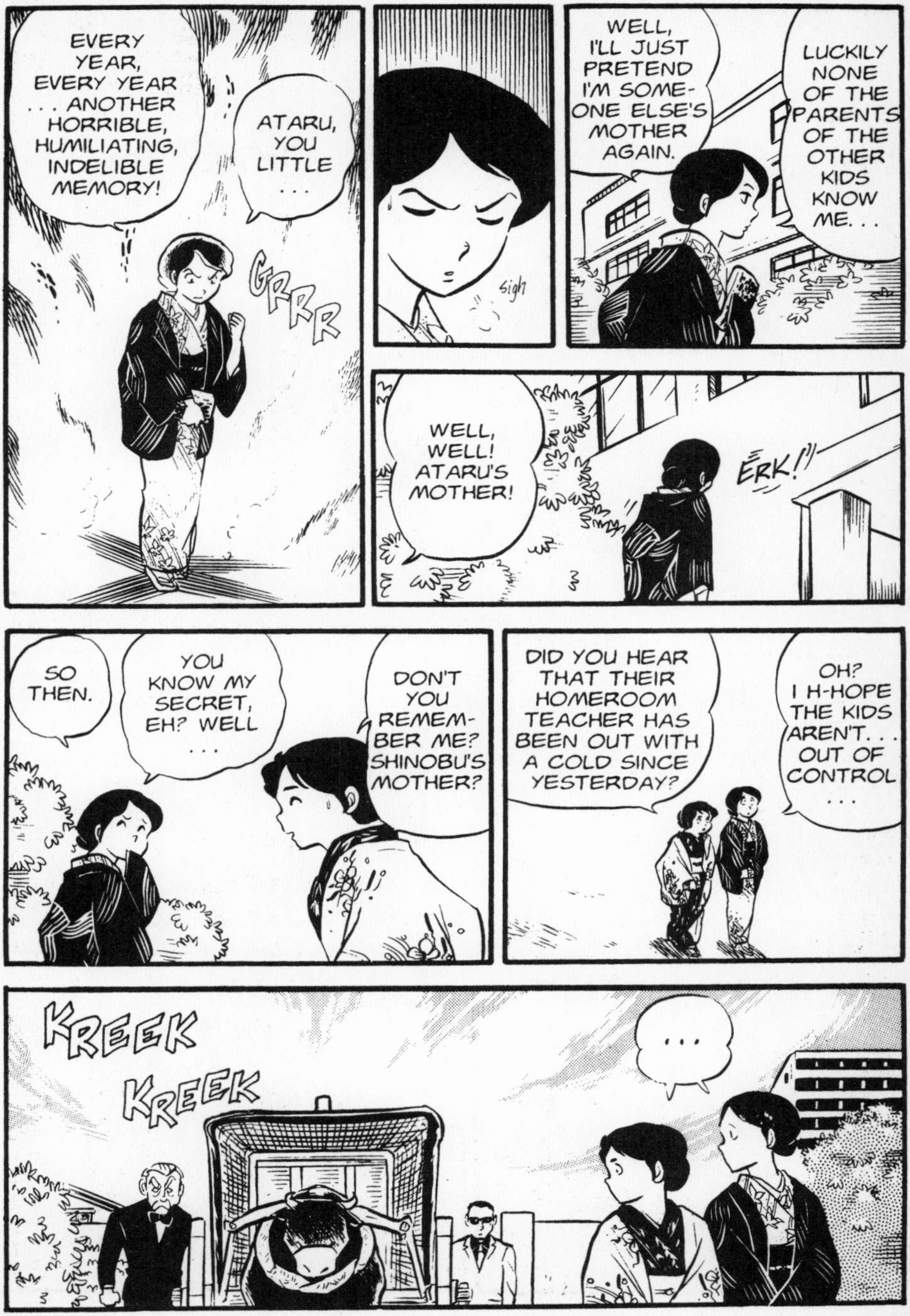
EVERY YEAR, EVERY YEAR . . . ANOTHER HORRIBLE, HUMILIATING, INDELIBLE MEMORY!
ATARU, YOU LITTLE . . .
GRRR
sigh
WELL, I'LL JUST PRETEND I'M SOME-ONE ELSE'S MOTHER AGAIN.
LUCKILY NONE OF THE PARENTS OF THE OTHER KIDS KNOW ME. . .
WELL, WELL! ATARU'S MOTHER!
ERK!
SO THEN.
YOU KNOW MY SECRET, EH? WELL . . .
DON'T YOU REMEM-BER ME? SHINOBU'S MOTHER?
DID YOU HEAR THAT THEIR HOMEROOM TEACHER HAS BEEN OUT WITH A COLD SINCE YESTERDAY?
OH? I H-HOPE THE KIDS AREN'T. . . OUT OF CONTROL . . .
KREEK
KREEK
. . .

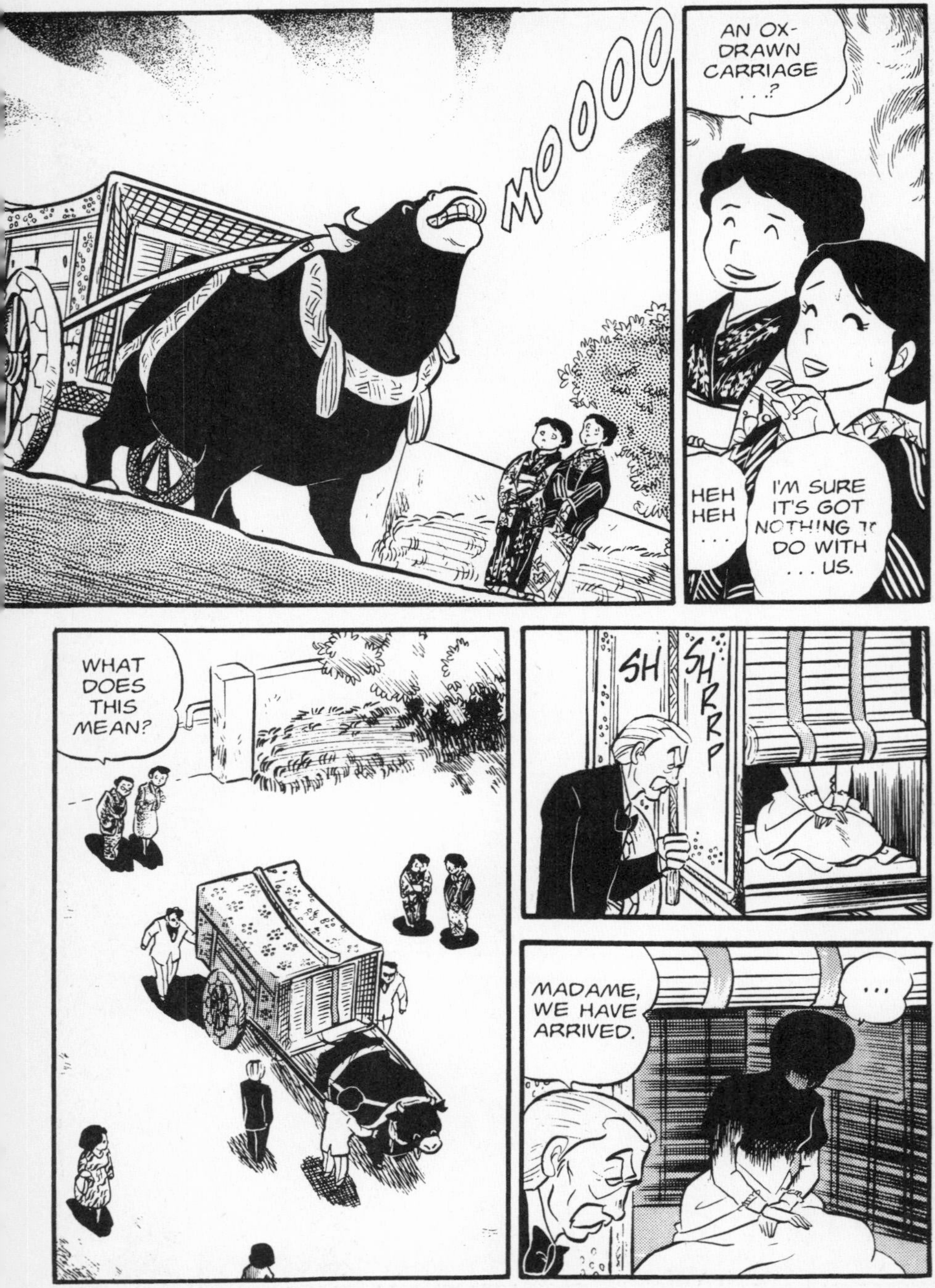
MOOOO
AN OX-DRAWN CARRIAGE . . .?
HEH HEH . . .
I'M SURE IT'S GOT NOTHING TO DO WITH . . . US.
WHAT DOES THIS MEAN?
SH SHRRP
MADAME, WE HAVE ARRIVED.
. . .

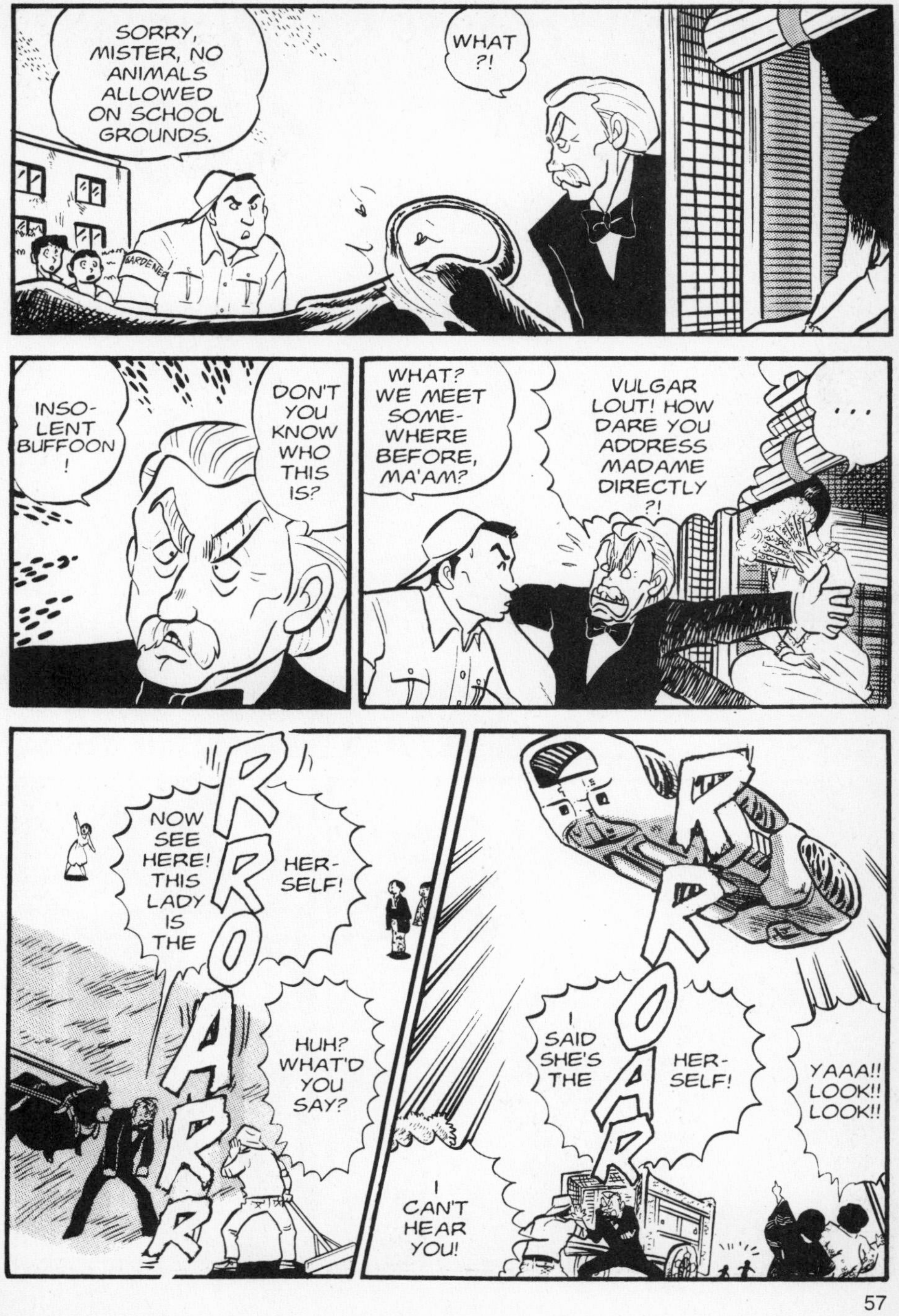

SORRY, MISTER, NO ANIMALS ALLOWED ON SCHOOL GROUNDS.
WHAT ?!
INSO-LENT BUFFOON !
DON'T YOU KNOW WHO THIS IS?
WHAT? WE MEET SOME-WHERE BEFORE, MA'AM?
VULGAR LOUT! HOW DARE YOU ADDRESS MADAME DIRECTLY ?!
. . .
NOW SEE HERE! THIS LADY IS THE
RROARR
HER-SELF!
HUH? WHAT'D YOU SAY?
RROOAR
I SAID SHE'S THE
HER-SELF!
YAAA!! LOOK!! LOOK!!
I CAN'T HEAR YOU!

TOOONG

AIYAAH! MADAME!

SQUISH

EEEEEEK!!

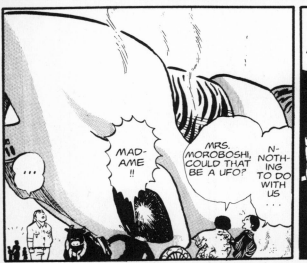

MAD-AME!!

MRS. MOROBOSHI, COULD THAT BE A UFO?

N-NOTH-ING TO DO WITH US...

WHAT A MESS.

FIRST BULLS, NOW UFOS.

WHY, WHY, *WHY* DO PEOPLE HATE GARDENERS?!

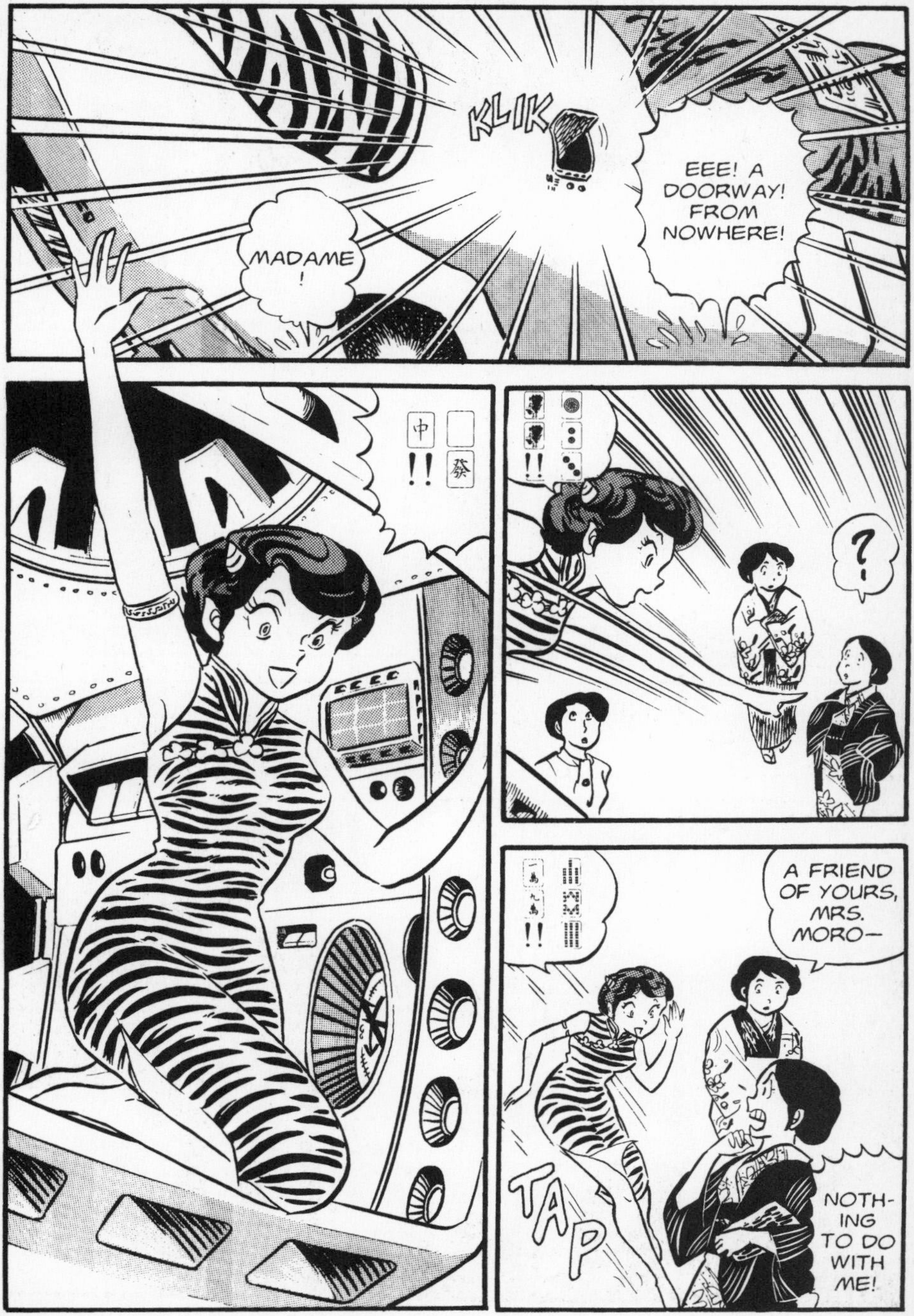
KLIK
MADAME !
EEE! A DOORWAY! FROM NOWHERE!
中 發 !!
?
一萬 九萬 !!
A FRIEND OF YOURS, MRS. MORO—
TAP
NOTH-ING TO DO WITH ME!

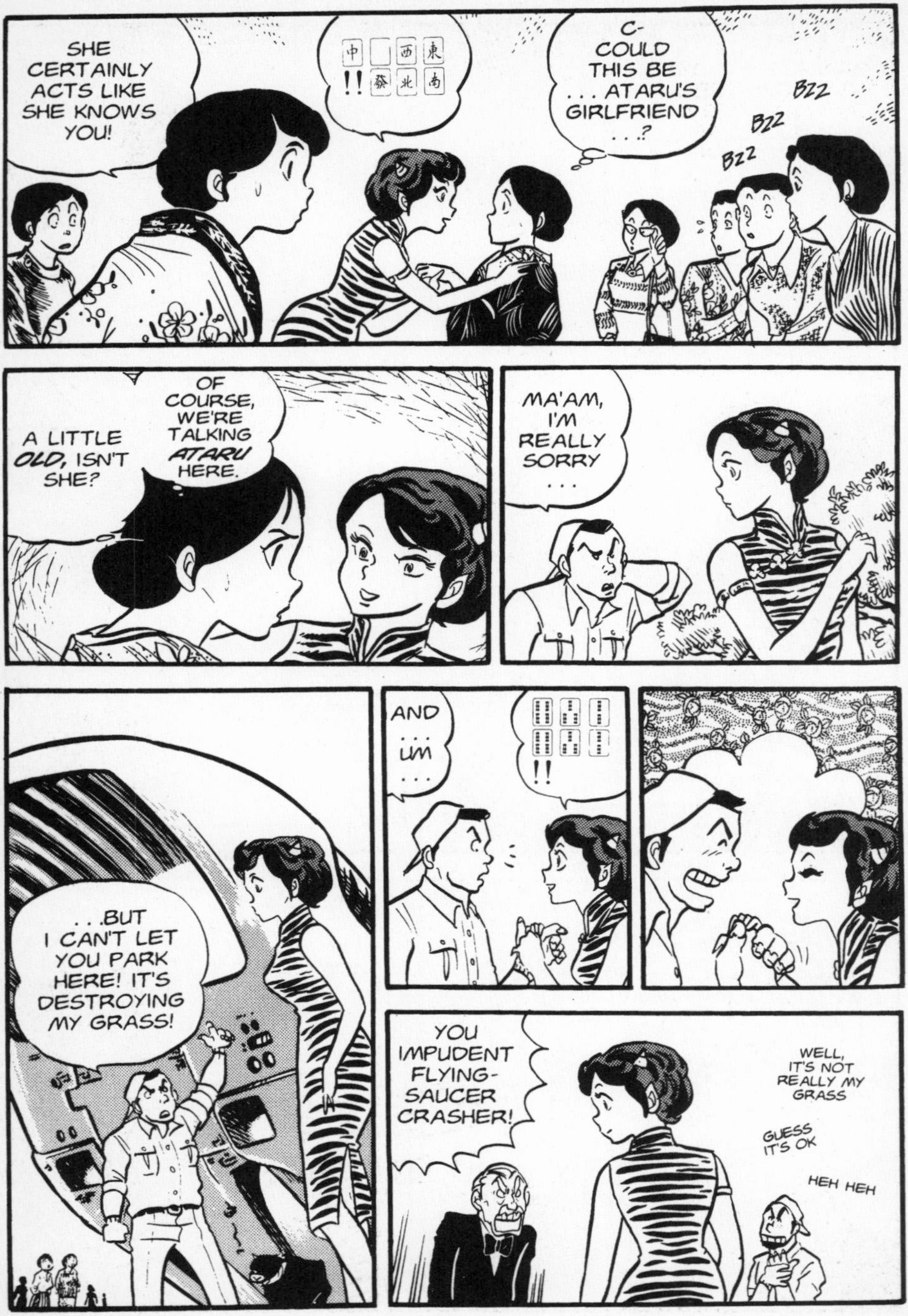

SHE CERTAINLY ACTS LIKE SHE KNOWS YOU!
!!
C- COULD THIS BE . . . ATARU'S GIRLFRIEND . . .?
BZZ
BZZ
BZZ
A LITTLE OLD, ISN'T SHE?
OF COURSE, WE'RE TALKING ATARU HERE.
MA'AM, I'M REALLY SORRY . . .
. . .BUT I CAN'T LET YOU PARK HERE! IT'S DESTROYING MY GRASS!
AND . . . UM . . .
!!
YOU IMPUDENT FLYING-SAUCER CRASHER!
WELL, IT'S NOT REALLY MY GRASS
GUESS IT'S OK
HEH HEH

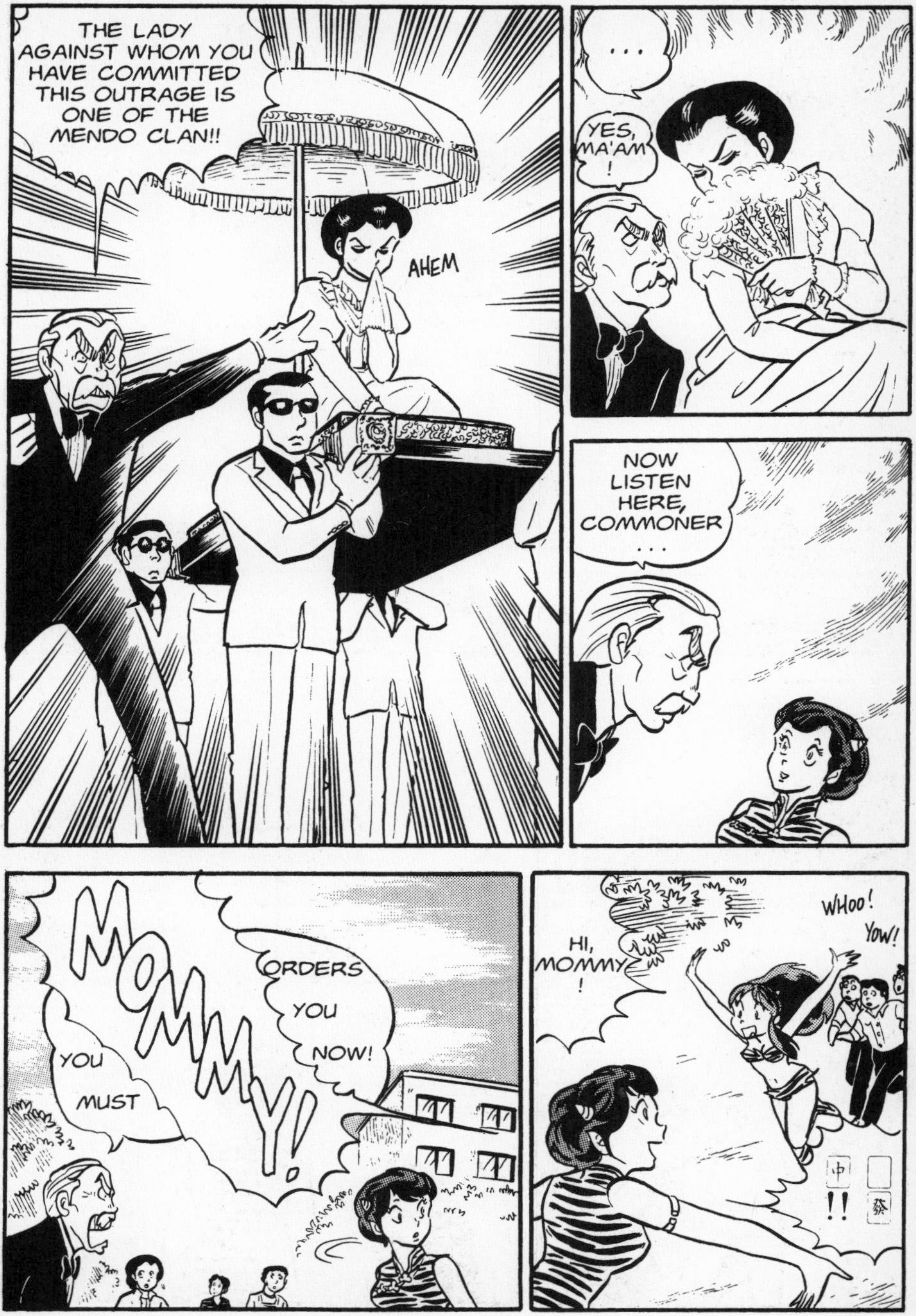
THE LADY AGAINST WHOM YOU HAVE COMMITTED THIS OUTRAGE IS ONE OF THE MENDO CLAN!!
AHEM
...
YES, MA'AM!
NOW LISTEN HERE, COMMONER...
YOU MUST
MOMMY!
ORDERS YOU NOW!
HI, MOMMY!
WHOO!
YOW!

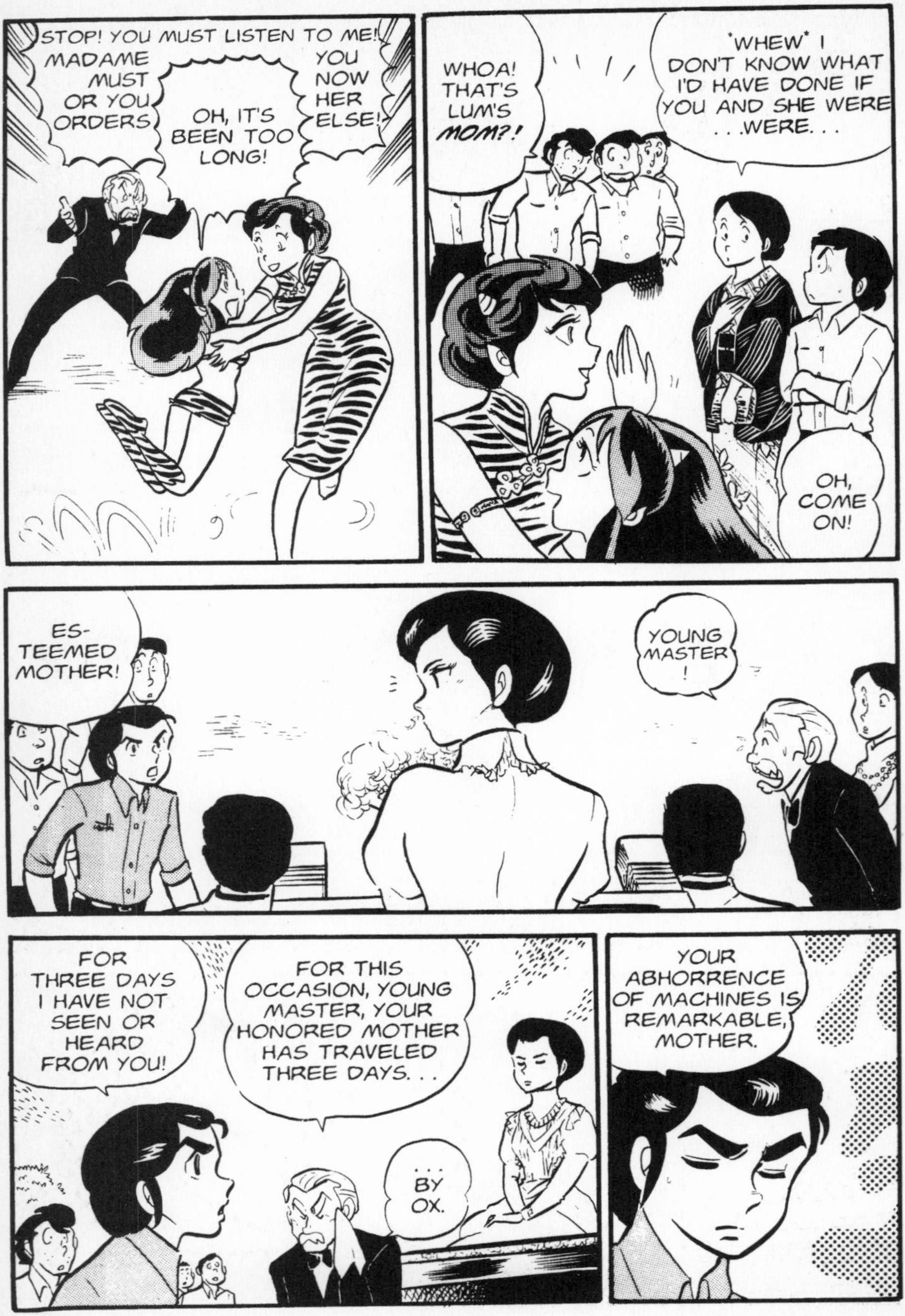
STOP! YOU MUST LISTEN TO ME!
MADAME MUST OR YOU ORDERS
OH, IT'S BEEN TOO LONG!
YOU NOW HER ELSE!
WHOA! THAT'S LUM'S MOM?!
WHEW I DON'T KNOW WHAT I'D HAVE DONE IF YOU AND SHE WERE WERE. . .WERE. . .
OH, COME ON!
ES-TEEMED MOTHER!
YOUNG MASTER!
FOR THREE DAYS I HAVE NOT SEEN OR HEARD FROM YOU!
FOR THIS OCCASION, YOUNG MASTER, YOUR HONORED MOTHER HAS TRAVELED THREE DAYS. . .
. . . BY OX.
YOUR ABHORRENCE OF MACHINES IS REMARKABLE, MOTHER.

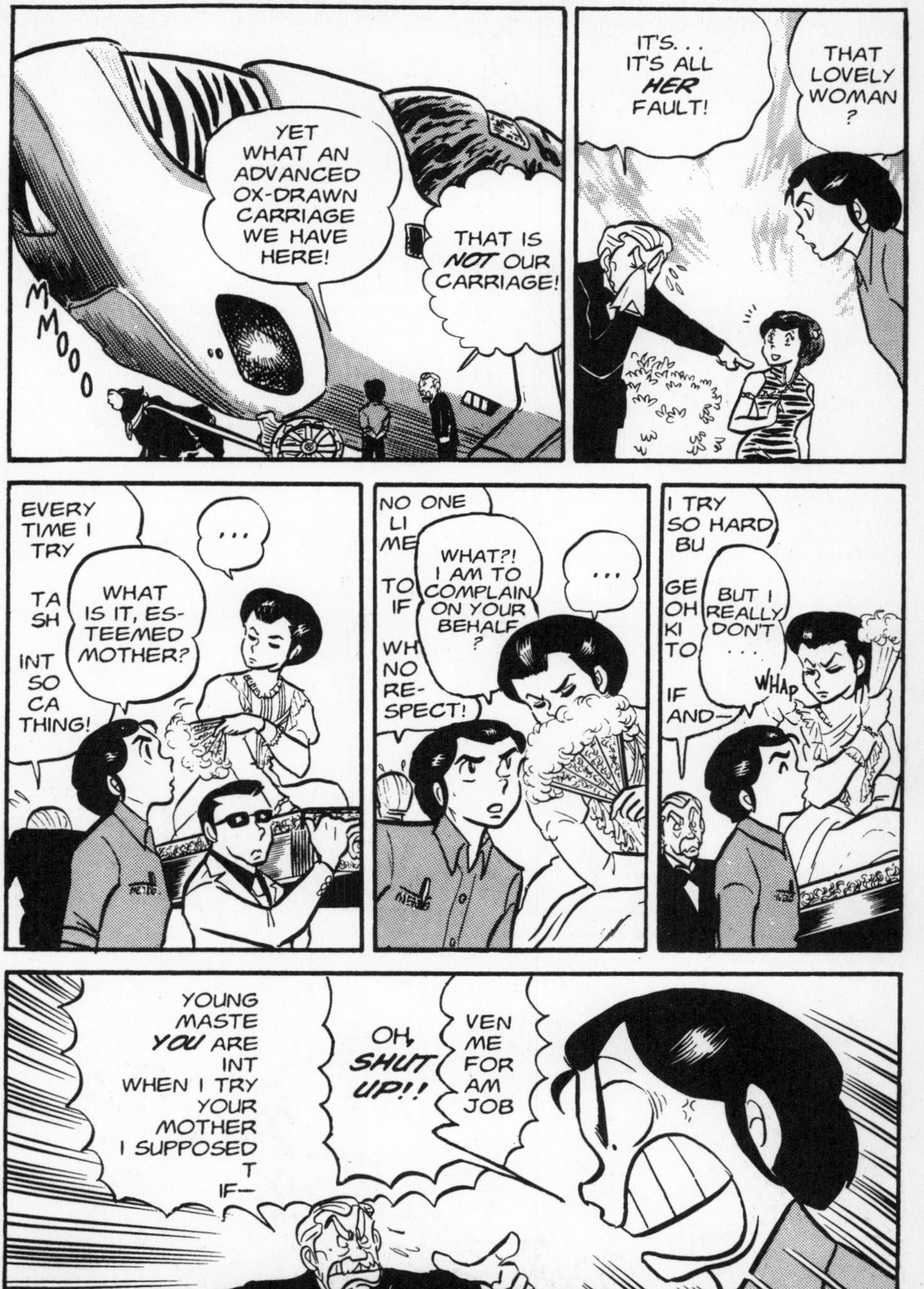
YET WHAT AN ADVANCED OX-DRAWN CARRIAGE WE HAVE HERE!
THAT IS NOT OUR CARRIAGE!
MMOOO
IT'S. . . IT'S ALL HER FAULT!
THAT LOVELY WOMAN ?
EVERY TIME I TRY TA SH INT SO CA THING!
. . .
WHAT IS IT, ES-TEEMED MOTHER?
NO ONE LI ME TO IF WH NO RE-SPECT!
WHAT?! I AM TO COMPLAIN ON YOUR BEHALF ?
. . .
I TRY SO HARD BU GE OH KI TO IF AND—
BUT I REALLY DON'T . . .
WHAP
YOUNG MASTE YOU ARE INT WHEN I TRY YOUR MOTHER I SUPPOSED T IF—
OH, SHUT UP!!
VEN ME FOR AM JOB

DEAR LUM, YOU MUST INTERPRET FOR ME!

OKAY!

...

HOW DARE YOU DESTROY OUR CARRIAGE?

<THANK YOU FOR DESTROYING OUR CARRIAGE!>

...

THE ENEMY OF MY CARRIAGE IS *MY* ENEMY!

<MY CARRIAGE IS MY ENEMY!>

...

SOMEDAY I WILL DEMAND PAYMENT!

<SOMEDAY I'LL REPAY YOU!>

！！

！！

CLASP

SHE SAYS, "THANK YOU FOR BEING SO UNDERSTANDING!"

ARE YOU SURE YOU TRANSLATED CORRECTLY?

WELL, THE GRAMMAR'S KIND OF TRICKY...

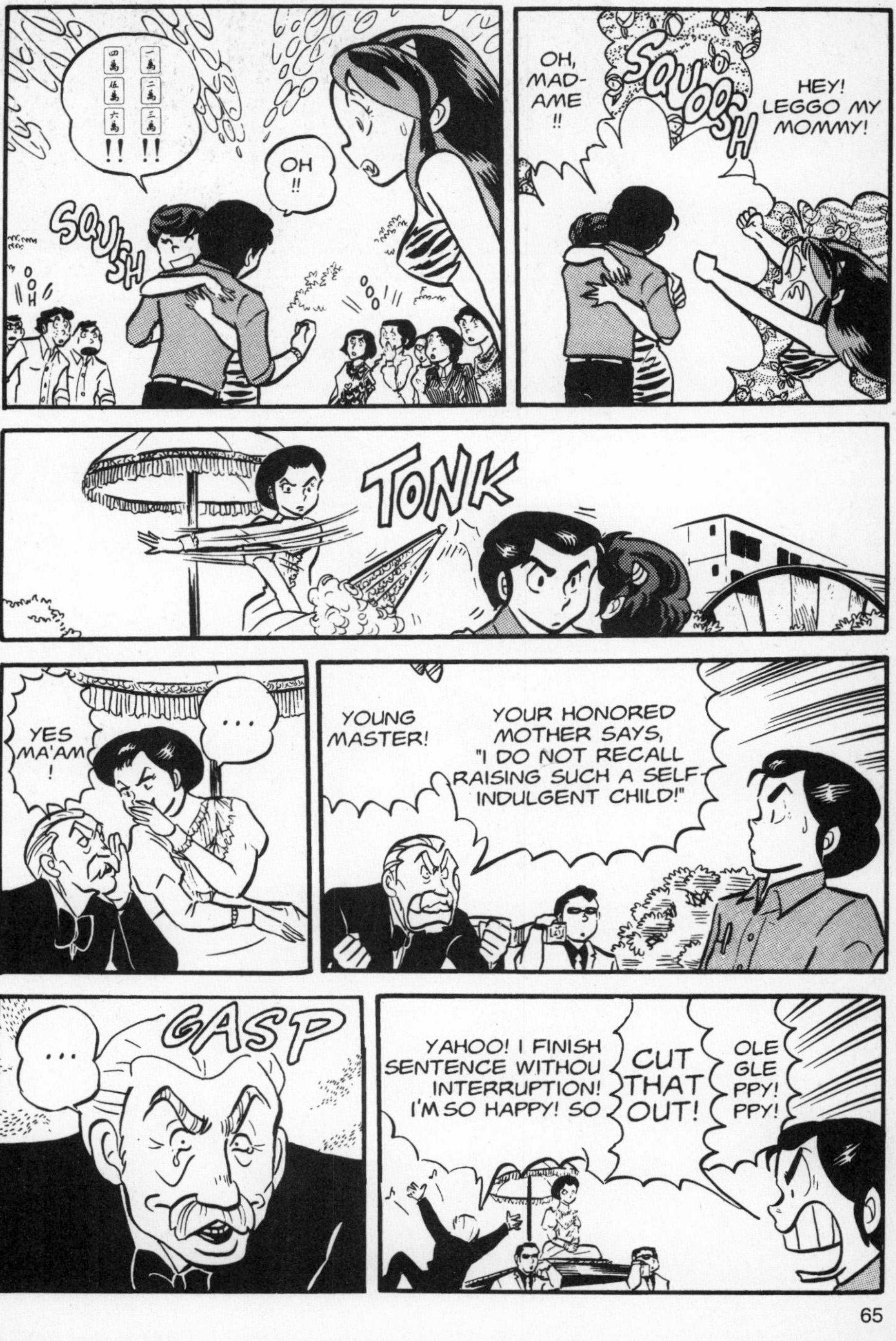
一萬二萬三萬!! 四萬伍萬六萬!!
OH !!
SQUISH
OOH
OOO
OH, MAD-AME !!
SQUOOSH
HEY! LEGGO MY MOMMY!
TONK
YES MA'AM !
...
YOUNG MASTER!
YOUR HONORED MOTHER SAYS, "I DO NOT RECALL RAISING SUCH A SELF-INDULGENT CHILD!"
...
GASP
YAHOO! I FINISH SENTENCE WITHOU INTERRUPTION! I'M SO HAPPY! SO
CUT THAT OUT!
OLE GLE PPY! PPY!

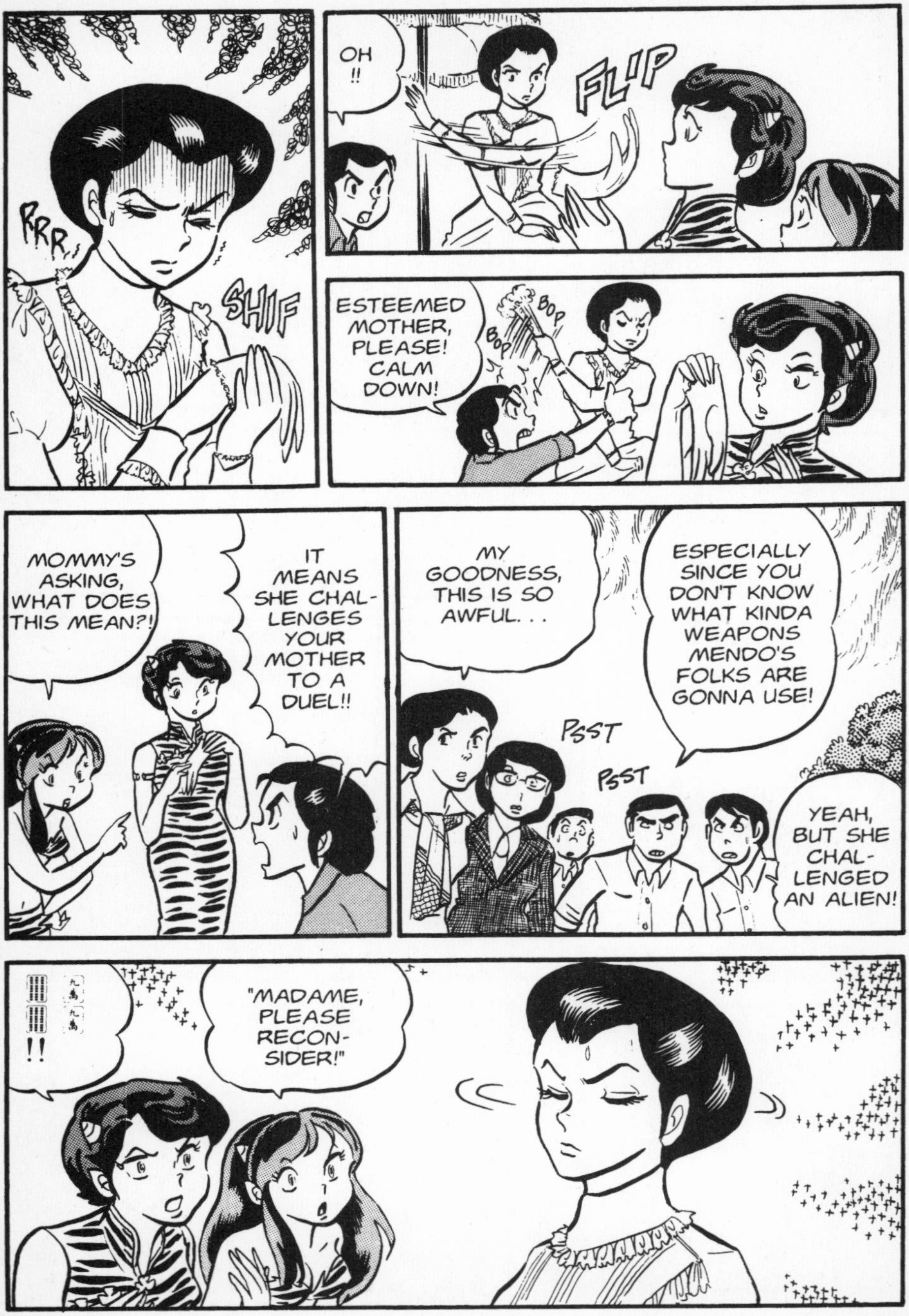
RRR
SHIF
OH !!
FLIP
ESTEEMED MOTHER, PLEASE! CALM DOWN!
BOP
BOP
MOMMY'S ASKING, WHAT DOES THIS MEAN?!
IT MEANS SHE CHAL- LENGES YOUR MOTHER TO A DUEL!!
MY GOODNESS, THIS IS SO AWFUL. . .
ESPECIALLY SINCE YOU DON'T KNOW WHAT KINDA WEAPONS MENDO'S FOLKS ARE GONNA USE!
PSST
PSST
YEAH, BUT SHE CHAL- LENGED AN ALIEN!
!!
"MADAME, PLEASE RECON- SIDER!"

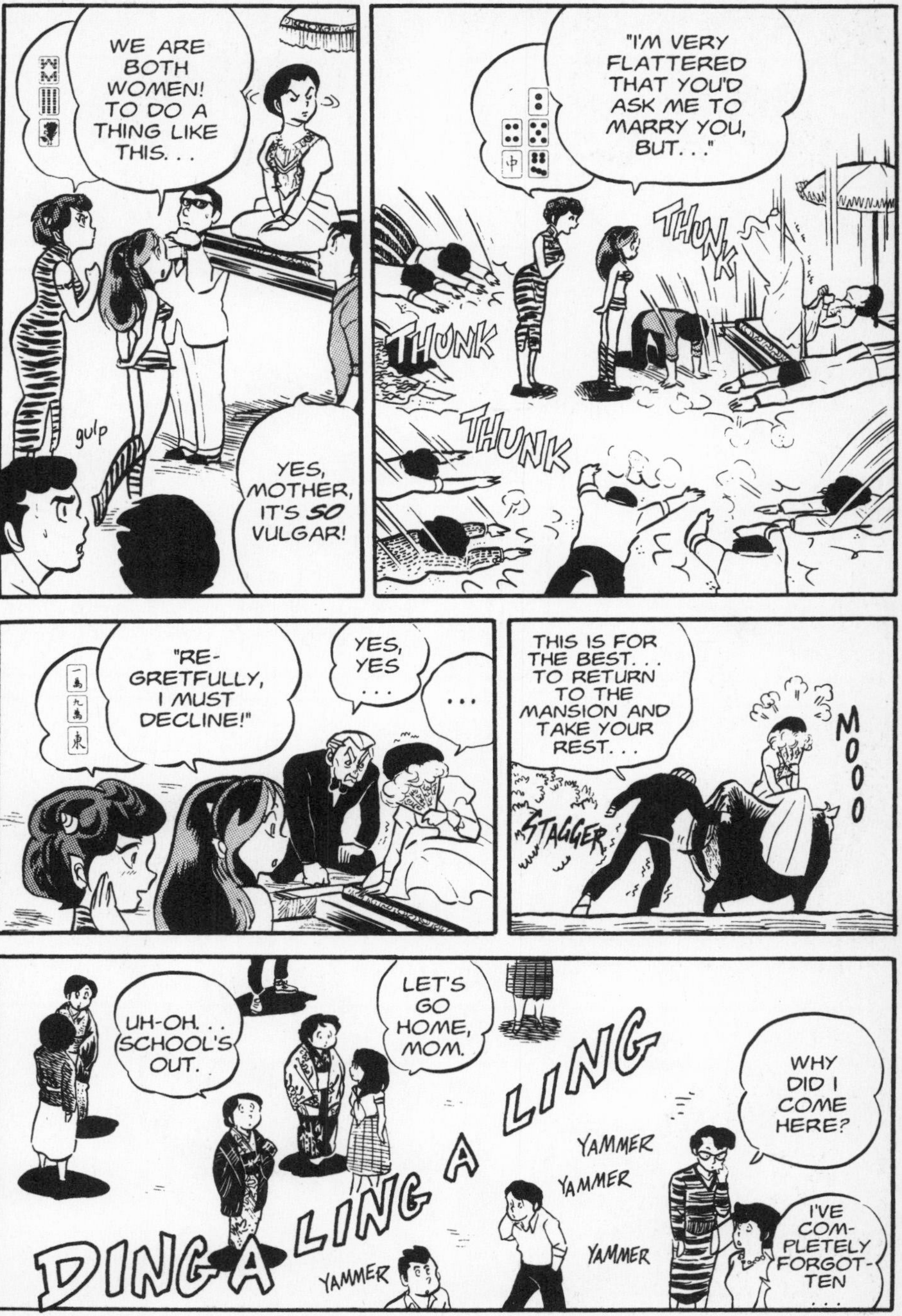
WE ARE BOTH WOMEN! TO DO A THING LIKE THIS. . .
gulp
YES, MOTHER, IT'S SO VULGAR!
"I'M VERY FLATTERED THAT YOU'D ASK ME TO MARRY YOU, BUT. . ."
THUNK
THUNK
THUNK
"RE-GRETFULLY, I MUST DECLINE!"
YES, YES . . .
. . .
THIS IS FOR THE BEST. . . TO RETURN TO THE MANSION AND TAKE YOUR REST. . .
STAGGER
MOOO
UH-OH. . . SCHOOL'S OUT.
LET'S GO HOME, MOM.
DING A LING A LING
WHY DID I COME HERE?
YAMMER
YAMMER
YAMMER
YAMMER
I'VE COM-PLETELY FORGOT-TEN . . .

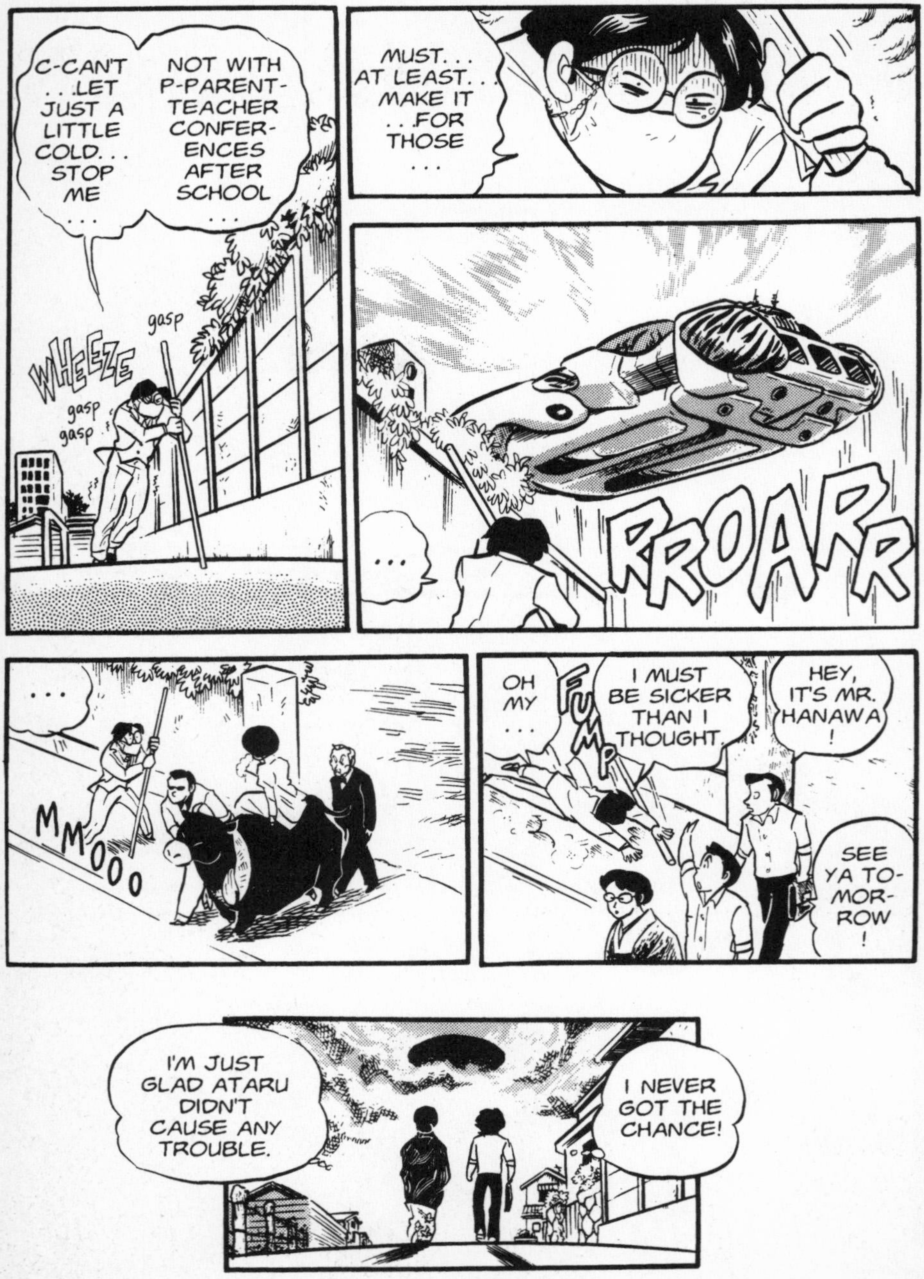
C-CAN'T . . .LET JUST A LITTLE COLD. . . STOP ME . . .
NOT WITH P-PARENT-TEACHER CONFERENCES AFTER SCHOOL . . .
WHEEZE
gasp
gasp gasp
MUST. . . AT LEAST. . . MAKE IT . . .FOR THOSE . . .
. . .
RROARR
. . .
MMOOO
OH MY . . .
FUMP
I MUST BE SICKER THAN I THOUGHT.
HEY, IT'S MR. HANAWA!
SEE YA TOMORROW!
I'M JUST GLAD ATARU DIDN'T CAUSE ANY TROUBLE.
I NEVER GOT THE CHANCE!

PART FIVE
RUN, NINJA, RUN

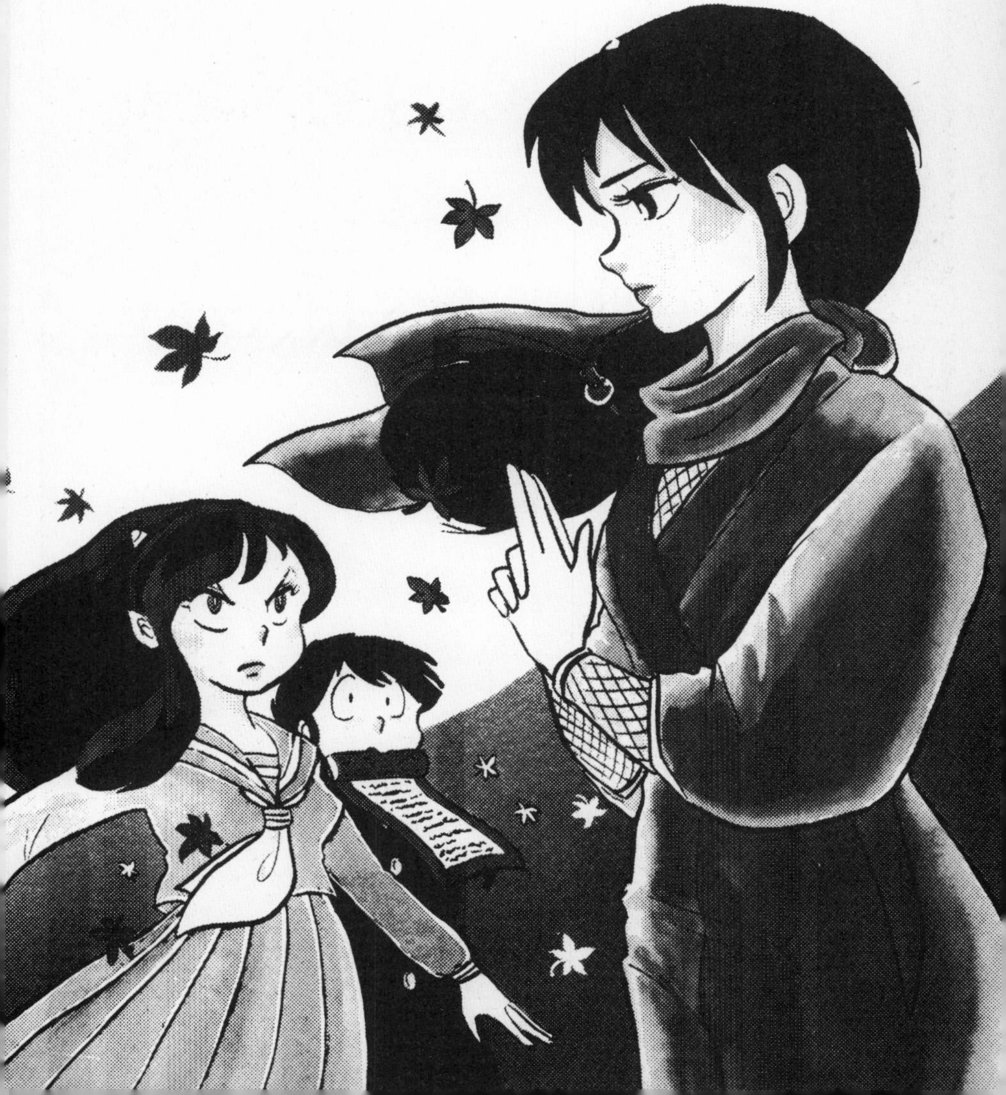

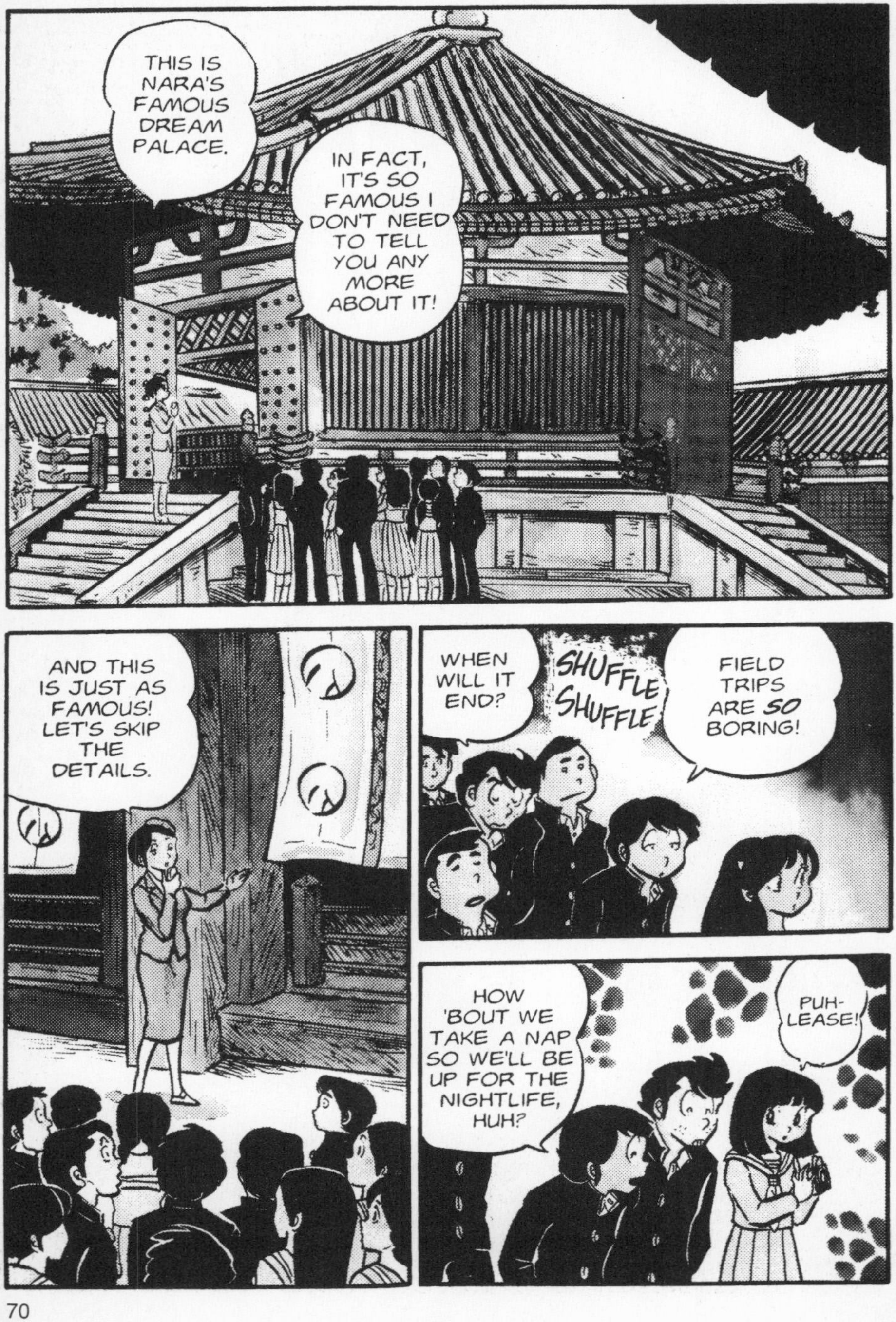
THIS IS NARA'S FAMOUS DREAM PALACE.
IN FACT, IT'S SO FAMOUS I DON'T NEED TO TELL YOU ANY MORE ABOUT IT!
AND THIS IS JUST AS FAMOUS! LET'S SKIP THE DETAILS.
WHEN WILL IT END?
SHUFFLE SHUFFLE
FIELD TRIPS ARE *SO* BORING!
HOW 'BOUT WE TAKE A NAP SO WE'LL BE UP FOR THE NIGHTLIFE, HUH?
PUH-LEASE!

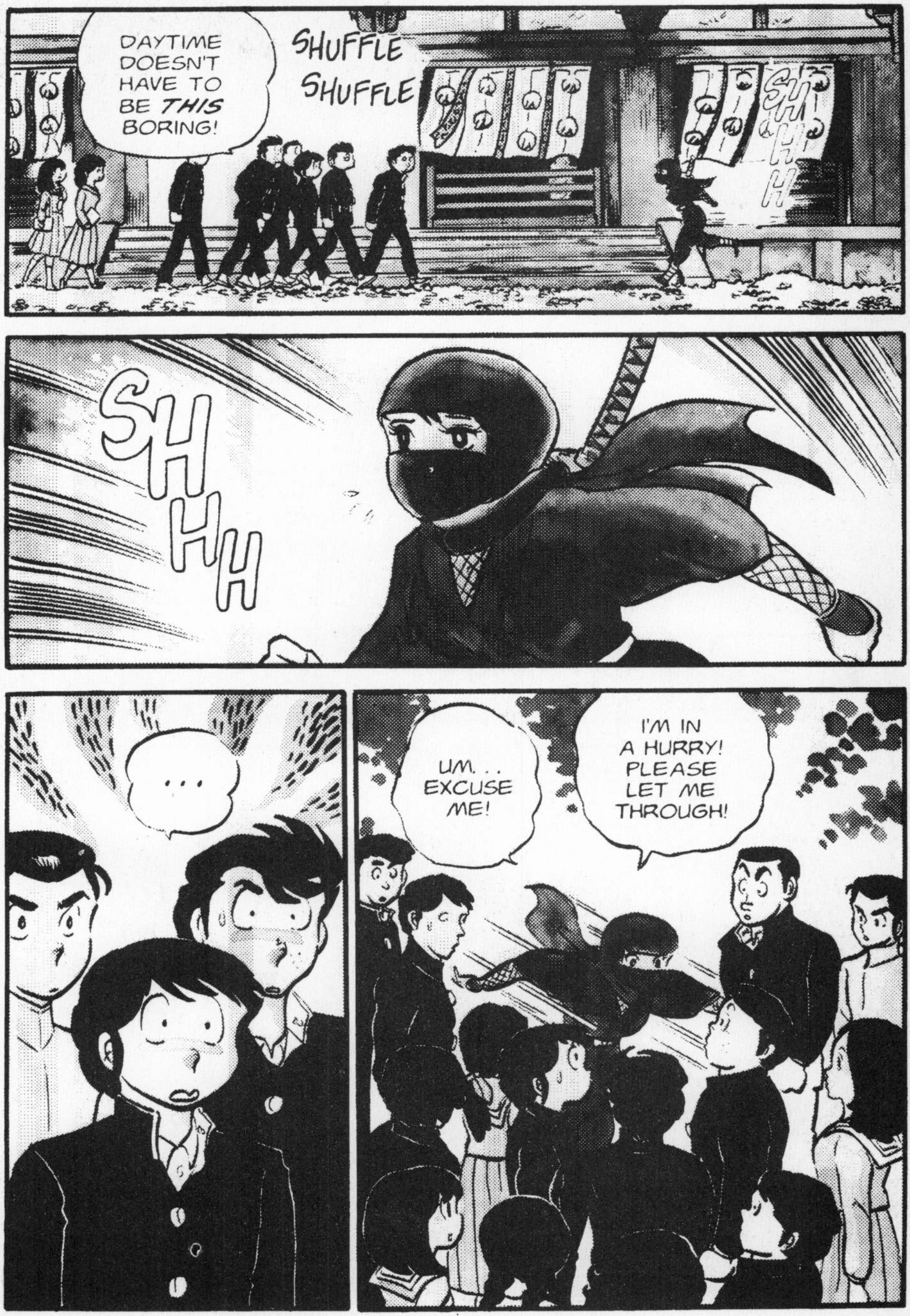
DAYTIME DOESN'T HAVE TO BE *THIS* BORING!
SHUFFLE SHUFFLE
SHHHH
SHHHH
. . .
UM. . . EXCUSE ME!
I'M IN A HURRY! PLEASE LET ME THROUGH!

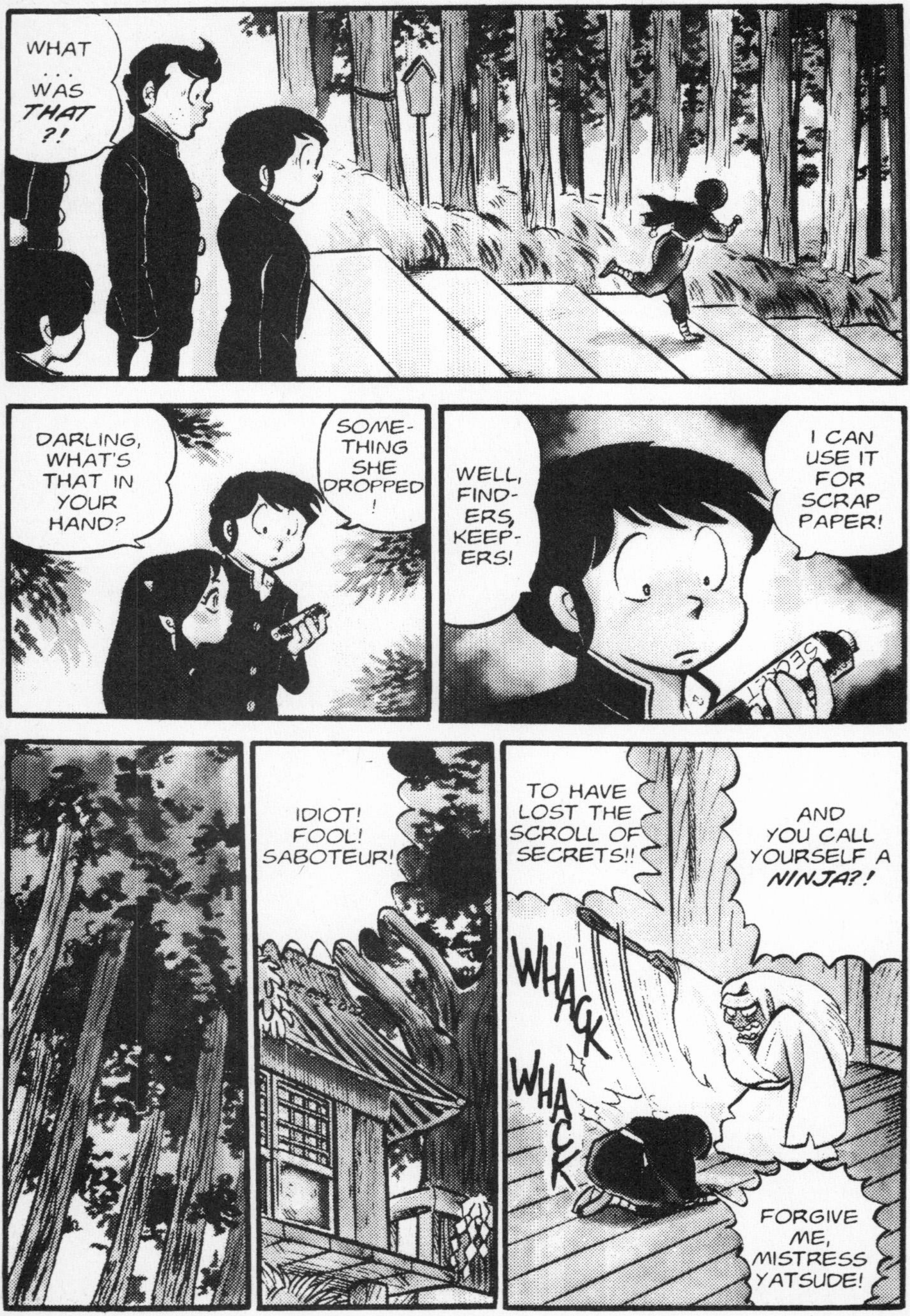

WHAT ... WAS *THAT* ?!
DARLING, WHAT'S THAT IN YOUR HAND?
SOME-THING SHE DROPPED!
WELL, FINDERS, KEEPERS!
I CAN USE IT FOR SCRAP PAPER!
IDIOT! FOOL! SABOTEUR!
TO HAVE LOST THE SCROLL OF SECRETS!!
AND YOU CALL YOURSELF A *NINJA?!*
WHACK
WHACK
FORGIVE ME, MISTRESS YATSUDE!

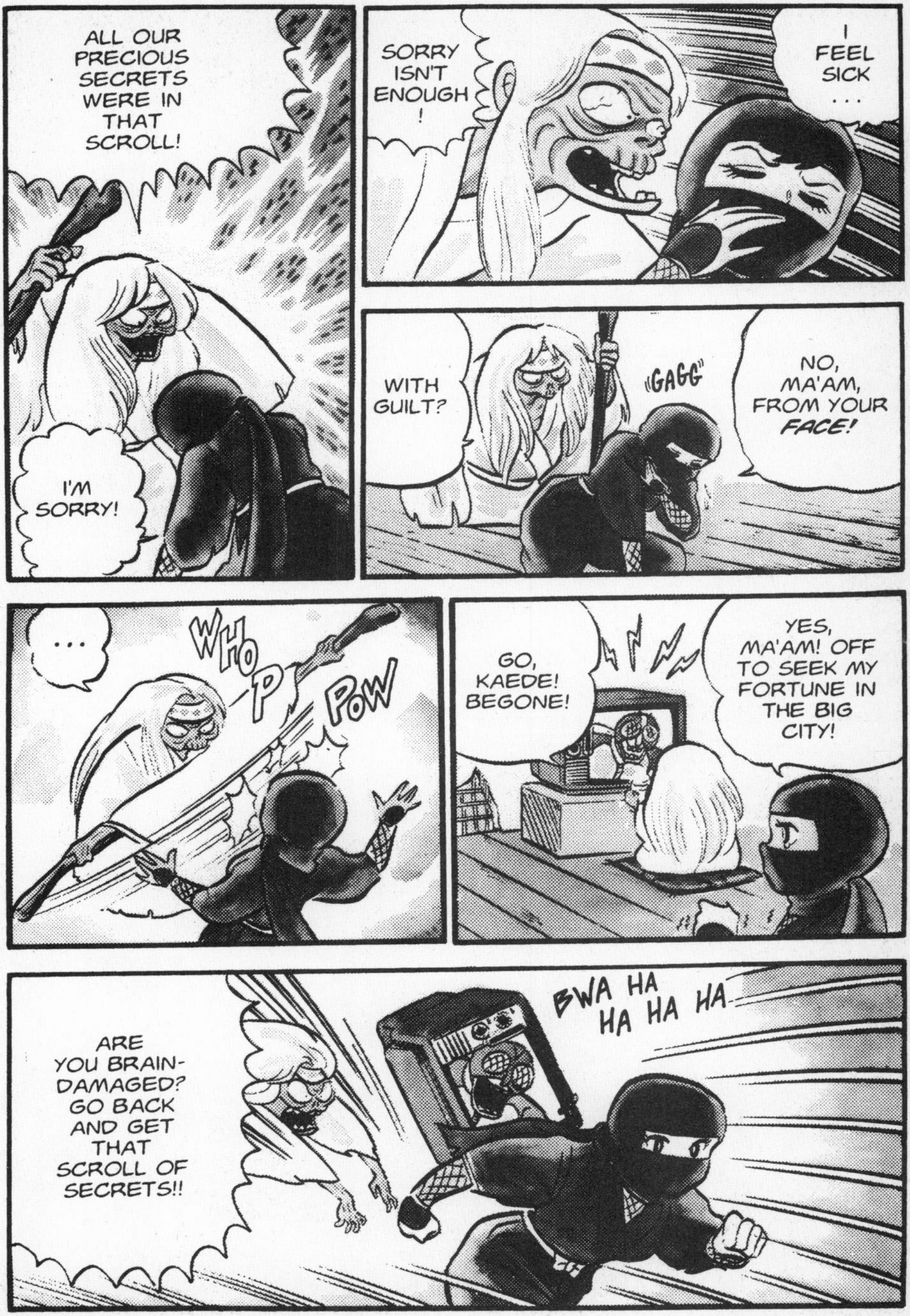
ALL OUR PRECIOUS SECRETS WERE IN THAT SCROLL!
I'M SORRY!
SORRY ISN'T ENOUGH!
I FEEL SICK . . .
WITH GUILT?
GAGG
NO, MA'AM, FROM YOUR FACE!
. . .
WHOP
POW
GO, KAEDE! BEGONE!
YES, MA'AM! OFF TO SEEK MY FORTUNE IN THE BIG CITY!
ARE YOU BRAIN-DAMAGED? GO BACK AND GET THAT SCROLL OF SECRETS!!
BWA HA HA HA HA

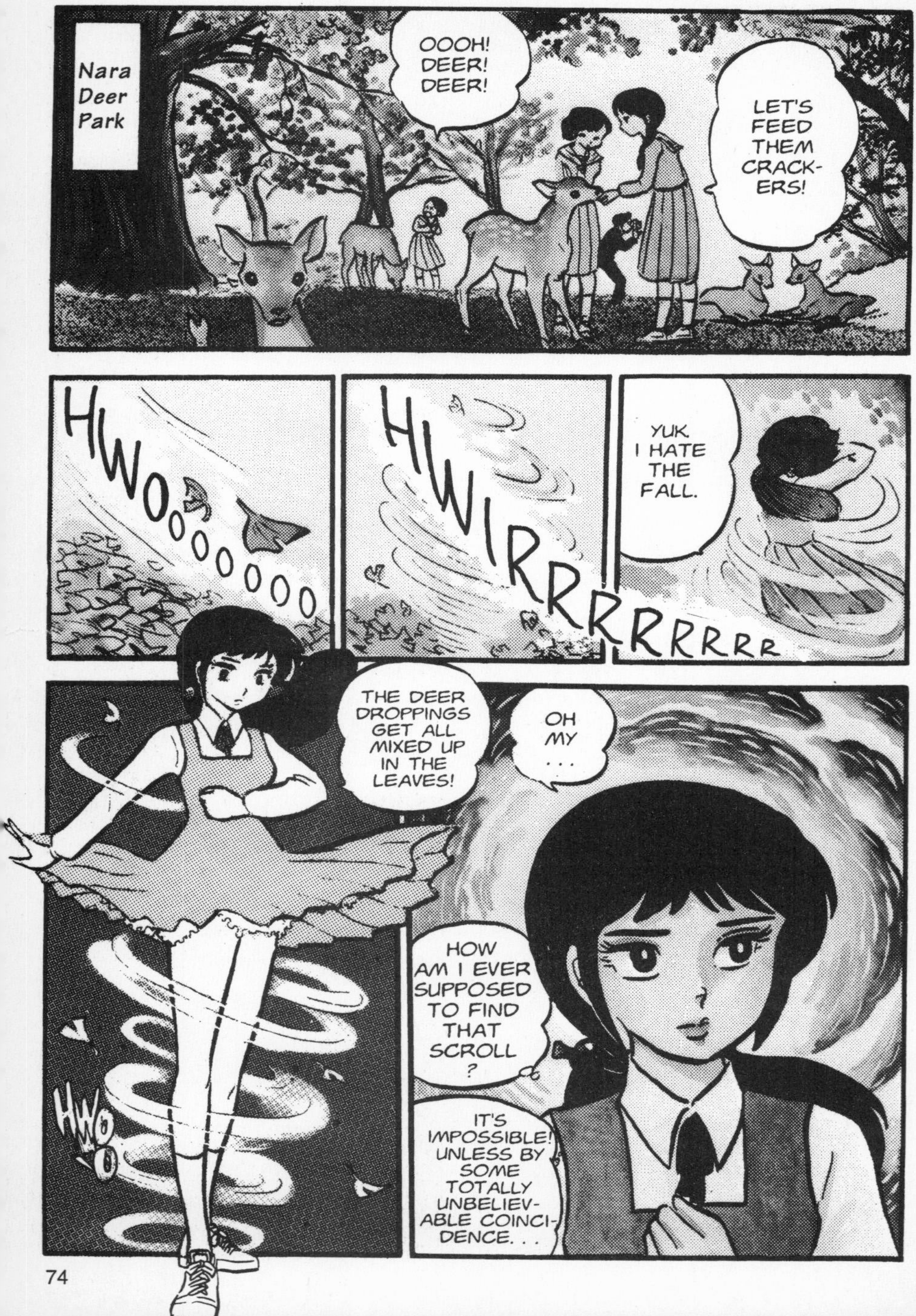

Nara Deer Park
OOOH! DEER! DEER!
LET'S FEED THEM CRACK- ERS!
HWOOOOOOOOO
HWIRRRRRRRRRR
YUK. I HATE THE FALL.
THE DEER DROPPINGS GET ALL MIXED UP IN THE LEAVES!
HWO
OH MY . . .
HOW AM I EVER SUPPOSED TO FIND THAT SCROLL ?
IT'S IMPOSSIBLE! UNLESS BY SOME TOTALLY UNBELIEV- ABLE COINCI- DENCE. . .

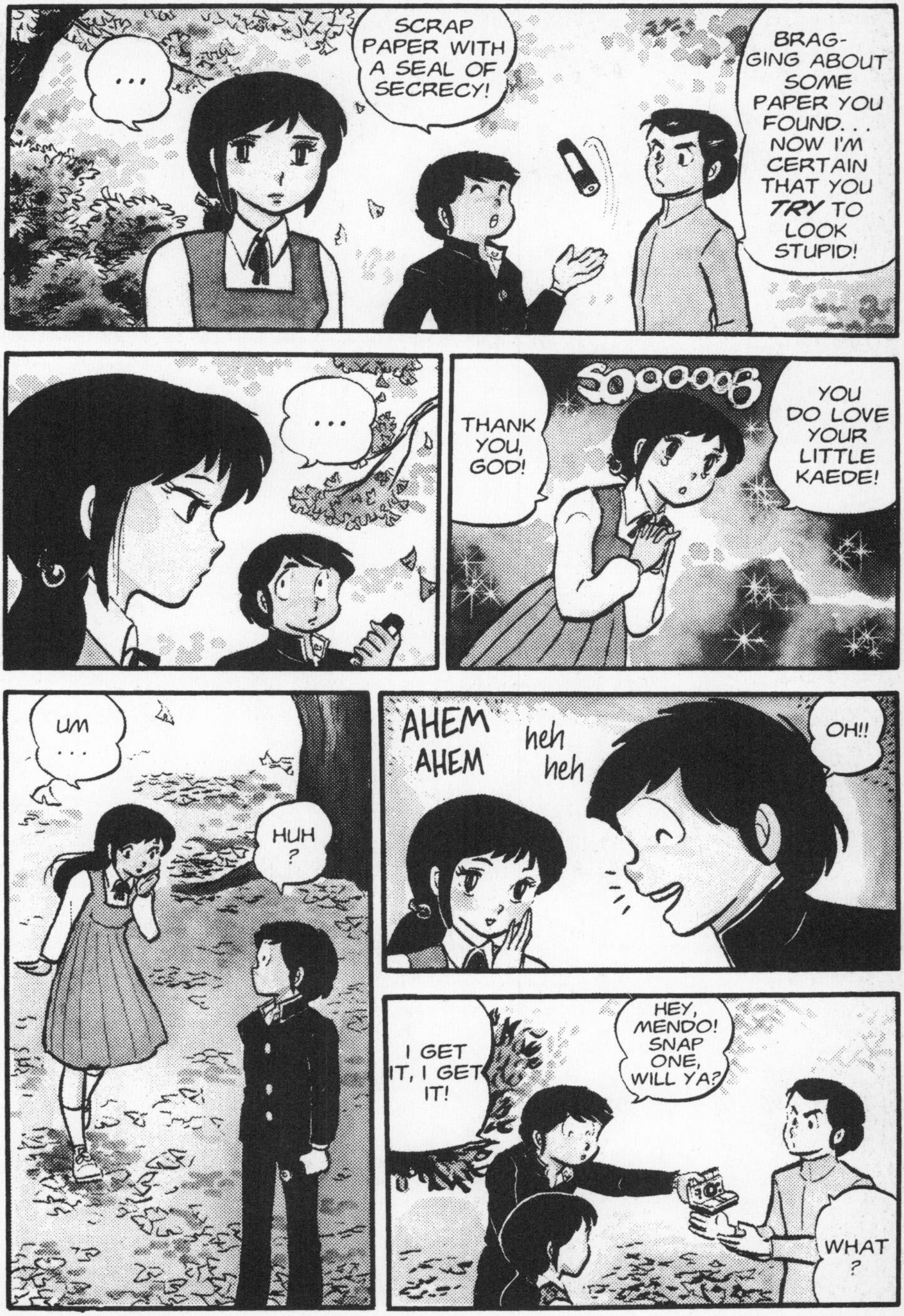
...
SCRAP PAPER WITH A SEAL OF SECRECY!
BRAGGING ABOUT SOME PAPER YOU FOUND... NOW I'M CERTAIN THAT YOU *TRY* TO LOOK STUPID!
...
SOOOOOB
THANK YOU, GOD!
YOU DO LOVE YOUR LITTLE KAEDE!
UM ...
HUH ?
AHEM AHEM
heh heh
OH!!
I GET IT, I GET IT!
HEY, MENDO! SNAP ONE, WILL YA?
WHAT ?

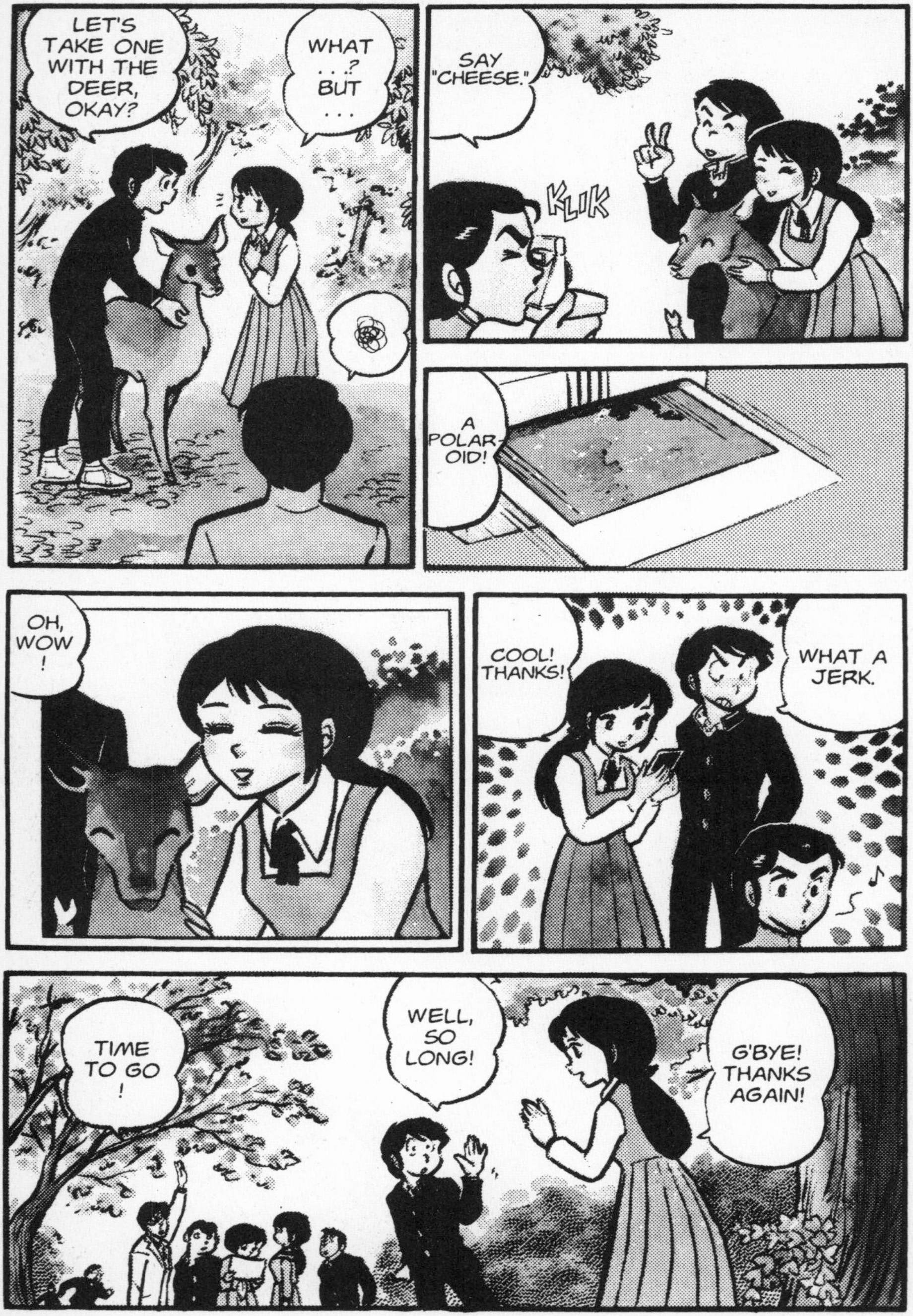

LET'S TAKE ONE WITH THE DEER, OKAY?
WHAT ...? BUT ...
SAY "CHEESE."
KLIK
A POLAR-OID!
OH, WOW!
COOL! THANKS!
WHAT A JERK.
TIME TO GO!
WELL, SO LONG!
G'BYE! THANKS AGAIN!

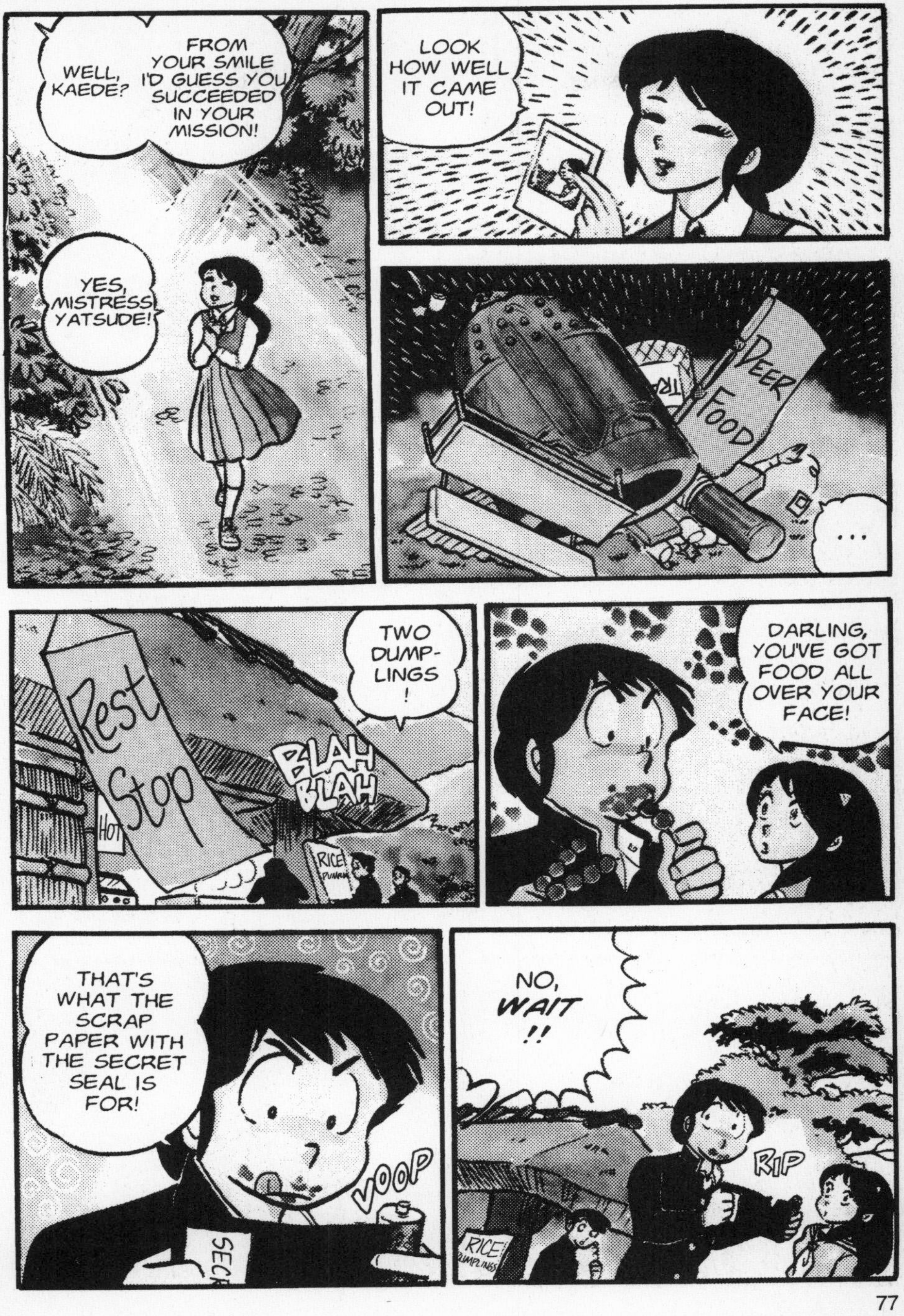

WELL, KAEDE?
FROM YOUR SMILE I'D GUESS YOU SUCCEEDED IN YOUR MISSION!
YES, MISTRESS YATSUDE!
LOOK HOW WELL IT CAME OUT!
DEER FOOD
...
Rest Stop
HOT
RICE!
TWO DUMPLINGS!
BLAH BLAH
DARLING, YOU'VE GOT FOOD ALL OVER YOUR FACE!
THAT'S WHAT THE SCRAP PAPER WITH THE SECRET SEAL IS FOR!
VOOP
NO, WAIT!!
RIP
RICE! DUMPLINGS

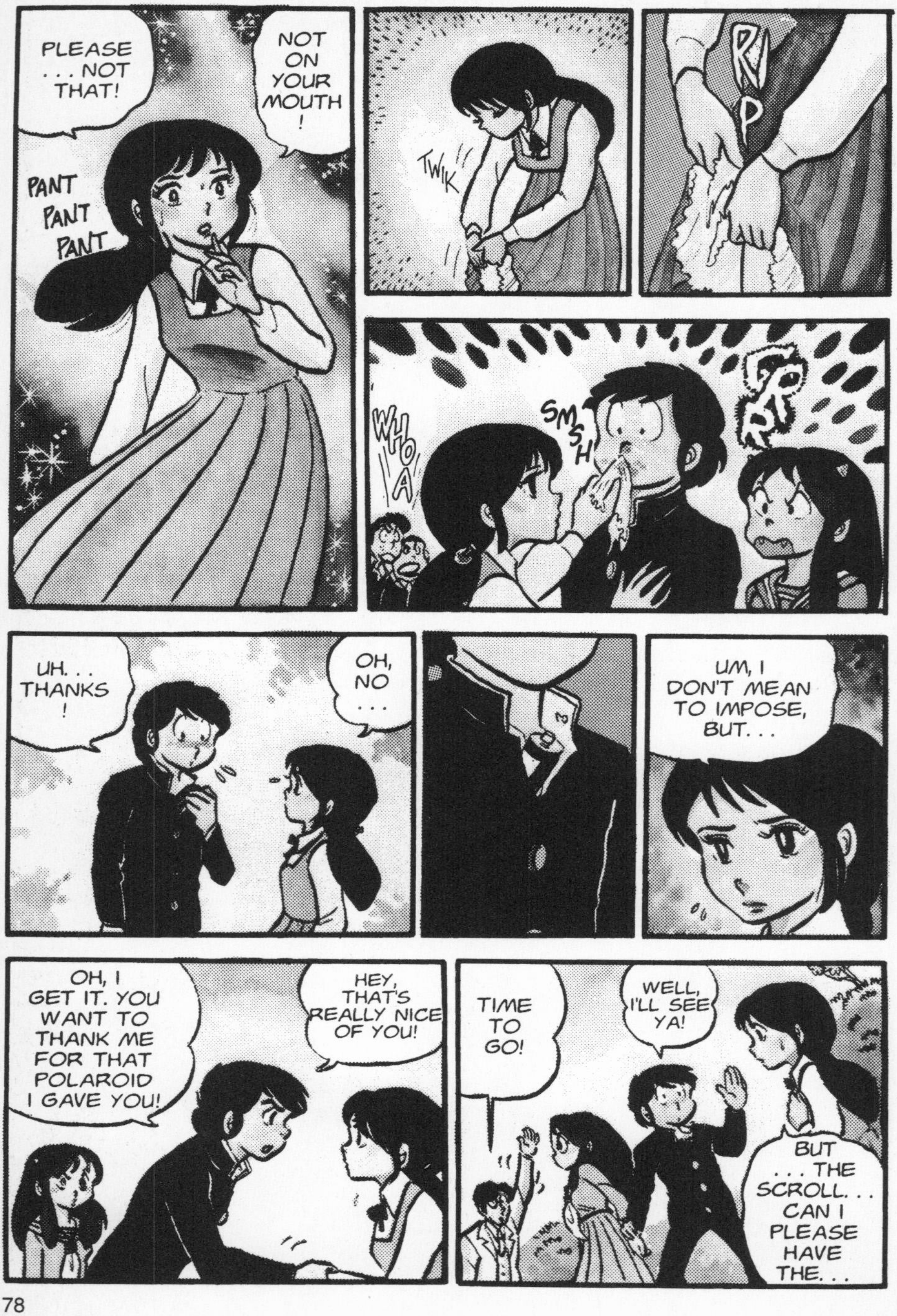

PLEASE . . . NOT THAT!
NOT ON YOUR MOUTH!
PANT PANT PANT
TWIK
RIP
WHOA
SMSH
RIP
UH. . . THANKS!
OH, NO . . .
UM, I DON'T MEAN TO IMPOSE, BUT. . .
OH, I GET IT. YOU WANT TO THANK ME FOR THAT POLAROID I GAVE YOU!
HEY, THAT'S REALLY NICE OF YOU!
TIME TO GO!
WELL, I'LL SEE YA!
BUT . . . THE SCROLL. . . CAN I PLEASE HAVE THE. . .

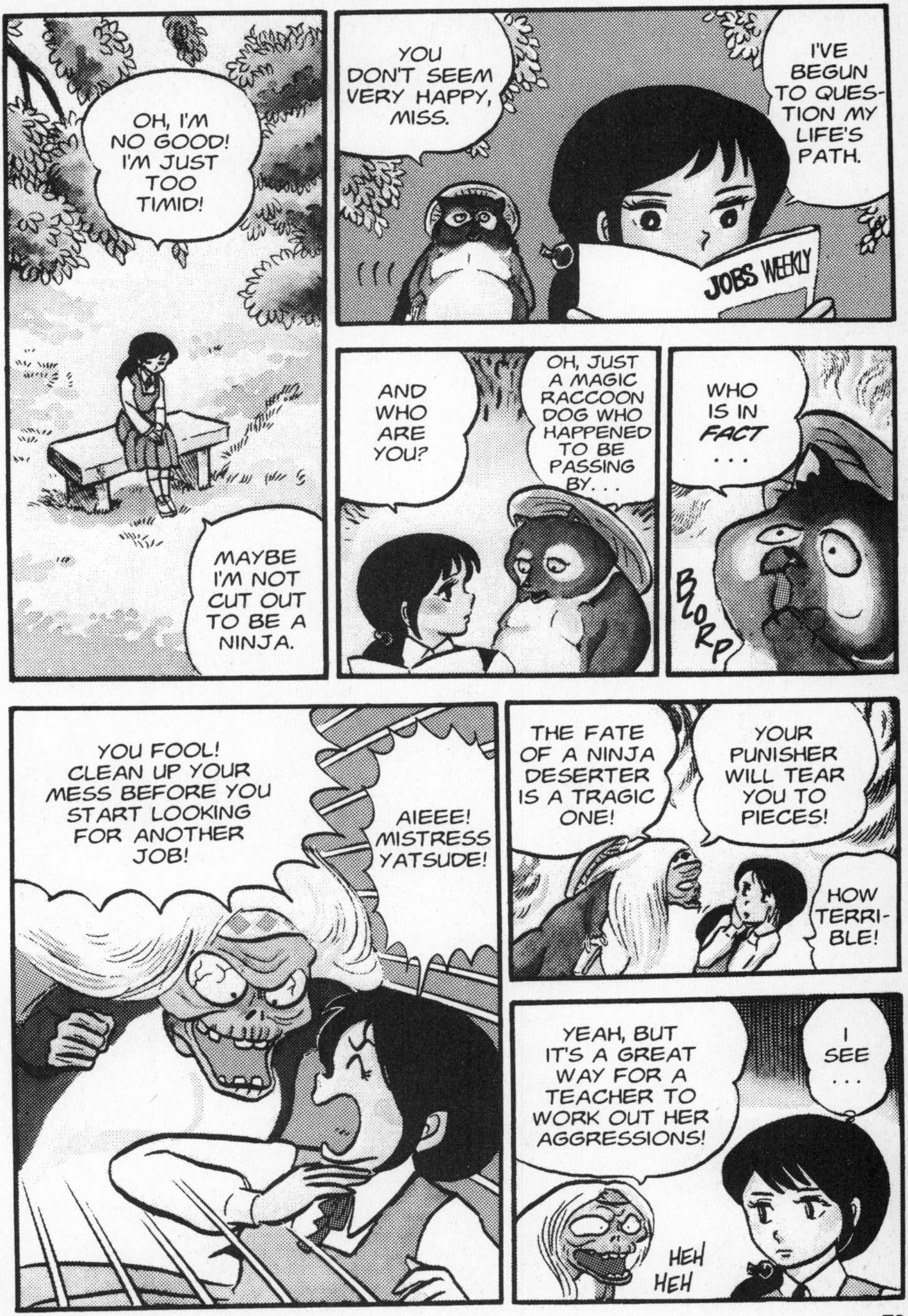
OH, I'M NO GOOD! I'M JUST TOO TIMID!
MAYBE I'M NOT CUT OUT TO BE A NINJA.
YOU DON'T SEEM VERY HAPPY, MISS.
I'VE BEGUN TO QUES- TION MY LIFE'S PATH.
JOBS WEEKLY
AND WHO ARE YOU?
OH, JUST A MAGIC RACCOON DOG WHO HAPPENED TO BE PASSING BY. . .
WHO IS IN *FACT* . . .
BLORP
YOU FOOL! CLEAN UP YOUR MESS BEFORE YOU START LOOKING FOR ANOTHER JOB!
AIEEE! MISTRESS YATSUDE!
THE FATE OF A NINJA DESERTER IS A TRAGIC ONE!
YOUR PUNISHER WILL TEAR YOU TO PIECES!
HOW TERRI- BLE!
YEAH, BUT IT'S A GREAT WAY FOR A TEACHER TO WORK OUT HER AGGRESSIONS!
I SEE . . .
HEH HEH

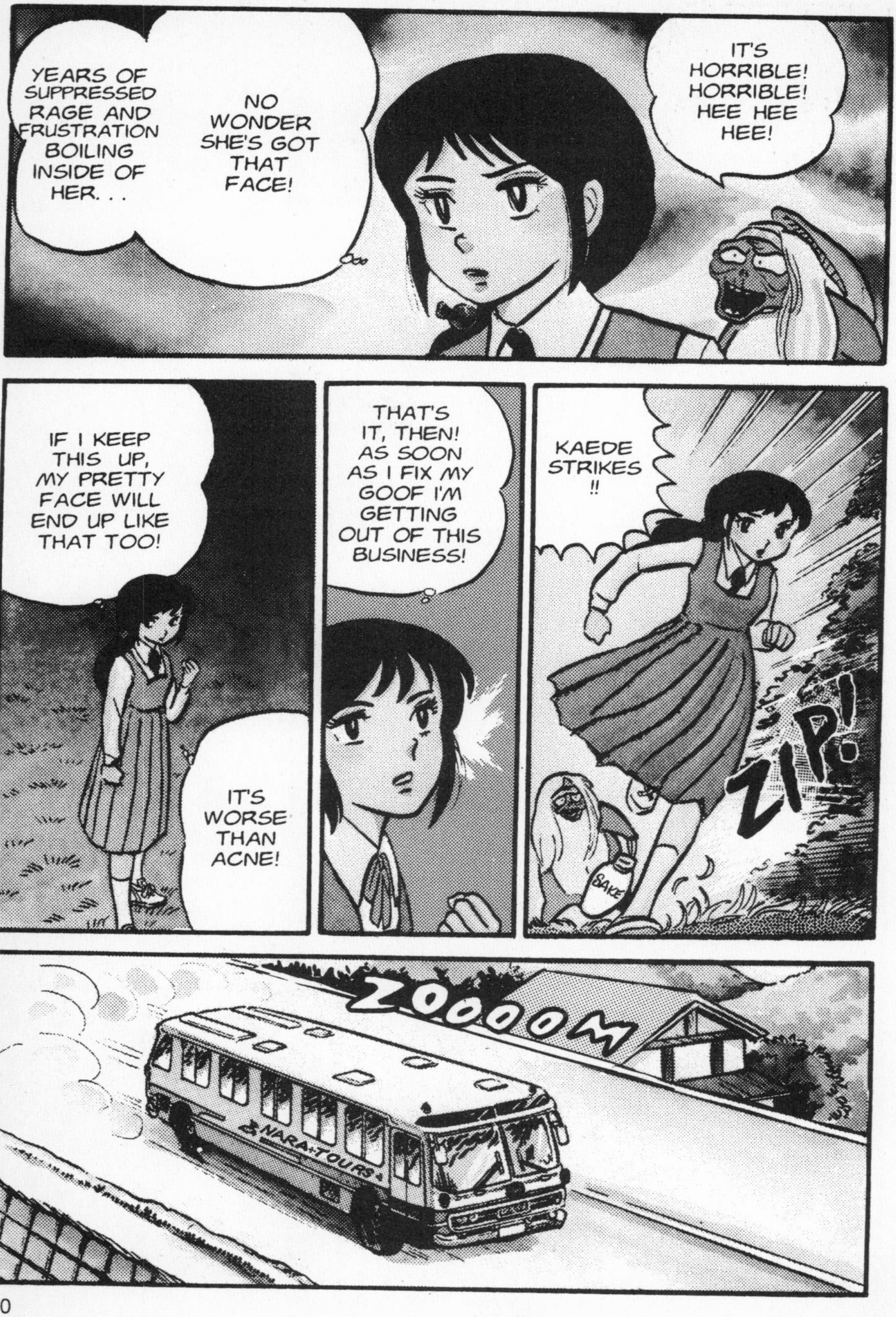
YEARS OF SUPPRESSED RAGE AND FRUSTRATION BOILING INSIDE OF HER. . .
NO WONDER SHE'S GOT THAT FACE!
IT'S HORRIBLE! HORRIBLE! HEE HEE HEE!
IF I KEEP THIS UP, MY PRETTY FACE WILL END UP LIKE THAT TOO!
IT'S WORSE THAN ACNE!
THAT'S IT, THEN! AS SOON AS I FIX MY GOOF I'M GETTING OUT OF THIS BUSINESS!
KAEDE STRIKES !!
SAKE
ZIP!
ZOOOOM
NARA-TOURS

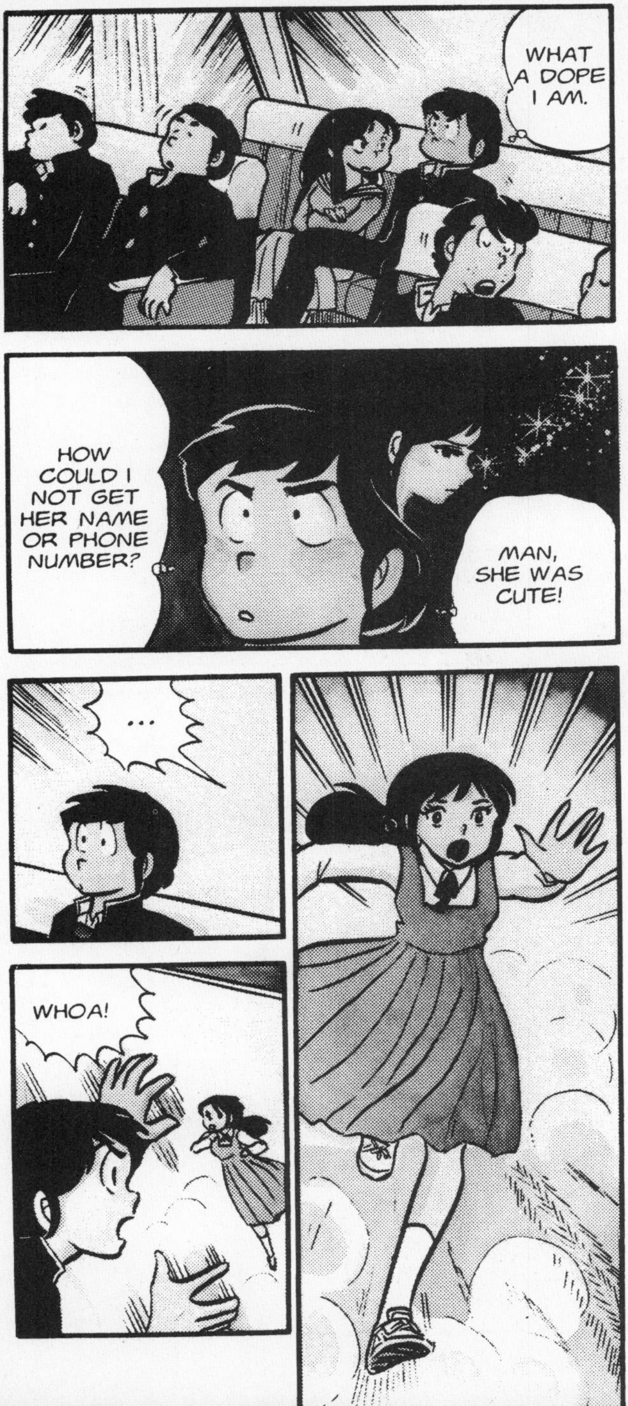
WHAT A DOPE I AM.
HOW COULD I NOT GET HER NAME OR PHONE NUMBER?
MAN, SHE WAS CUTE!
...
WHOA!
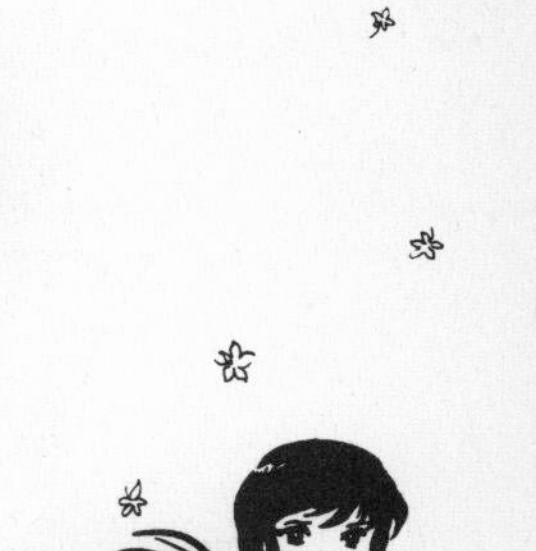

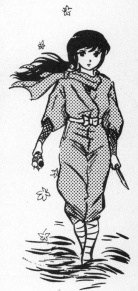

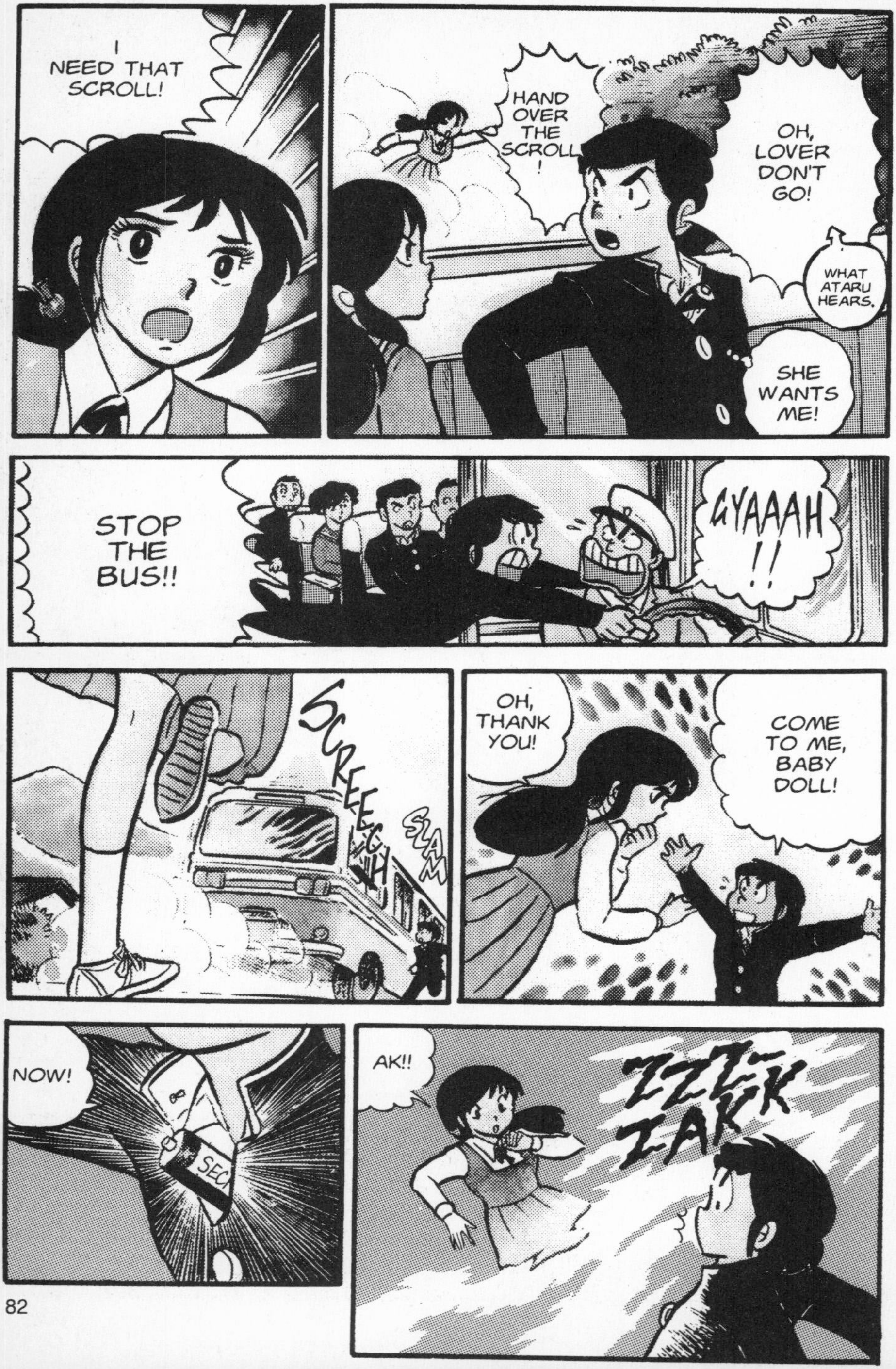

I NEED THAT SCROLL!
HAND OVER THE SCROLL!
OH, LOVER DON'T GO!
WHAT ATARU HEARS.
SHE WANTS ME!
STOP THE BUS!!
GYAAAH!!
SCREEEGH
SLAM
OH, THANK YOU!
COME TO ME, BABY DOLL!
NOW!
SEC
AK!!
ZZZEK ZAK

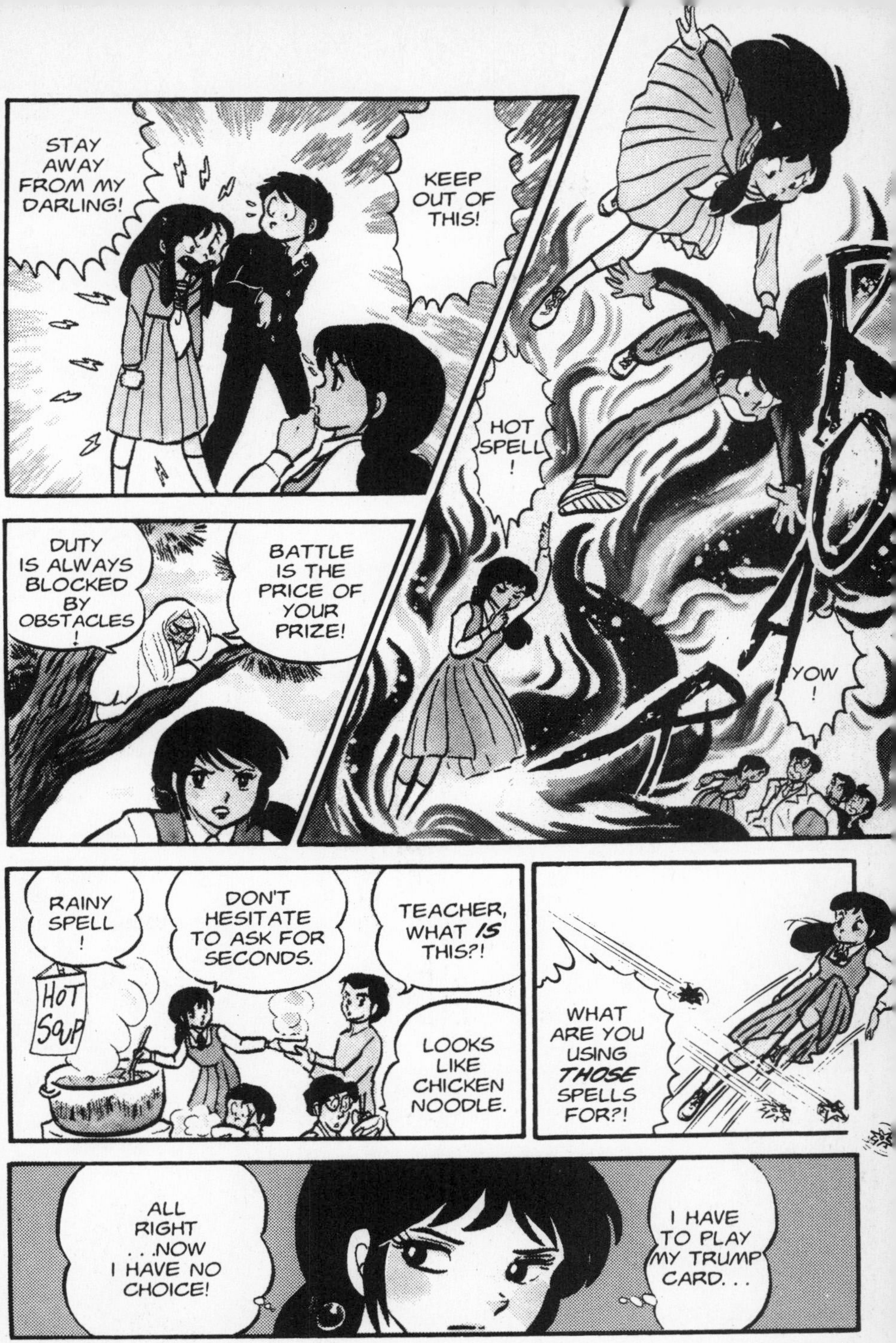
STAY AWAY FROM MY DARLING!
KEEP OUT OF THIS!
HOT SPELL!
DUTY IS ALWAYS BLOCKED BY OBSTACLES!
BATTLE IS THE PRICE OF YOUR PRIZE!
YOW!
RAINY SPELL!
DON'T HESITATE TO ASK FOR SECONDS.
TEACHER, WHAT *IS* THIS?!
HOT SOUP
LOOKS LIKE CHICKEN NOODLE.
WHAT ARE YOU USING ***THOSE*** SPELLS FOR?!
ALL RIGHT . . .NOW I HAVE NO CHOICE!
I HAVE TO PLAY MY TRUMP CARD. . .

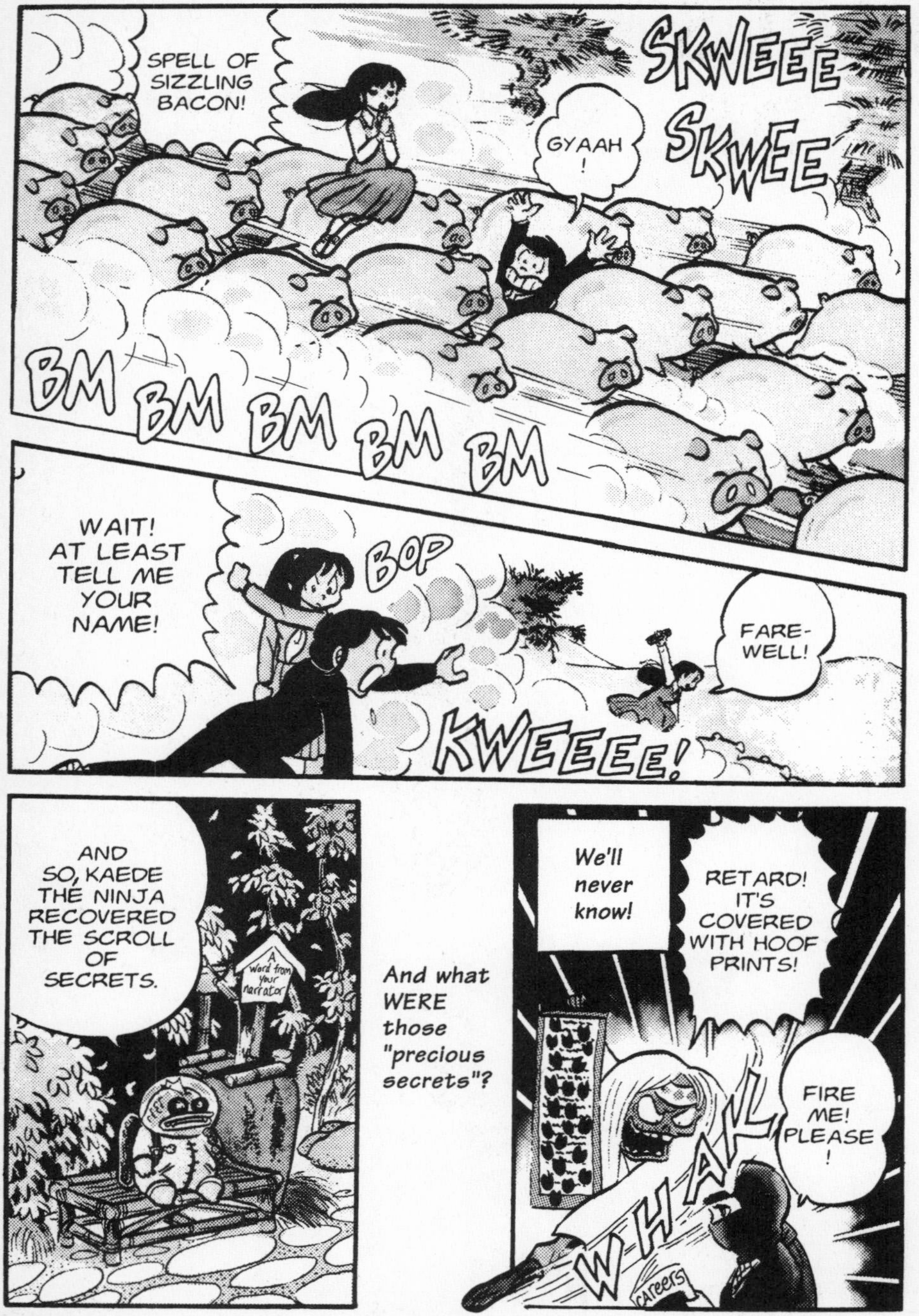
SPELL OF SIZZLING BACON!
GYAAH!
SKWEEE
SKWEE
BM BM BM BM BM
WAIT! AT LEAST TELL ME YOUR NAME!
BOP
FARE-WELL!
KWEEEEE!
AND SO, KAEDE THE NINJA RECOVERED THE SCROLL OF SECRETS.
A Word from your narrator
And what WERE those "precious secrets"?
We'll never know!
RETARD! IT'S COVERED WITH HOOF PRINTS!
FIRE ME! PLEASE!
careers

PART SIX
HIDE, NINJA, HIDE

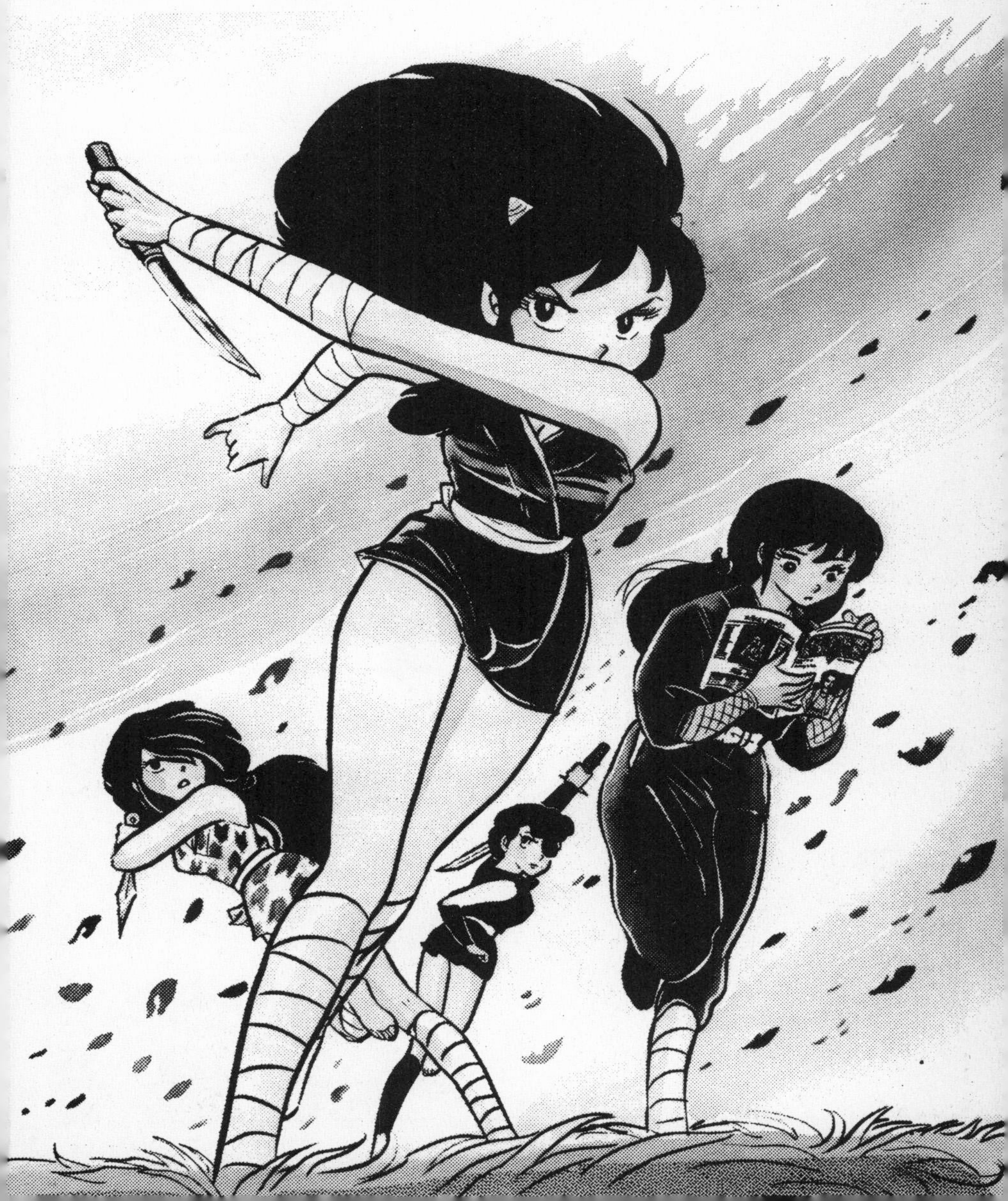

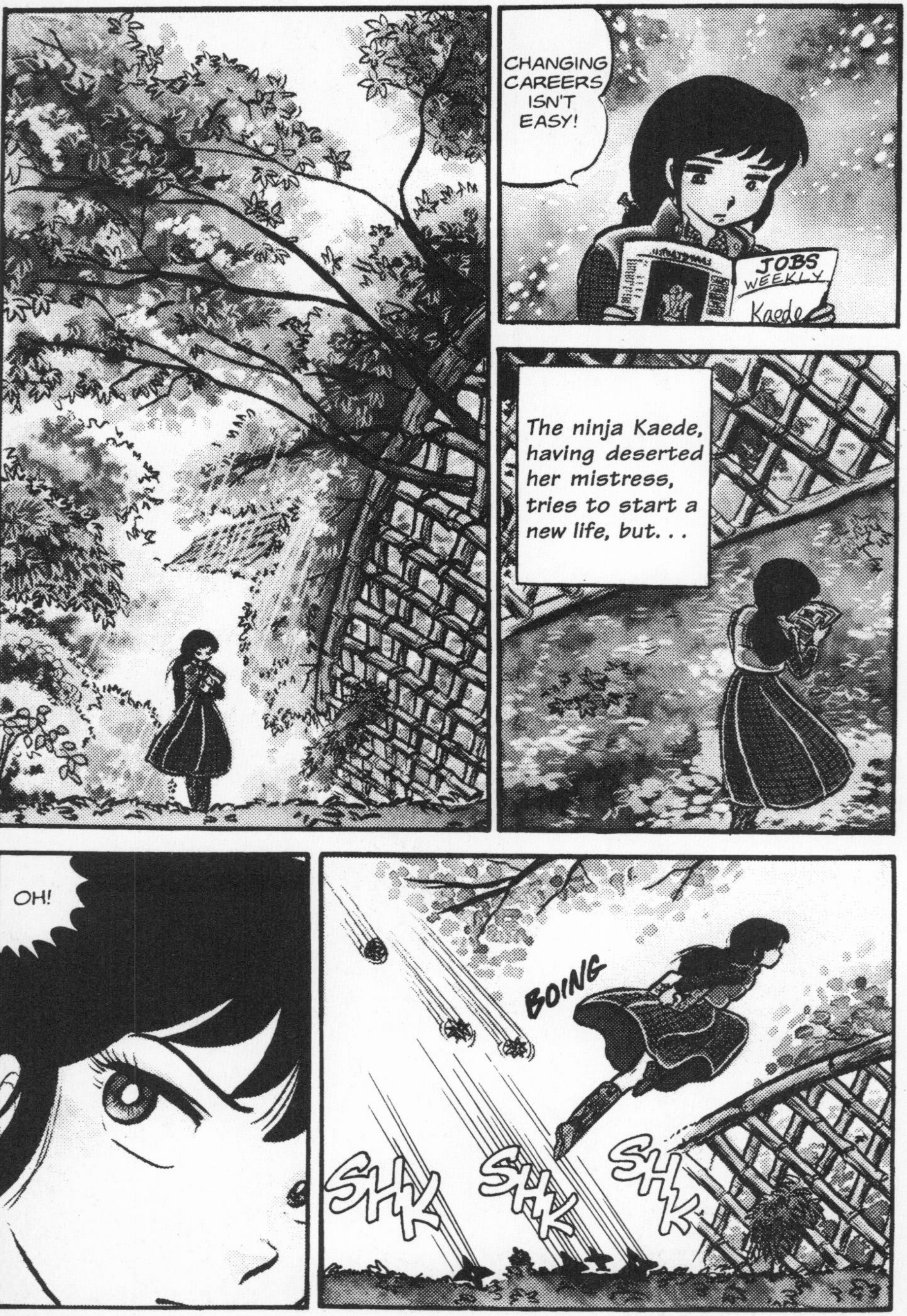
CHANGING CAREERS ISN'T EASY!
JOBS WEEKLY
Kaede
The ninja Kaede, having deserted her mistress, tries to start a new life, but. . .
OH!
BOING
SHK SHK SHK

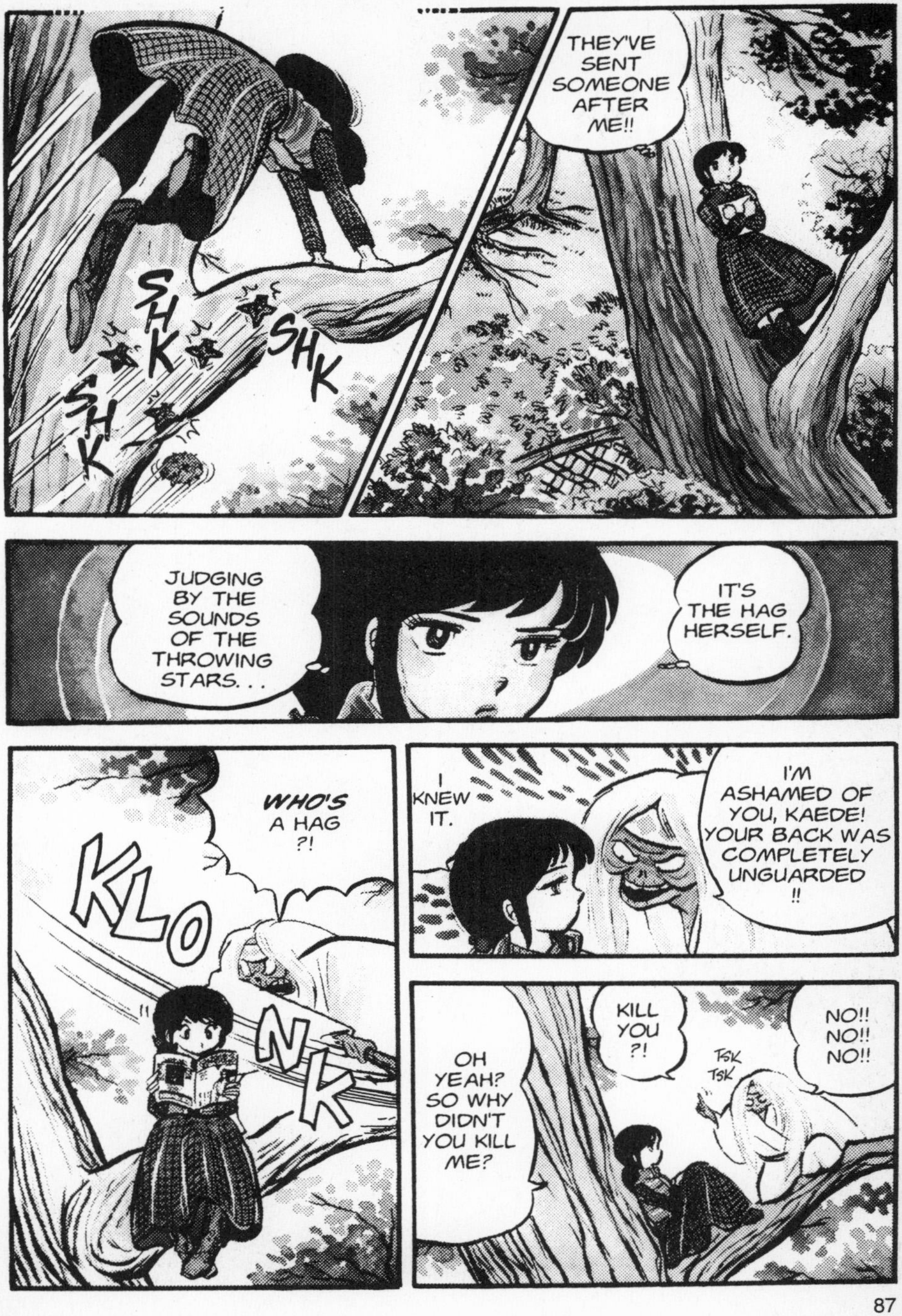
SHK
SHK
SHK
THEY'VE SENT SOMEONE AFTER ME!!
JUDGING BY THE SOUNDS OF THE THROWING STARS. . .
IT'S THE HAG HERSELF.
WHO'S A HAG ?!
KLONK
I KNEW IT.
I'M ASHAMED OF YOU, KAEDE! YOUR BACK WAS COMPLETELY UNGUARDED !!
OH YEAH? SO WHY DIDN'T YOU KILL ME?
KILL YOU ?!
TSK TSK
NO!! NO!! NO!!

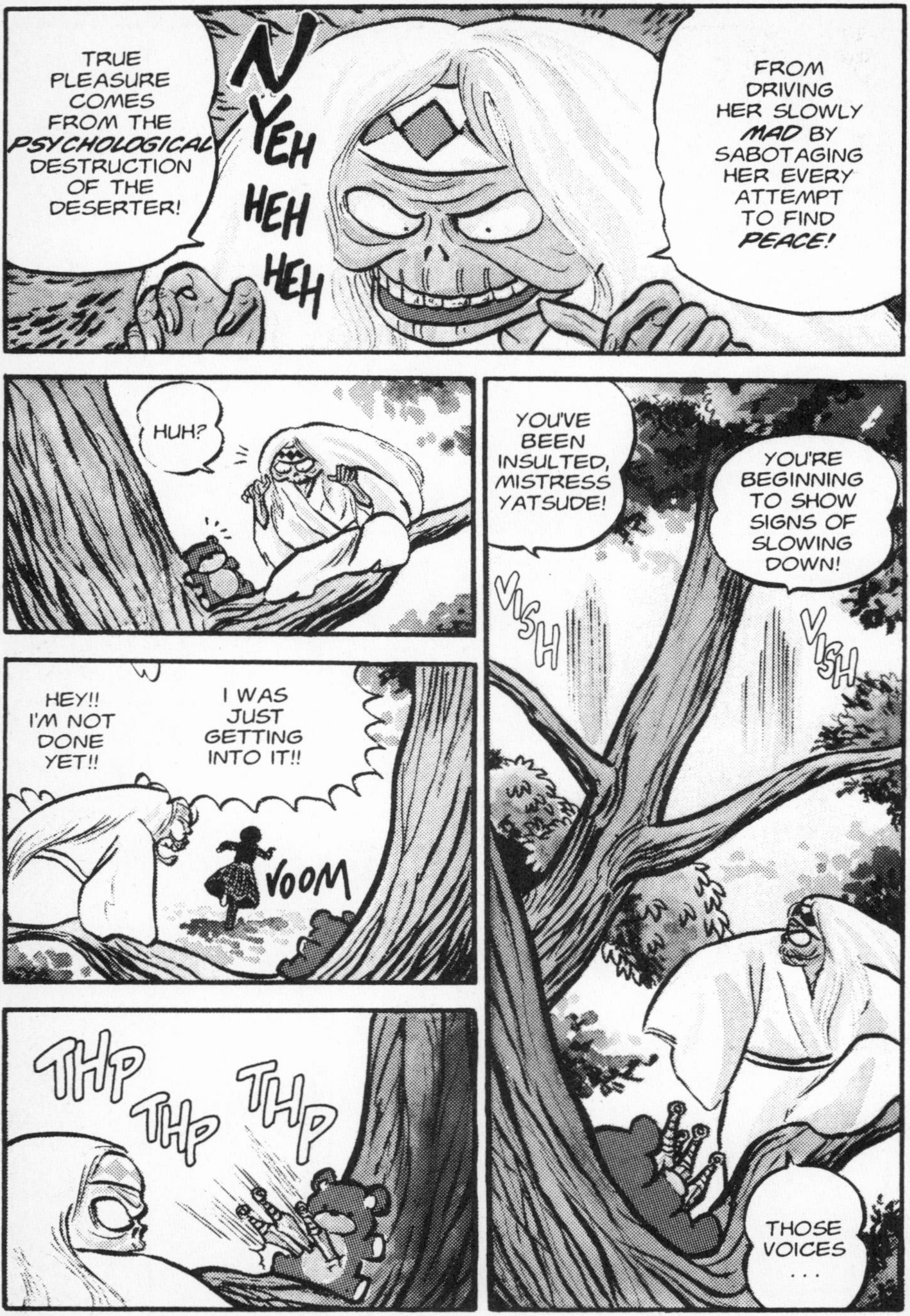
TRUE PLEASURE COMES FROM THE PSYCHOLOGICAL DESTRUCTION OF THE DESERTER!
N YEH HEH HEH
FROM DRIVING HER SLOWLY MAD BY SABOTAGING HER EVERY ATTEMPT TO FIND PEACE!
HUH?
HEY!! I'M NOT DONE YET!!
I WAS JUST GETTING INTO IT!!
VOOM
THP THP THP
YOU'VE BEEN INSULTED, MISTRESS YATSUDE!
YOU'RE BEGINNING TO SHOW SIGNS OF SLOWING DOWN!
VISH
VISH
THOSE VOICES . . .

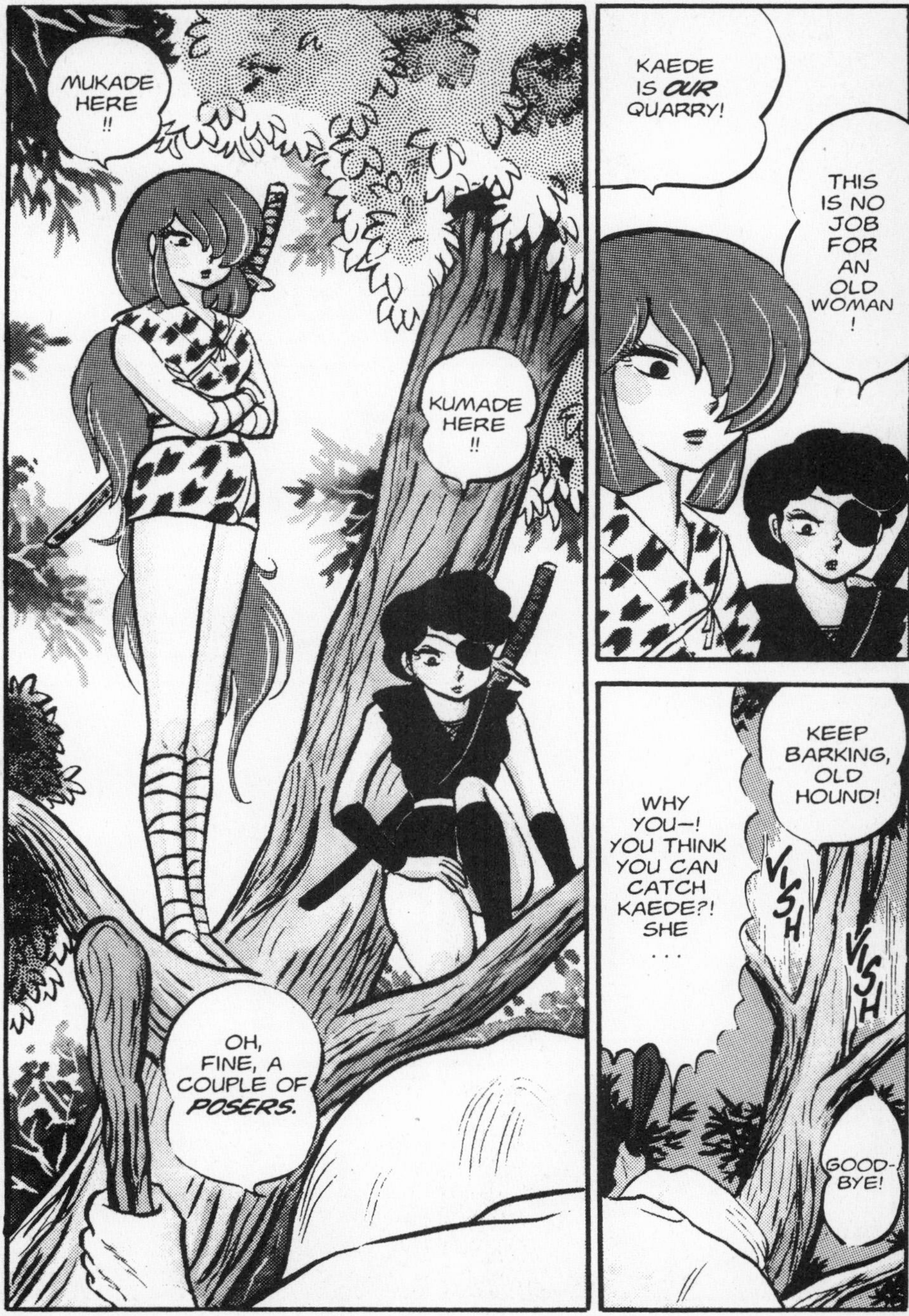
MUKADE HERE !!
KUMADE HERE !!
OH, FINE, A COUPLE OF *POSERS.*
KAEDE IS *OUR* QUARRY!
THIS IS NO JOB FOR AN OLD WOMAN!
WHY YOU—! YOU THINK YOU CAN CATCH KAEDE?! SHE . . .
KEEP BARKING, OLD HOUND!
VISH
VISH
GOOD-BYE!

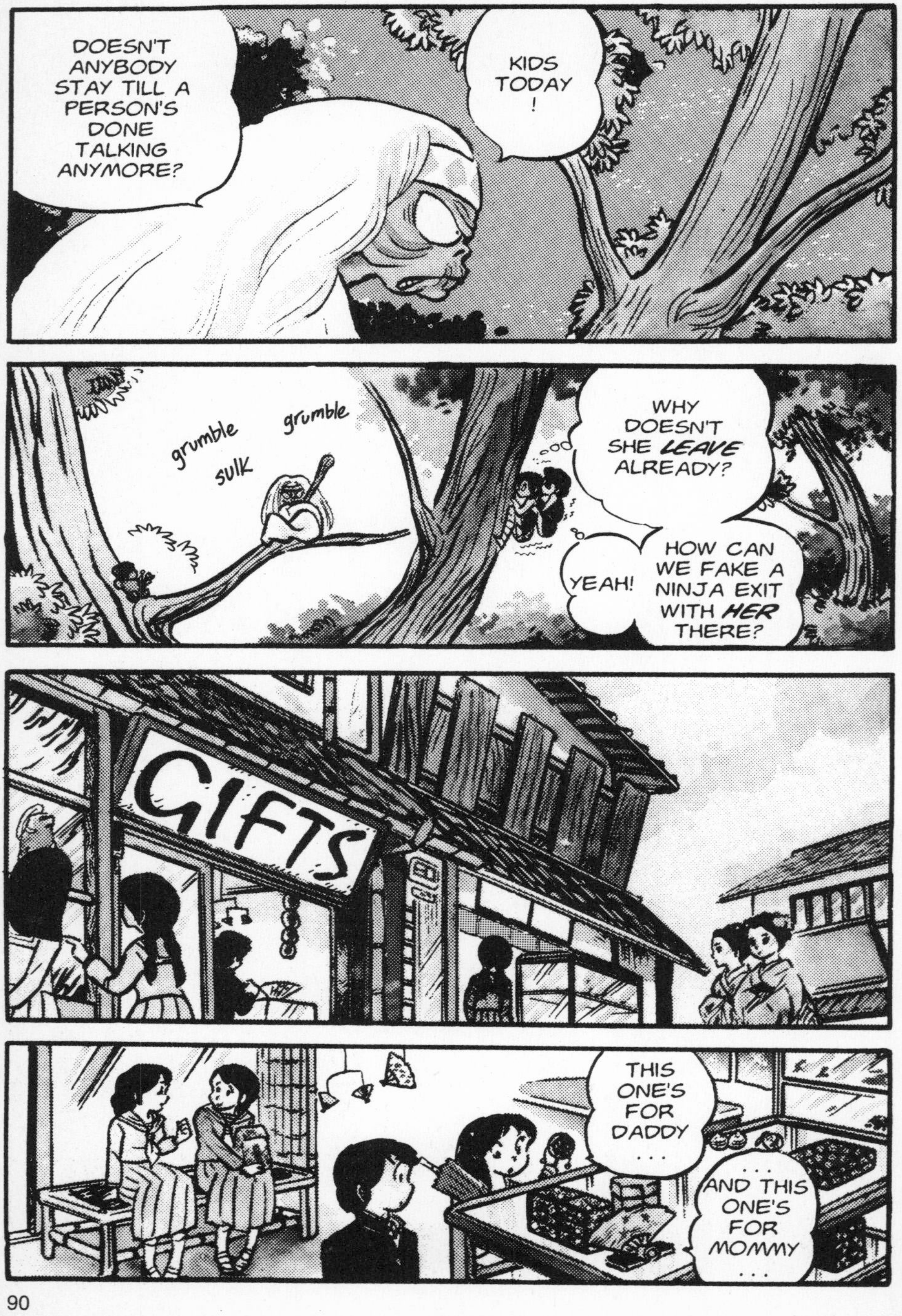
DOESN'T ANYBODY STAY TILL A PERSON'S DONE TALKING ANYMORE?
KIDS TODAY !
grumble
grumble
sulk
WHY DOESN'T SHE *LEAVE* ALREADY?
YEAH!
HOW CAN WE FAKE A NINJA EXIT WITH *HER* THERE?
GIFTS
THIS ONE'S FOR DADDY . . .
. . . AND THIS ONE'S FOR MOMMY . . .

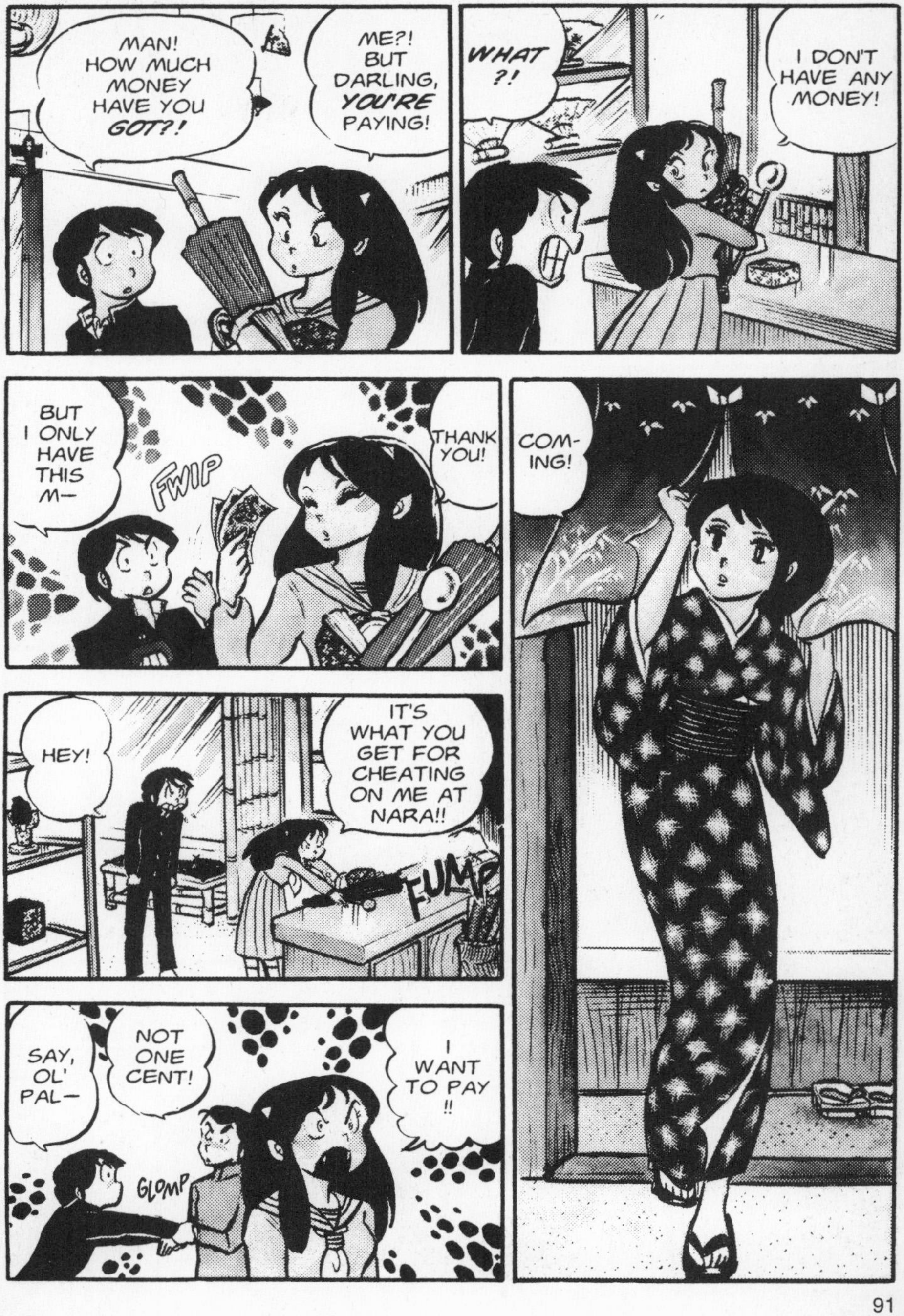

MAN! HOW MUCH MONEY HAVE YOU GOT?!
ME?! BUT DARLING, YOU'RE PAYING!
WHAT ?!
I DON'T HAVE ANY MONEY!
BUT I ONLY HAVE THIS M—
FWIP
THANK YOU!
HEY!
IT'S WHAT YOU GET FOR CHEATING ON ME AT NARA!!
FUMP
SAY, OL' PAL—
NOT ONE CENT!
GLOMP
I WANT TO PAY !!
COM-ING!

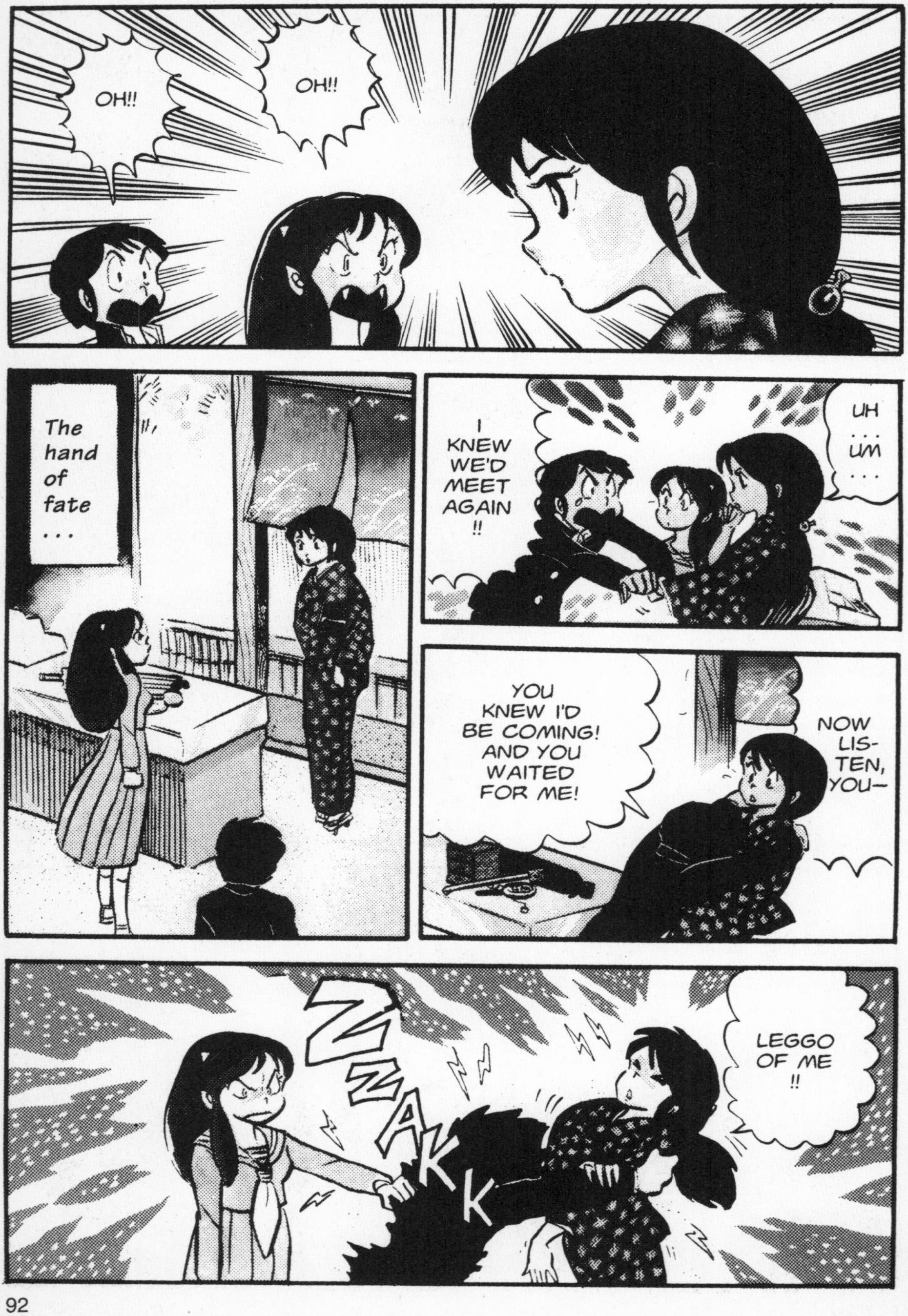
OH!!
OH!!
The hand of fate . . .
I KNEW WE'D MEET AGAIN !!
UH . . . UM . . .
YOU KNEW I'D BE COMING! AND YOU WAITED FOR ME!
NOW LIS- TEN, YOU—
ZZAKK
LEGGO OF ME !!

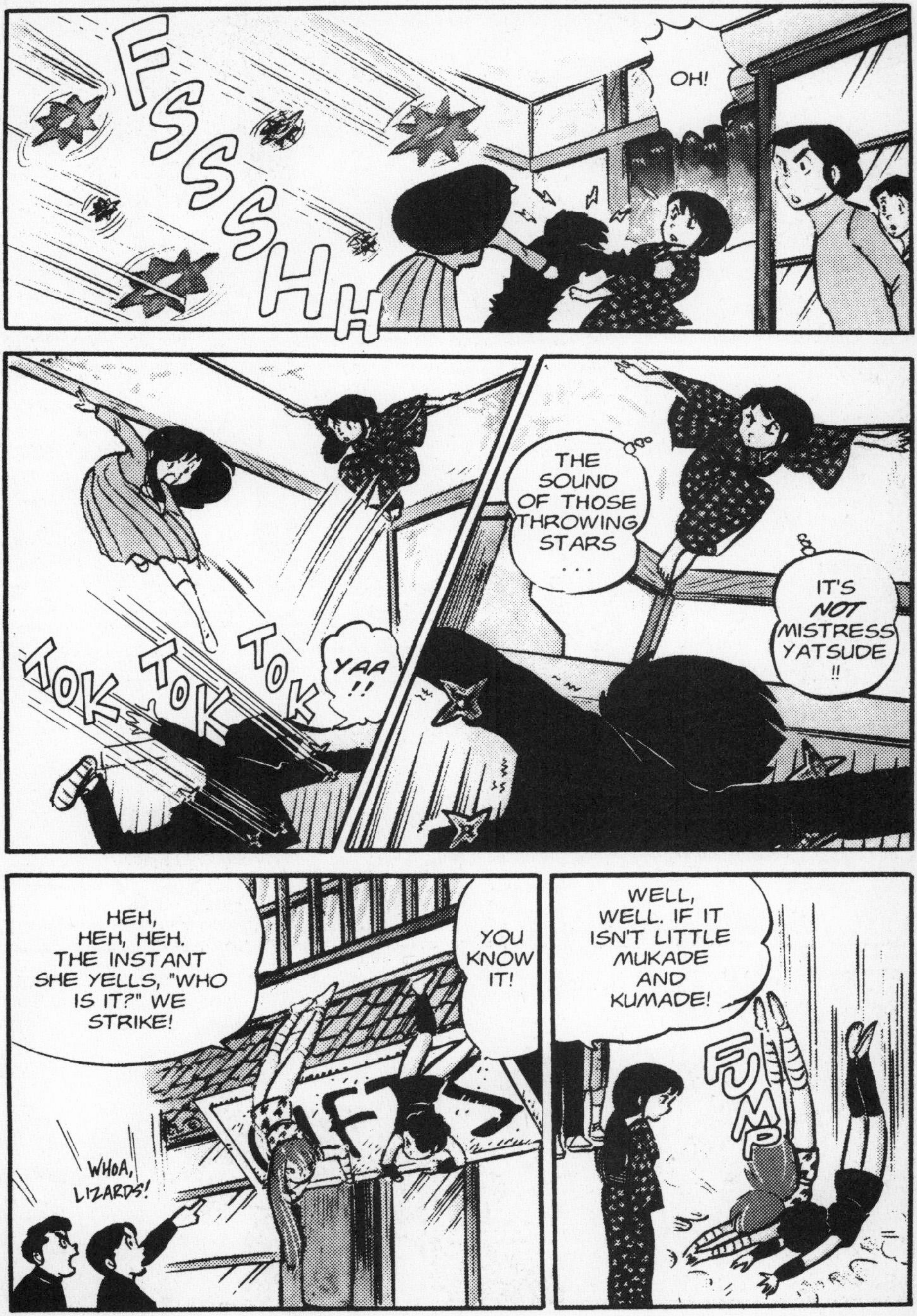
FSSSHH
OH!
TOK TOK TOK
YAA!!
THE SOUND OF THOSE THROWING STARS . . .
IT'S NOT MISTRESS YATSUDE!!
HEH, HEH, HEH. THE INSTANT SHE YELLS, "WHO IS IT?" WE STRIKE!
YOU KNOW IT!
WHOA, LIZARDS!
WELL, WELL. IF IT ISN'T LITTLE MUKADE AND KUMADE!
FUMP

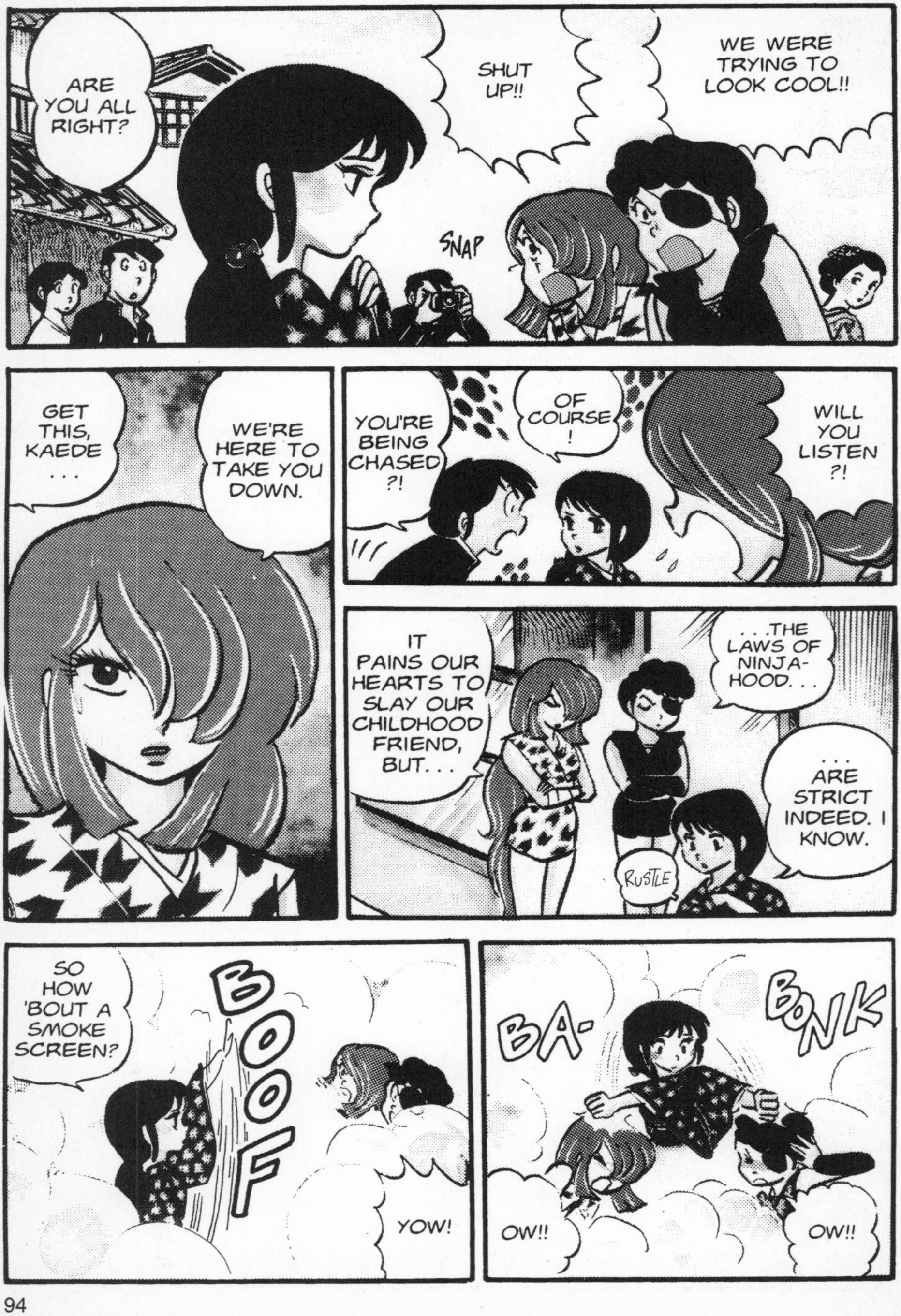

ARE YOU ALL RIGHT?
SHUT UP!!
WE WERE TRYING TO LOOK COOL!!
SNAP
GET THIS, KAEDE . . .
WE'RE HERE TO TAKE YOU DOWN.
YOU'RE BEING CHASED ?!
OF COURSE !
WILL YOU LISTEN ?!
IT PAINS OUR HEARTS TO SLAY OUR CHILDHOOD FRIEND, BUT. . .
. . .THE LAWS OF NINJA-HOOD. . .
. . . ARE STRICT INDEED. I KNOW.
RUSTLE
SO HOW 'BOUT A SMOKE SCREEN?
BOOOF
YOW!
BA-BONK
OW!!
OW!!

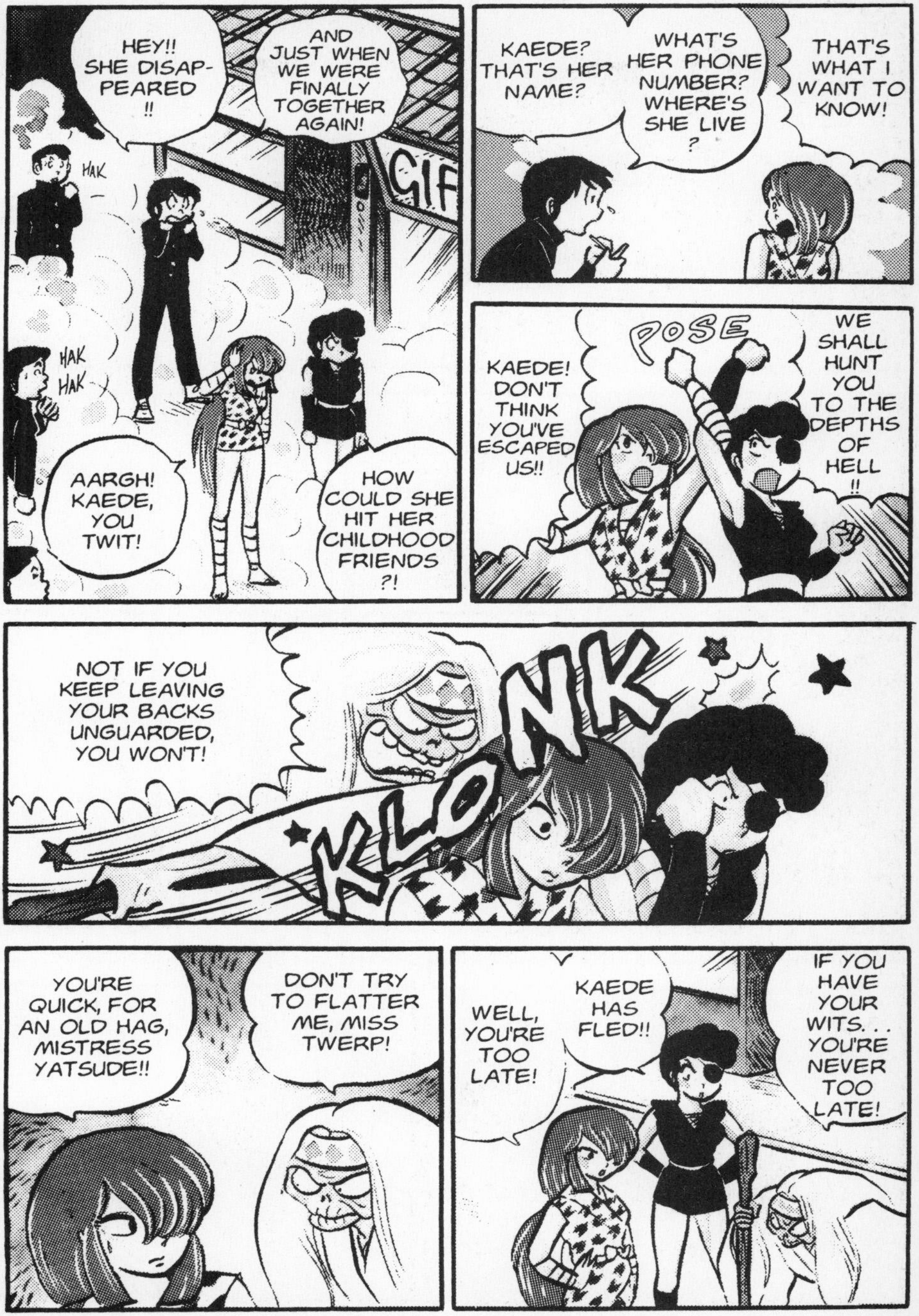
HEY!! SHE DISAP-PEARED !!
AND JUST WHEN WE WERE FINALLY TOGETHER AGAIN!
HAK
HAK HAK
AARGH! KAEDE, YOU TWIT!
HOW COULD SHE HIT HER CHILDHOOD FRIENDS ?!
KAEDE? THAT'S HER NAME?
WHAT'S HER PHONE NUMBER? WHERE'S SHE LIVE ?
THAT'S WHAT I WANT TO KNOW!
KAEDE! DON'T THINK YOU'VE ESCAPED US!!
POSE
WE SHALL HUNT YOU TO THE DEPTHS OF HELL !!
NOT IF YOU KEEP LEAVING YOUR BACKS UNGUARDED, YOU WON'T!
KLONK
YOU'RE QUICK, FOR AN OLD HAG, MISTRESS YATSUDE!!
DON'T TRY TO FLATTER ME, MISS TWERP!
WELL, YOU'RE TOO LATE!
KAEDE HAS FLED!!
IF YOU HAVE YOUR WITS. . . YOU'RE NEVER TOO LATE!

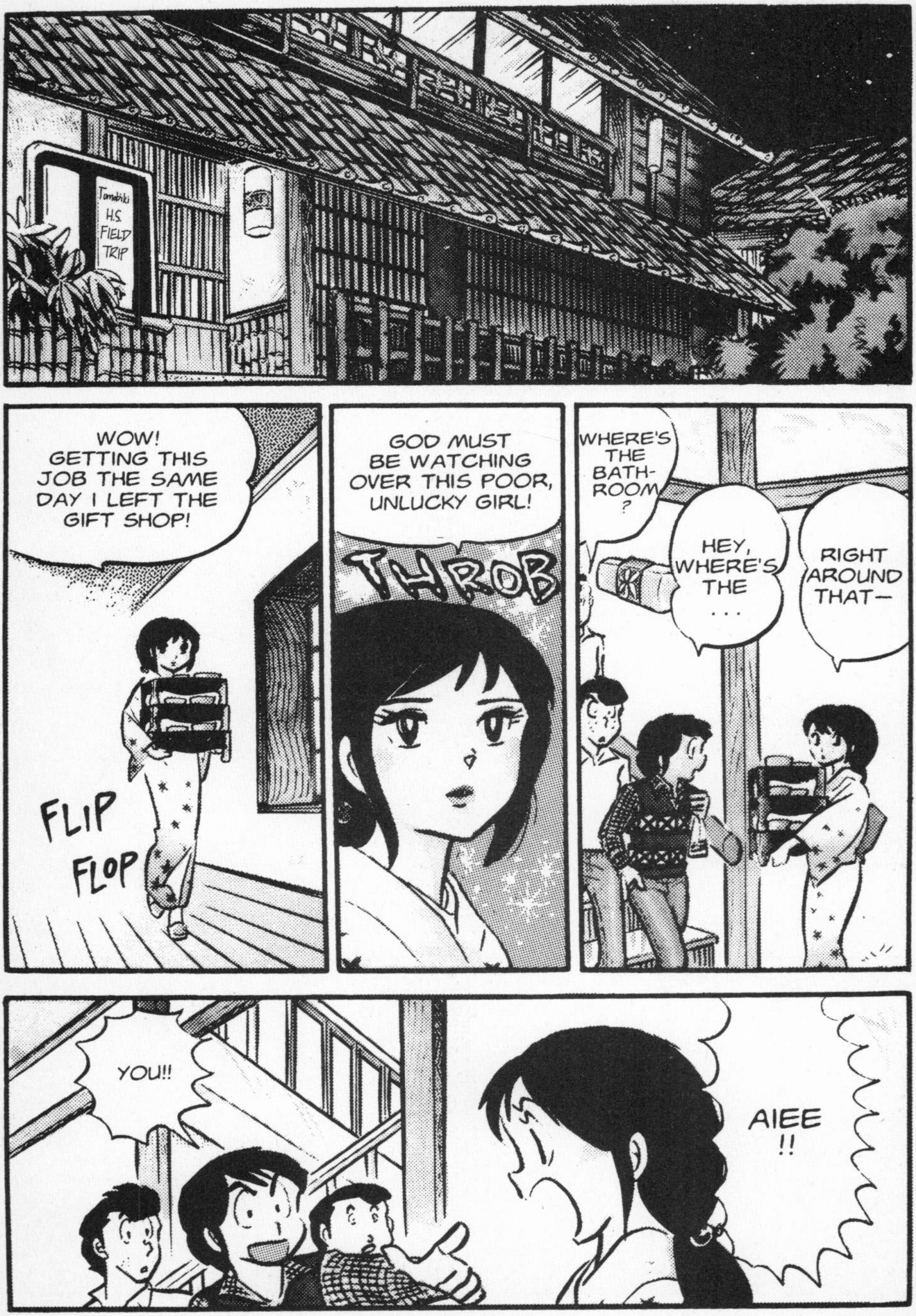
Tomobiki H.S. FIELD TRIP
WOW! GETTING THIS JOB THE SAME DAY I LEFT THE GIFT SHOP!
FLIP
FLOP
GOD MUST BE WATCHING OVER THIS POOR, UNLUCKY GIRL!
THROB
WHERE'S THE BATH-ROOM?
HEY, WHERE'S THE . . .
RIGHT AROUND THAT—
YOU!!
AIEE !!

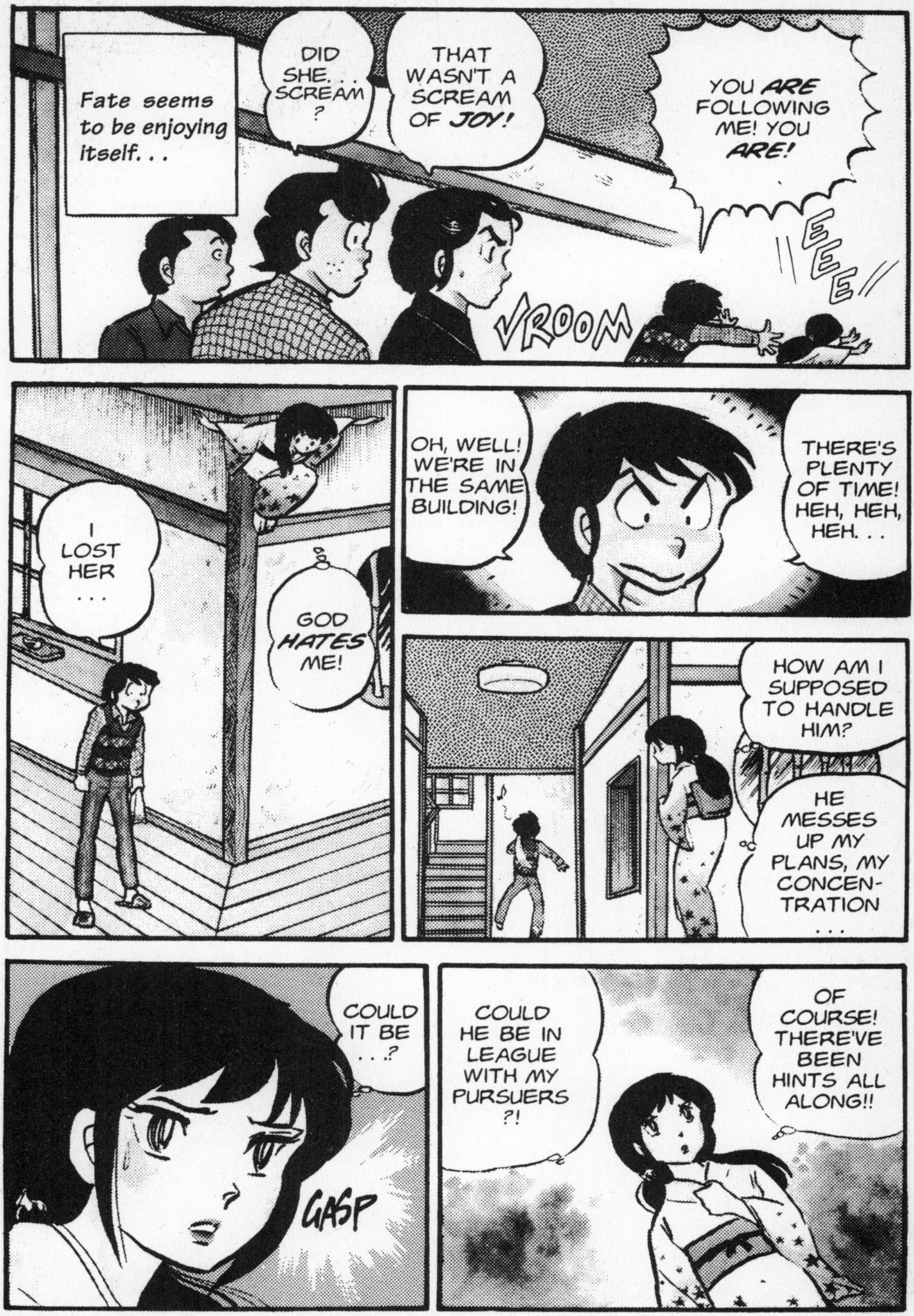
Fate seems to be enjoying itself. . .
DID SHE. . . SCREAM ?
THAT WASN'T A SCREAM OF JOY!
YOU ARE FOLLOWING ME! YOU ARE!
EEE
VROOM
I LOST HER . . .
GOD HATES ME!
OH, WELL! WE'RE IN THE SAME BUILDING!
THERE'S PLENTY OF TIME! HEH, HEH, HEH. . .
HOW AM I SUPPOSED TO HANDLE HIM?
HE MESSES UP MY PLANS, MY CONCEN-TRATION . . .
COULD IT BE . . .?
GASP
COULD HE BE IN LEAGUE WITH MY PURSUERS ?!
OF COURSE! THERE'VE BEEN HINTS ALL ALONG!!

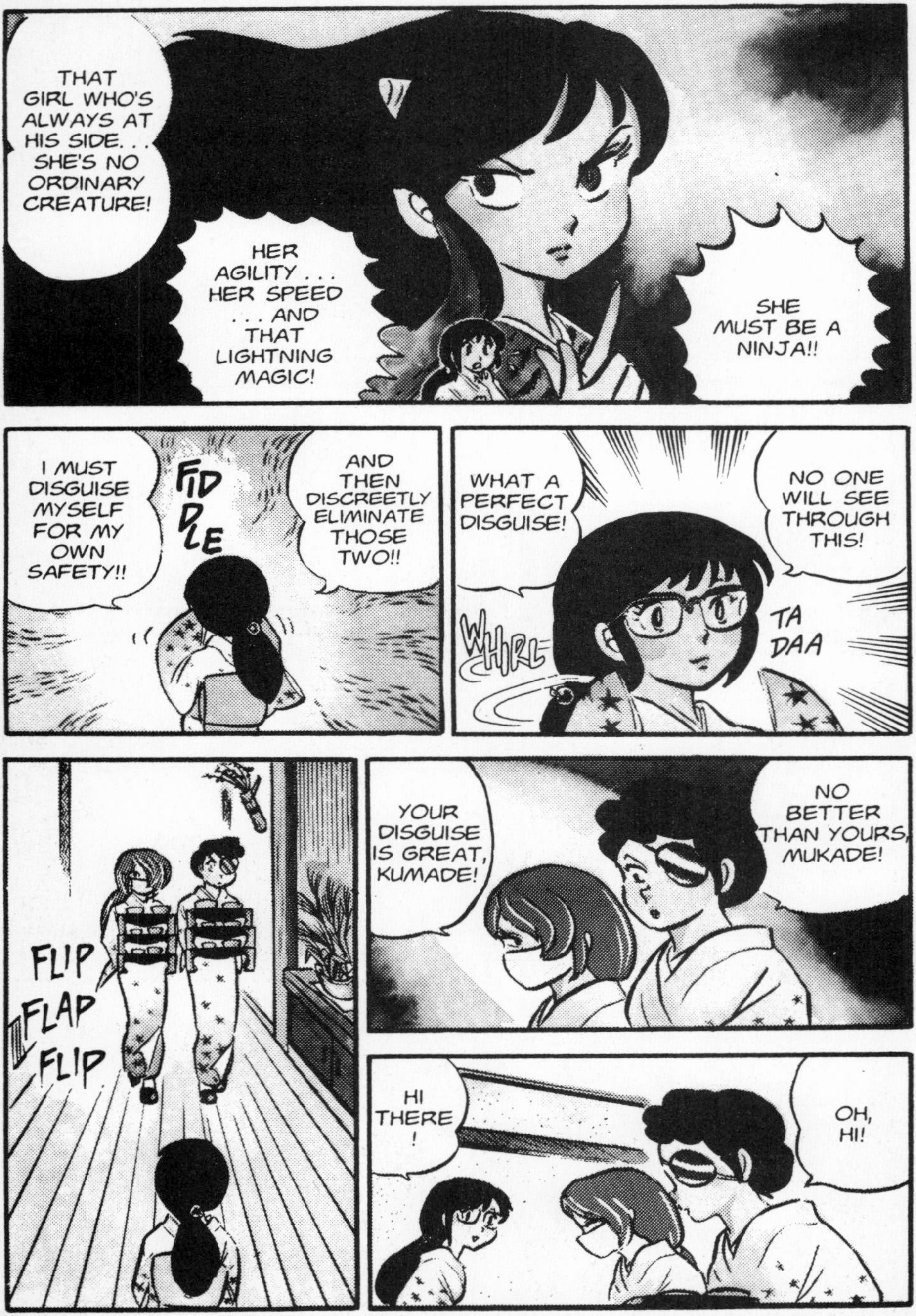
THAT GIRL WHO'S ALWAYS AT HIS SIDE. . . SHE'S NO ORDINARY CREATURE!
HER AGILITY . . . HER SPEED . . . AND THAT LIGHTNING MAGIC!
SHE MUST BE A NINJA!!
I MUST DISGUISE MYSELF FOR MY OWN SAFETY!!
FIDDLE
AND THEN DISCREETLY ELIMINATE THOSE TWO!!
WHAT A PERFECT DISGUISE!
NO ONE WILL SEE THROUGH THIS!
WHIRL
TA DAA
FLIP
FLAP
FLIP
YOUR DISGUISE IS GREAT, KUMADE!
NO BETTER THAN YOURS, MUKADE!
HI THERE !
OH, HI!

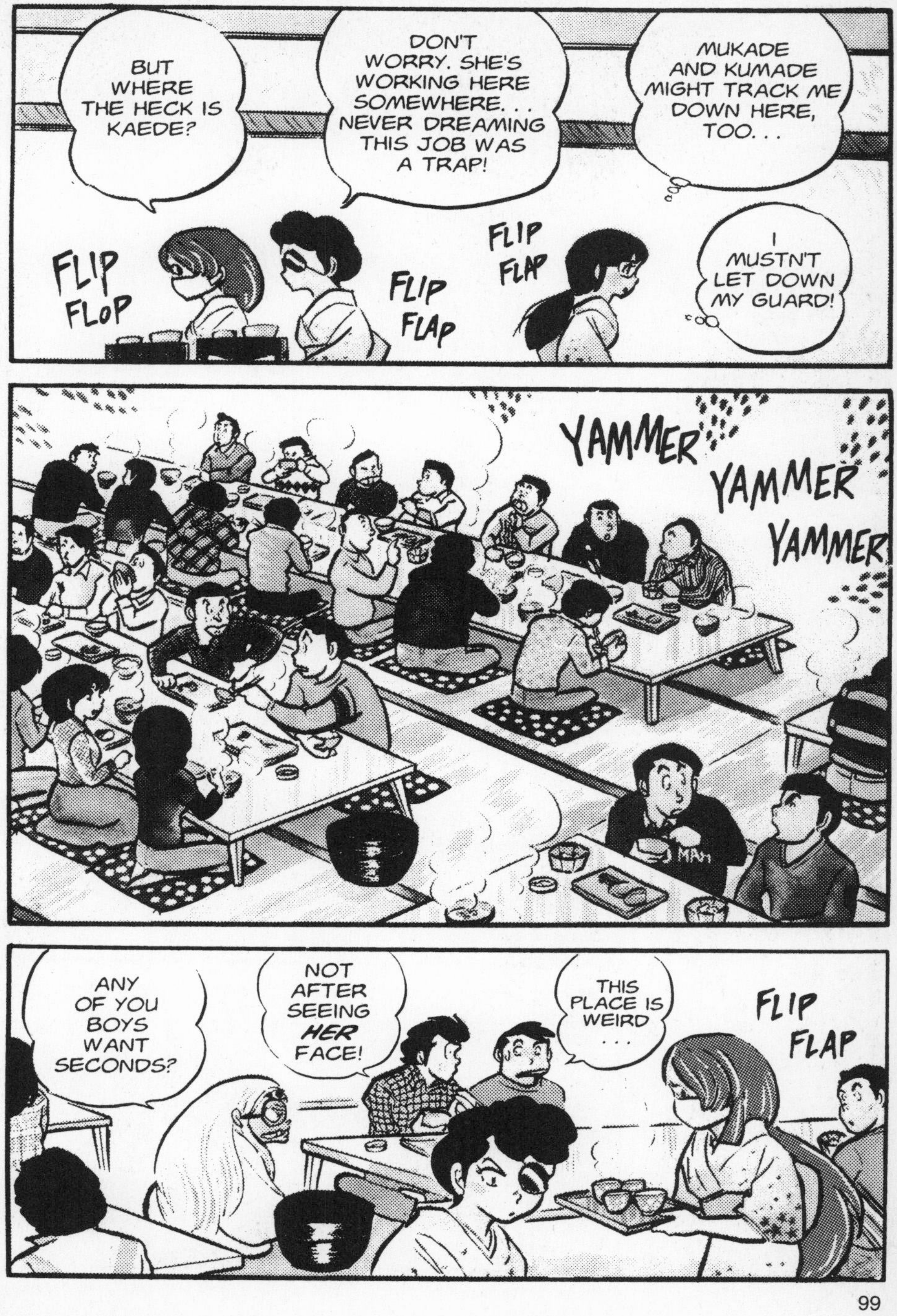
BUT WHERE THE HECK IS KAEDE?
DON'T WORRY. SHE'S WORKING HERE SOMEWHERE. . . NEVER DREAMING THIS JOB WAS A TRAP!
MUKADE AND KUMADE MIGHT TRACK ME DOWN HERE, TOO. . .
FLIP FLOP
FLIP FLAP
FLIP FLAP
I MUSTN'T LET DOWN MY GUARD!
YAMMER
YAMMER
YAMMER
ANY OF YOU BOYS WANT SECONDS?
NOT AFTER SEEING *HER* FACE!
THIS PLACE IS WEIRD . . .
FLIP FLAP

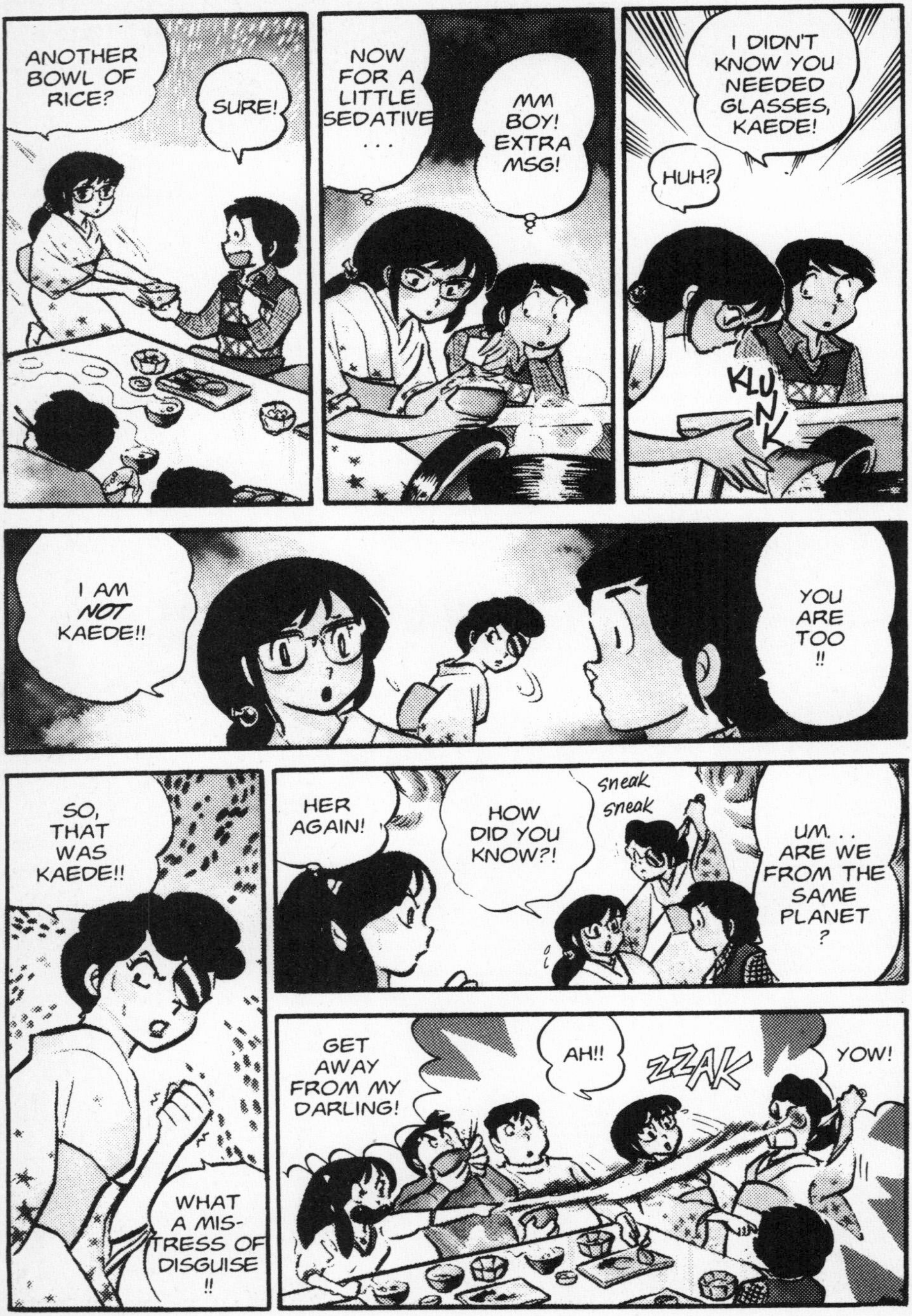
ANOTHER BOWL OF RICE?
SURE!
NOW FOR A LITTLE SEDATIVE . . .
MM BOY! EXTRA MSG!
I DIDN'T KNOW YOU NEEDED GLASSES, KAEDE!
HUH?
KLUNK
I AM NOT KAEDE!!
YOU ARE TOO !!
SO, THAT WAS KAEDE!!
WHAT A MIS-TRESS OF DISGUISE !!
HER AGAIN!
HOW DID YOU KNOW?!
sneak sneak
UM. . . ARE WE FROM THE SAME PLANET ?
GET AWAY FROM MY DARLING!
AH!!
ZZAK
YOW!

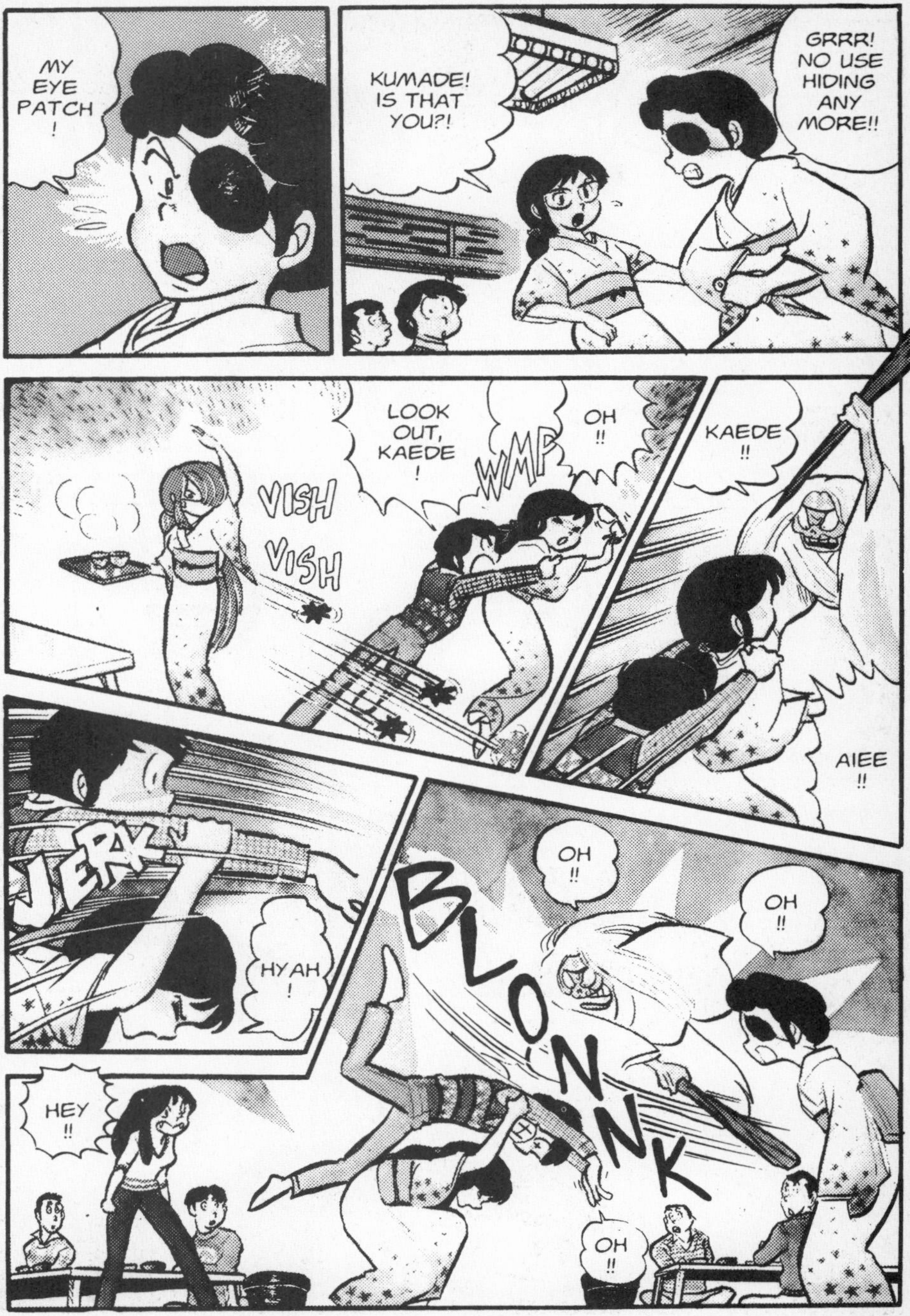
MY EYE PATCH !
KUMADE! IS THAT YOU?!
GRRR! NO USE HIDING ANY MORE!!
VISH
VISH
LOOK OUT, KAEDE !
WMP
OH !!
KAEDE !!
AIEE !!
JERK
HYAH !
OH !!
BLONNK
OH !!
HEY !!
OH !!

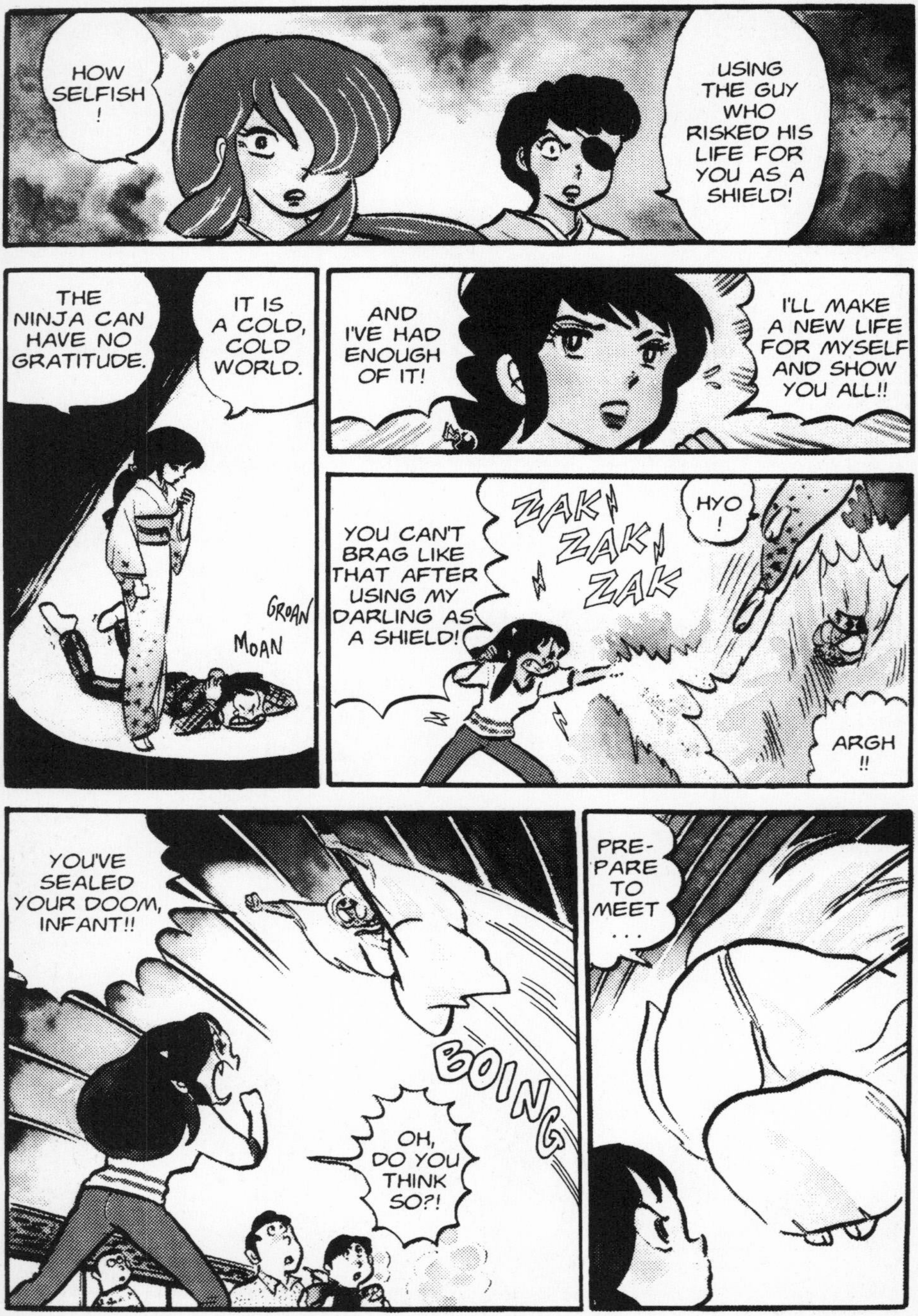
HOW SELFISH !
USING THE GUY WHO RISKED HIS LIFE FOR YOU AS A SHIELD!
THE NINJA CAN HAVE NO GRATITUDE.
IT IS A COLD, COLD WORLD.
GROAN
MOAN
AND I'VE HAD ENOUGH OF IT!
I'LL MAKE A NEW LIFE FOR MYSELF AND SHOW YOU ALL!!
YOU CAN'T BRAG LIKE THAT AFTER USING MY DARLING AS A SHIELD!
ZAK ZAK ZAK
HYO !
ARGH !!
YOU'VE SEALED YOUR DOOM, INFANT!!
BOING
OH, DO YOU THINK SO?!
PRE- PARE TO MEET . . .

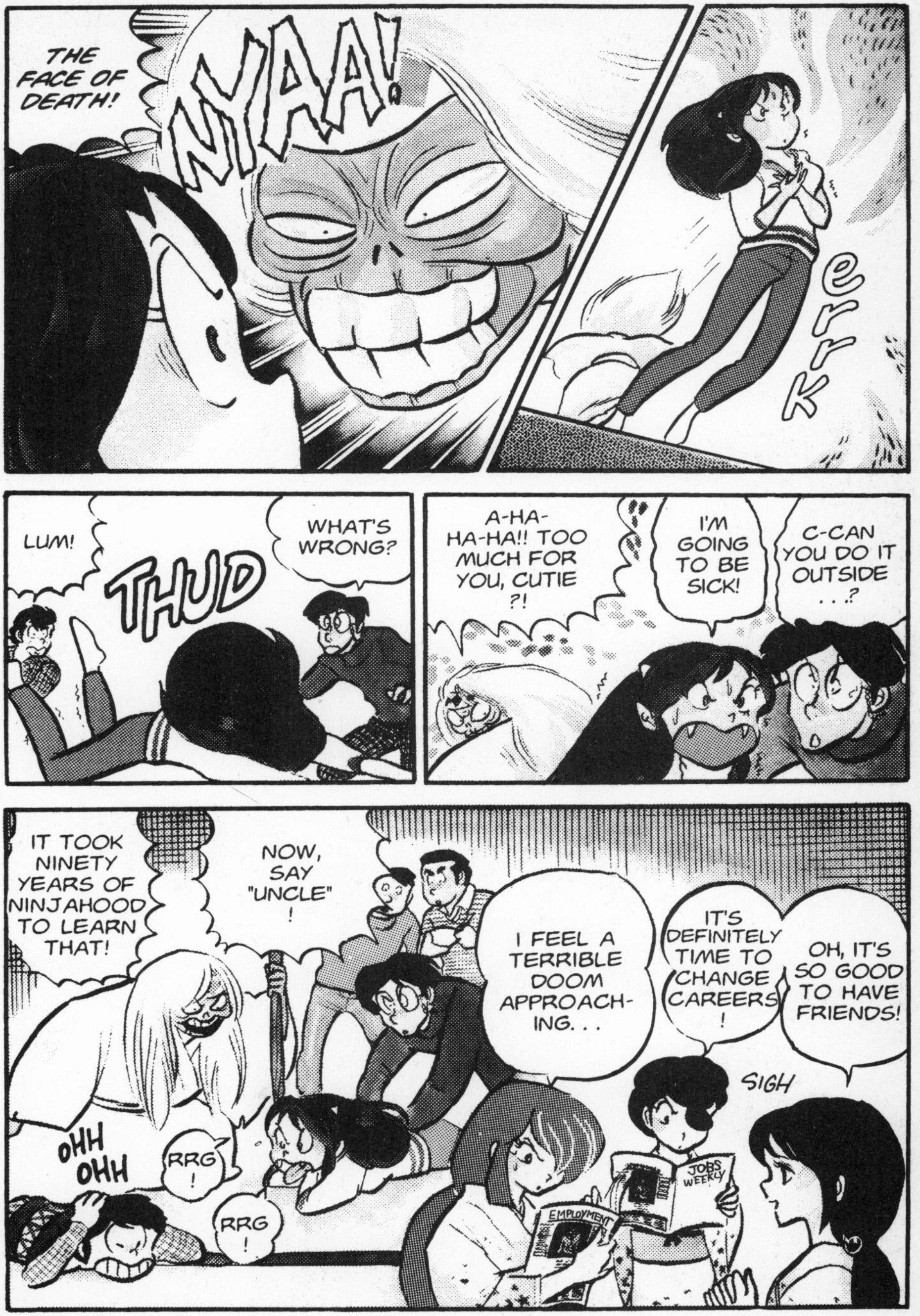
THE FACE OF DEATH!
NYAA!
errrk
LUM!
THUD
WHAT'S WRONG?
A-HA-HA-HA!! TOO MUCH FOR YOU, CUTIE ?!
I'M GOING TO BE SICK!
C-CAN YOU DO IT OUTSIDE . . .?
IT TOOK NINETY YEARS OF NINJAHOOD TO LEARN THAT!
NOW, SAY "UNCLE" !
OHH OHH
RRG !
RRG !
I FEEL A TERRIBLE DOOM APPROACH-ING. . .
EMPLOYMENT
IT'S DEFINITELY TIME TO CHANGE CAREERS !
JOBS WEEKLY
SIGH
OH, IT'S SO GOOD TO HAVE FRIENDS!

PART SEVEN
NINJA FOREVER

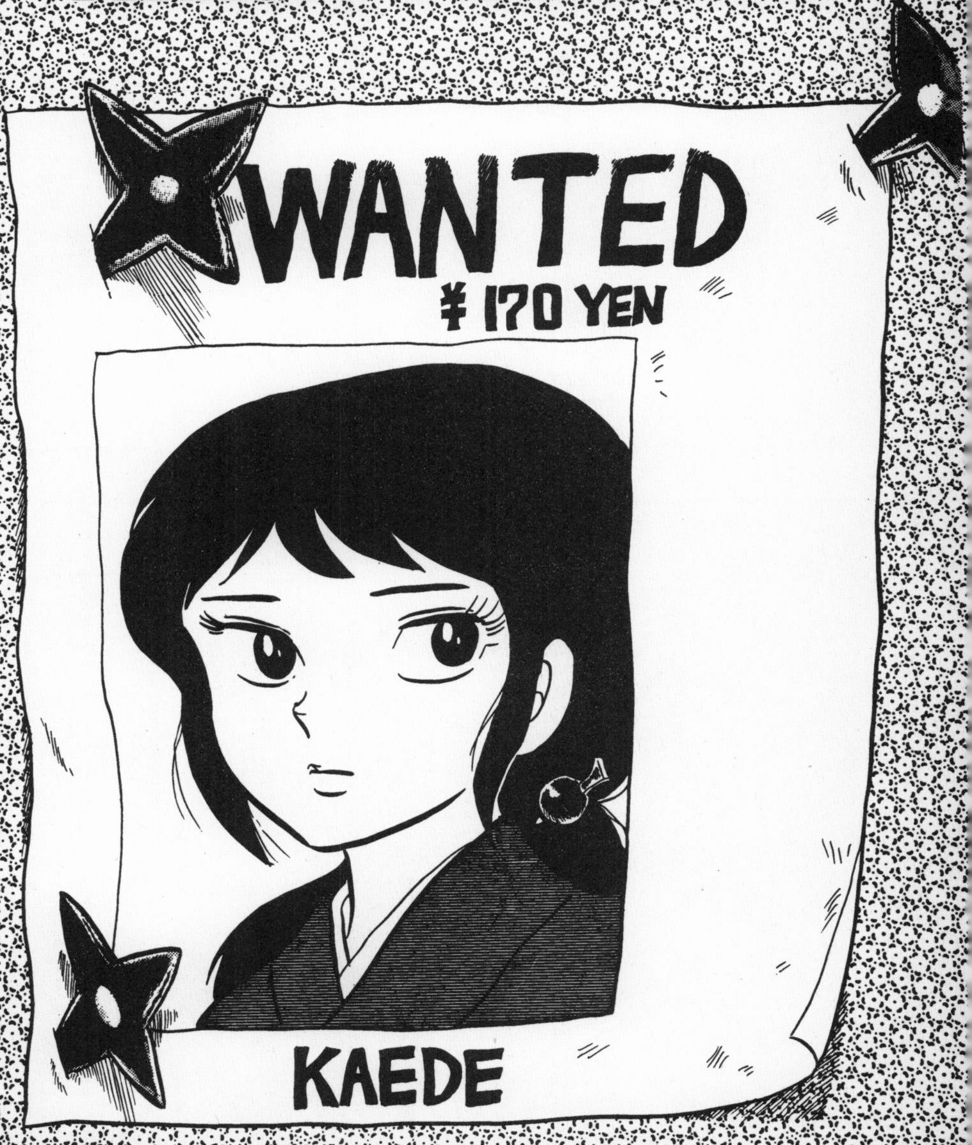
WANTED
¥ 170 YEN
KAEDE

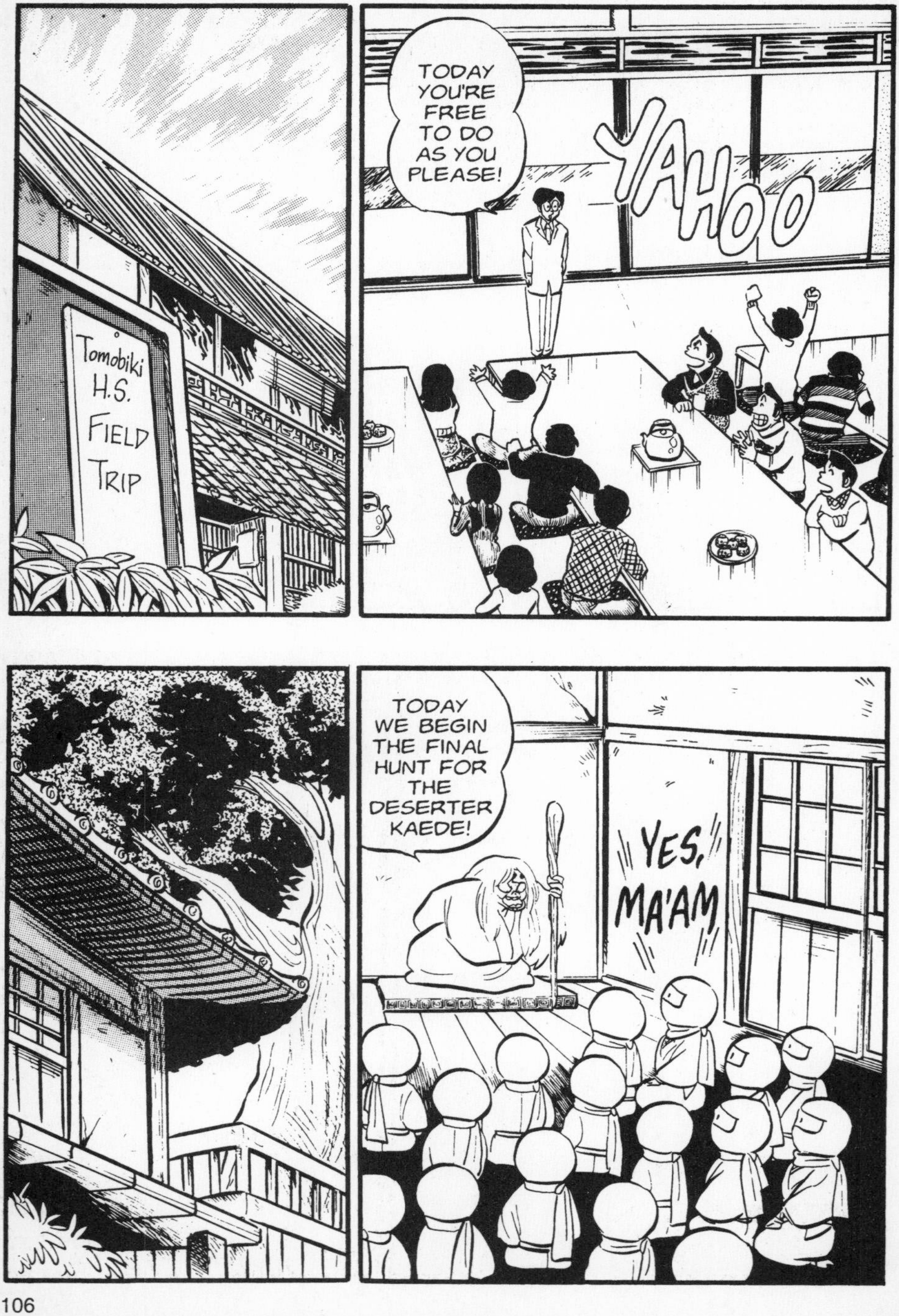

Tomobiki H.S. FIELD TRIP
TODAY YOU'RE FREE TO DO AS YOU PLEASE!
YAHOO
TODAY WE BEGIN THE FINAL HUNT FOR THE DESERTER KAEDE!
YES, MA'AM

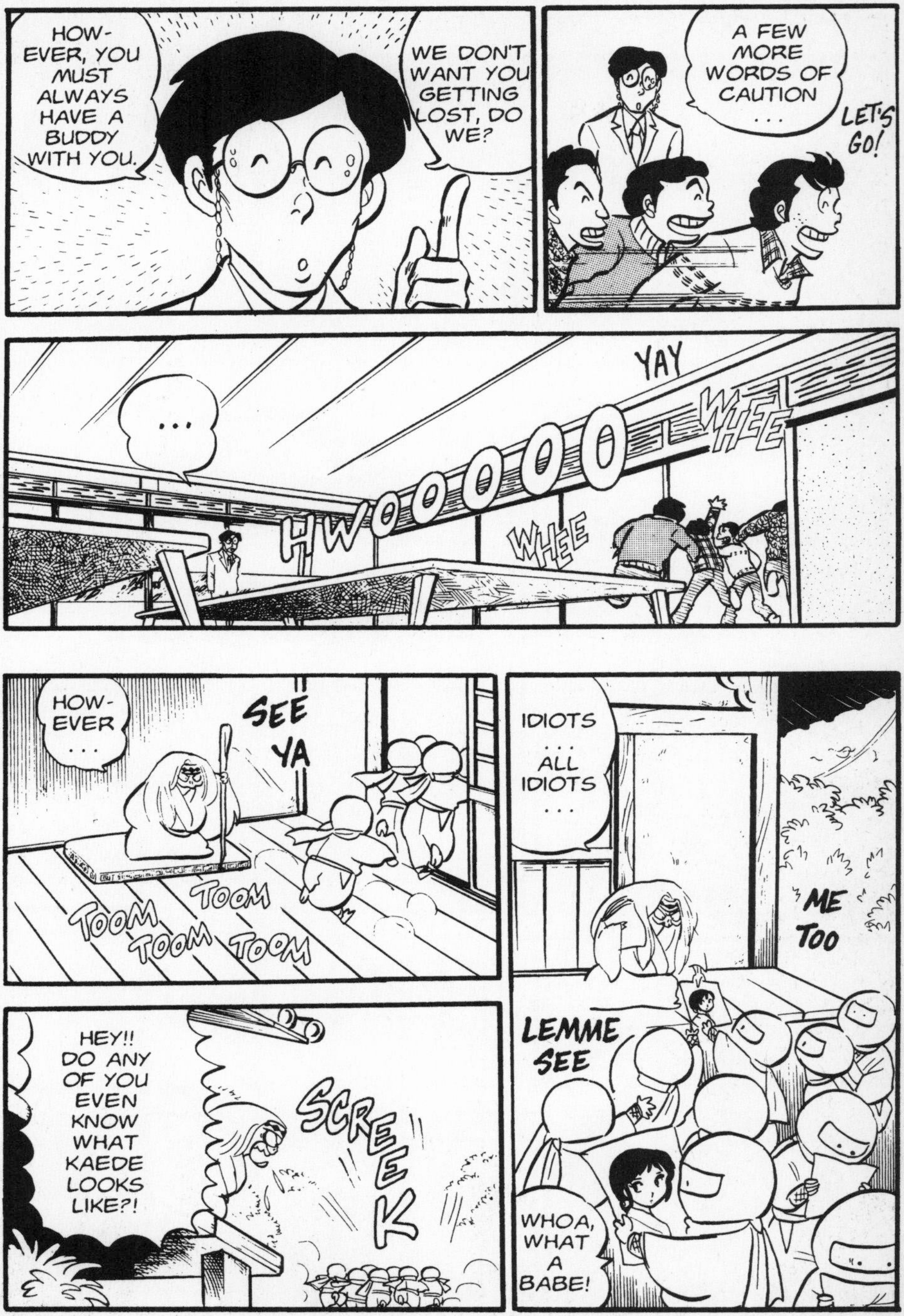
HOW-EVER, YOU MUST ALWAYS HAVE A BUDDY WITH YOU.
WE DON'T WANT YOU GETTING LOST, DO WE?
A FEW MORE WORDS OF CAUTION . . .
LET'S GO!
...
YAY
HWOOOOOO
WHEE
WHEE
HOW-EVER . . .
SEE YA
TOOM TOOM
TOOM TOOM
IDIOTS . . . ALL IDIOTS . . .
ME TOO
HEY!! DO ANY OF YOU EVEN KNOW WHAT KAEDE LOOKS LIKE?!
SCREEEK
LEMME SEE
WHOA, WHAT A BABE!

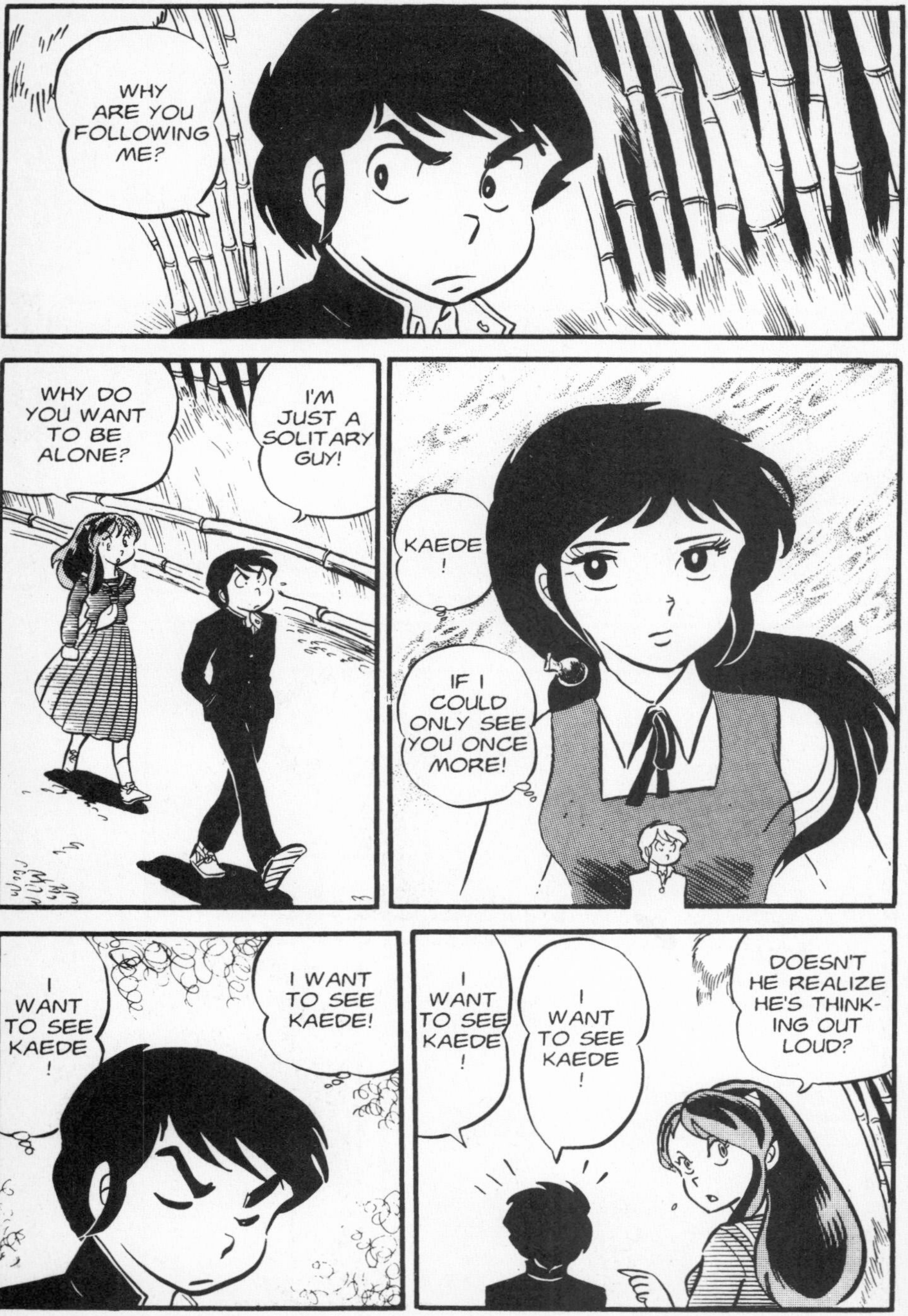
WHY ARE YOU FOLLOWING ME?
WHY DO YOU WANT TO BE ALONE?
I'M JUST A SOLITARY GUY!
KAEDE!
IF I COULD ONLY SEE YOU ONCE MORE!
I WANT TO SEE KAEDE!
I WANT TO SEE KAEDE!
I WANT TO SEE KAEDE!
I WANT TO SEE KAEDE!
DOESN'T HE REALIZE HE'S THINKING-ING OUT LOUD?

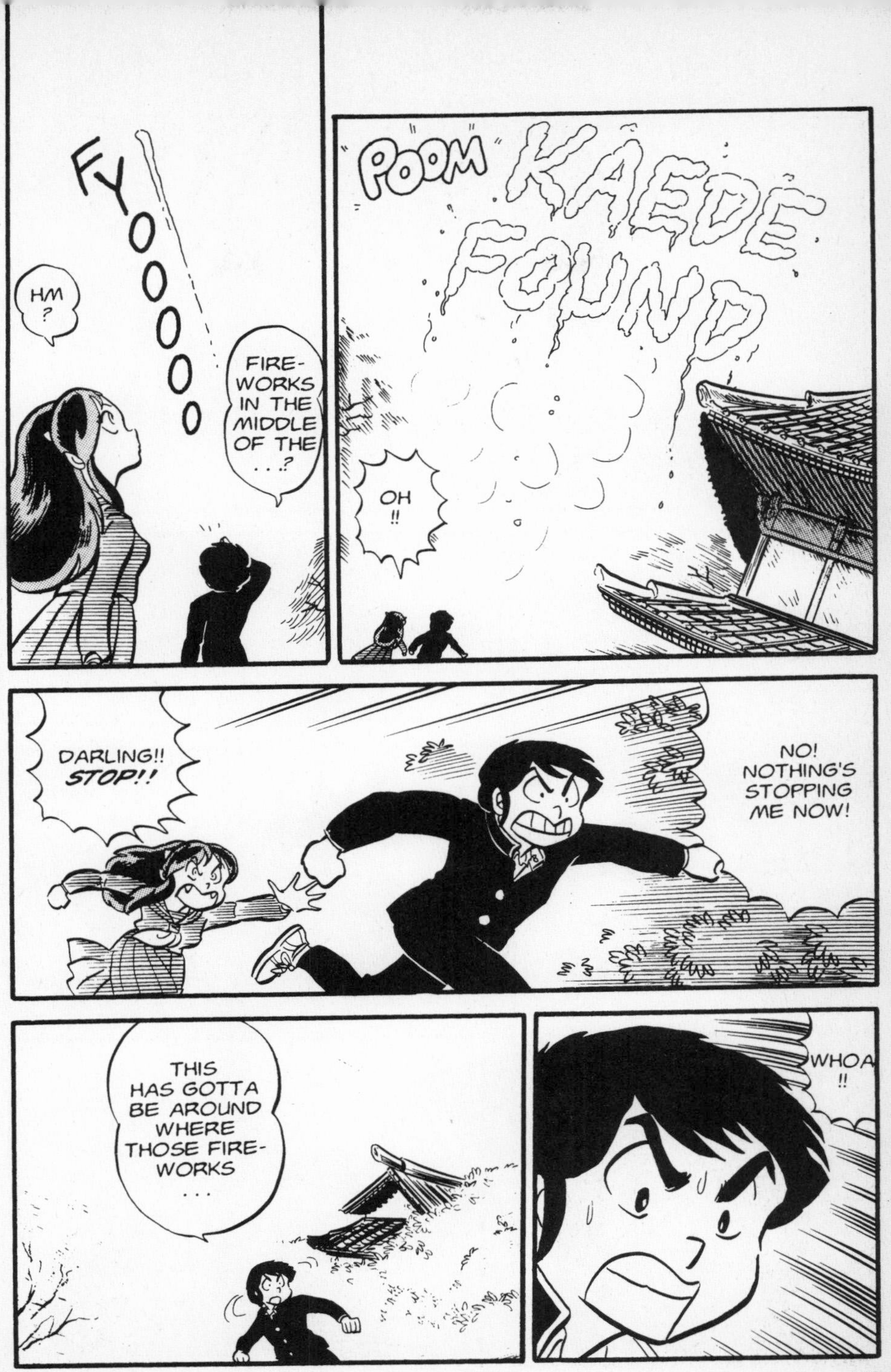
FYOOOOOO
HM ?
FIRE-WORKS IN THE MIDDLE OF THE . . .?
POOM
KAEDE FOUND
OH !!
DARLING!! *STOP!!*
NO! NOTHING'S STOPPING ME NOW!
THIS HAS GOTTA BE AROUND WHERE THOSE FIRE-WORKS . . .
WHOA !!

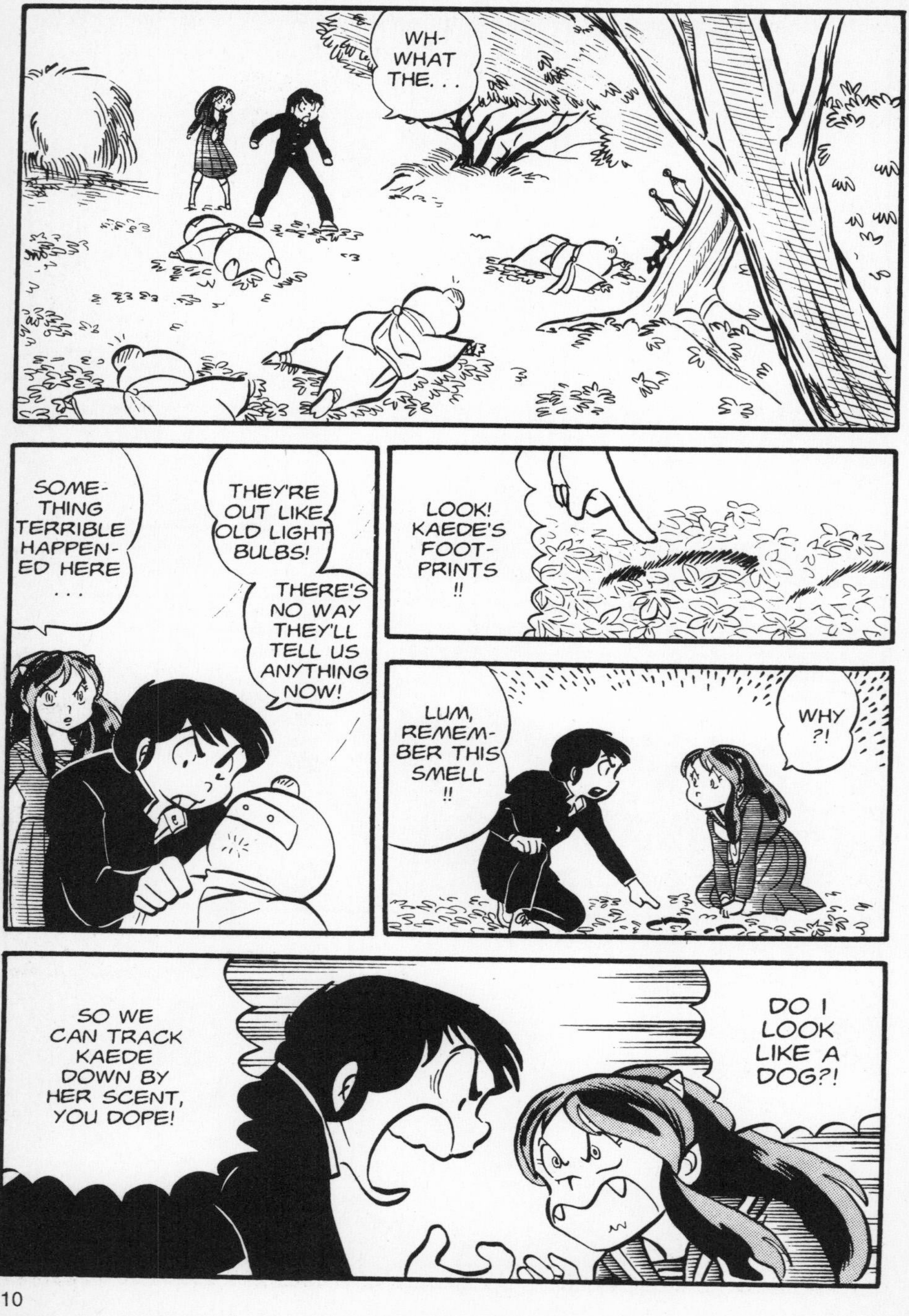
WH-WHAT THE. . .
SOME-THING TERRIBLE HAPPEN-ED HERE . . .
THEY'RE OUT LIKE OLD LIGHT BULBS!
THERE'S NO WAY THEY'LL TELL US ANYTHING NOW!
LOOK! KAEDE'S FOOT-PRINTS !!
LUM, REMEM-BER THIS SMELL !!
WHY ?!
SO WE CAN TRACK KAEDE DOWN BY HER SCENT, YOU DOPE!
DO I LOOK LIKE A DOG?!

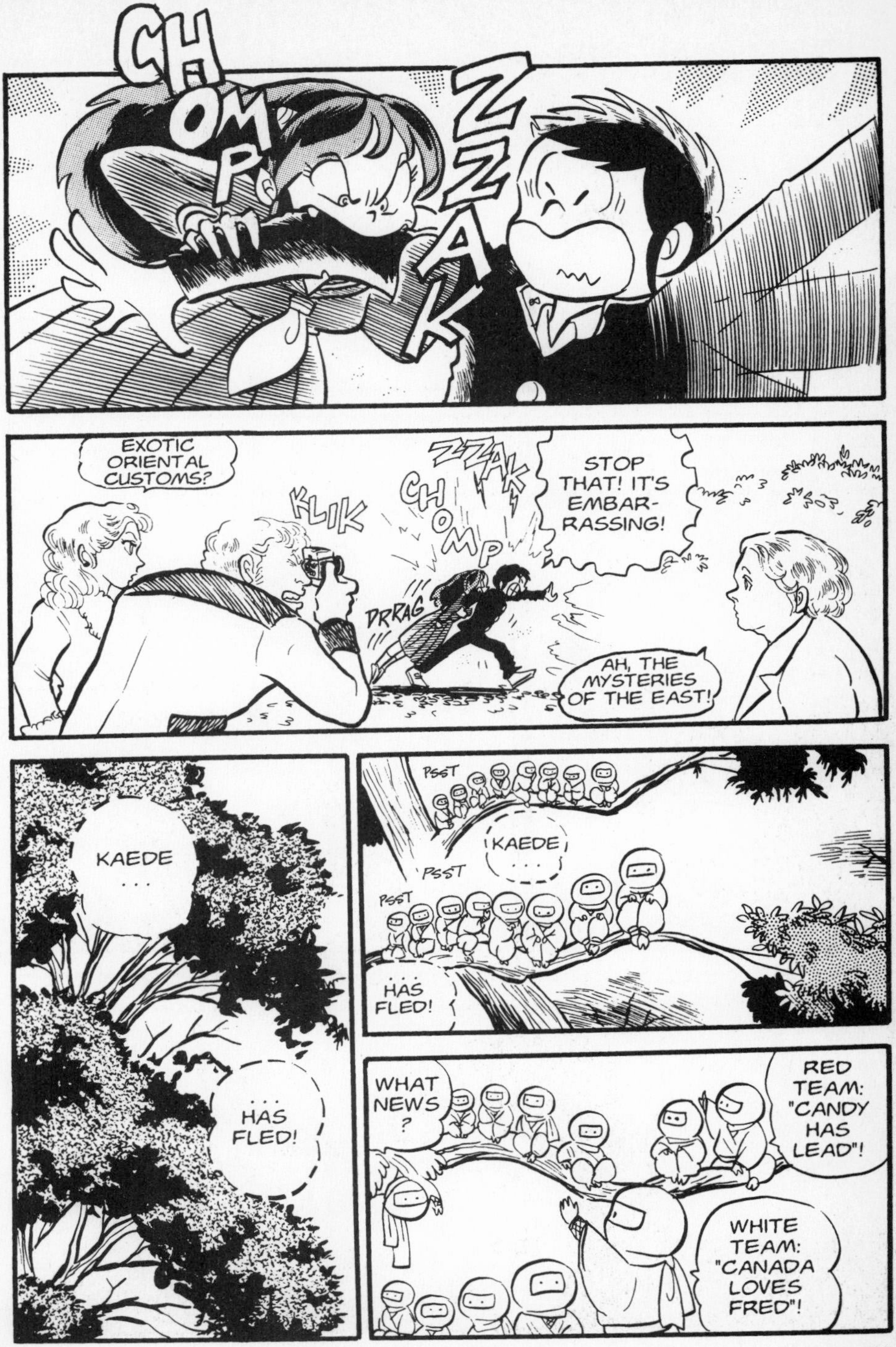
CHOMP
ZZAK
EXOTIC ORIENTAL CUSTOMS?
KLIK
ZZZAK
CHOMP
DRRAG
STOP THAT! IT'S EMBAR-RASSING!
AH, THE MYSTERIES OF THE EAST!
KAEDE . . .
. . . HAS FLED!
PSST
KAEDE . . .
PSST
PSST
. . . HAS FLED!
WHAT NEWS?
RED TEAM: "CANDY HAS LEAD"!
WHITE TEAM: "CANADA LOVES FRED"!

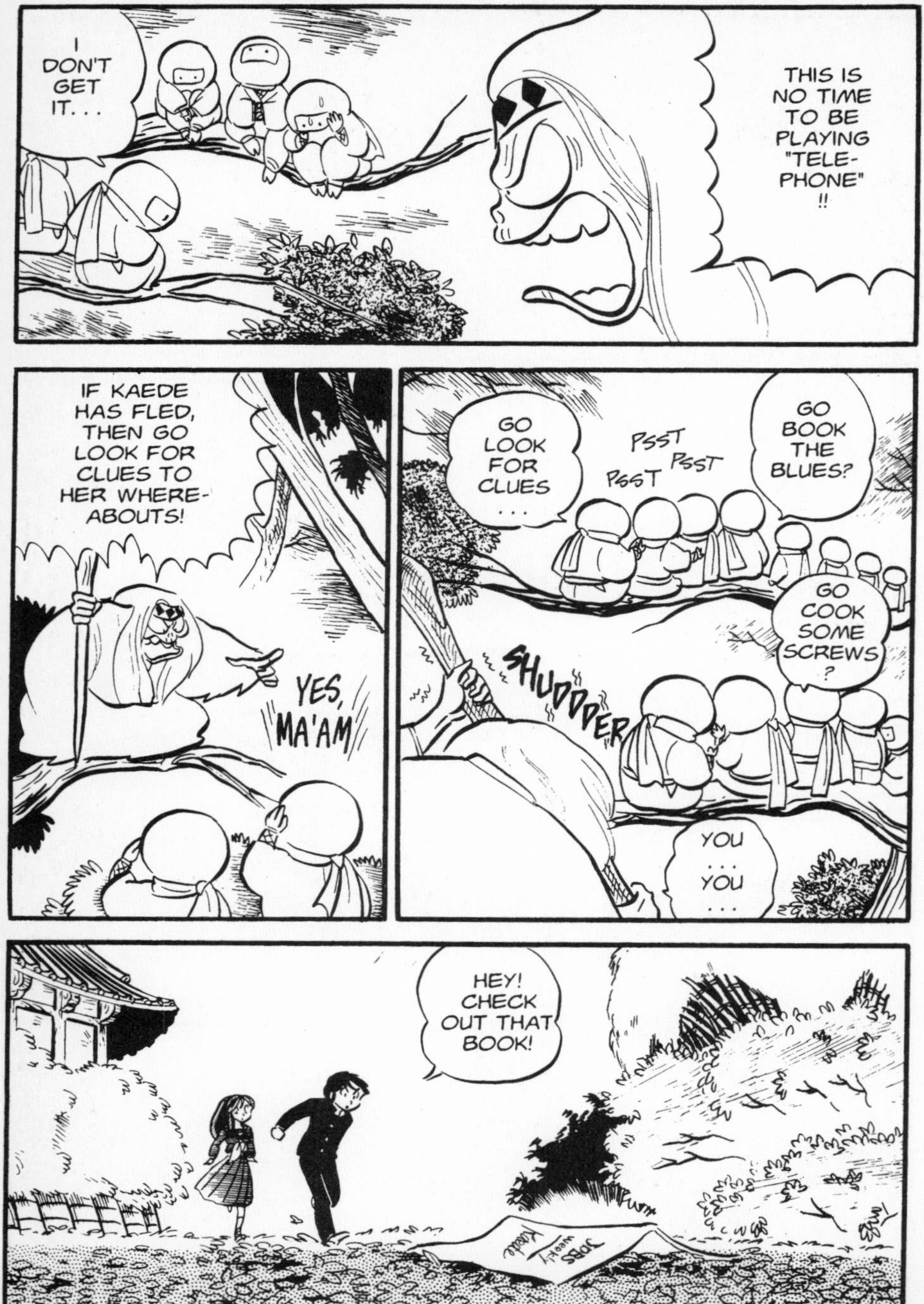
I DON'T GET IT. . .
THIS IS NO TIME TO BE PLAYING "TELE-PHONE" !!
IF KAEDE HAS FLED, THEN GO LOOK FOR CLUES TO HER WHERE-ABOUTS!
YES, MA'AM
GO LOOK FOR CLUES . . .
PSST PSST PSST
GO BOOK THE BLUES?
GO COOK SOME SCREWS ?
SHUDDDER
YOU . . . YOU . . .
HEY! CHECK OUT THAT BOOK!
JOBS weekly Kaede

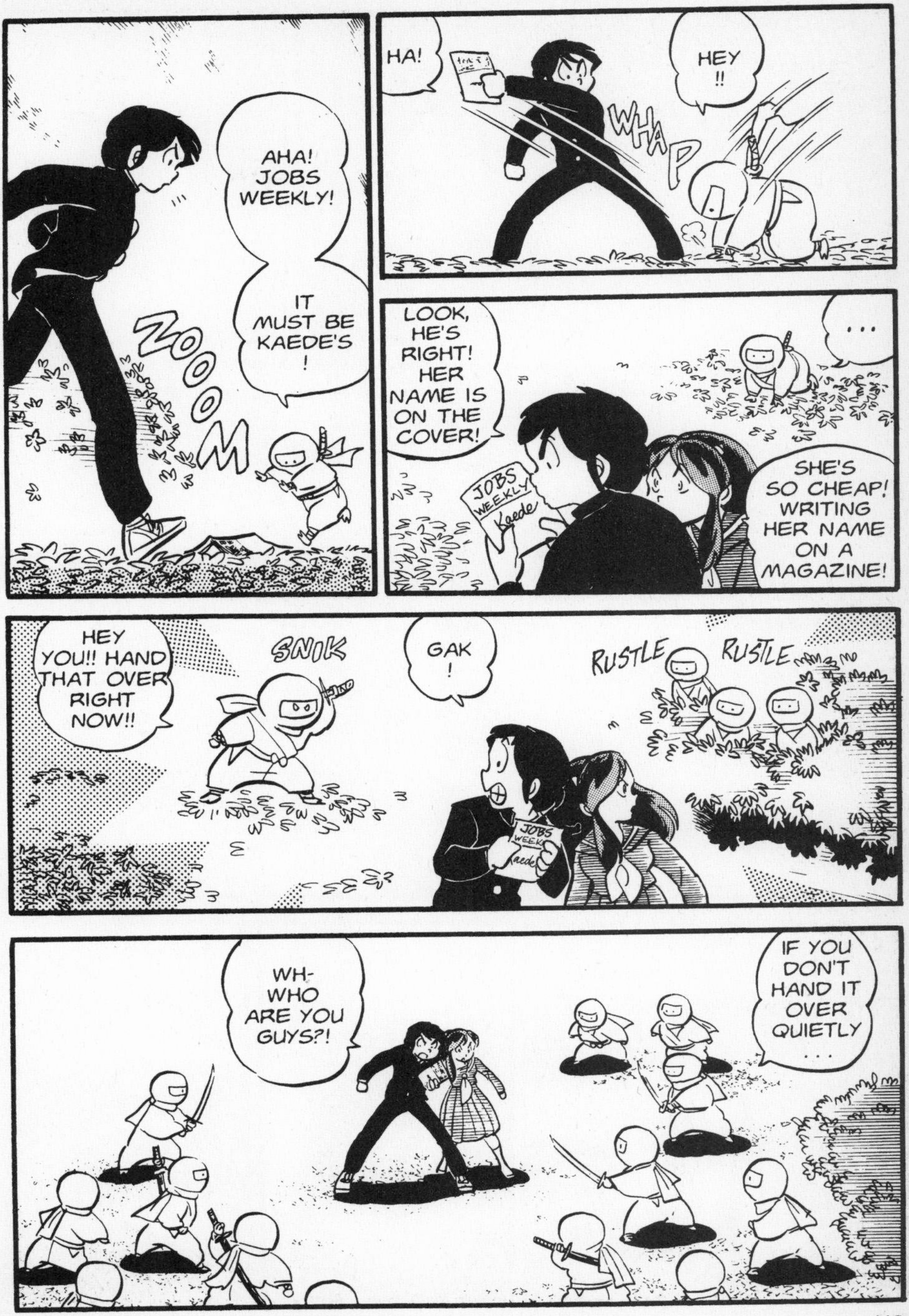
AHA! JOBS WEEKLY!
IT MUST BE KAEDE'S!
ZOOOM
HA!
HEY!!
WHAP
LOOK, HE'S RIGHT! HER NAME IS ON THE COVER!
...
JOBS WEEKLY Kaede
SHE'S SO CHEAP! WRITING HER NAME ON A MAGAZINE!
HEY YOU!! HAND THAT OVER RIGHT NOW!!
SNIK
GAK!
RUSTLE RUSTLE
WH-WHO ARE YOU GUYS?!
IF YOU DON'T HAND IT OVER QUIETLY...

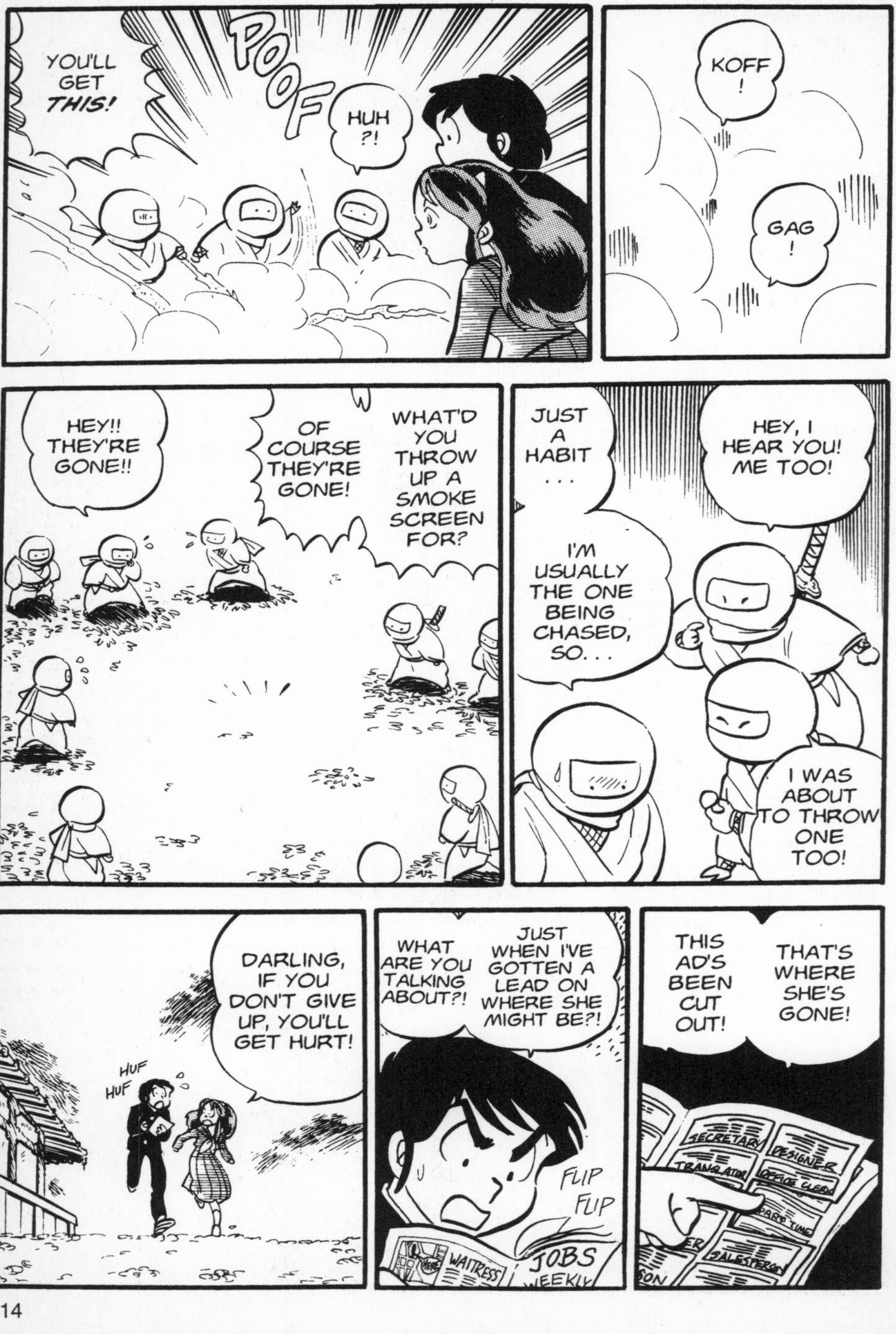
YOU'LL GET THIS!
POOF
HUH ?!
KOFF !
GAG !
HEY!! THEY'RE GONE!!
OF COURSE THEY'RE GONE!
WHAT'D YOU THROW UP A SMOKE SCREEN FOR?
JUST A HABIT . . .
I'M USUALLY THE ONE BEING CHASED, SO. . .
HEY, I HEAR YOU! ME TOO!
I WAS ABOUT TO THROW ONE TOO!
DARLING, IF YOU DON'T GIVE UP, YOU'LL GET HURT!
HUF HUF
WHAT ARE YOU TALKING ABOUT?!
JUST WHEN I'VE GOTTEN A LEAD ON WHERE SHE MIGHT BE?!
FLIP FLIP
WAITRESS
JOBS WEEKLY
THIS AD'S BEEN CUT OUT!
THAT'S WHERE SHE'S GONE!
SECRETARY
DESIGNER
TRANSLATOR
OFFICE CLERK
PART TIME
SALESPERSON

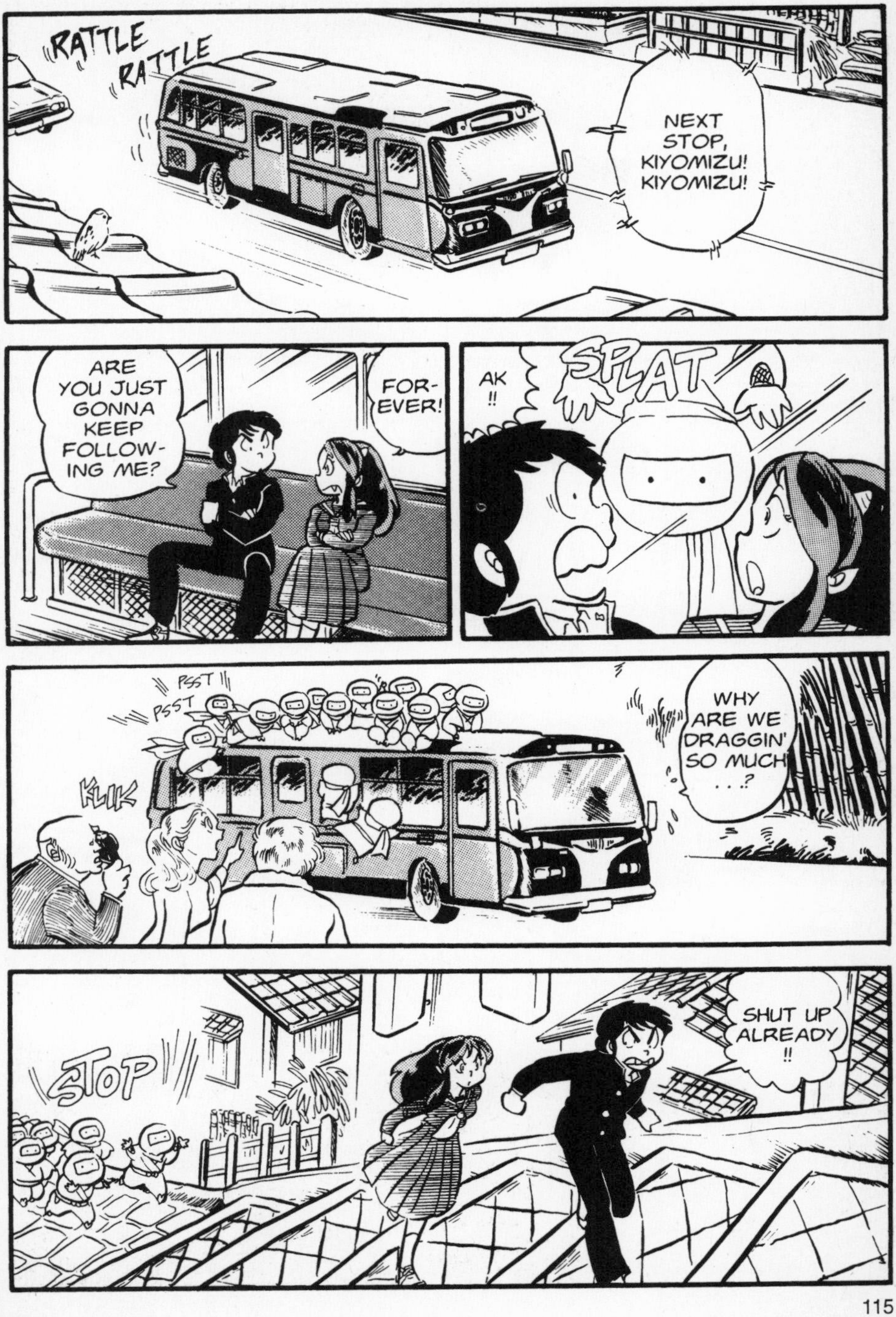
RATTLE RATTLE
NEXT STOP, KIYOMIZU! KIYOMIZU!
ARE YOU JUST GONNA KEEP FOLLOW-ING ME?
FOR-EVER!
AK !!
SPLAT
PSST PSST
KLIK
WHY ARE WE DRAGGIN' SO MUCH . . .?
STOP
SHUT UP ALREADY !!

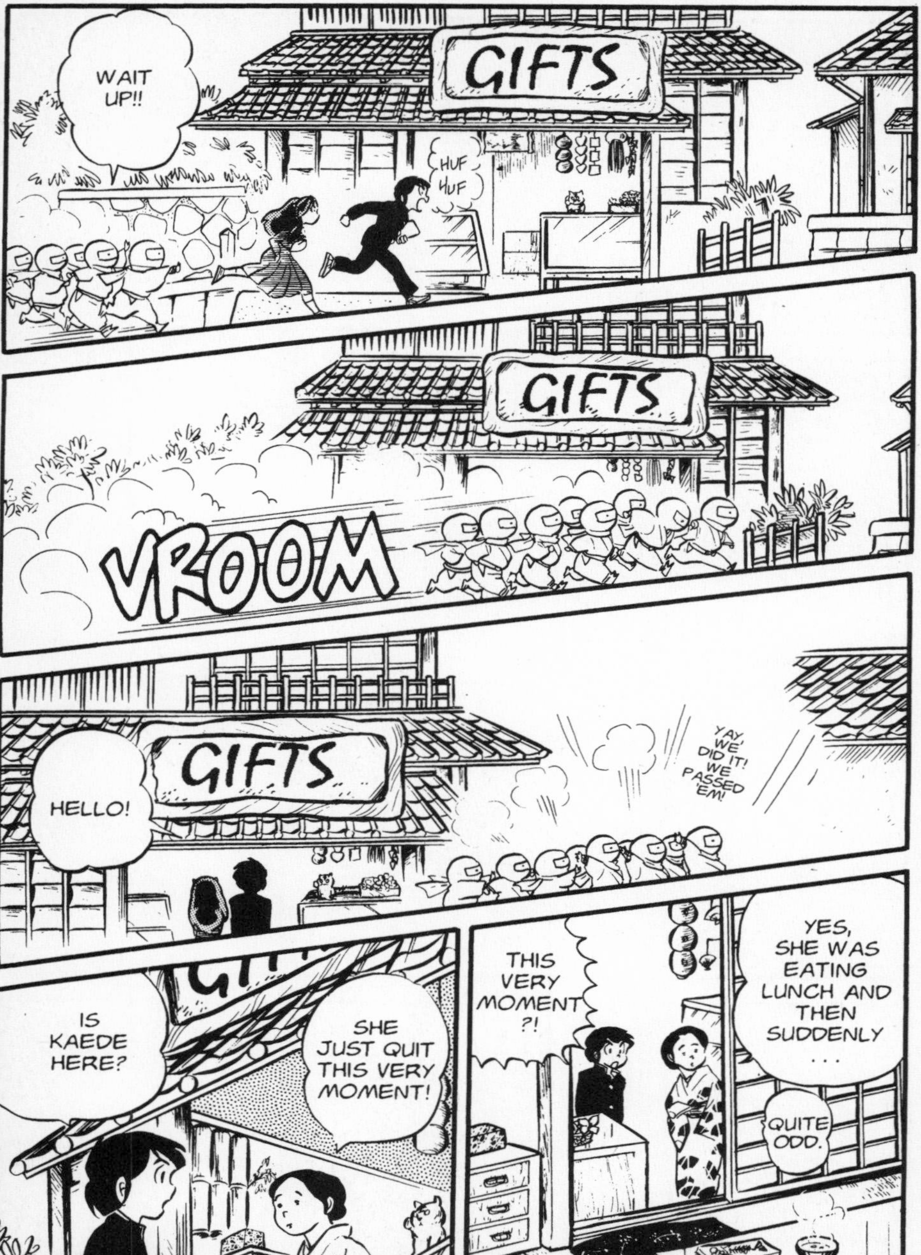
GIFTS
WAIT UP!!
HUF HUF
GIFTS
VROOM
GIFTS
HELLO!
YAY, WE DID IT! WE PASSED 'EM!
IS KAEDE HERE?
SHE JUST QUIT THIS VERY MOMENT!
THIS VERY MOMENT ?!
YES, SHE WAS EATING LUNCH AND THEN SUDDENLY . . .
QUITE ODD.

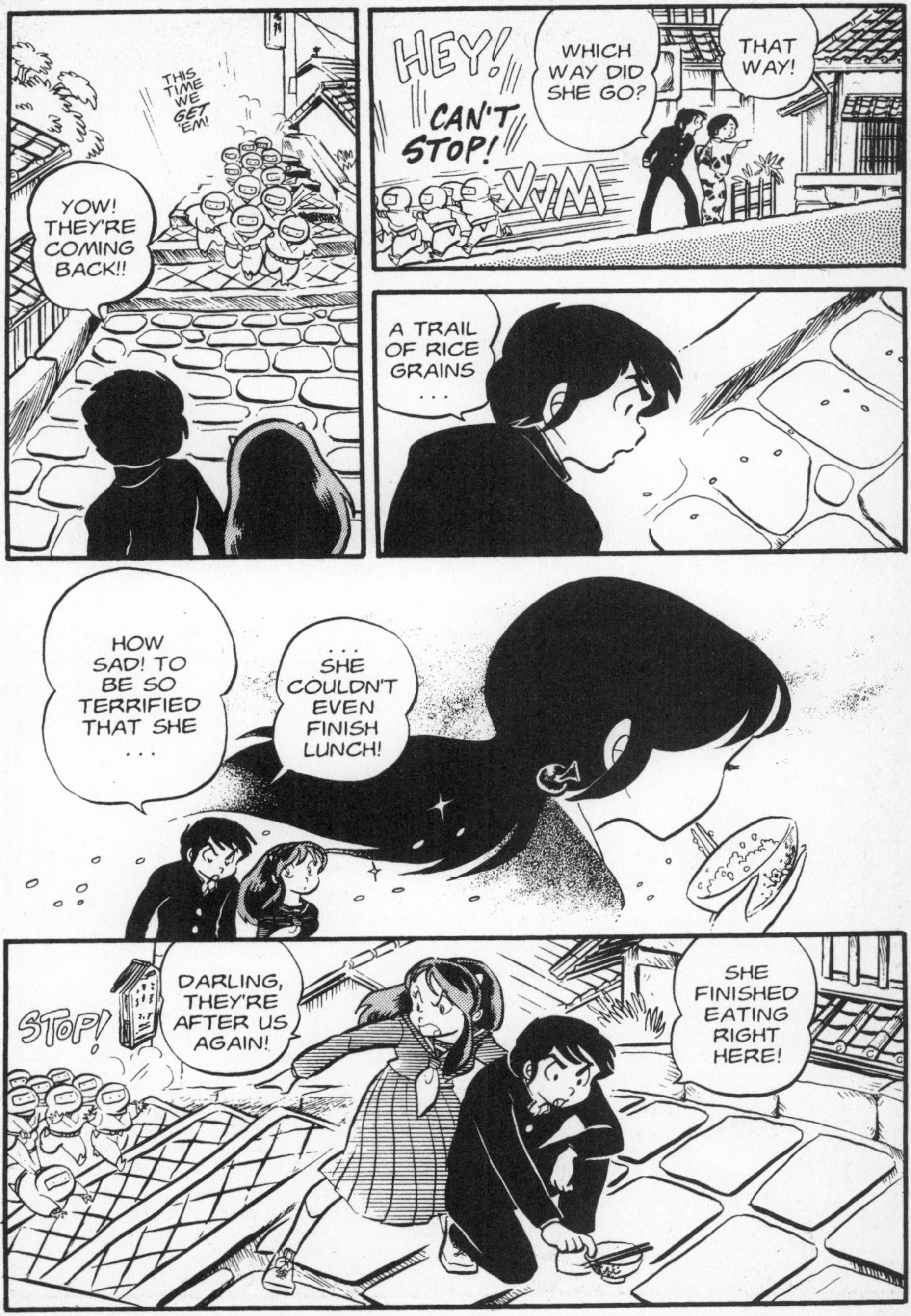
THIS TIME WE GET 'EM!
YOW! THEY'RE COMING BACK!!
HEY!
CAN'T STOP!
WHICH WAY DID SHE GO?
THAT WAY!
A TRAIL OF RICE GRAINS . . .
HOW SAD! TO BE SO TERRIFIED THAT SHE . . .
. . . SHE COULDN'T EVEN FINISH LUNCH!
STOP!
DARLING, THEY'RE AFTER US AGAIN!
SHE FINISHED EATING RIGHT HERE!

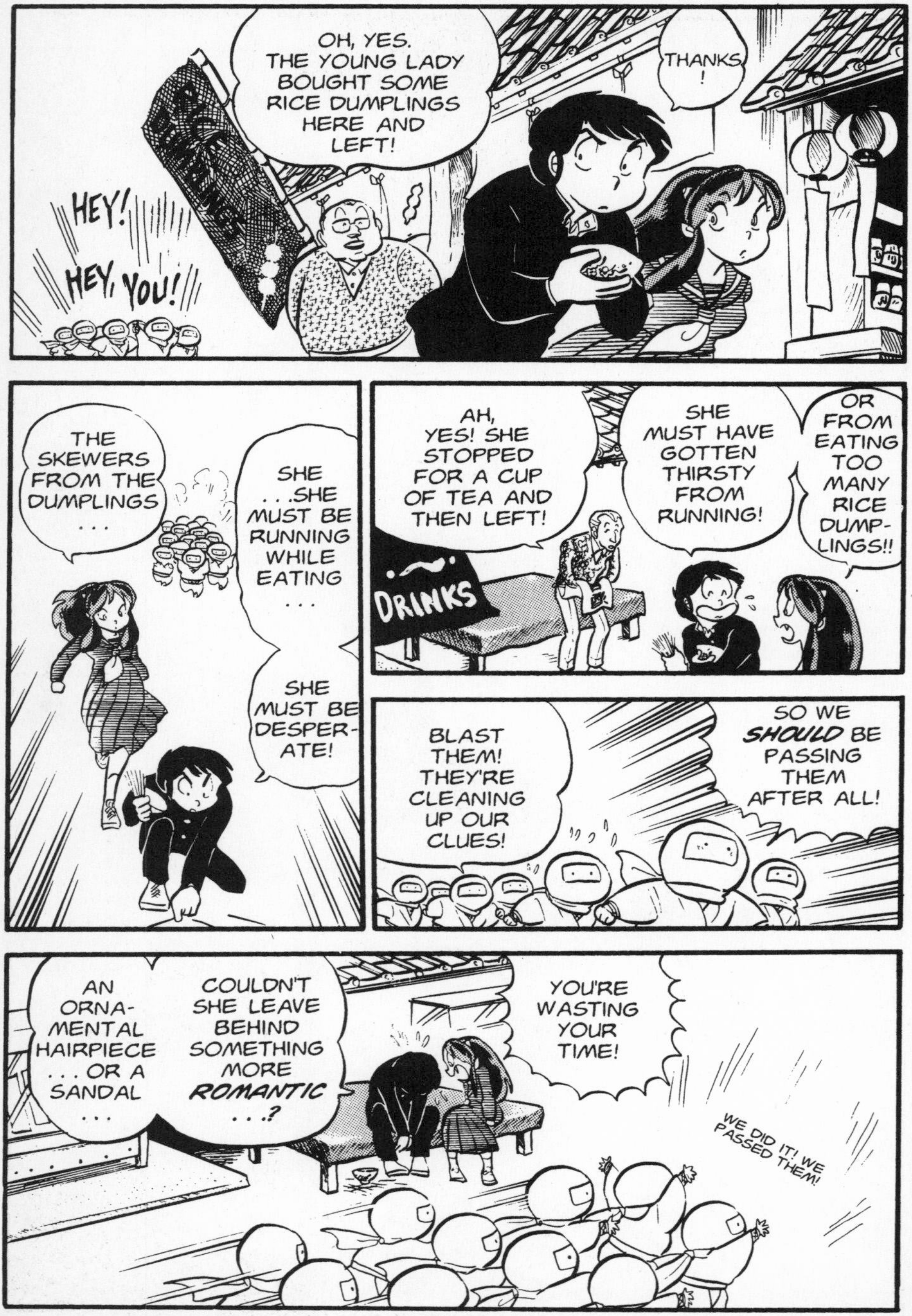
HEY!
HEY, YOU!
OH, YES. THE YOUNG LADY BOUGHT SOME RICE DUMPLINGS HERE AND LEFT!
THANKS!
THE SKEWERS FROM THE DUMPLINGS . . .
SHE . . .SHE MUST BE RUNNING WHILE EATING . . .
SHE MUST BE DESPERATE!
AH, YES! SHE STOPPED FOR A CUP OF TEA AND THEN LEFT!
DRINKS
SHE MUST HAVE GOTTEN THIRSTY FROM RUNNING!
OR FROM EATING TOO MANY RICE DUMPLINGS!!
BLAST THEM! THEY'RE CLEANING UP OUR CLUES!
SO WE *SHOULD* BE PASSING THEM AFTER ALL!
AN ORNAMENTAL HAIRPIECE . . . OR A SANDAL . . .
COULDN'T SHE LEAVE BEHIND SOMETHING MORE *ROMANTIC* . . .?
YOU'RE WASTING YOUR TIME!
WE DID IT! WE PASSED THEM!

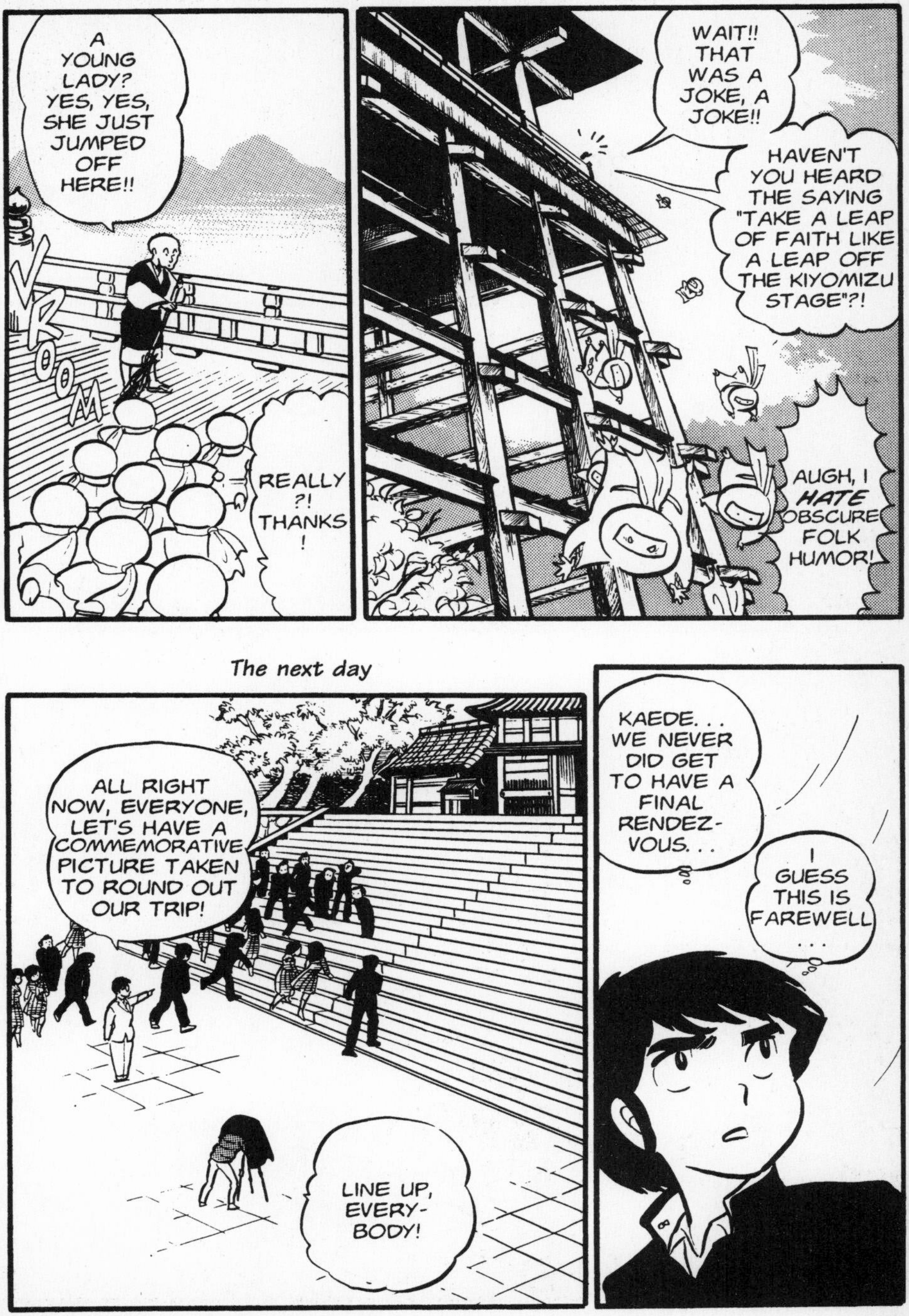
A YOUNG LADY? YES, YES, SHE JUST JUMPED OFF HERE!!
VROOM
REALLY ?! THANKS !
WAIT!! THAT WAS A JOKE, A JOKE!!
HAVEN'T YOU HEARD THE SAYING "TAKE A LEAP OF FAITH LIKE A LEAP OFF THE KIYOMIZU STAGE"?!
AUGH, I HATE OBSCURE FOLK HUMOR!
The next day
ALL RIGHT NOW, EVERYONE, LET'S HAVE A COMMEMORATIVE PICTURE TAKEN TO ROUND OUT OUR TRIP!
LINE UP, EVERY-BODY!
KAEDE. . . WE NEVER DID GET TO HAVE A FINAL RENDEZ-VOUS. . .
I GUESS THIS IS FAREWELL . . .

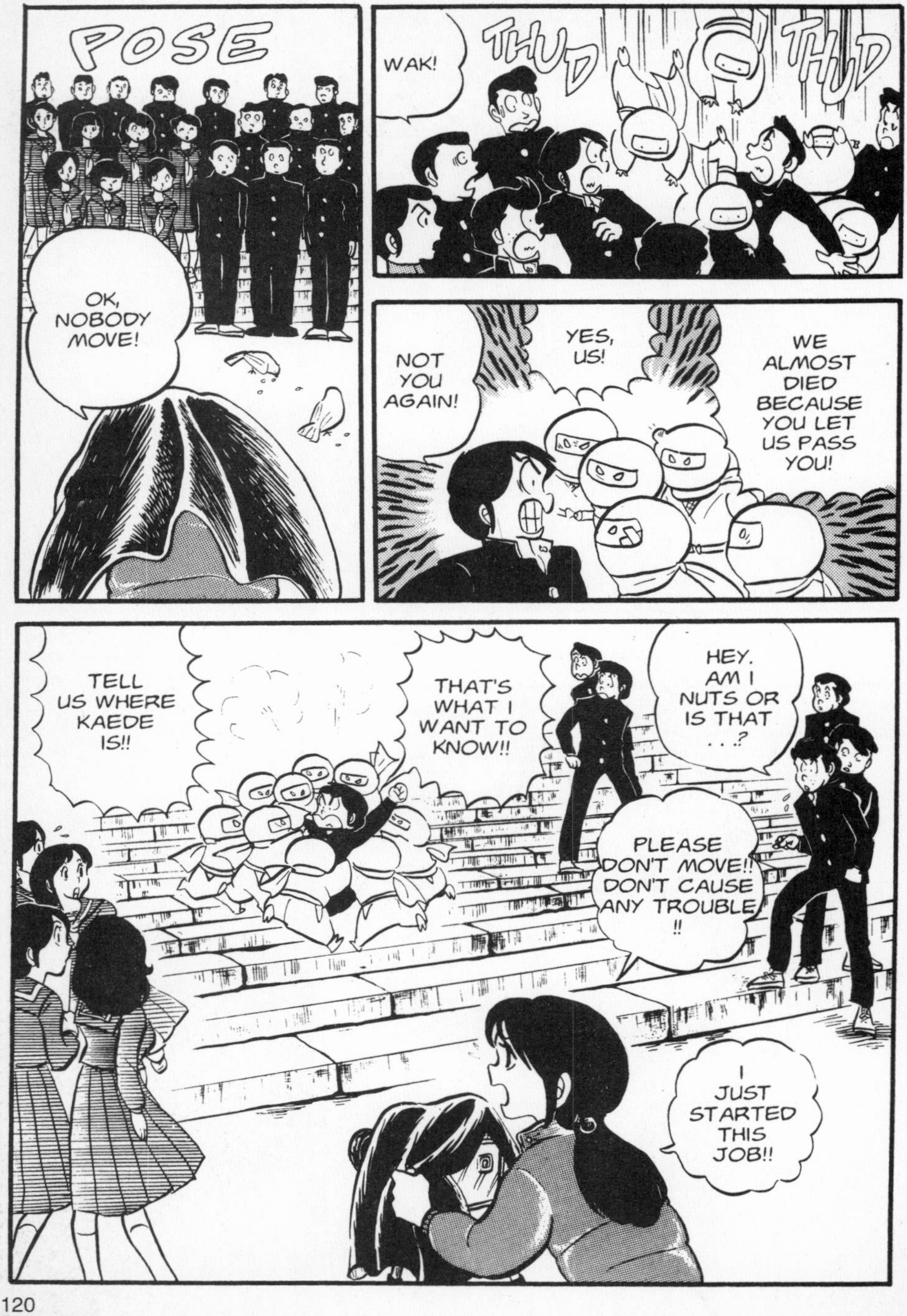
POSE
OK, NOBODY MOVE!
WAK!
THUD
THUD
NOT YOU AGAIN!
YES, US!
WE ALMOST DIED BECAUSE YOU LET US PASS YOU!
TELL US WHERE KAEDE IS!!
THAT'S WHAT I WANT TO KNOW!!
HEY. AM I NUTS OR IS THAT . . .?
PLEASE DON'T MOVE!! DON'T CAUSE ANY TROUBLE !!
I JUST STARTED THIS JOB!!

PART EIGHT
A NECK-AND-NECK FINISH

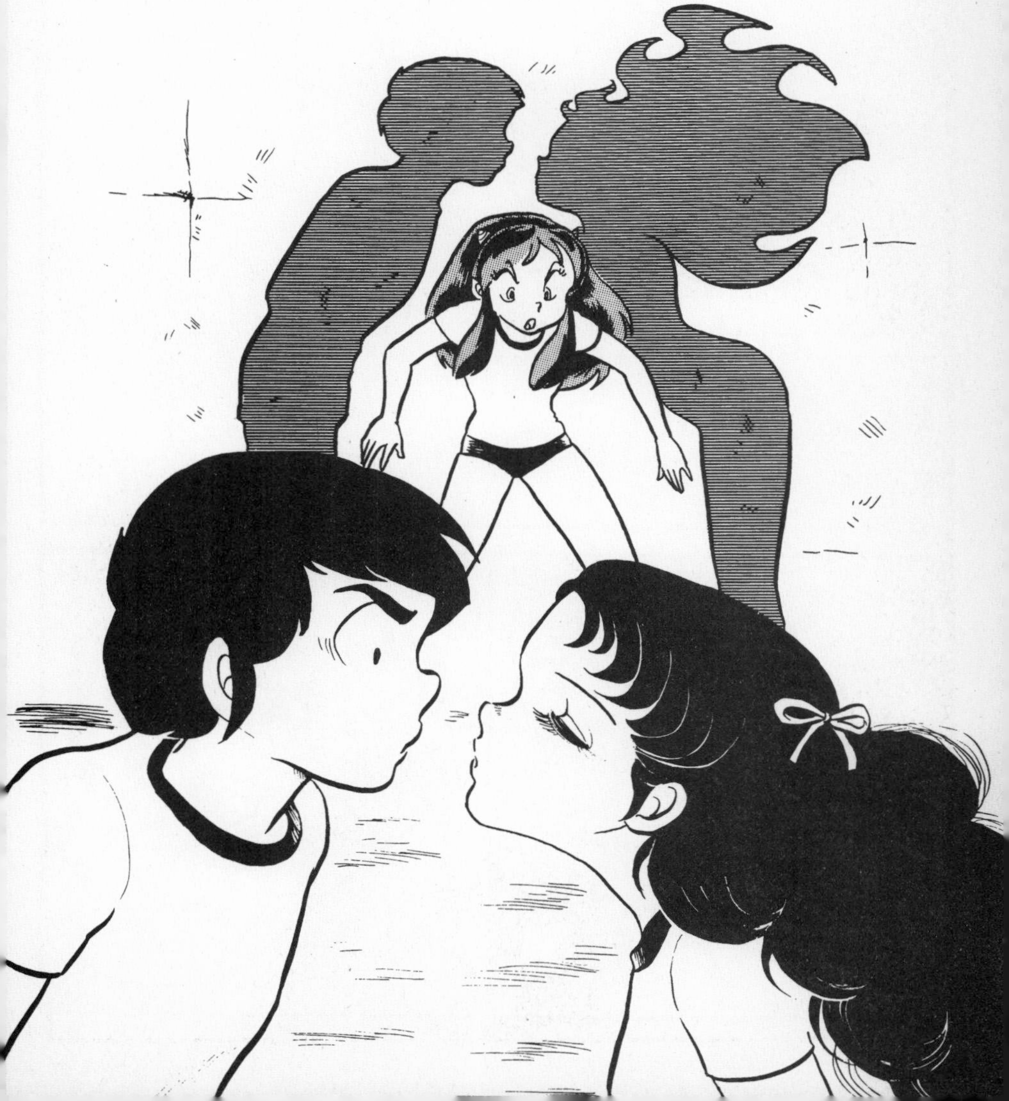

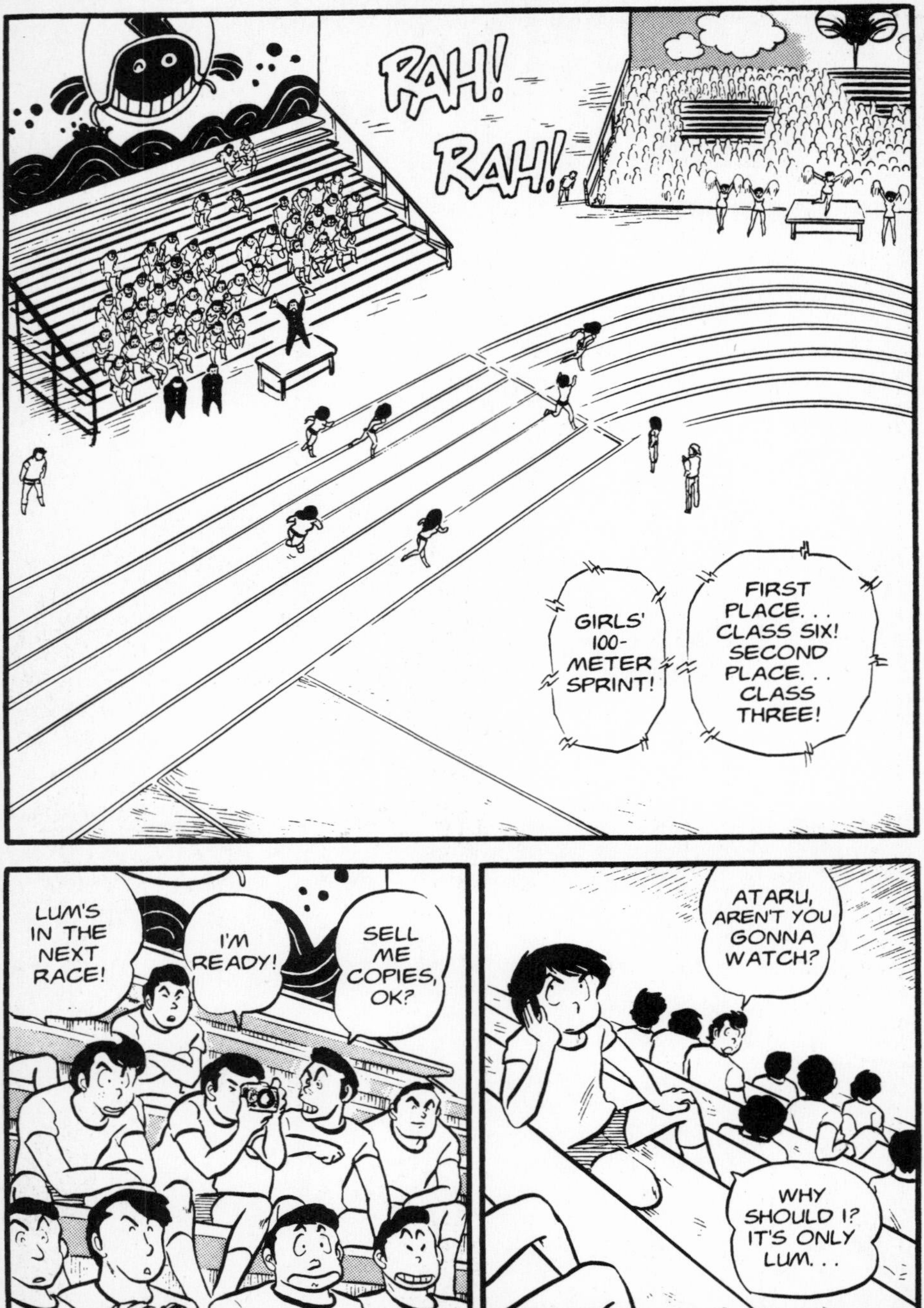
RAH! RAH!
GIRLS' 100-METER SPRINT!
FIRST PLACE. . . CLASS SIX! SECOND PLACE. . . CLASS THREE!
LUM'S IN THE NEXT RACE!
I'M READY!
SELL ME COPIES, OK?
ATARU, AREN'T YOU GONNA WATCH?
WHY SHOULD I? IT'S ONLY LUM. . .

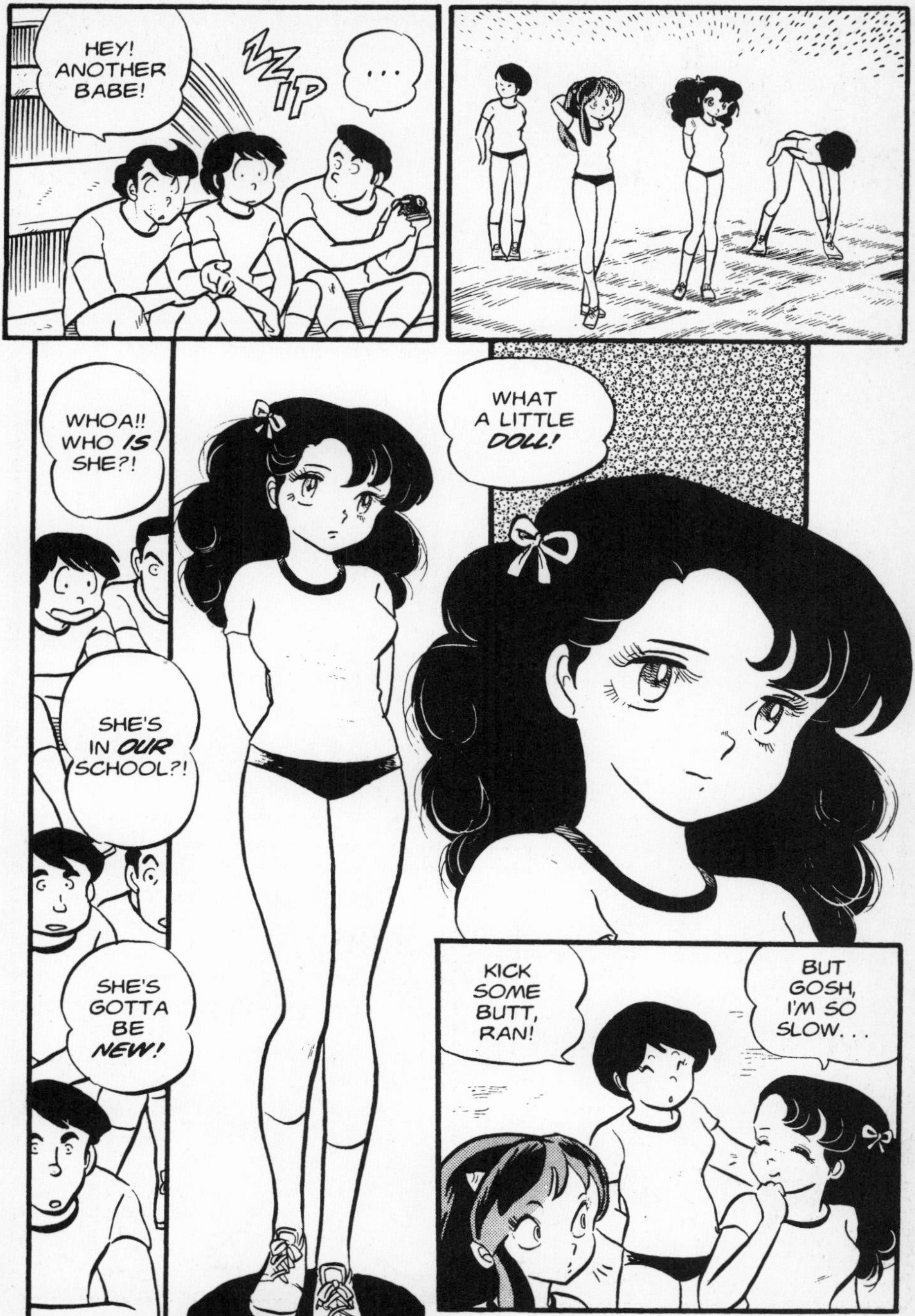
HEY! ANOTHER BABE!
ZZIP
...
WHOA!! WHO *IS* SHE?!
SHE'S IN *OUR* SCHOOL?!
SHE'S GOTTA BE *NEW!*
WHAT A LITTLE *DOLL!*
KICK SOME BUTT, RAN!
BUT GOSH, I'M SO SLOW...

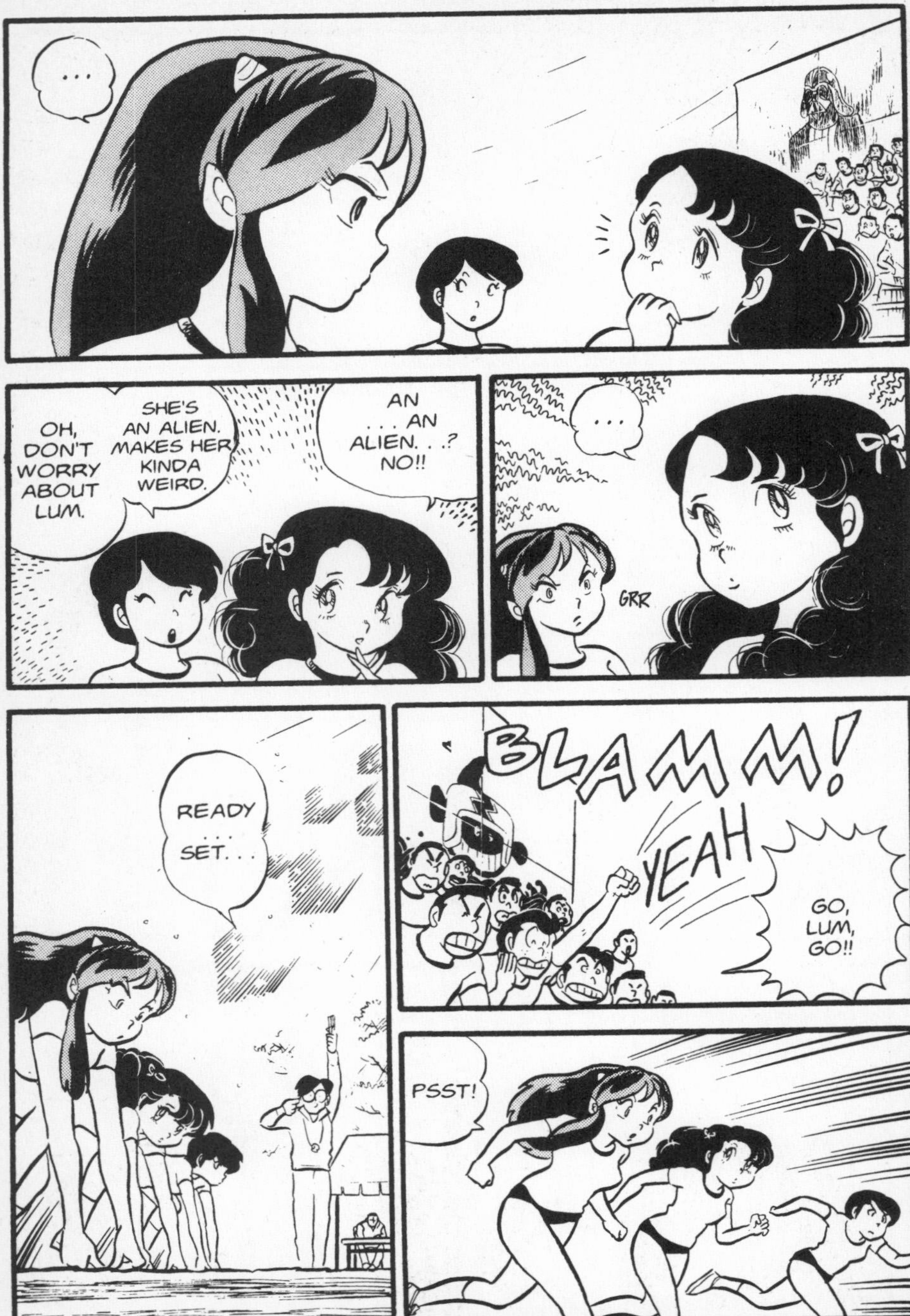

. . .
OH, DON'T WORRY ABOUT LUM.
SHE'S AN ALIEN. MAKES HER KINDA WEIRD.
AN . . . AN ALIEN. . .? NO!!
. . .
GRR
READY . . . SET. . .
BLAMM!
YEAH
GO, LUM, GO!!
PSST!

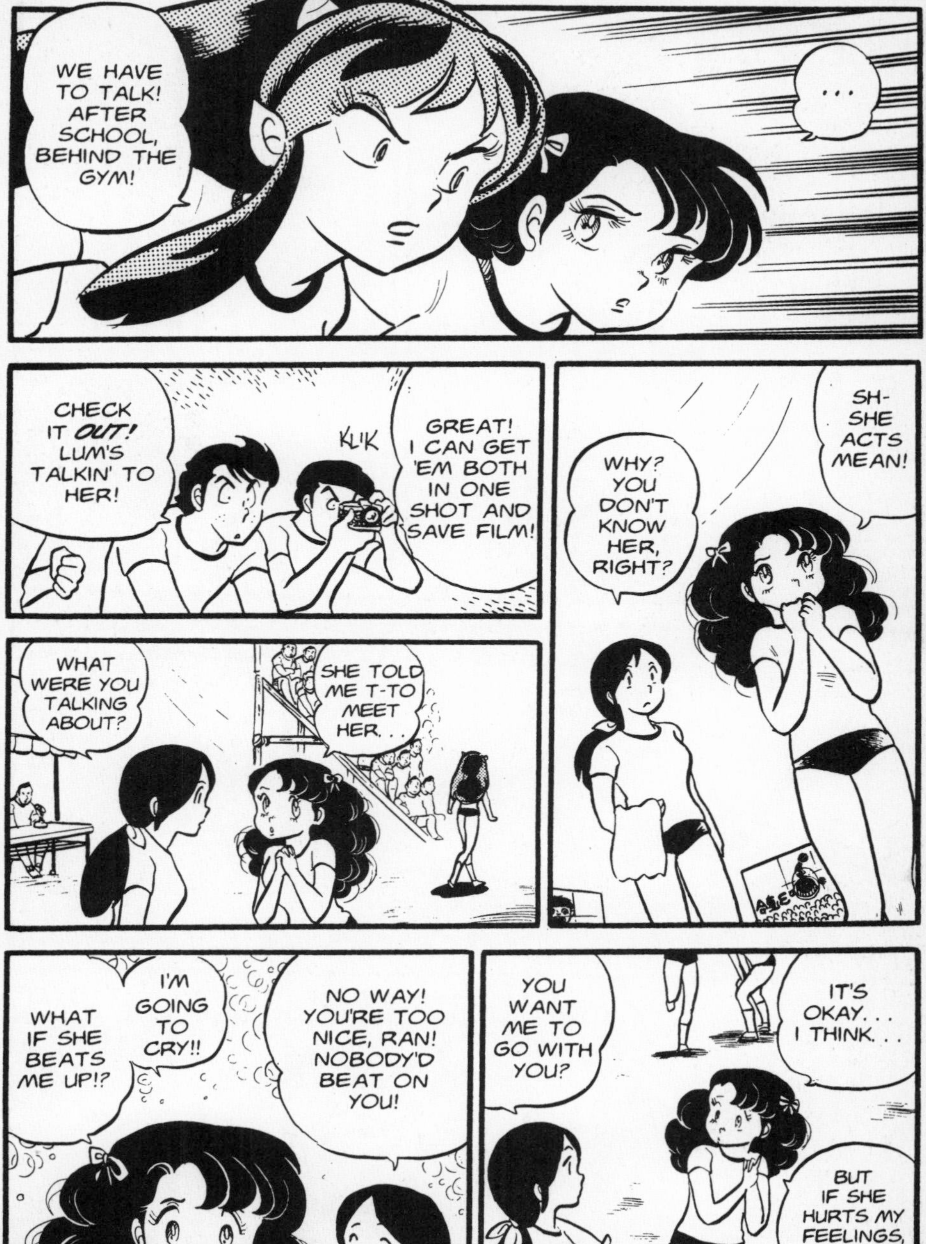
WE HAVE TO TALK! AFTER SCHOOL, BEHIND THE GYM!
...
CHECK IT *OUT!* LUM'S TALKIN' TO HER!
KLIK
GREAT! I CAN GET 'EM BOTH IN ONE SHOT AND SAVE FILM!
WHAT WERE YOU TALKING ABOUT?
SHE TOLD ME T-TO MEET HER...
SH- SHE ACTS MEAN!
WHY? YOU DON'T KNOW HER, RIGHT?
WHAT IF SHE BEATS ME UP!?
I'M GOING TO CRY!!
NO WAY! YOU'RE TOO NICE, RAN! NOBODY'D BEAT ON YOU!
YOU WANT ME TO GO WITH YOU?
IT'S OKAY... I THINK...
BUT IF SHE HURTS MY FEELINGS, CAN I CRY ON YOUR SHOULDER?

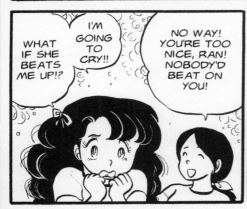

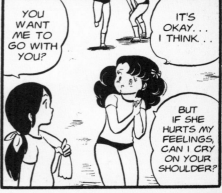

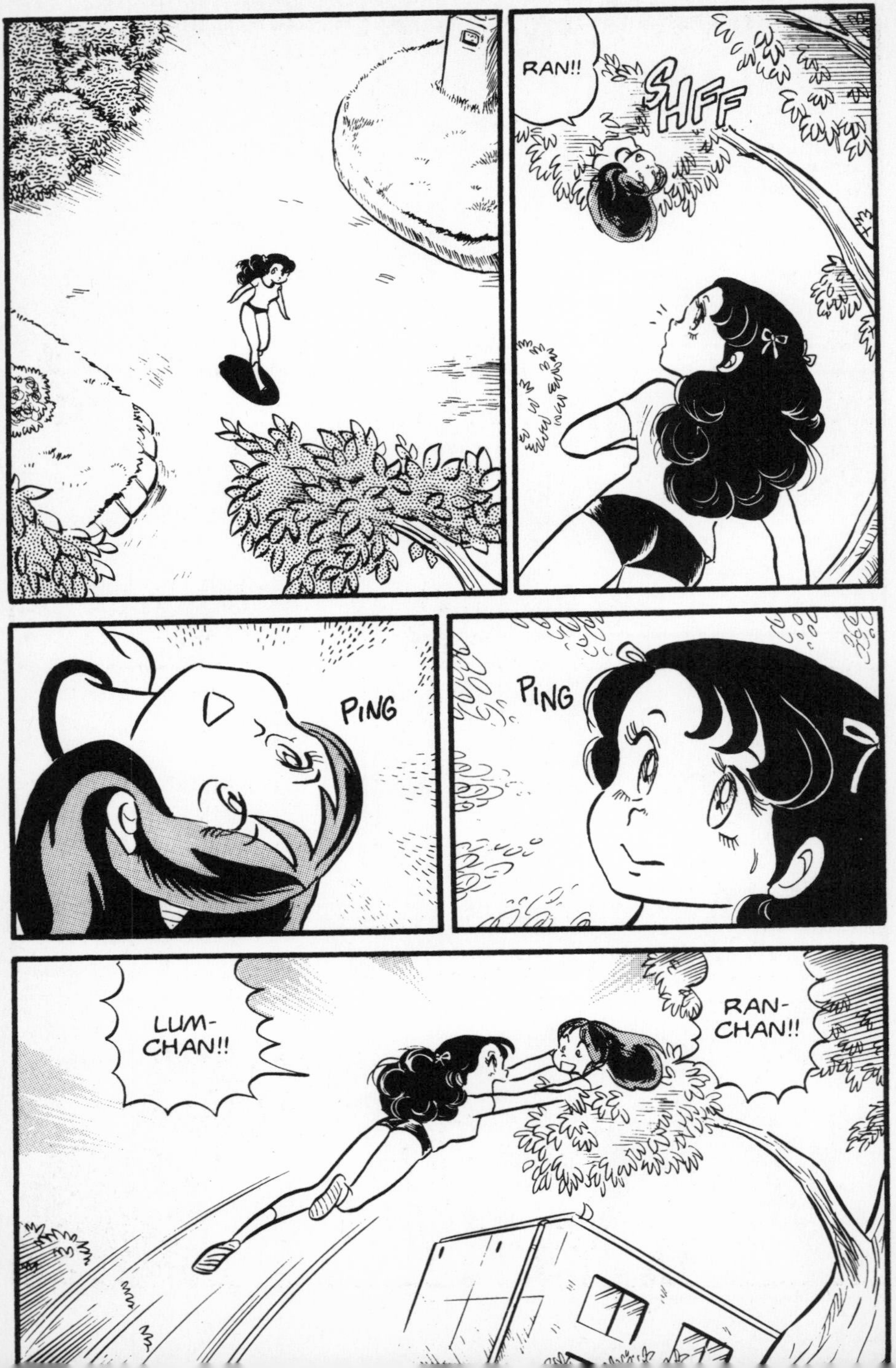
RAN!!
SHFF
PING
PING
LUM-
CHAN!!
RAN-
CHAN!!

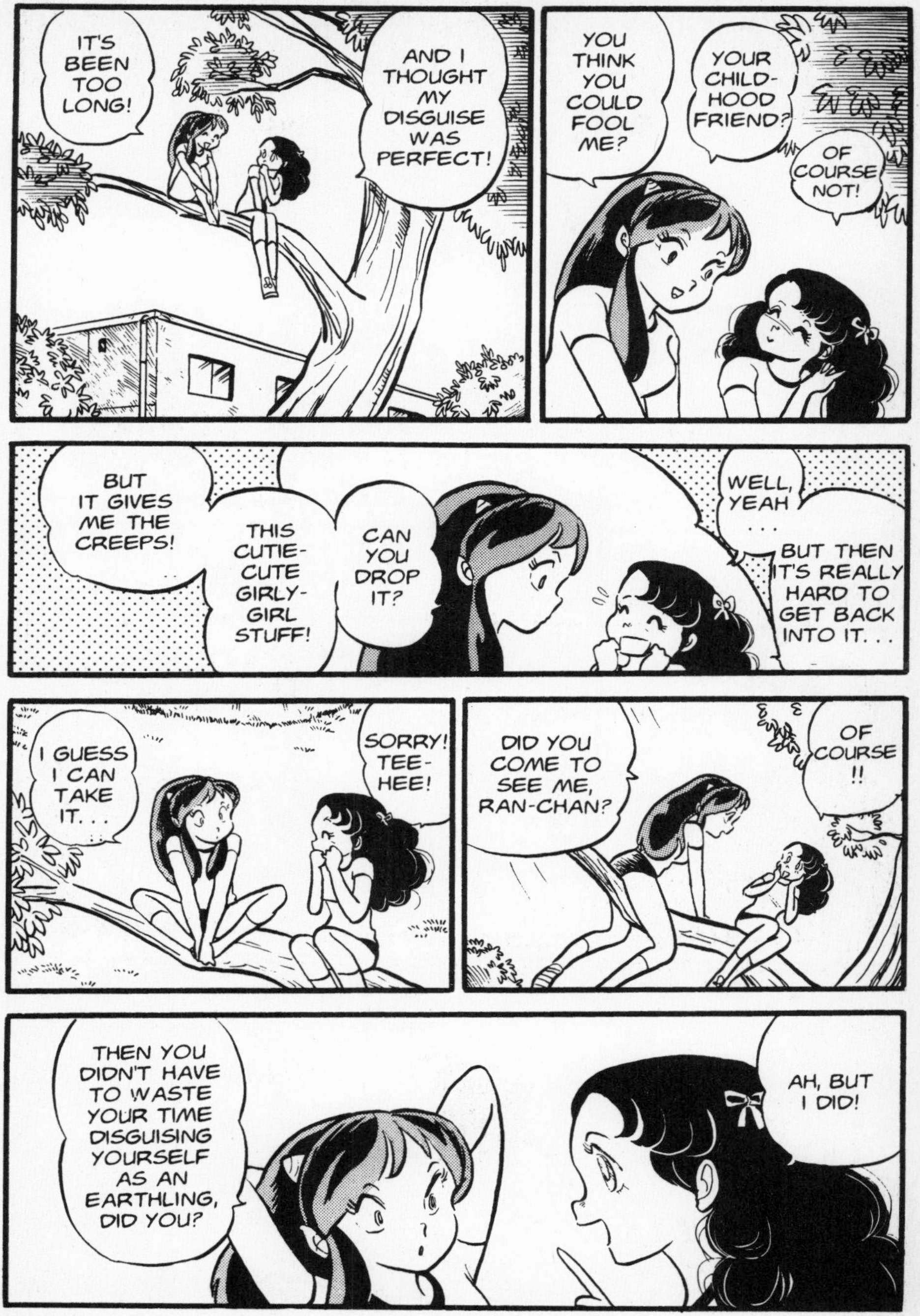
IT'S BEEN TOO LONG!
AND I THOUGHT MY DISGUISE WAS PERFECT!
YOU THINK YOU COULD FOOL ME?
YOUR CHILD-HOOD FRIEND?
OF COURSE NOT!
BUT IT GIVES ME THE CREEPS!
THIS CUTIE-CUTE GIRLY-GIRL STUFF!
CAN YOU DROP IT?
WELL, YEAH . . .
BUT THEN IT'S REALLY HARD TO GET BACK INTO IT. . .
I GUESS I CAN TAKE IT. . .
SORRY! TEE-HEE!
DID YOU COME TO SEE ME, RAN-CHAN?
OF COURSE !!
THEN YOU DIDN'T HAVE TO WASTE YOUR TIME DISGUISING YOURSELF AS AN EARTHLING, DID YOU?
AH, BUT I DID!

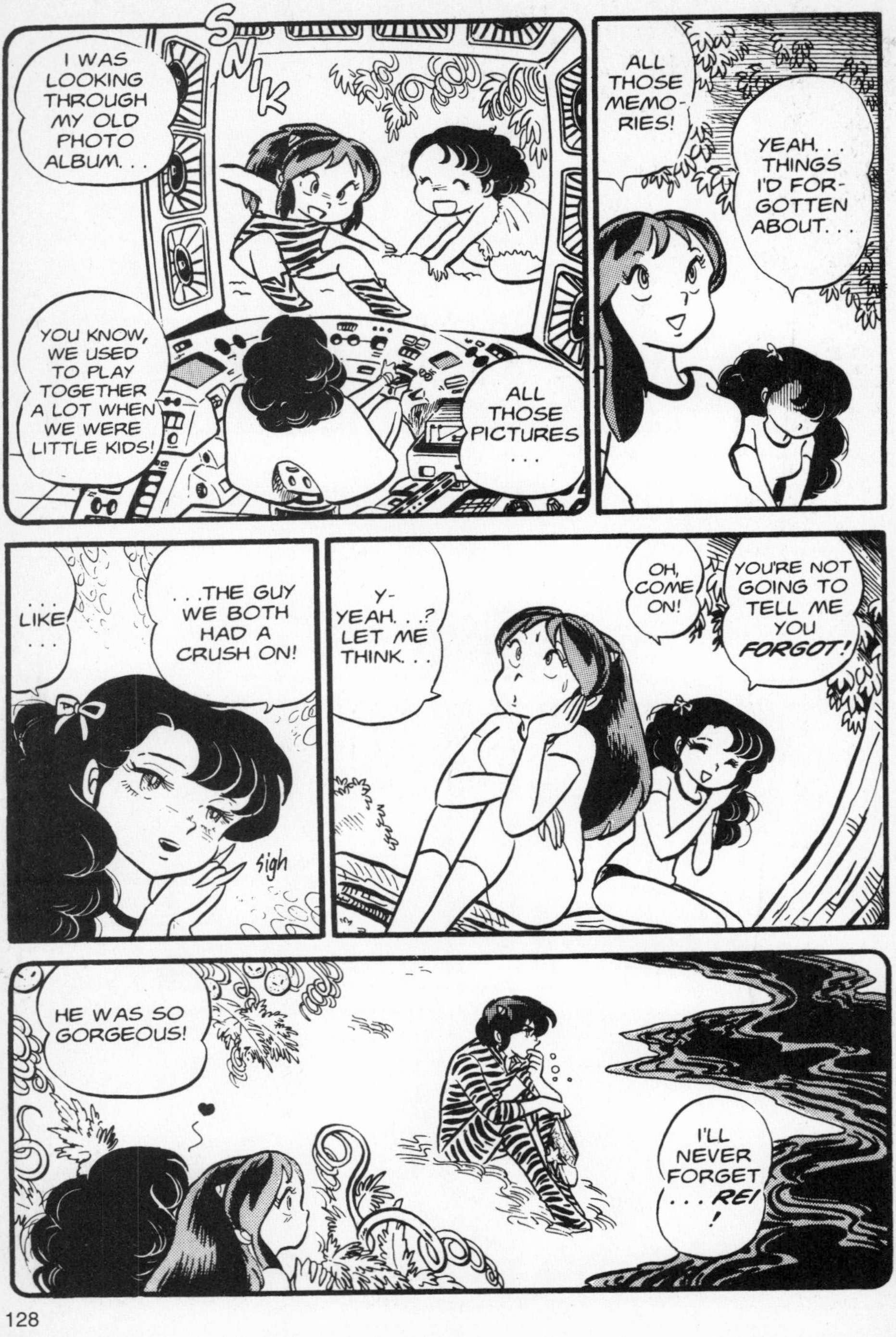
SNIK
I WAS LOOKING THROUGH MY OLD PHOTO ALBUM...
YOU KNOW, WE USED TO PLAY TOGETHER A LOT WHEN WE WERE LITTLE KIDS!
ALL THOSE PICTURES...
ALL THOSE MEMO-RIES!
YEAH... THINGS I'D FOR-GOTTEN ABOUT...
...LIKE...
...THE GUY WE BOTH HAD A CRUSH ON!
sigh
Y-YEAH...? LET ME THINK...
OH, COME ON!
YOU'RE NOT GOING TO TELL ME YOU *FORGOT!*
HE WAS SO GORGEOUS!
I'LL NEVER FORGET ...*REI*!

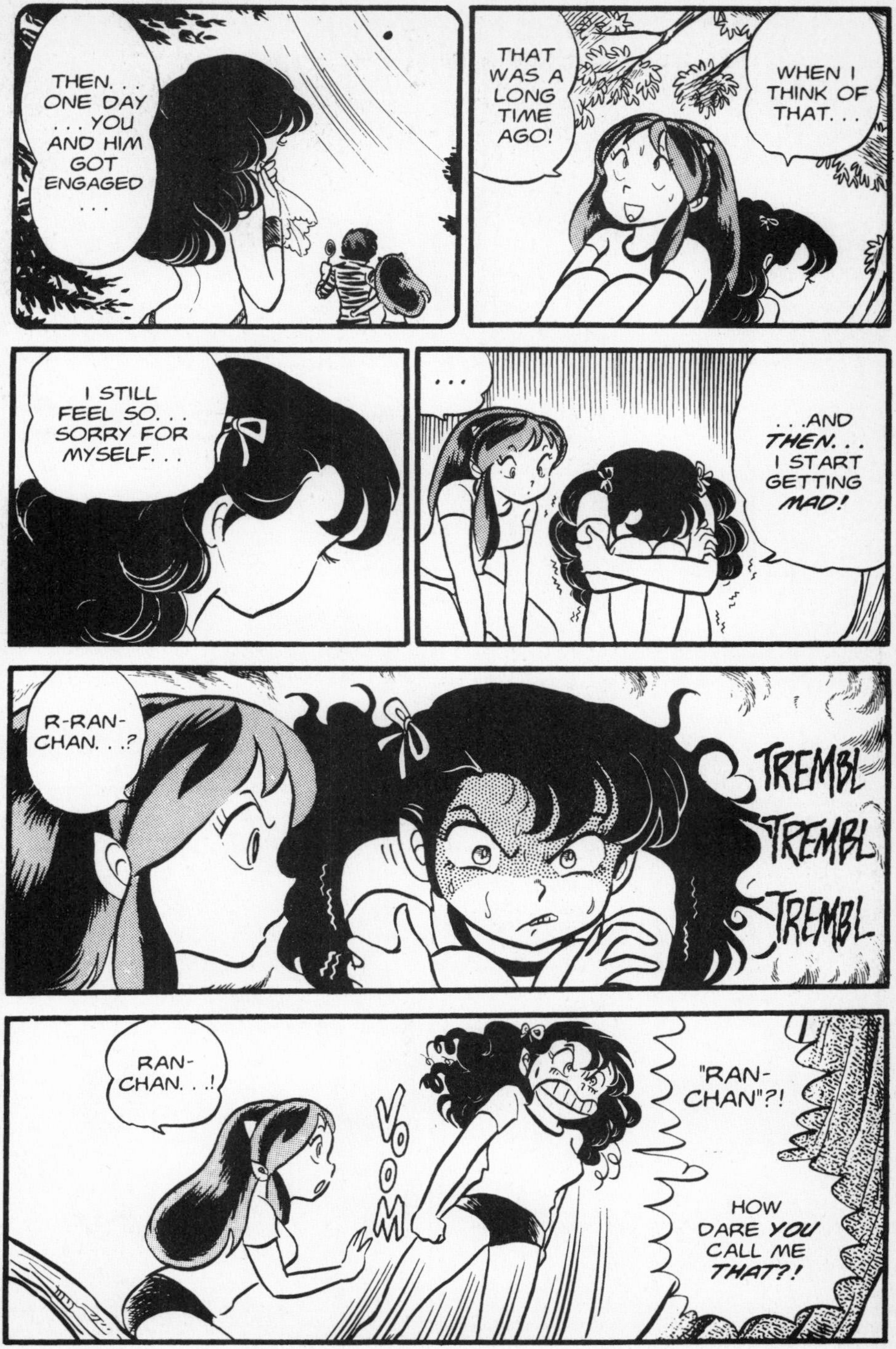
THEN. . . ONE DAY . . . YOU AND HIM GOT ENGAGED . . .
THAT WAS A LONG TIME AGO!
WHEN I THINK OF THAT. . .
I STILL FEEL SO. . . SORRY FOR MYSELF. . .
. . .
. . .AND THEN. . . I START GETTING MAD!
R-RAN-CHAN. . .?
TREMBL
TREMBL
TREMBL
RAN-CHAN. . .!
VOOM
"RAN-CHAN"?!
HOW DARE YOU CALL ME THAT?!

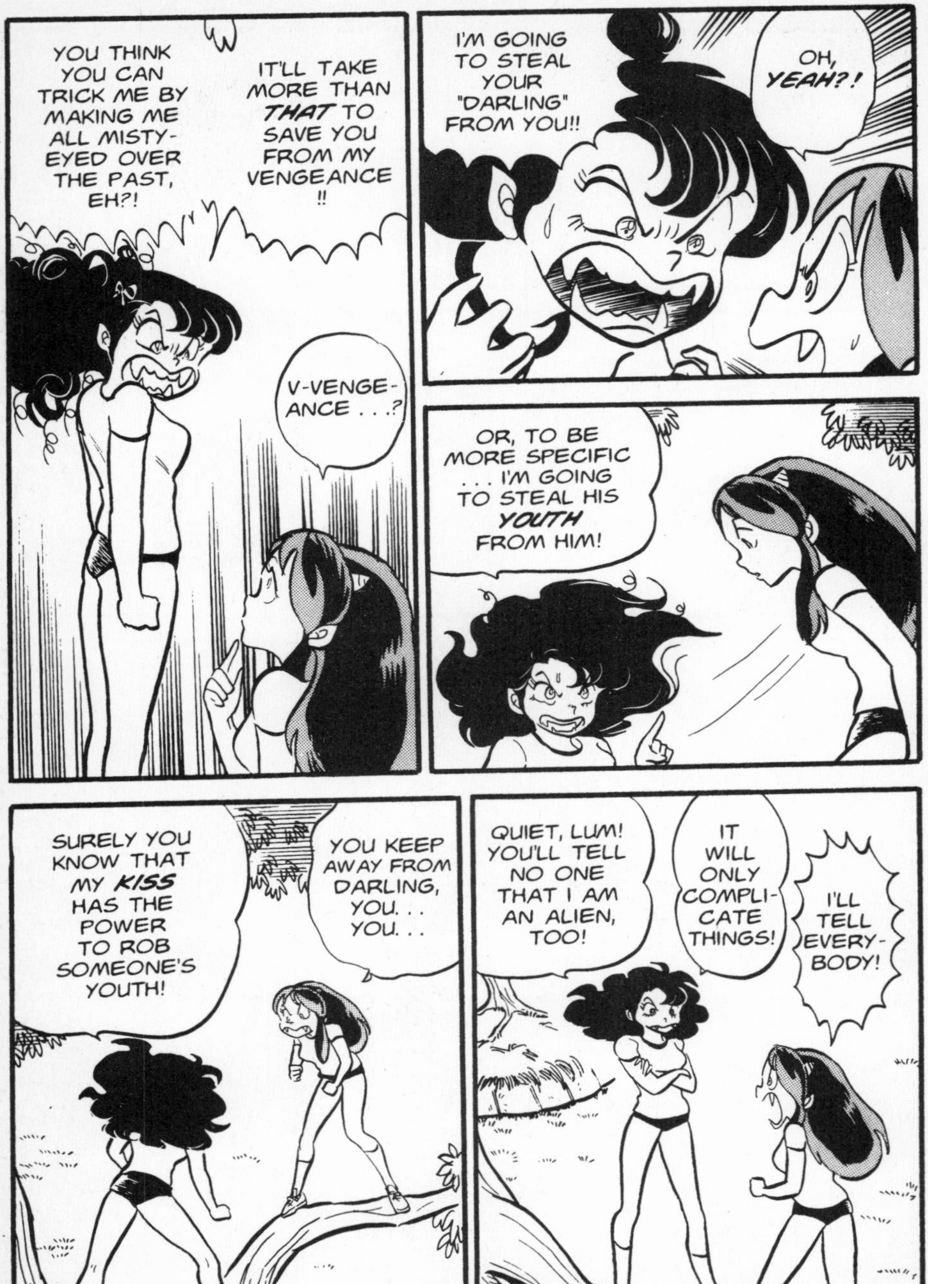
YOU THINK YOU CAN TRICK ME BY MAKING ME ALL MISTY-EYED OVER THE PAST, EH?!
IT'LL TAKE MORE THAN *THAT* TO SAVE YOU FROM MY VENGEANCE !!
V-VENGE-ANCE . . .?
I'M GOING TO STEAL YOUR "DARLING" FROM YOU!!
OH, *YEAH?!*
OR, TO BE MORE SPECIFIC . . . I'M GOING TO STEAL HIS *YOUTH* FROM HIM!
SURELY YOU KNOW THAT MY *KISS* HAS THE POWER TO ROB SOMEONE'S YOUTH!
YOU KEEP AWAY FROM DARLING, YOU. . . YOU. . .
QUIET, LUM! YOU'LL TELL NO ONE THAT I AM AN ALIEN, TOO!
IT WILL ONLY COMPLI-CATE THINGS!
I'LL TELL EVERY-BODY!

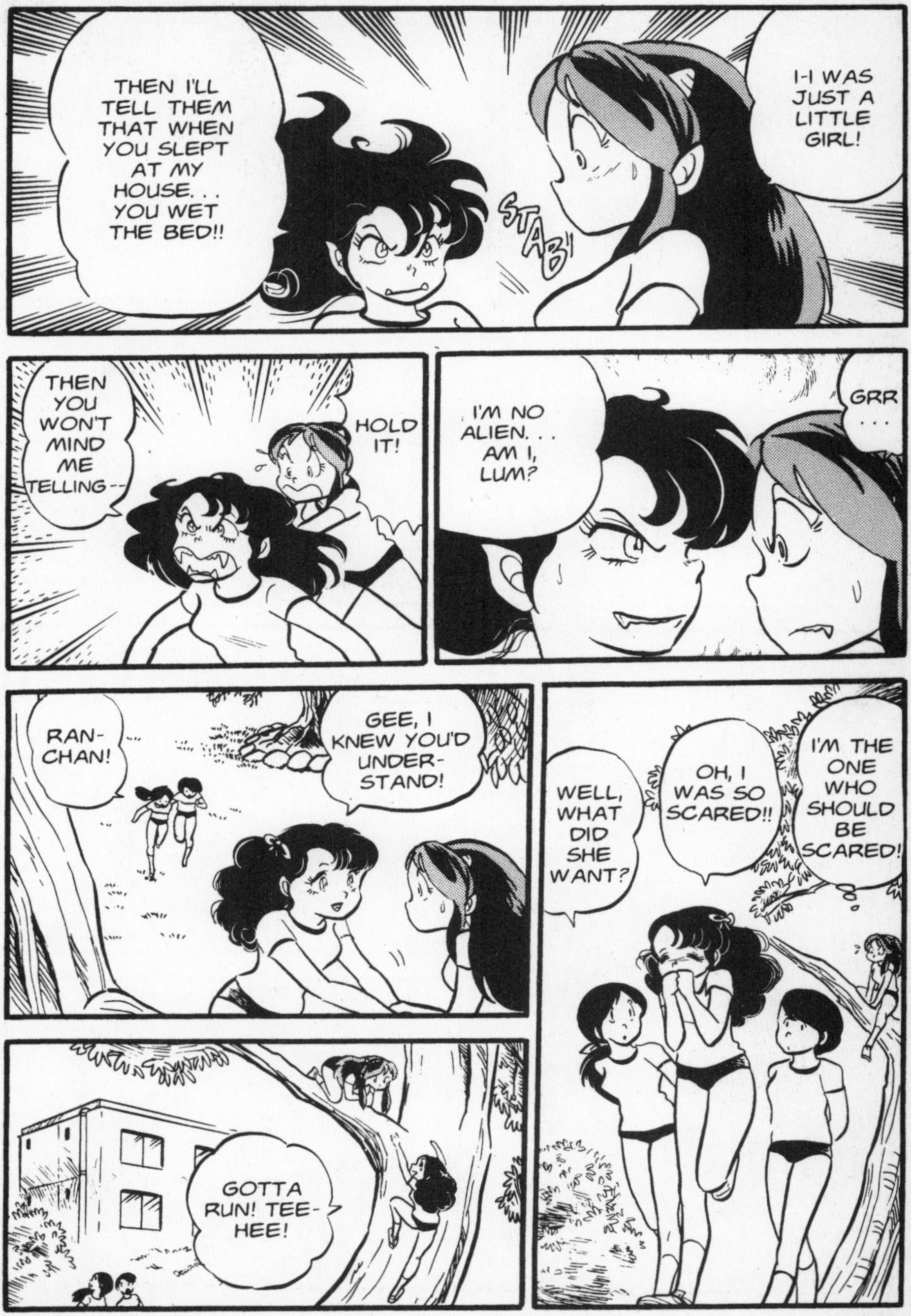
THEN I'LL TELL THEM THAT WHEN YOU SLEPT AT MY HOUSE. . . YOU WET THE BED!!
STAB!
I-I WAS JUST A LITTLE GIRL!
THEN YOU WON'T MIND ME TELLING--
HOLD IT!
I'M NO ALIEN. . . AM I, LUM?
GRR . . .
RAN-CHAN!
GEE, I KNEW YOU'D UNDER-STAND!
GOTTA RUN! TEE-HEE!
WELL, WHAT DID SHE WANT?
OH, I WAS SO SCARED!!
I'M THE ONE WHO SHOULD BE SCARED!

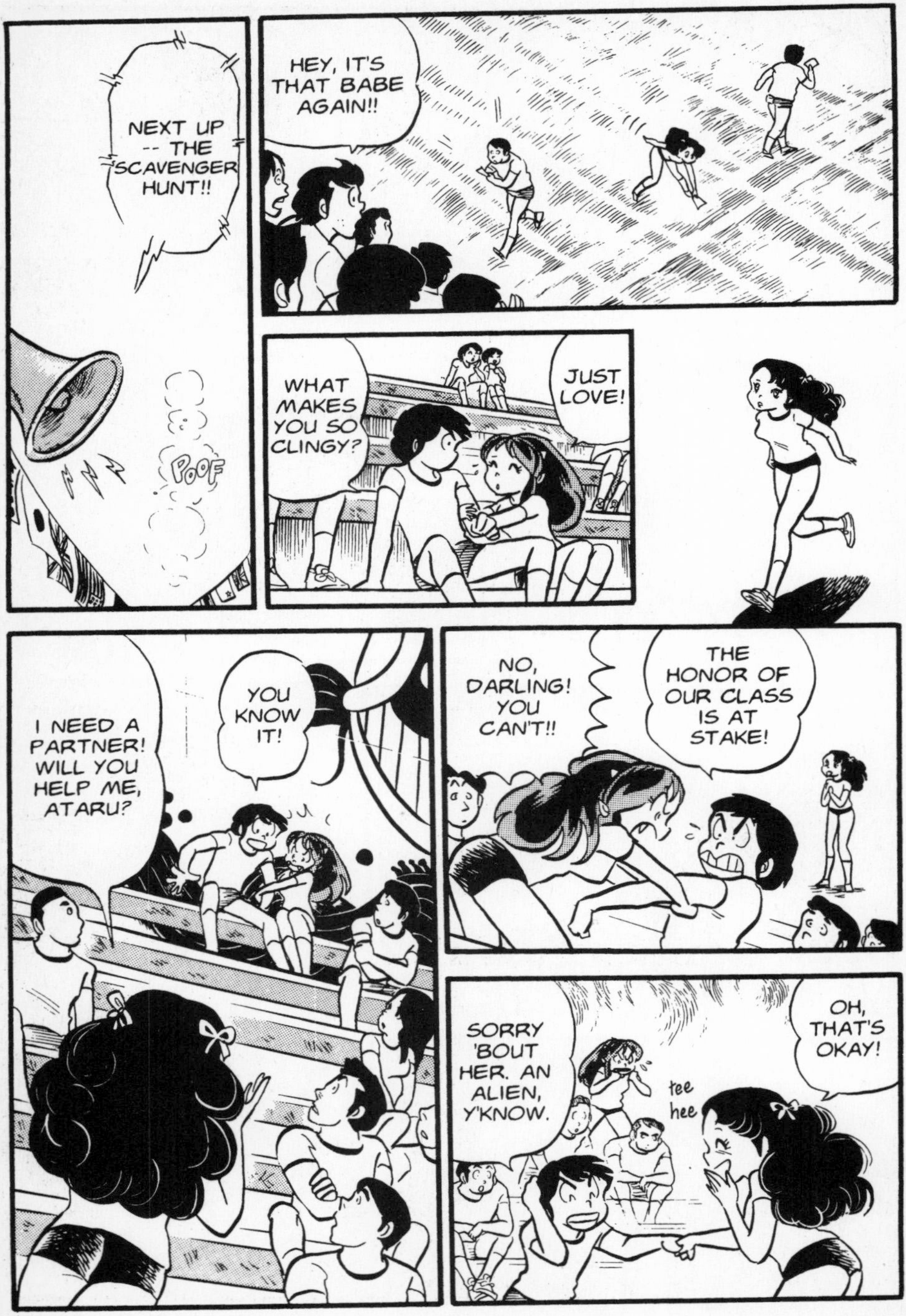
NEXT UP -- THE SCAVENGER HUNT!!
HEY, IT'S THAT BABE AGAIN!!
WHAT MAKES YOU SO CLINGY?
JUST LOVE!
POOF
I NEED A PARTNER! WILL YOU HELP ME, ATARU?
YOU KNOW IT!
NO, DARLING! YOU CAN'T!!
THE HONOR OF OUR CLASS IS AT STAKE!
SORRY 'BOUT HER. AN ALIEN, Y'KNOW.
tee hee
OH, THAT'S OKAY!

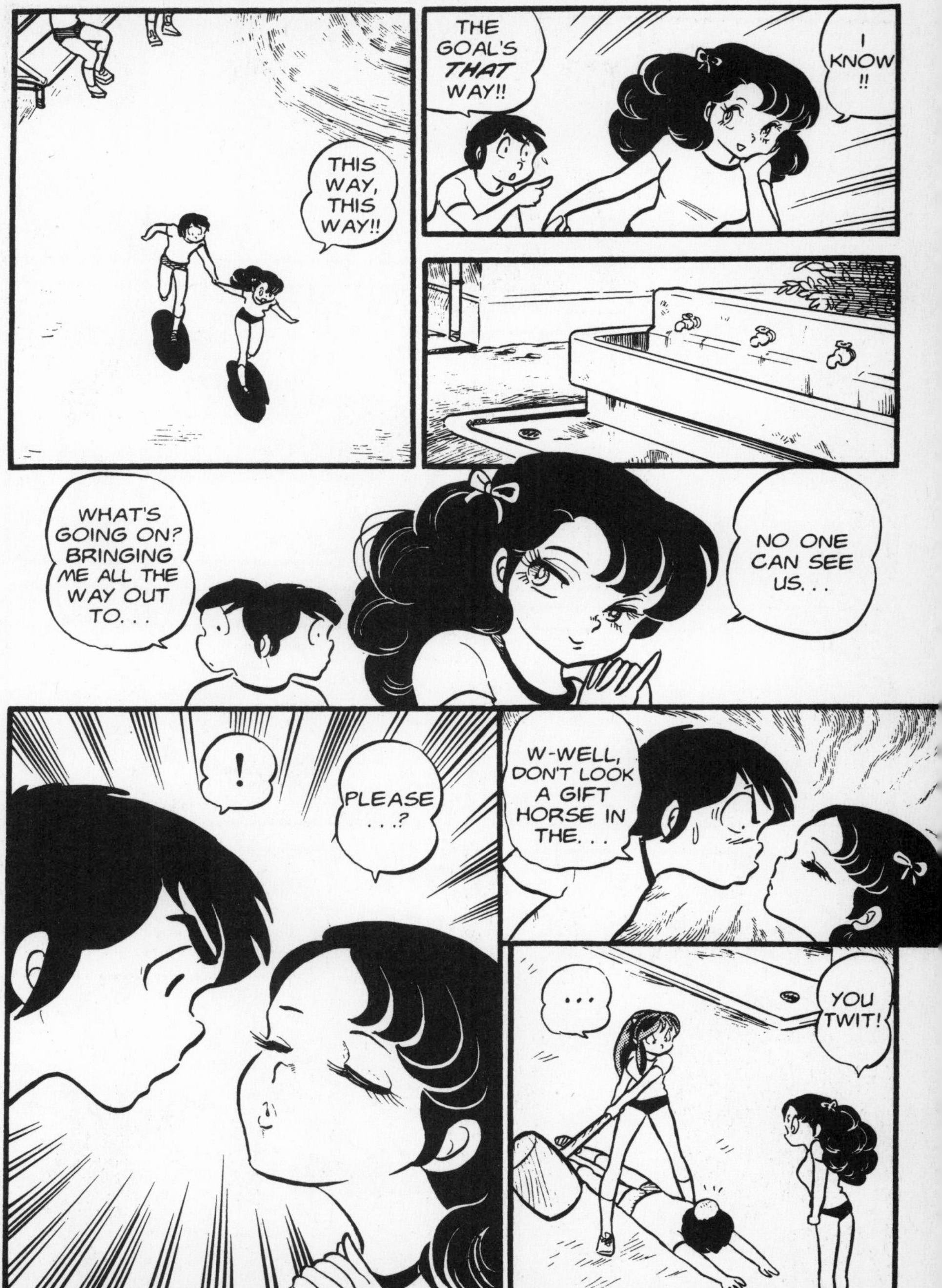
THIS WAY, THIS WAY!!
THE GOAL'S *THAT* WAY!!
I KNOW !!
WHAT'S GOING ON? BRINGING ME ALL THE WAY OUT TO...
NO ONE CAN SEE US...
!
PLEASE ...?
W-WELL, DON'T LOOK A GIFT HORSE IN THE...
...
YOU TWIT!

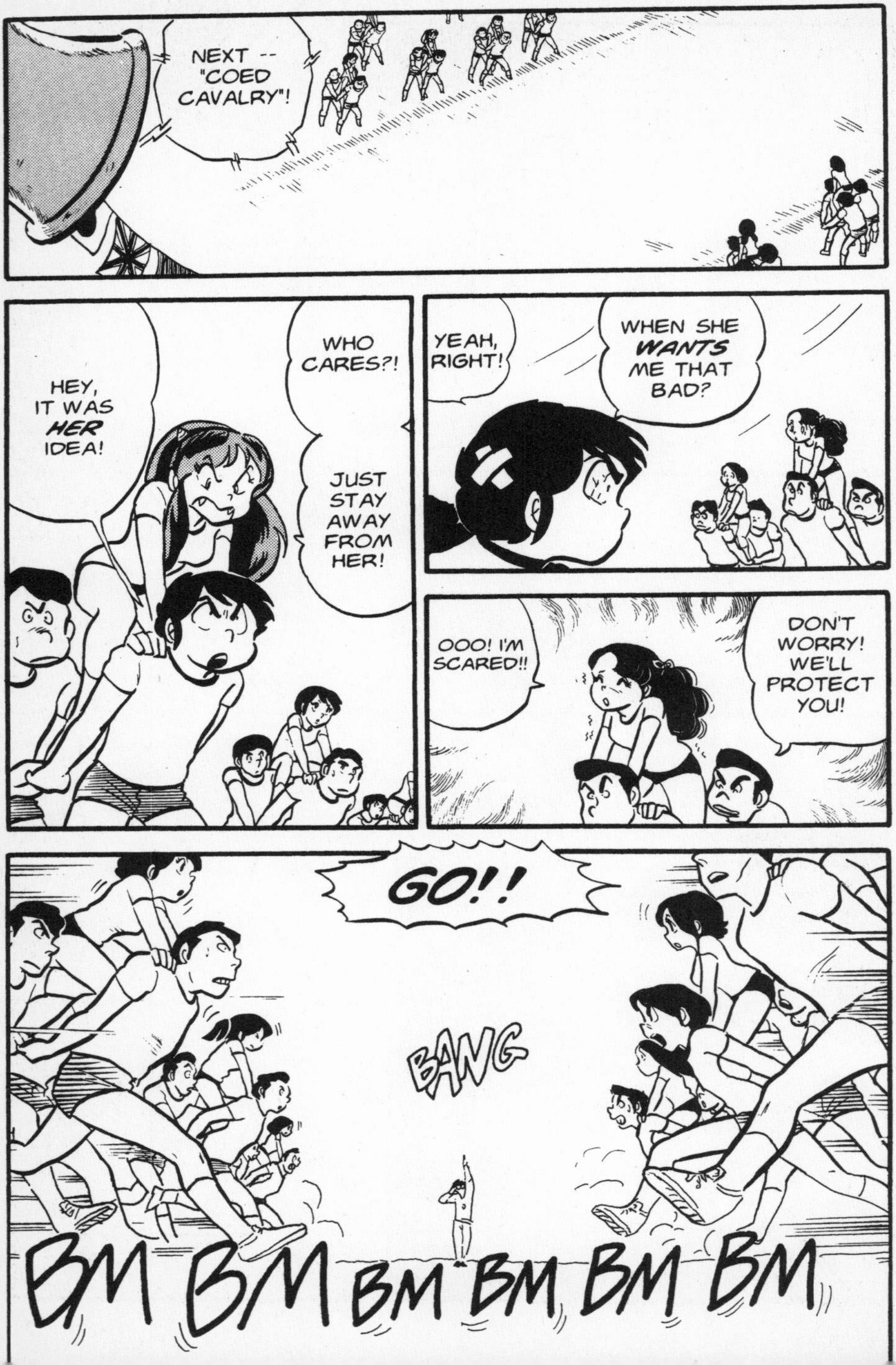

NEXT -- "COED CAVALRY"!
HEY, IT WAS **HER** IDEA!
WHO CARES?!
JUST STAY AWAY FROM HER!
YEAH, RIGHT!
WHEN SHE **WANTS** ME THAT BAD?
OOO! I'M SCARED!!
DON'T WORRY! WE'LL PROTECT YOU!
GO!!
BANG
BM BM BM BM BM BM

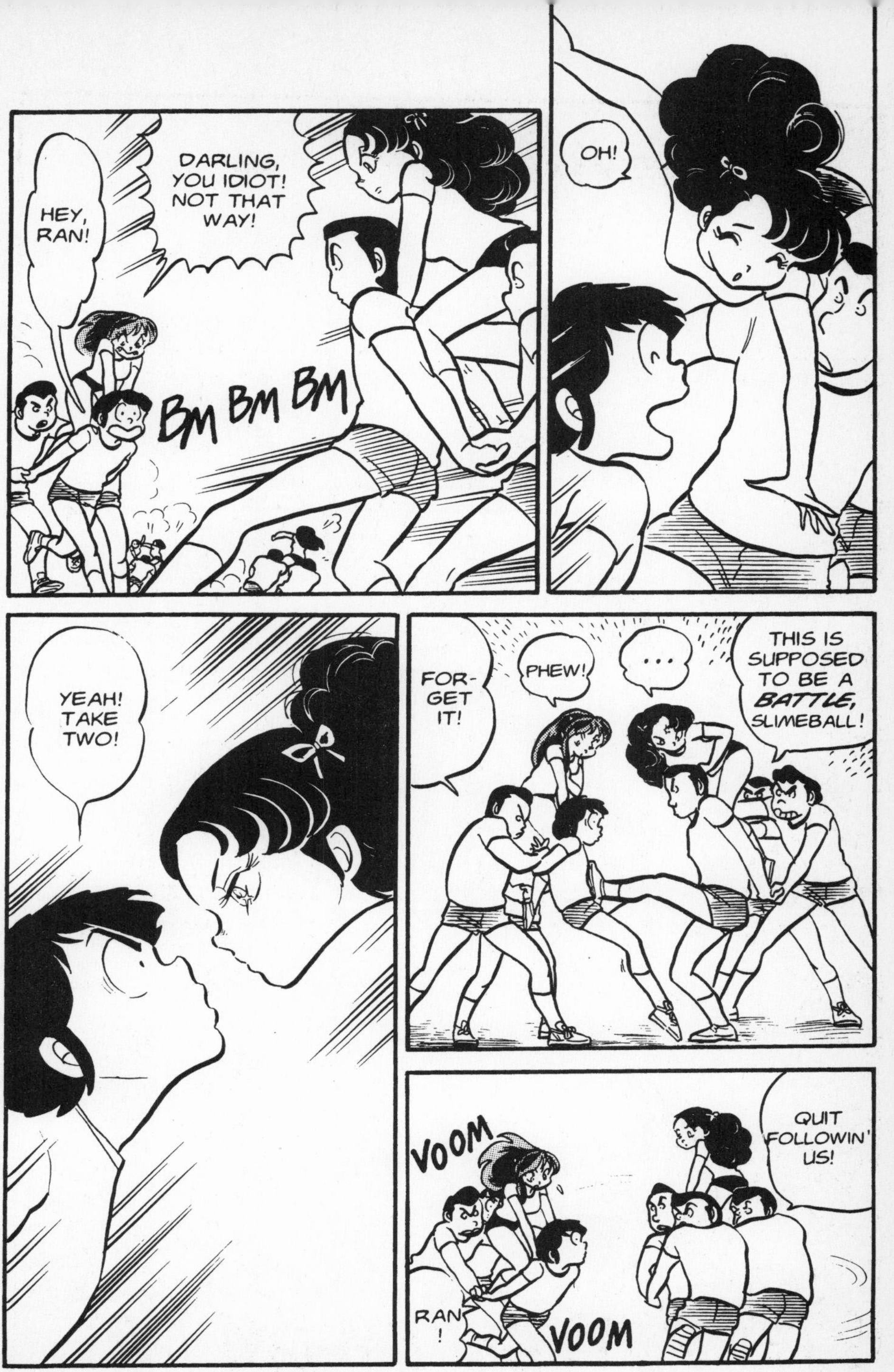
HEY, RAN!
DARLING, YOU IDIOT! NOT THAT WAY!
BM BM BM
OH!
YEAH! TAKE TWO!
FOR-GET IT!
PHEW!
...
THIS IS SUPPOSED TO BE A *BATTLE*, SLIMEBALL!
VOOM
QUIT FOLLOWIN' US!
RAN!
VOOM

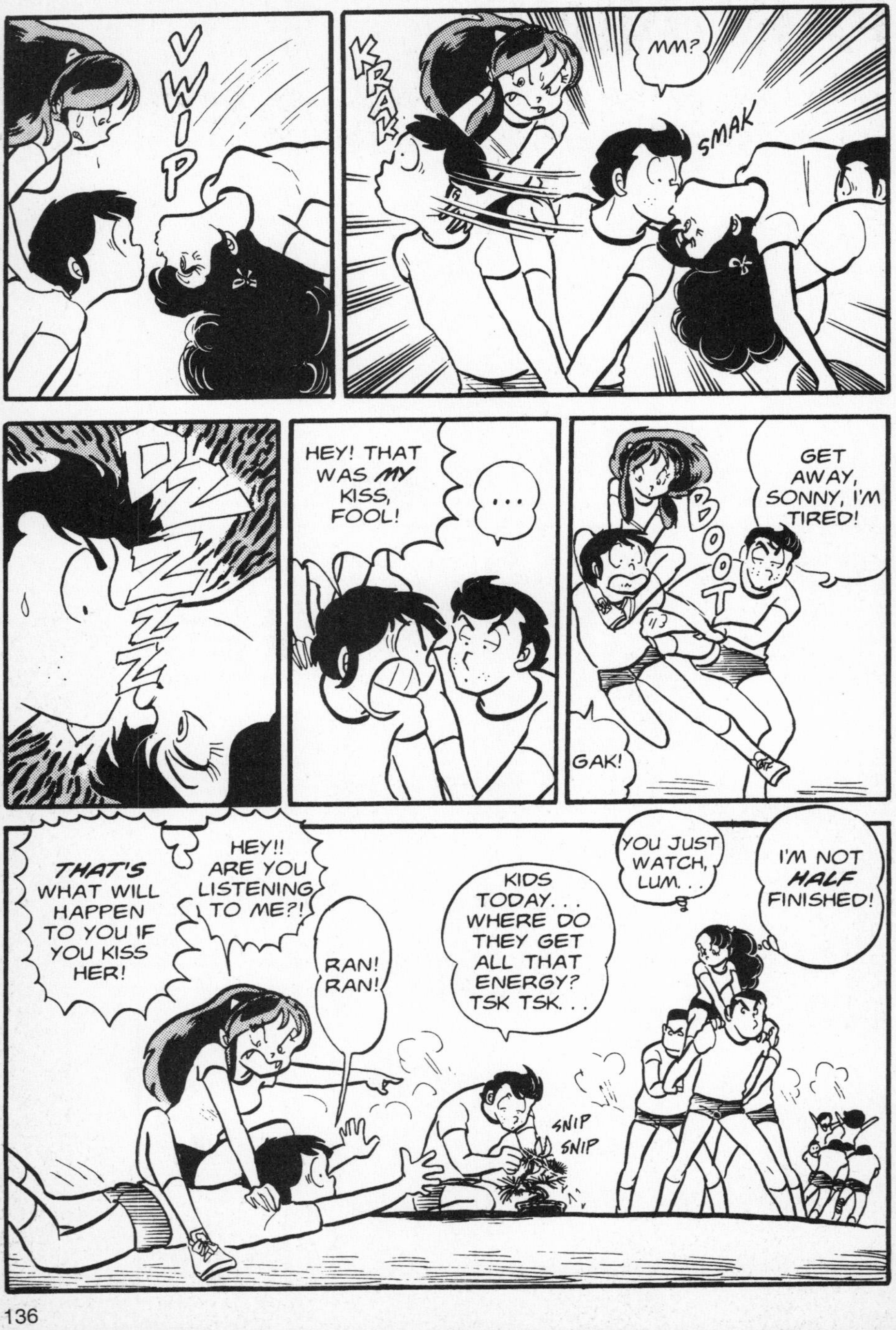
VWIP
KRAK
MM?
SMAK
HEY! THAT WAS *MY* KISS, FOOL!
...
GET AWAY, SONNY, I'M TIRED!
BOOT
GAK!
THAT'S WHAT WILL HAPPEN TO YOU IF YOU KISS HER!
HEY!! ARE YOU LISTENING TO ME?!
RAN! RAN!
KIDS TODAY... WHERE DO THEY GET ALL THAT ENERGY? TSK TSK...
SNIP SNIP
YOU JUST WATCH, LUM...
I'M NOT *HALF* FINISHED!

PART NINE
CLOSER...CLOSER...
CLOSER...

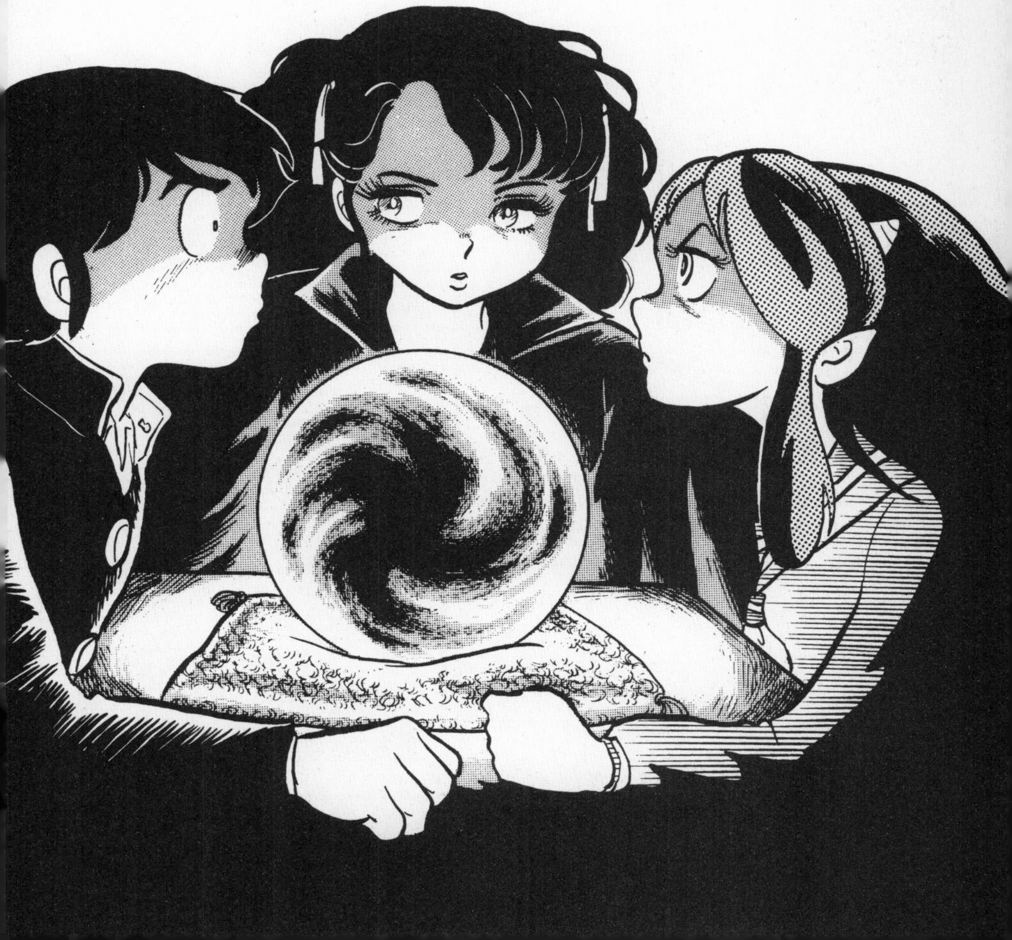

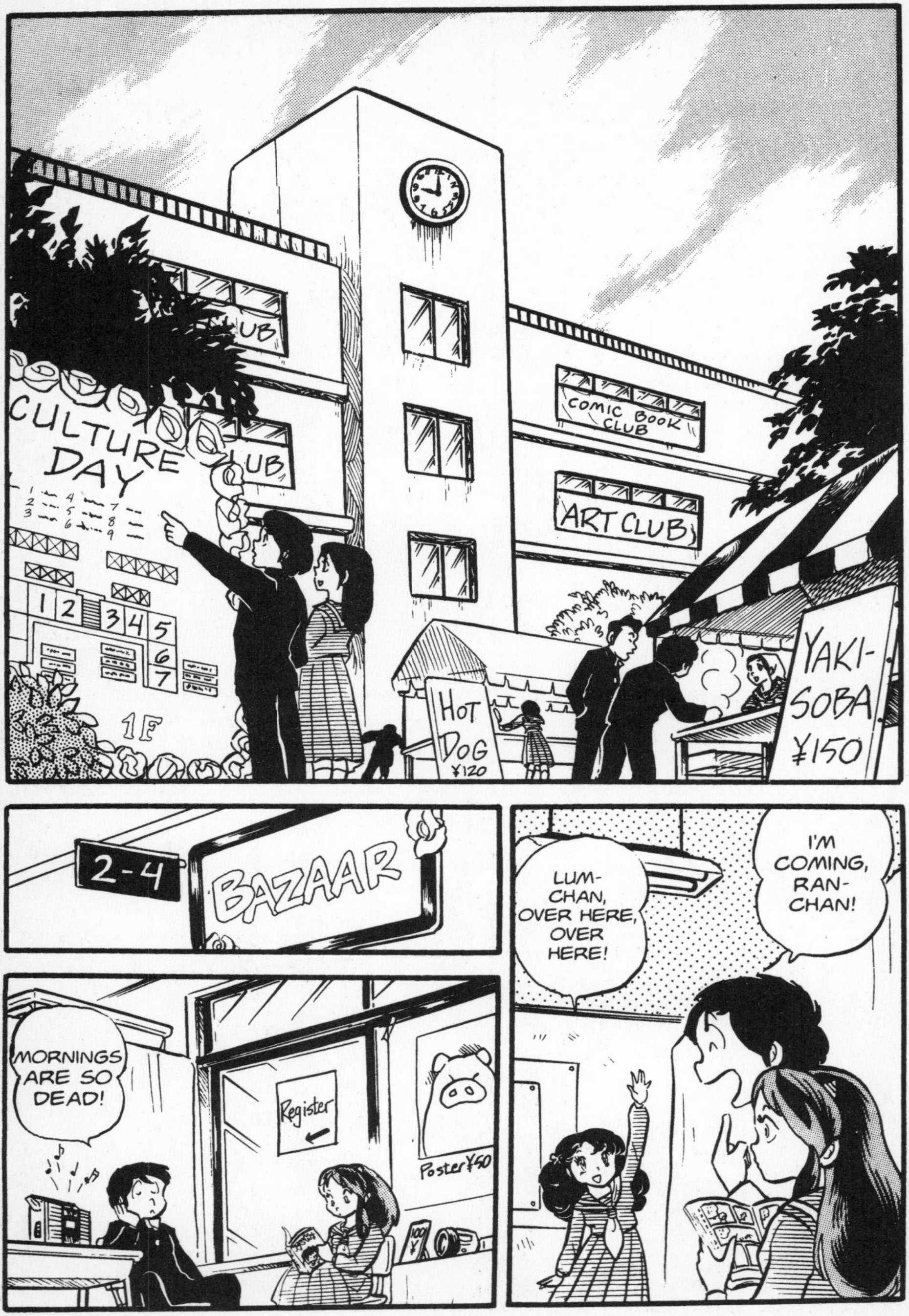
CULTURE DAY
UB
UB
COMIC BOOK CLUB
ART CLUB
1F
HOT DOG ¥120
YAKI-SOBA ¥150
2-4
BAZAAR
MORNINGS ARE SO DEAD!
Register
Poster ¥50
LUM-CHAN, OVER HERE, OVER HERE!
I'M COMING, RAN-CHAN!

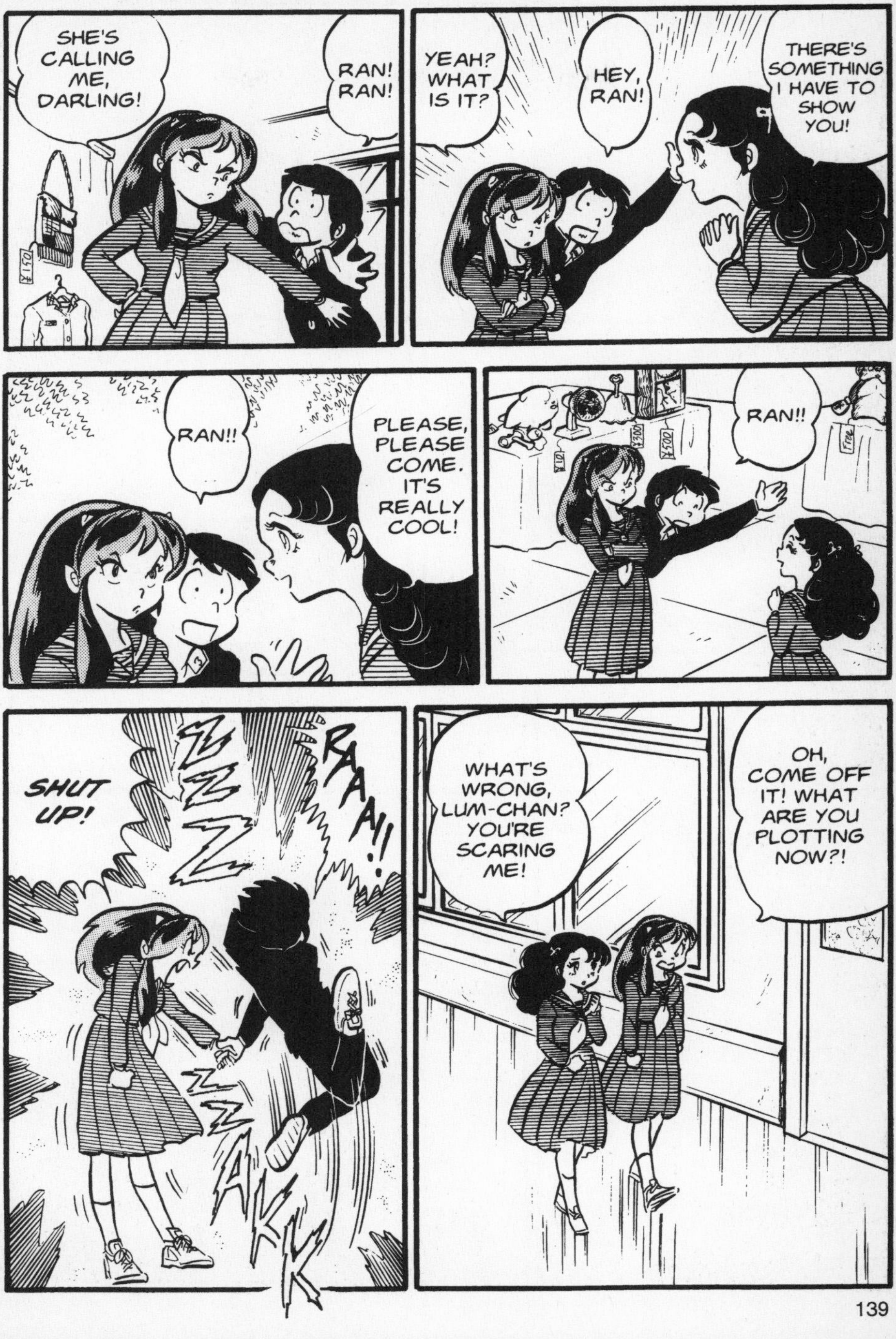
SHE'S CALLING ME, DARLING!
RAN! RAN!
YEAH? WHAT IS IT?
HEY, RAN!
THERE'S SOMETHING I HAVE TO SHOW YOU!
RAN!!
PLEASE, PLEASE COME. IT'S REALLY COOL!
RAN!!
SHUT UP!
WHAT'S WRONG, LUM-CHAN? YOU'RE SCARING ME!
OH, COME OFF IT! WHAT ARE YOU PLOTTING NOW?!

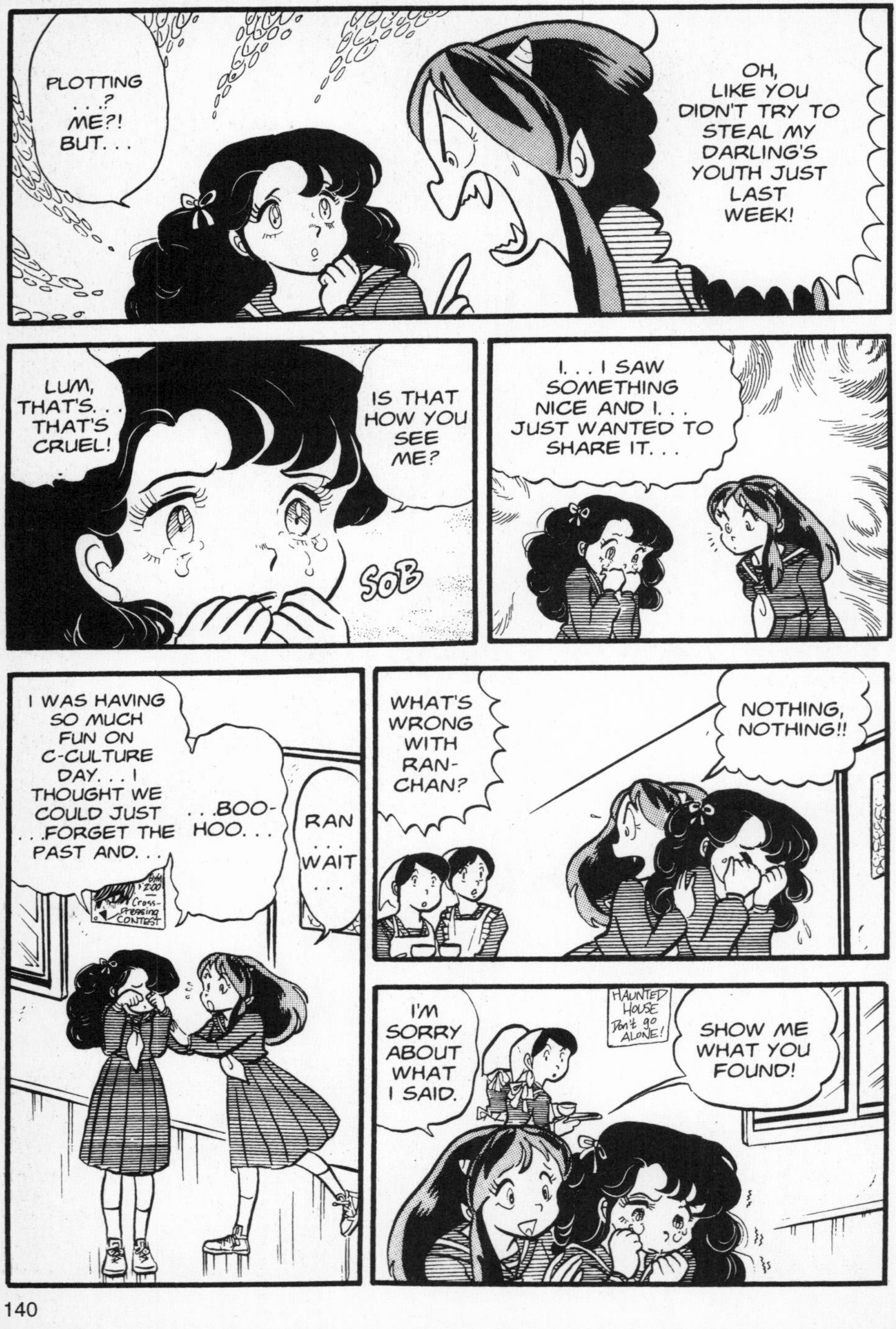

PLOTTING . . .? ME?! BUT. . .
OH, LIKE YOU DIDN'T TRY TO STEAL MY DARLING'S YOUTH JUST LAST WEEK!
LUM, THAT'S. . . THAT'S CRUEL!
IS THAT HOW YOU SEE ME?
SOB
I. . . I SAW SOMETHING NICE AND I. . . JUST WANTED TO SHARE IT. . .
I WAS HAVING SO MUCH FUN ON C-CULTURE DAY. . . I THOUGHT WE COULD JUST . . .FORGET THE PAST AND. . .
. . .BOO-HOO. . .
Cross-Dressing CONTEST
RAN . . . WAIT . . .
WHAT'S WRONG WITH RAN-CHAN?
NOTHING, NOTHING!!
I'M SORRY ABOUT WHAT I SAID.
HAUNTED HOUSE Don't go ALONE!
SHOW ME WHAT YOU FOUND!

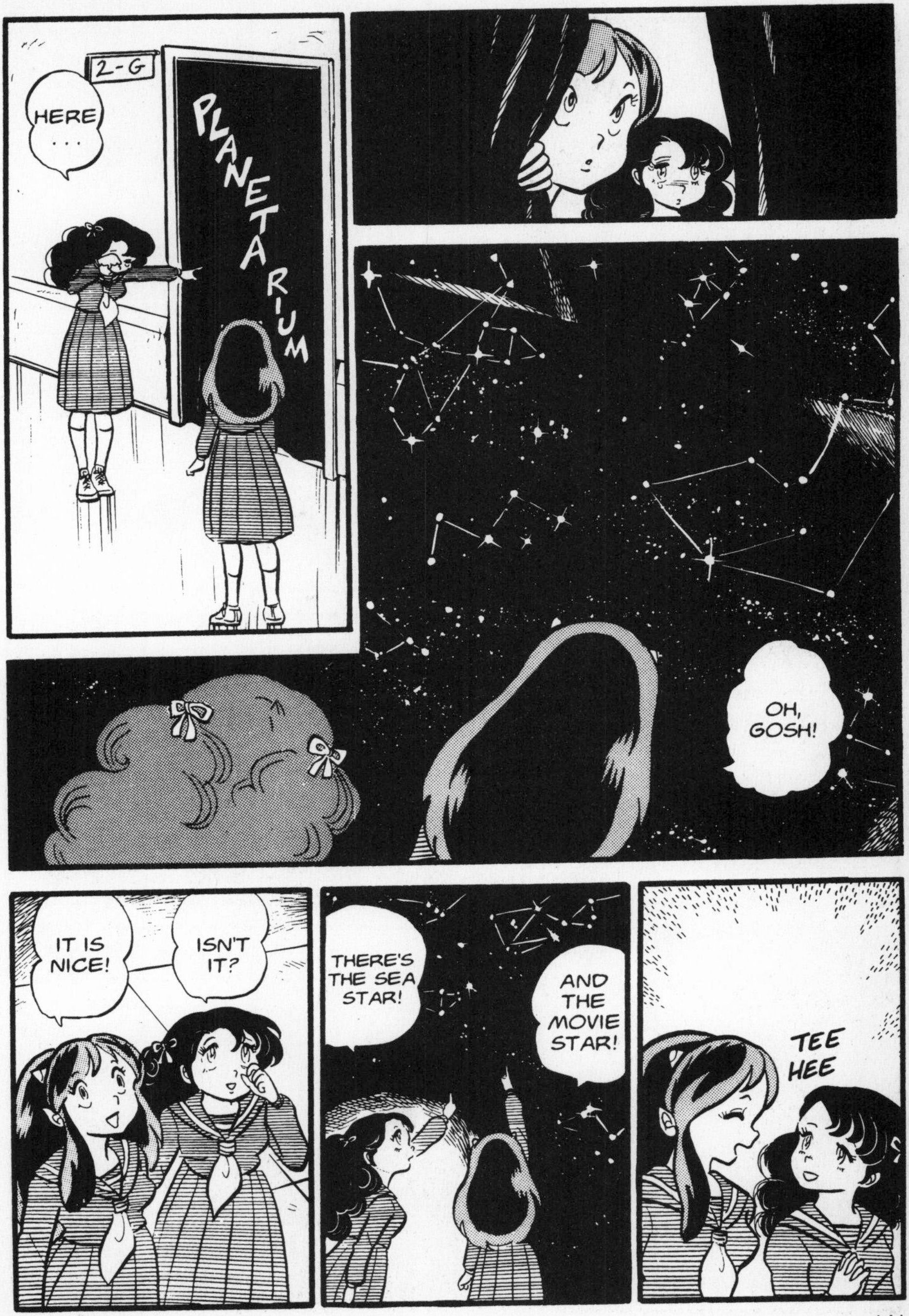
2-G
HERE . . .
PLANETARIUM
OH, GOSH!
IT IS NICE!
ISN'T IT?
THERE'S THE SEA STAR!
AND THE MOVIE STAR!
TEE HEE

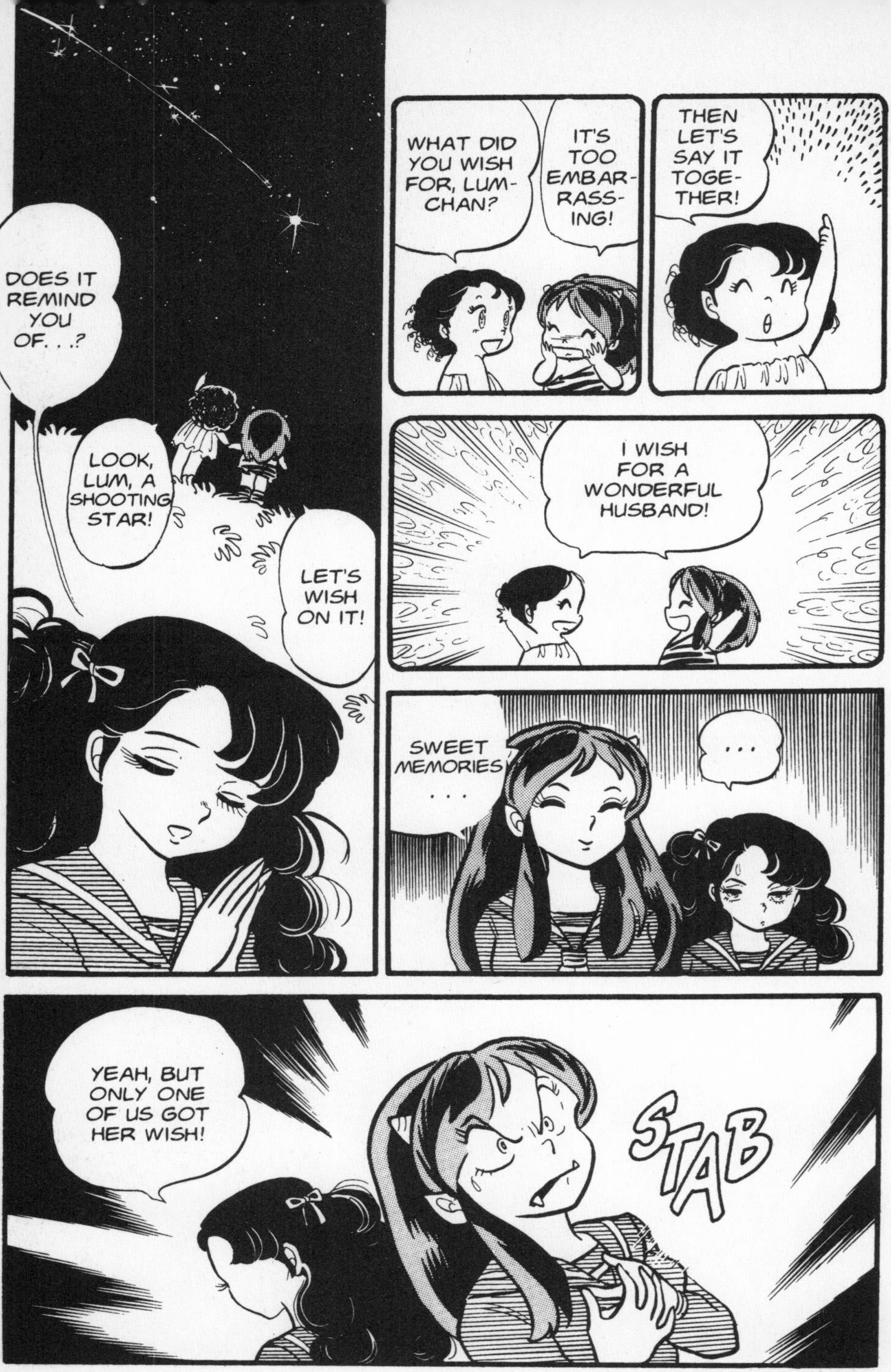
DOES IT REMIND YOU OF. . .?
LOOK, LUM, A SHOOTING STAR!
LET'S WISH ON IT!
WHAT DID YOU WISH FOR, LUM-CHAN?
IT'S TOO EMBARRASSING!
THEN LET'S SAY IT TOGETHER!
I WISH FOR A WONDERFUL HUSBAND!
SWEET MEMORIES . . .
. . .
YEAH, BUT ONLY ONE OF US GOT HER WISH!
STAB

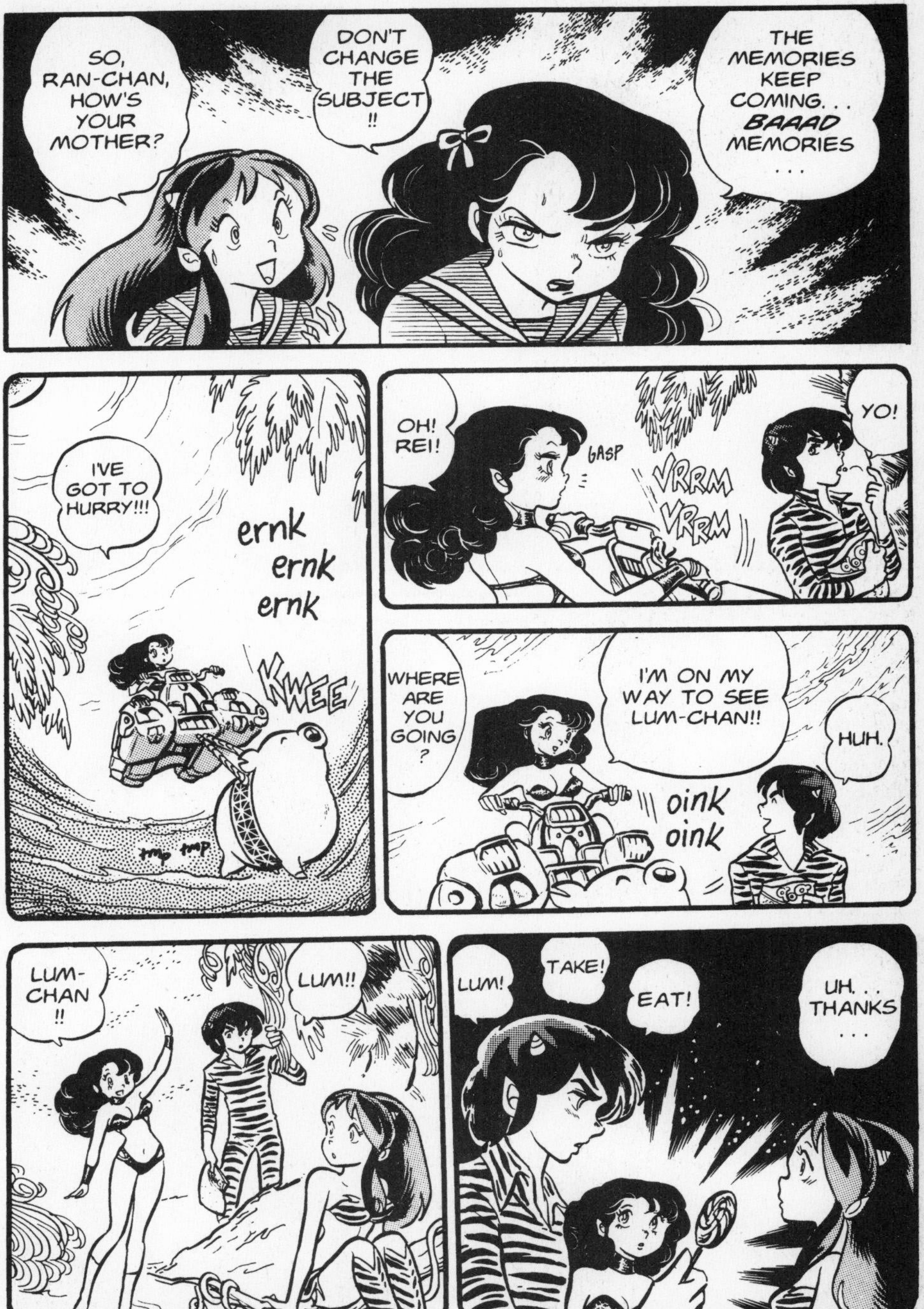
SO, RAN-CHAN, HOW'S YOUR MOTHER?
DON'T CHANGE THE SUBJECT !!
THE MEMORIES KEEP COMING. . . BAAAD MEMORIES . . .
I'VE GOT TO HURRY!!!
ernk ernk ernk
KWEE
OH! REI!
GASP
VRRM VRRM
YO!
WHERE ARE YOU GOING ?
I'M ON MY WAY TO SEE LUM-CHAN!!
HUH.
oink oink
LUM-CHAN !!
LUM!!
LUM!
TAKE!
EAT!
UH. . . THANKS . . .

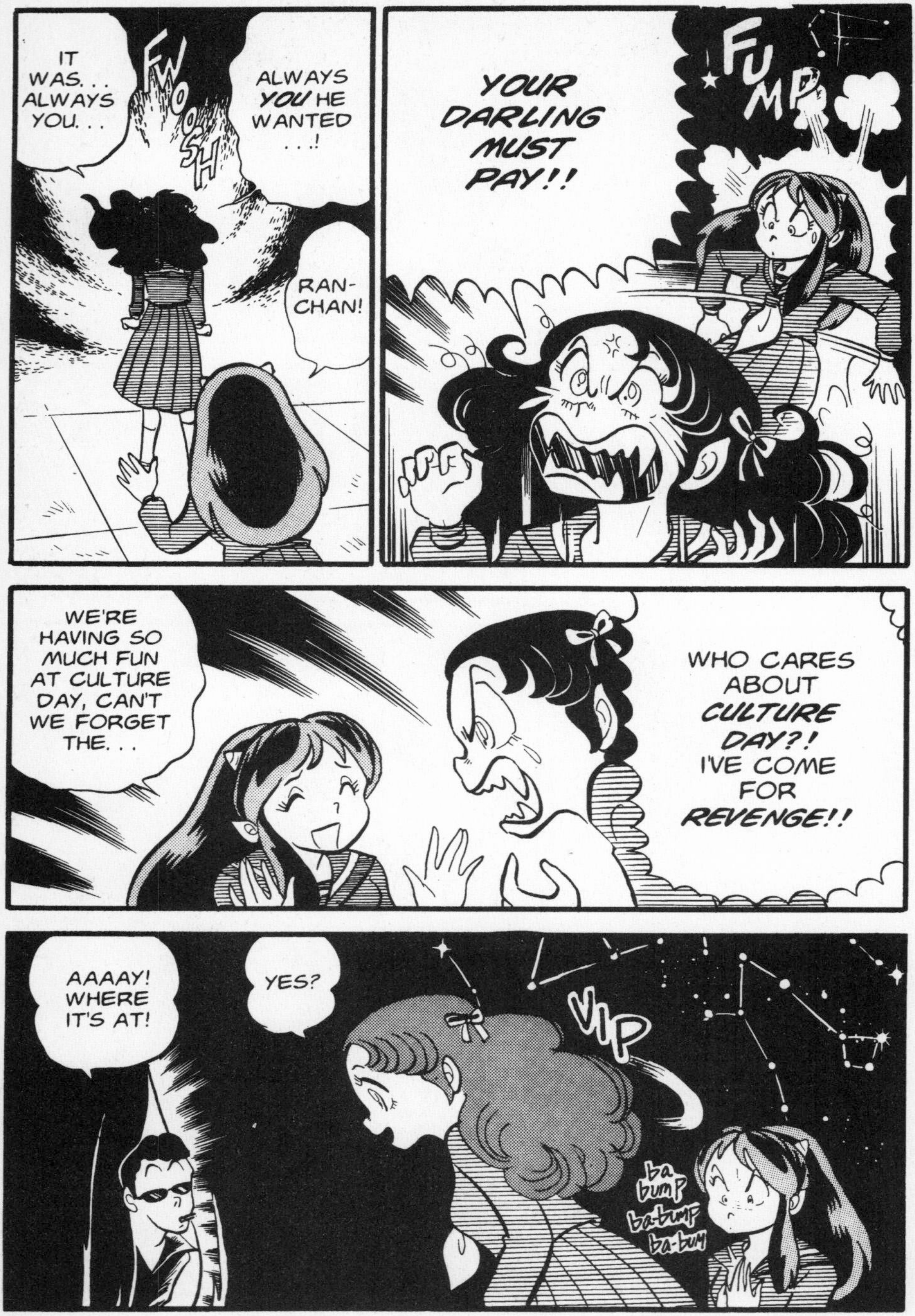
IT WAS. . . ALWAYS YOU. . .
FWOOSH
ALWAYS YOU HE WANTED . . .!
RAN-CHAN!
YOUR DARLING MUST PAY!!
FUMP
WE'RE HAVING SO MUCH FUN AT CULTURE DAY, CAN'T WE FORGET THE. . .
WHO CARES ABOUT CULTURE DAY?! I'VE COME FOR REVENGE!!
AAAAY! WHERE IT'S AT!
YES?
VIP
ba bump ba-bump ba-bum

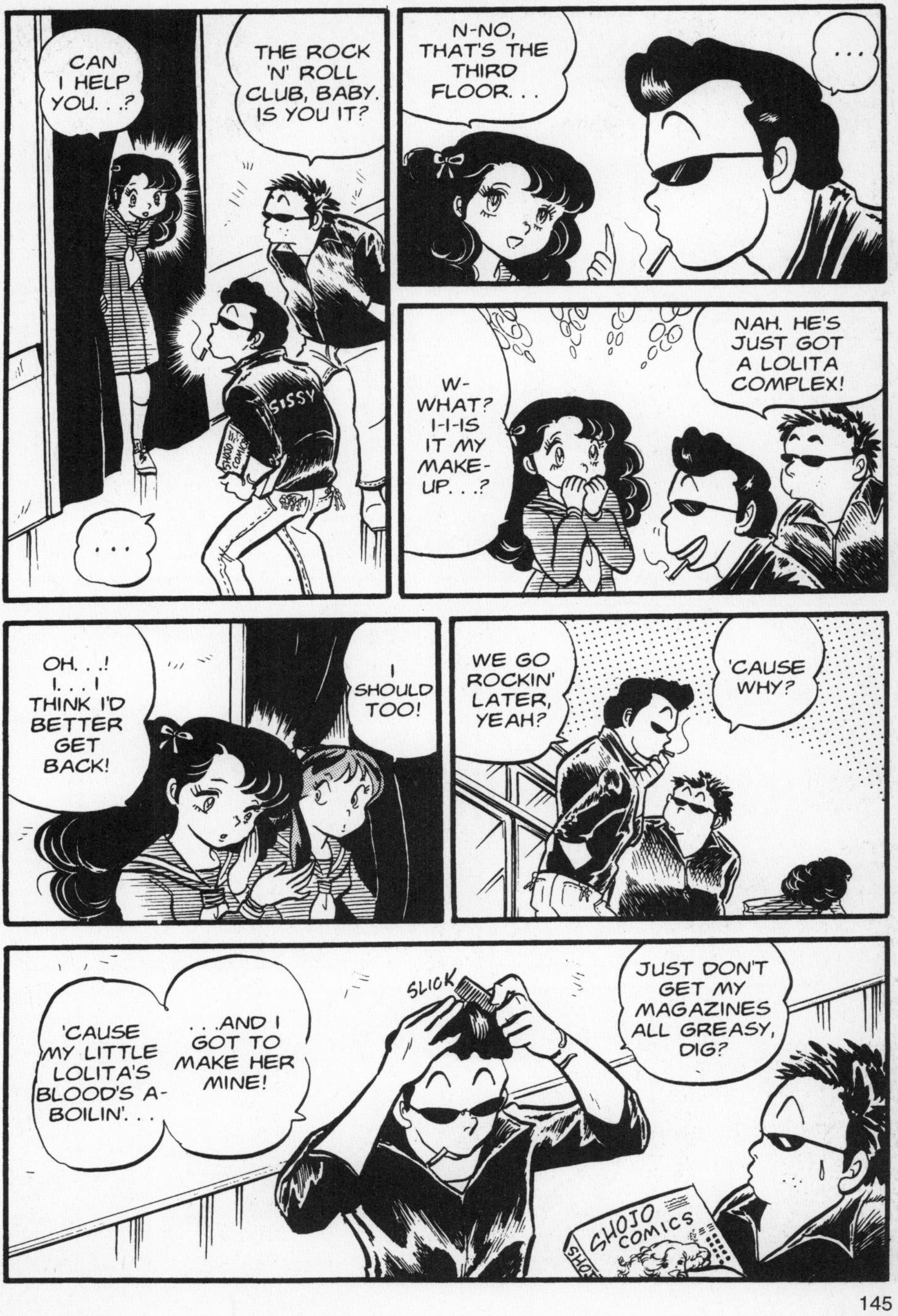
CAN I HELP YOU. . .?
THE ROCK 'N' ROLL CLUB, BABY. IS YOU IT?
SISSY
SHOJO COMICS
. . .
N-NO, THAT'S THE THIRD FLOOR. . .
. . .
W-WHAT? I-I-IS IT MY MAKE-UP. . .?
NAH. HE'S JUST GOT A LOLITA COMPLEX!
OH. . .! I. . . I THINK I'D BETTER GET BACK!
I SHOULD TOO!
WE GO ROCKIN' LATER, YEAH?
'CAUSE WHY?
'CAUSE MY LITTLE LOLITA'S BLOOD'S A-BOILIN'. . .
. . .AND I GOT TO MAKE HER MINE!
SLICK
JUST DON'T GET MY MAGAZINES ALL GREASY, DIG?
SHOJO COMICS

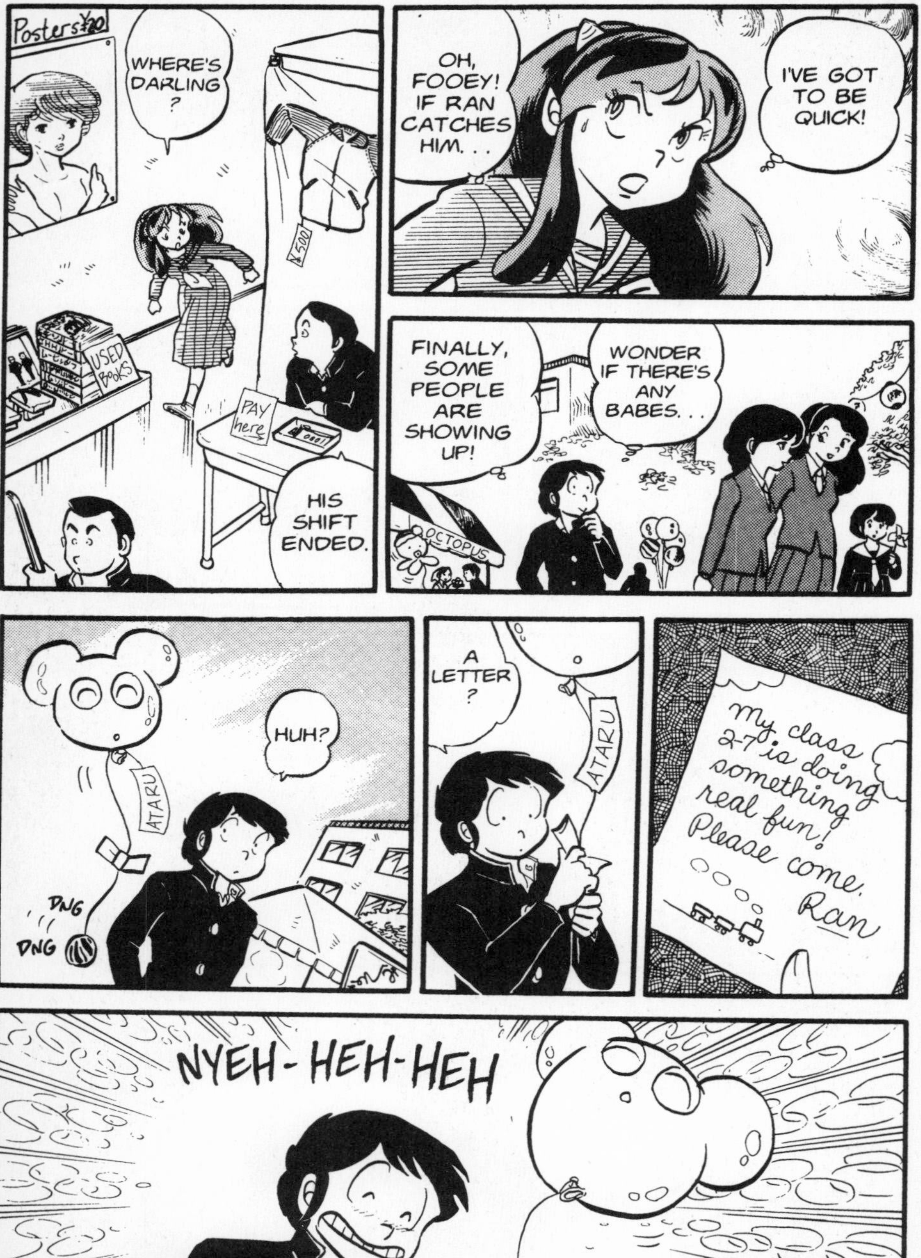
Posters ¥20
WHERE'S DARLING?
¥500
USED BOOKS
PAY here
HIS SHIFT ENDED.
OH, FOOEY! IF RAN CATCHES HIM. . .
I'VE GOT TO BE QUICK!
FINALLY, SOME PEOPLE ARE SHOWING UP!
WONDER IF THERE'S ANY BABES. . .
OCTOPUS
HUH?
ATARU
DNG
DNG
A LETTER?
ATARU
My class 2-7 is doing something real fun! Please come.
Ran
NYEH-HEH-HEH

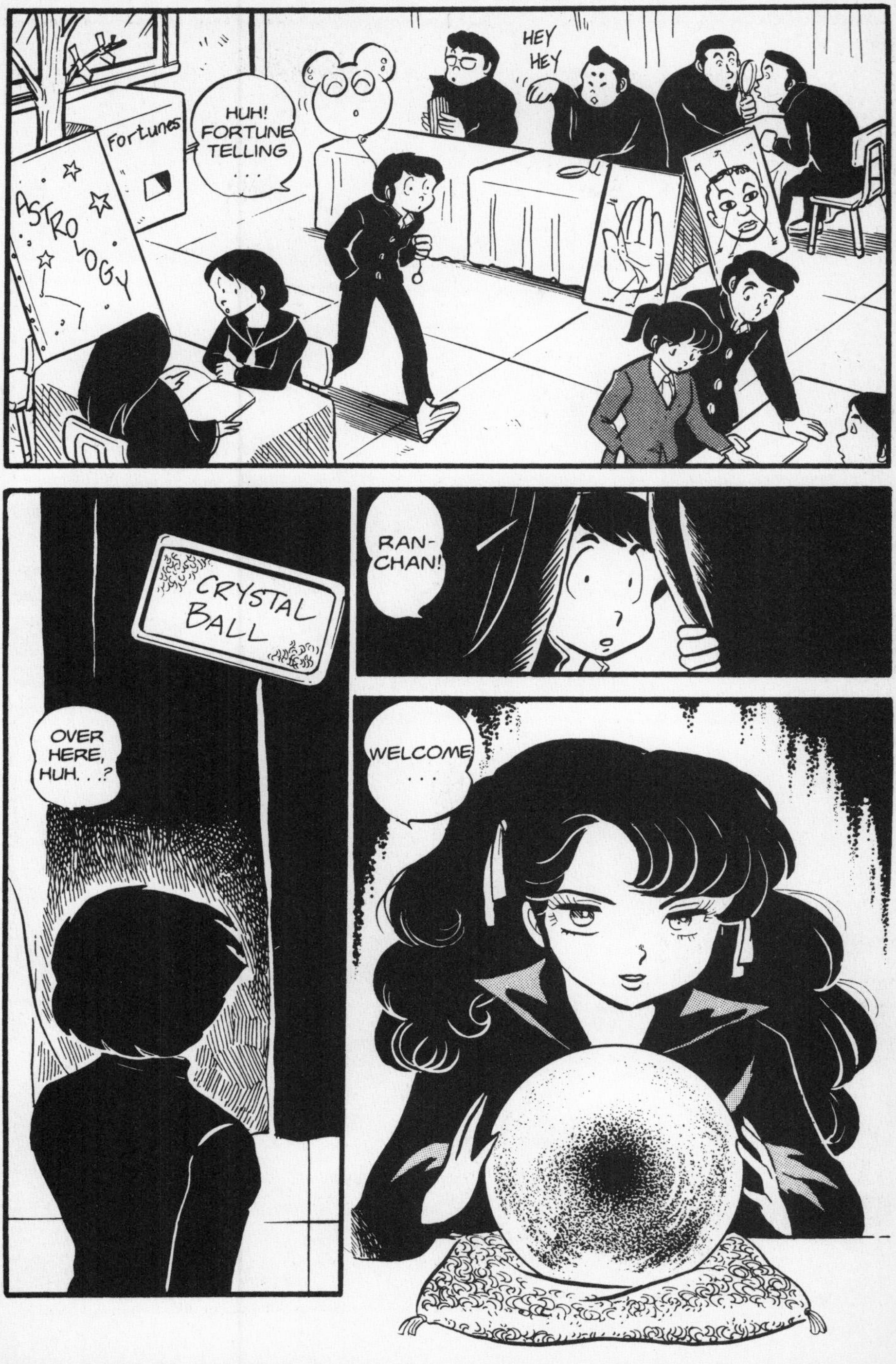
Fortunes
HUH! FORTUNE TELLING . . .
HEY HEY
ASTROLOGY
CRYSTAL BALL
OVER HERE, HUH. . .?
RAN-CHAN!
WELCOME . . .

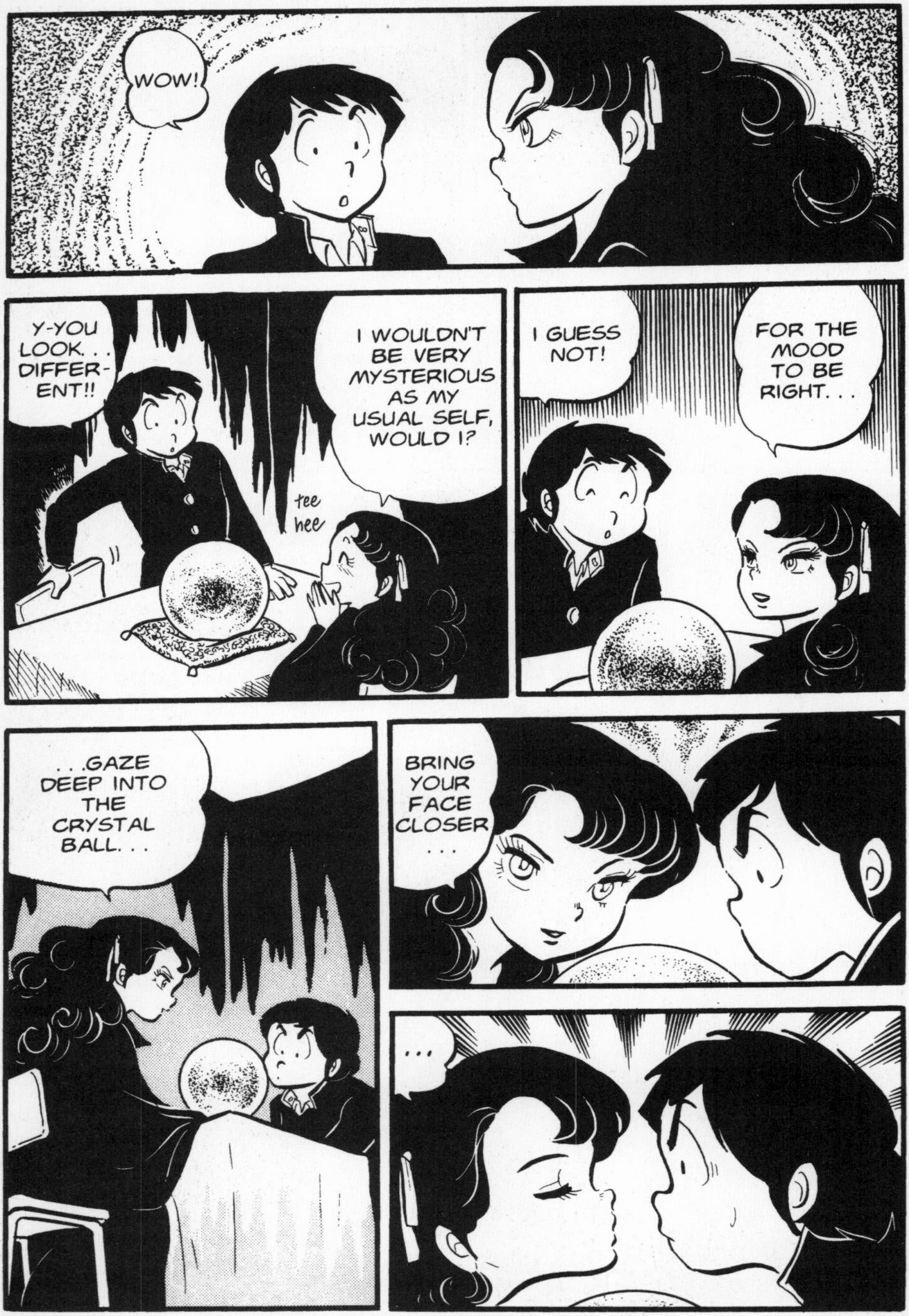
WOW!
Y-YOU LOOK. . . DIFFERENT!!
I WOULDN'T BE VERY MYSTERIOUS AS MY USUAL SELF, WOULD I?
tee hee
I GUESS NOT!
FOR THE MOOD TO BE RIGHT. . .
. . .GAZE DEEP INTO THE CRYSTAL BALL. . .
BRING YOUR FACE CLOSER . . .
. . .

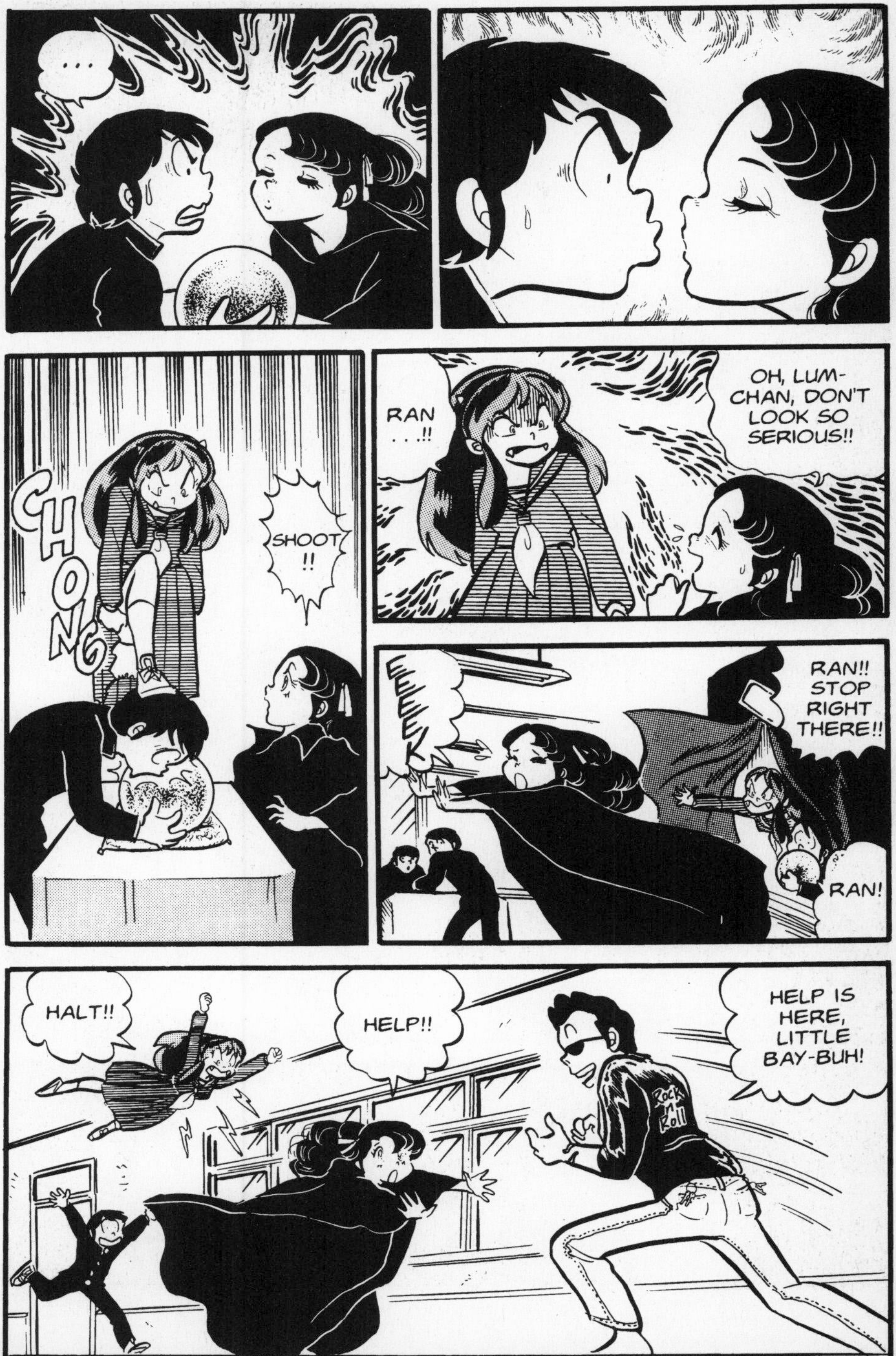
. . .
CHONG
SHOOT !!
RAN . . .!!
OH, LUM-CHAN, DON'T LOOK SO SERIOUS!!
EEEEK
RAN!! STOP RIGHT THERE!!
RAN!
HALT!!
HELP!!
HELP IS HERE, LITTLE BAY-BUH!
Rock 'n Roll

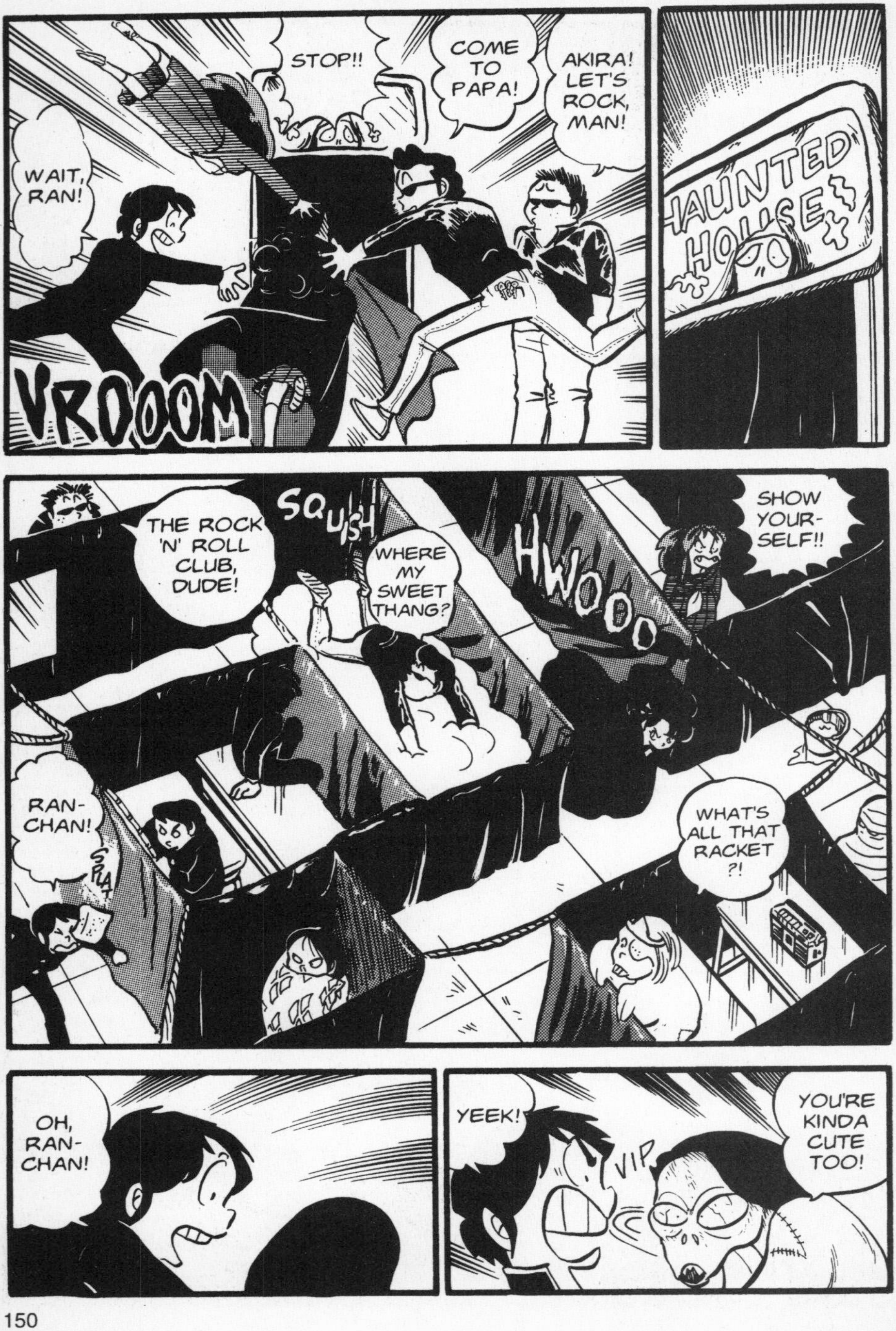
STOP!!
COME TO PAPA!
AKIRA! LET'S ROCK, MAN!
WAIT, RAN!
VROOOM
HAUNTED HOUSE
THE ROCK 'N' ROLL CLUB, DUDE!
SQUISH
WHERE MY SWEET THANG?
HWOOO
SHOW YOURSELF!!
RAN-CHAN!
SPLAT
WHAT'S ALL THAT RACKET ?!
OH, RAN-CHAN!
YEEK!
VIP
YOU'RE KINDA CUTE TOO!

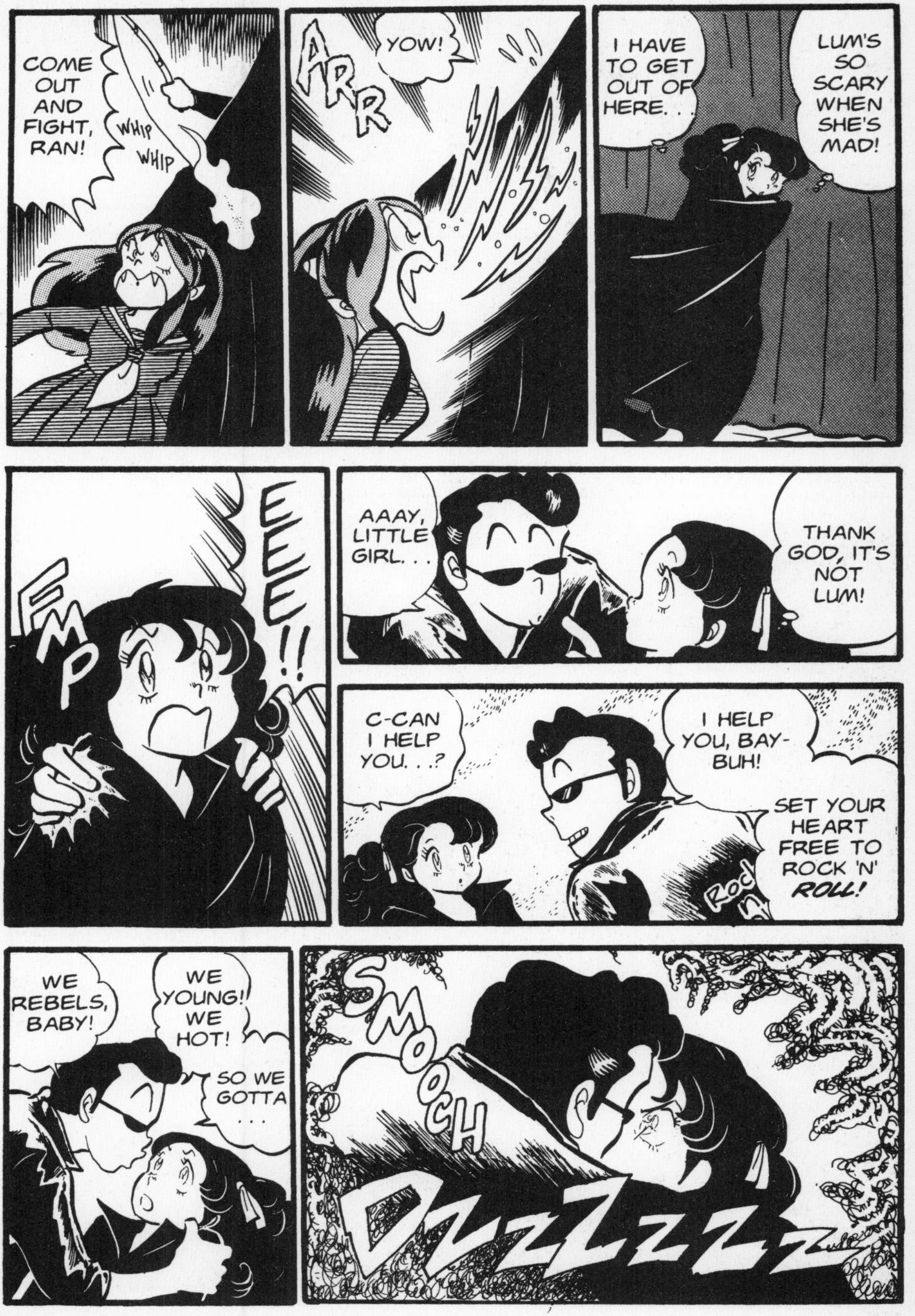
COME OUT AND FIGHT, RAN!
WHIP WHIP
ARR
YOW!
I HAVE TO GET OUT OF HERE. . .
LUM'S SO SCARY WHEN SHE'S MAD!
FMP
EEEE!!
AAAY, LITTLE GIRL. . .
THANK GOD, IT'S NOT LUM!
C-CAN I HELP YOU. . .?
I HELP YOU, BAY-BUH!
SET YOUR HEART FREE TO ROCK 'N' ROLL!
WE REBELS, BABY!
WE YOUNG! WE HOT!
SO WE GOTTA . . .
SMOOCH
DZZZZZZ

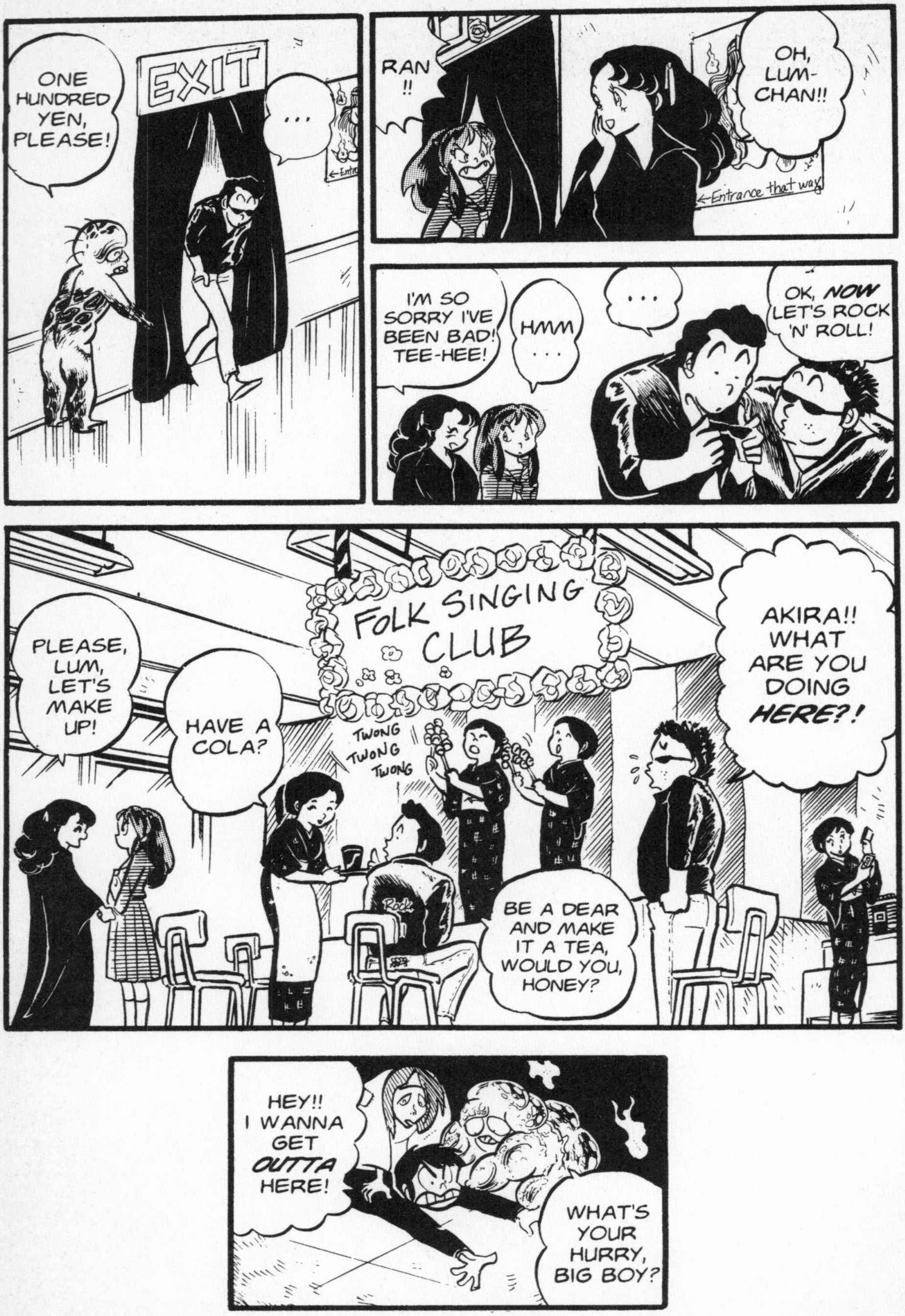
ONE HUNDRED YEN, PLEASE!
EXIT
...
RAN !!
OH, LUM-CHAN!!
←Entrance that way
I'M SO SORRY I'VE BEEN BAD! TEE-HEE!
HMM ...
...
OK, NOW LET'S ROCK 'N' ROLL!
FOLK SINGING CLUB
PLEASE, LUM, LET'S MAKE UP!
HAVE A COLA?
TWONG TWONG TWONG
AKIRA!! WHAT ARE YOU DOING HERE?!
BE A DEAR AND MAKE IT A TEA, WOULD YOU, HONEY?
HEY!! I WANNA GET OUTTA HERE!
WHAT'S YOUR HURRY, BIG BOY?

PART TEN
A DRAMATIC ESCAPE

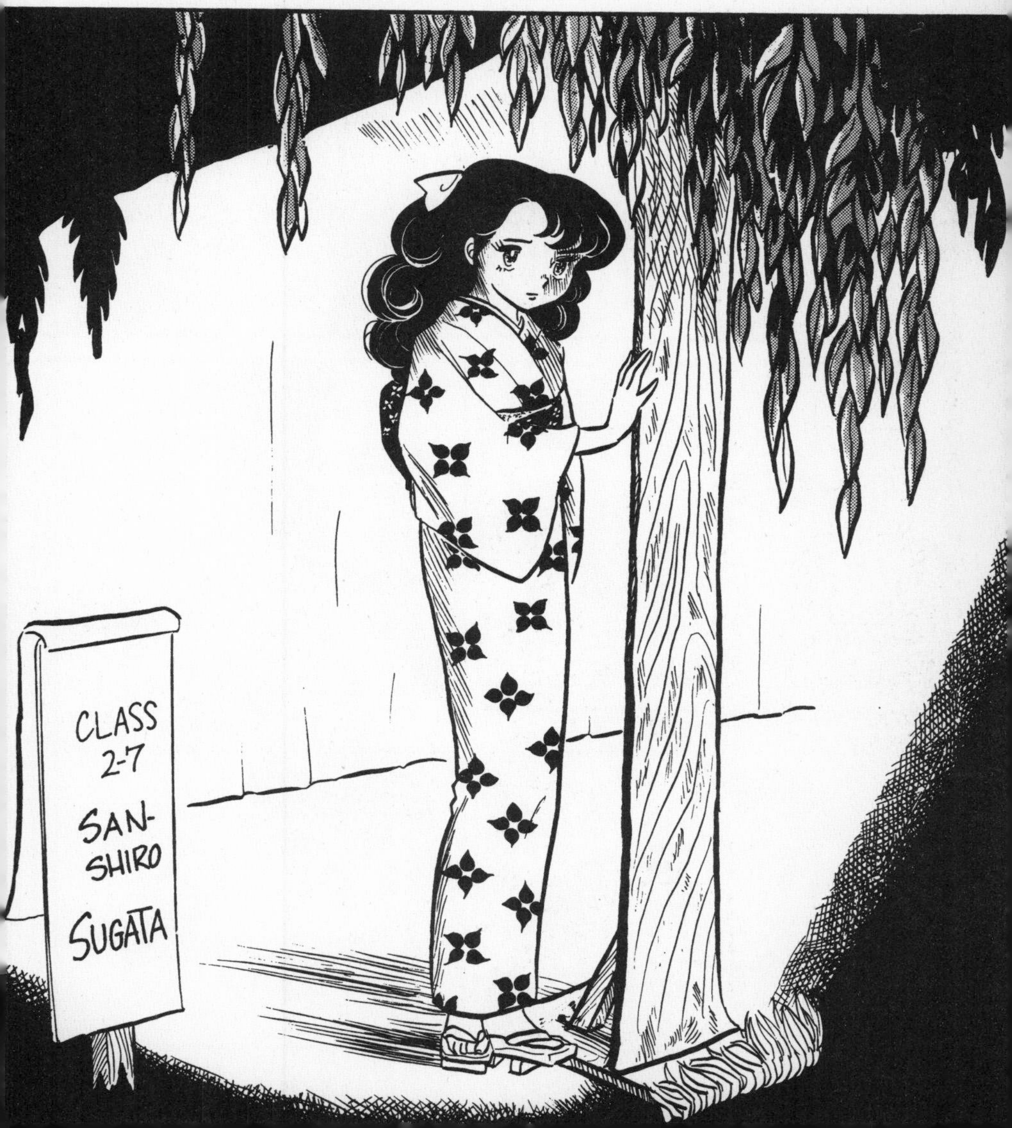
CLASS 2-7
SAN-SHIRO
SUGATA

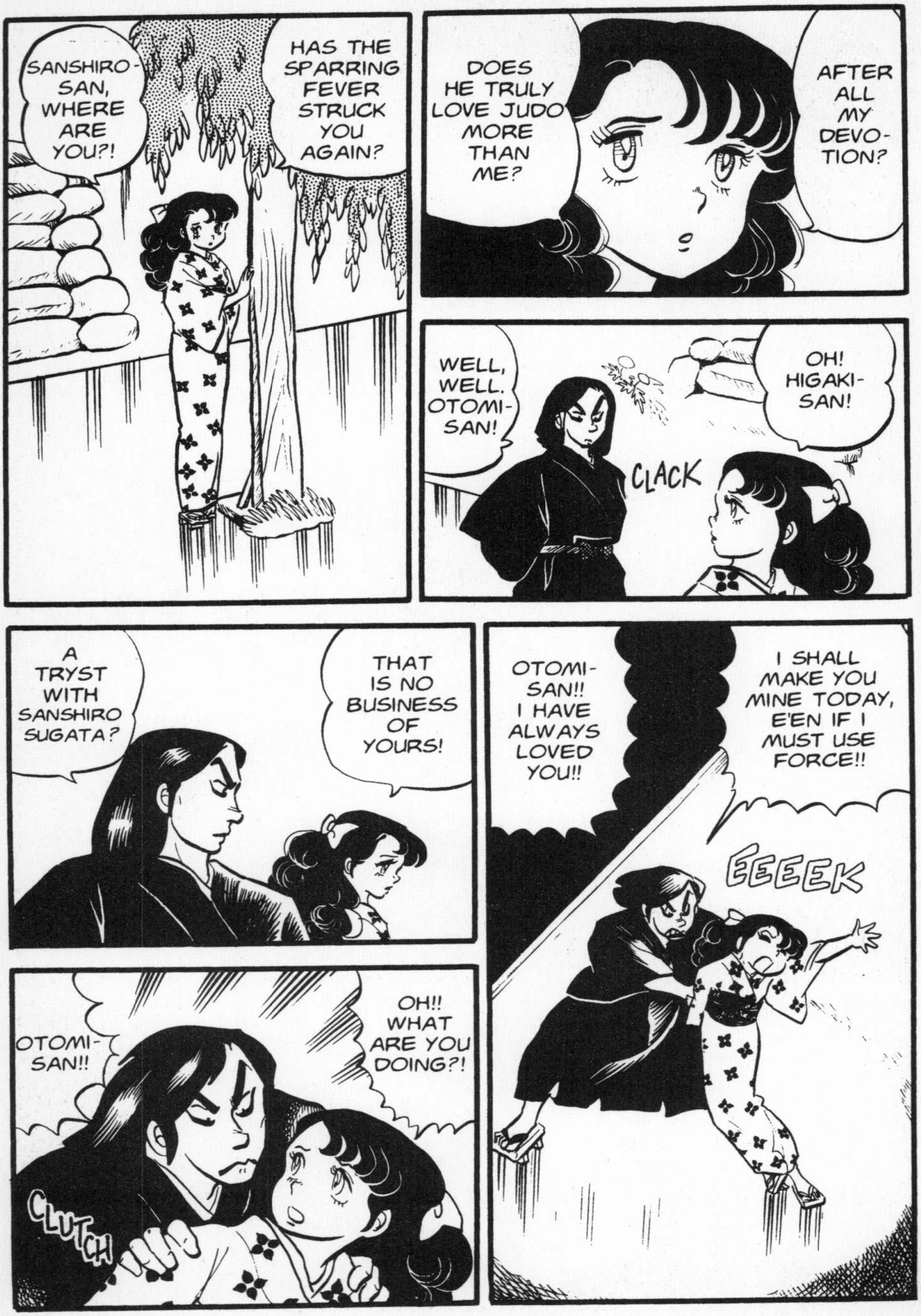
SANSHIRO-SAN, WHERE ARE YOU?!
HAS THE SPARRING FEVER STRUCK YOU AGAIN?
DOES HE TRULY LOVE JUDO MORE THAN ME?
AFTER ALL MY DEVOTION?
WELL, WELL. OTOMI-SAN!
OH! HIGAKI-SAN!
CLACK
A TRYST WITH SANSHIRO SUGATA?
THAT IS NO BUSINESS OF YOURS!
OTOMI-SAN!! I HAVE ALWAYS LOVED YOU!!
I SHALL MAKE YOU MINE TODAY, E'EN IF I MUST USE FORCE!!
EEEEK
OTOMI-SAN!!
OH!! WHAT ARE YOU DOING?!
CLUTCH

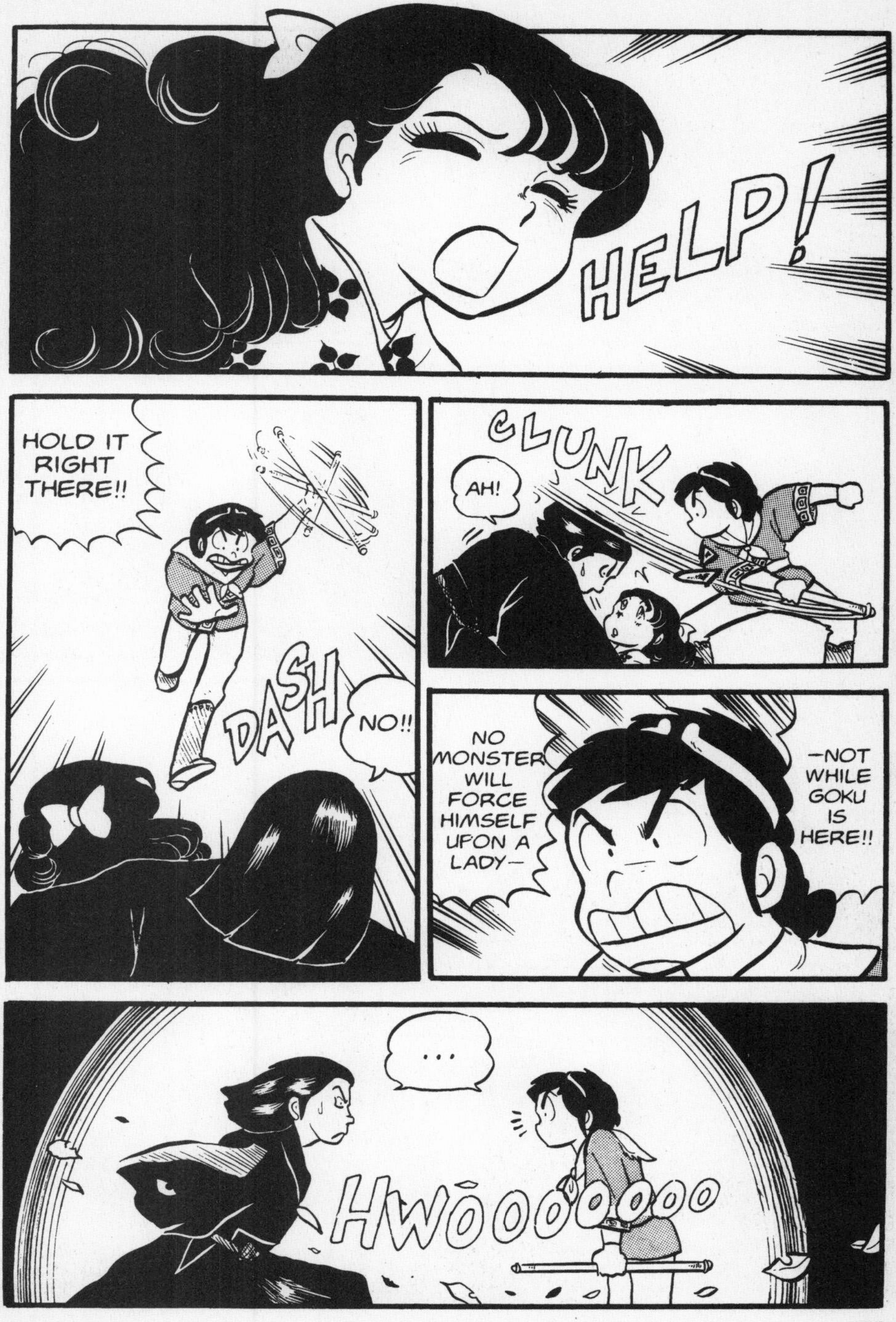
HELP!
HOLD IT RIGHT THERE!!
DASH
NO!!
CLUNK
AH!
NO MONSTER WILL FORCE HIMSELF UPON A LADY—
—NOT WHILE GOKU IS HERE!!
...
HWOOOOOOOO

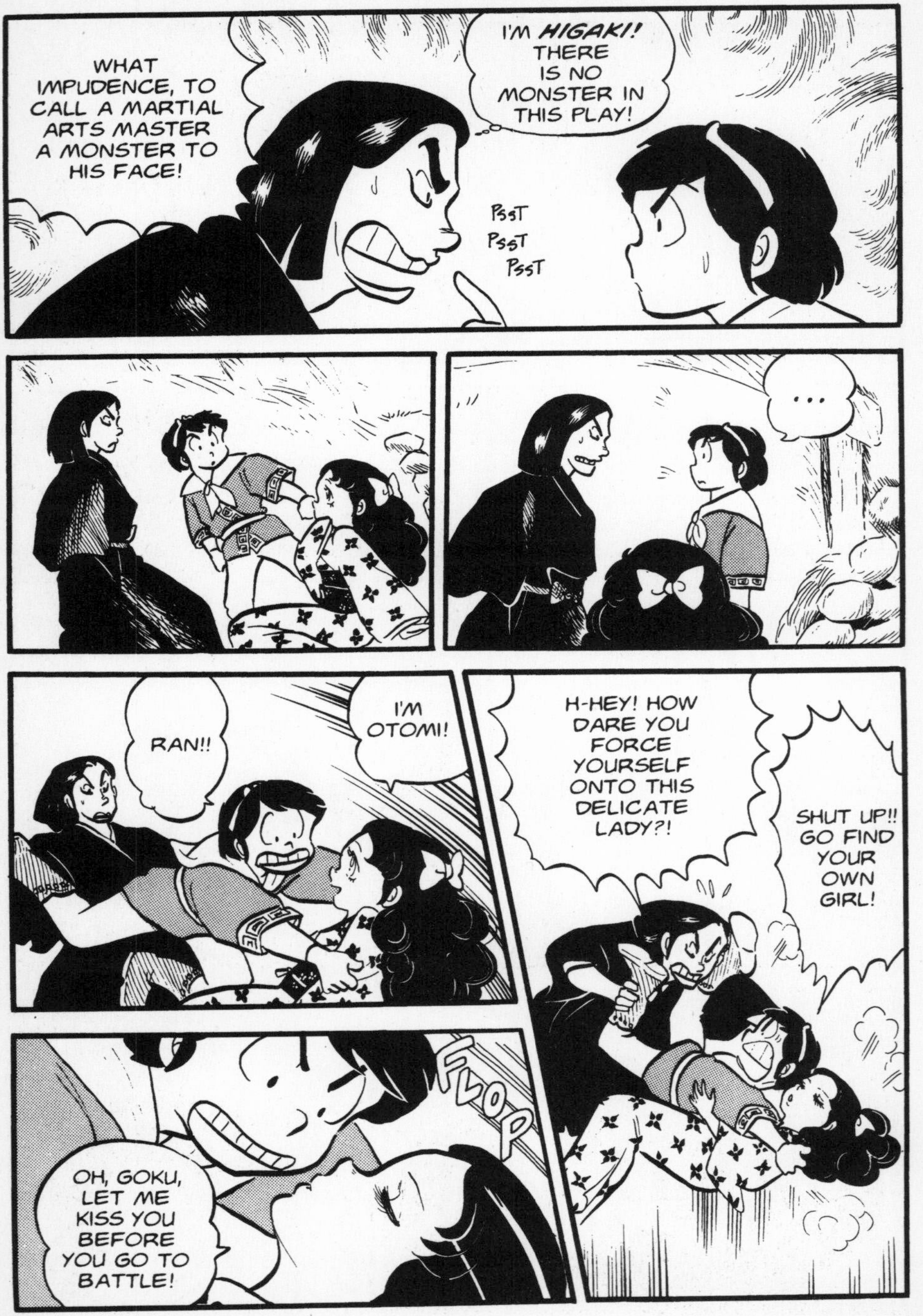
WHAT IMPUDENCE, TO CALL A MARTIAL ARTS MASTER A MONSTER TO HIS FACE!
I'M ***HIGAKI!*** THERE IS NO MONSTER IN THIS PLAY!
PSST
PSST
PSST
...
RAN!!
I'M OTOMI!
FWOP
OH, GOKU, LET ME KISS YOU BEFORE YOU GO TO BATTLE!
H-HEY! HOW DARE YOU FORCE YOURSELF ONTO THIS DELICATE LADY?!
SHUT UP!! GO FIND YOUR OWN GIRL!

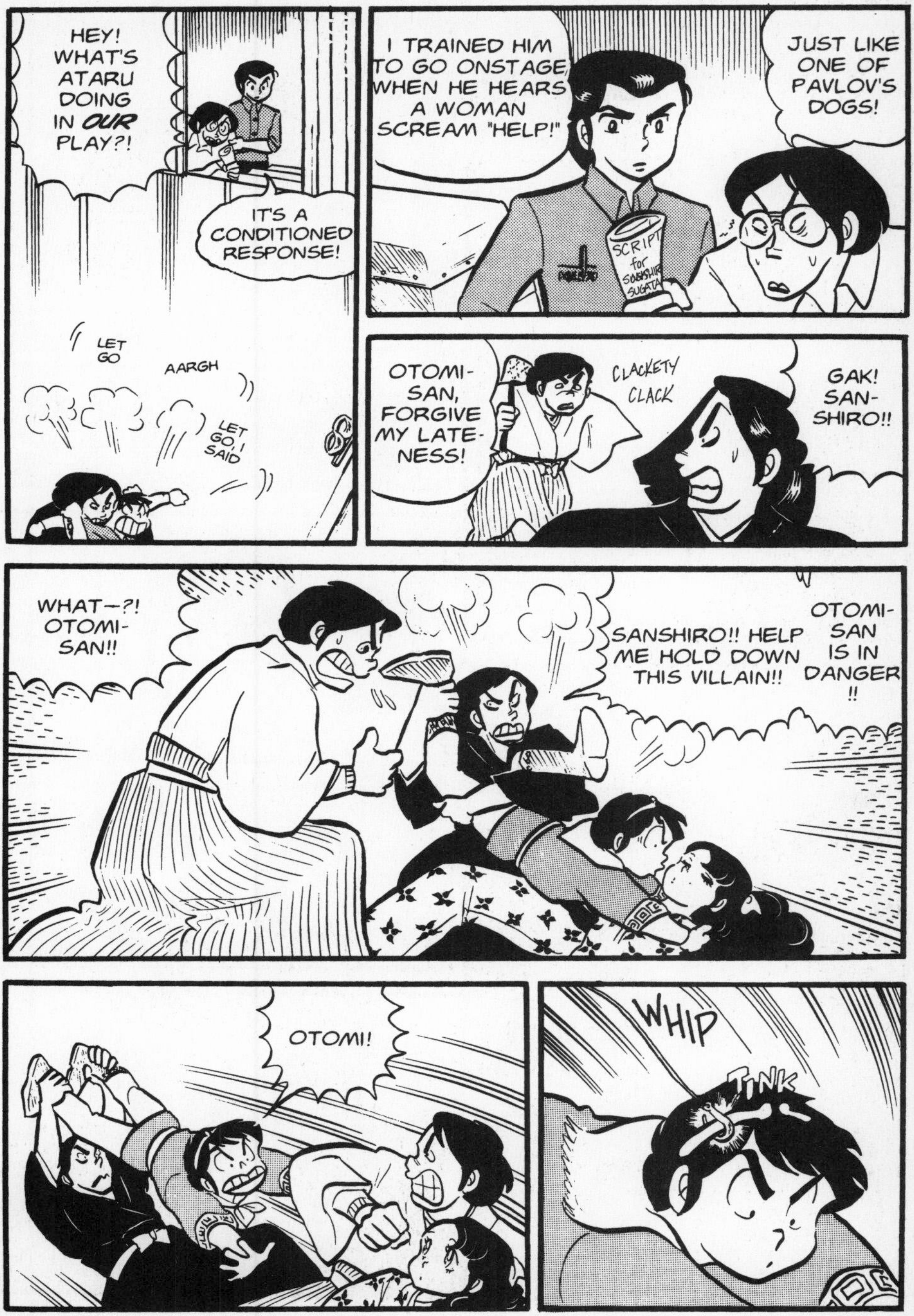

HEY! WHAT'S ATARU DOING IN OUR PLAY?!
IT'S A CONDITIONED RESPONSE!
LET GO
AARGH
LET GO, I SAID
I TRAINED HIM TO GO ONSTAGE WHEN HE HEARS A WOMAN SCREAM "HELP!"
SCRIPT for SANSHIRO SUGATA
JUST LIKE ONE OF PAVLOV'S DOGS!
OTOMI-SAN, FORGIVE MY LATENESS!
CLACKETY CLACK
GAK! SAN-SHIRO!!
WHAT—?! OTOMI-SAN!!
SANSHIRO!! HELP ME HOLD DOWN THIS VILLAIN!!
OTOMI-SAN IS IN DANGER!!
OTOMI!
WHIP
TINK

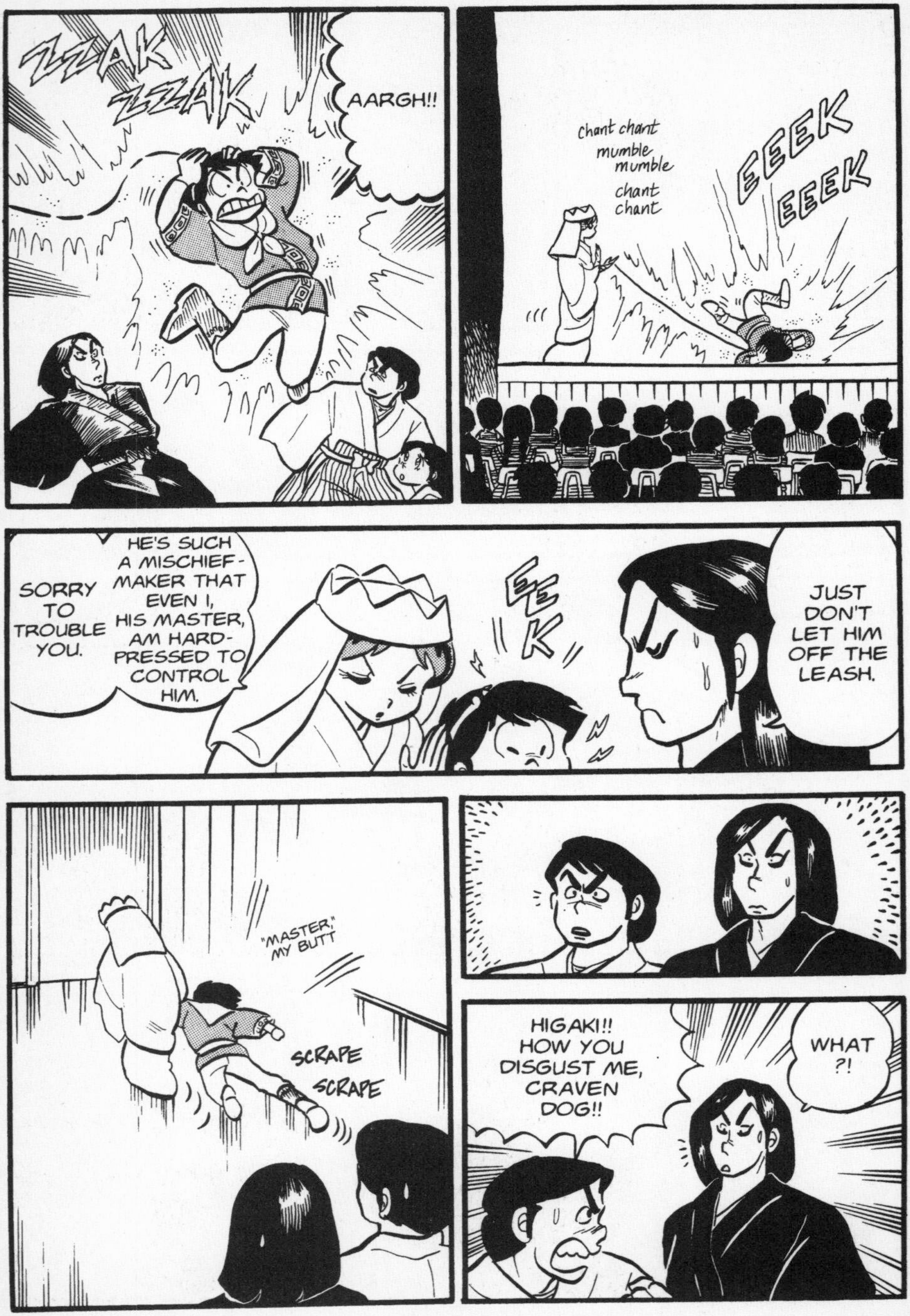
ZZAK ZZAK
AARGH!!
chant chant
mumble mumble
chant chant
EEEK EEEK
SORRY TO TROUBLE YOU.
HE'S SUCH A MISCHIEF-MAKER THAT EVEN I, HIS MASTER, AM HARD-PRESSED TO CONTROL HIM.
EEK
JUST DON'T LET HIM OFF THE LEASH.
"MASTER," MY BUTT
SCRAPE SCRAPE
HIGAKI!! HOW YOU DISGUST ME, CRAVEN DOG!!
WHAT ?!

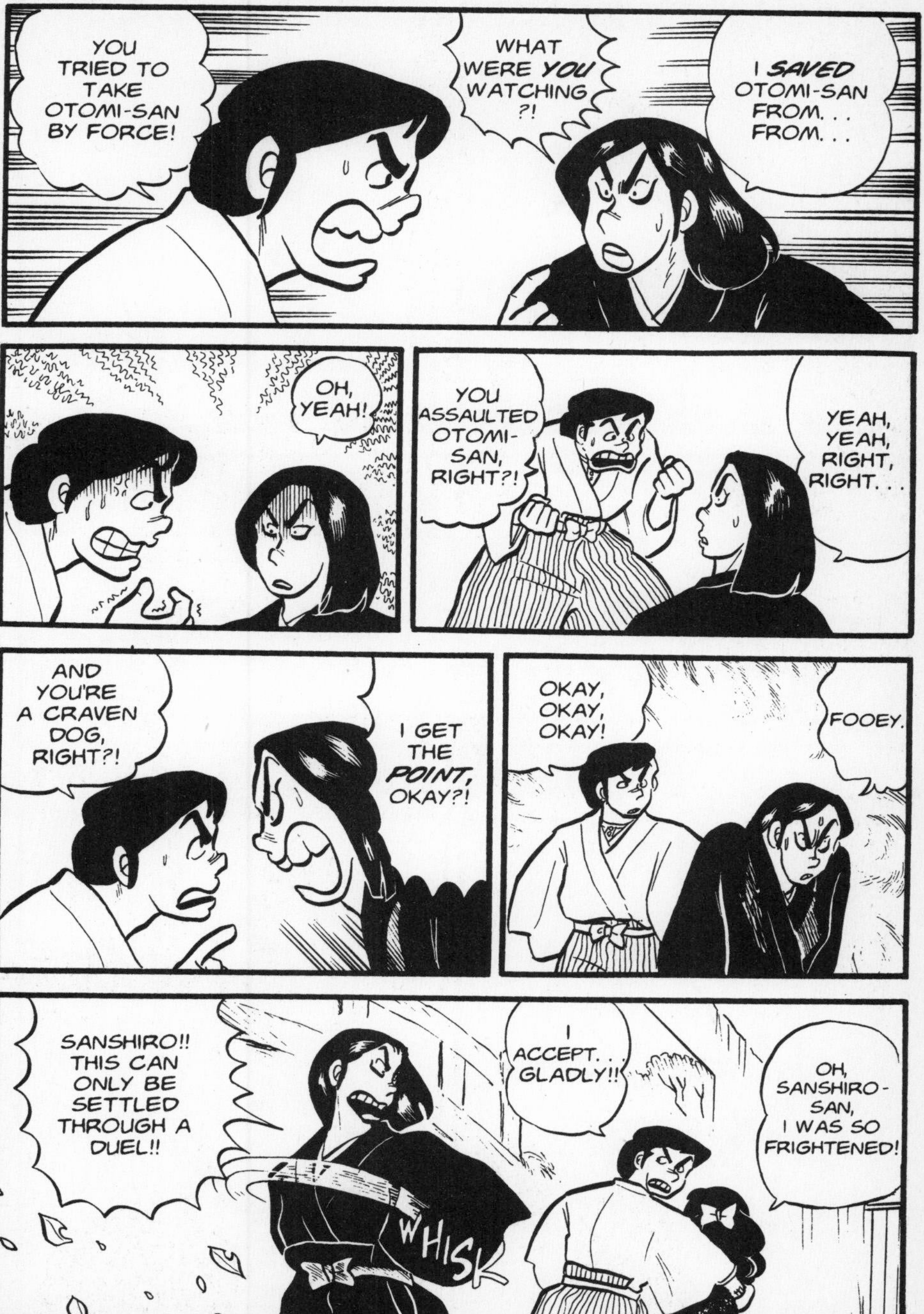

YOU TRIED TO TAKE OTOMI-SAN BY FORCE!
WHAT WERE YOU WATCHING ?!
I SAVED OTOMI-SAN FROM. . . FROM. . .
OH, YEAH!
YOU ASSAULTED OTOMI-SAN, RIGHT?!
YEAH, YEAH, RIGHT, RIGHT. . .
AND YOU'RE A CRAVEN DOG, RIGHT?!
I GET THE POINT, OKAY?!
OKAY, OKAY, OKAY!
FOOEY.
SANSHIRO!! THIS CAN ONLY BE SETTLED THROUGH A DUEL!!
WHISK
I ACCEPT. . . GLADLY!!
OH, SANSHIRO-SAN, I WAS SO FRIGHTENED!

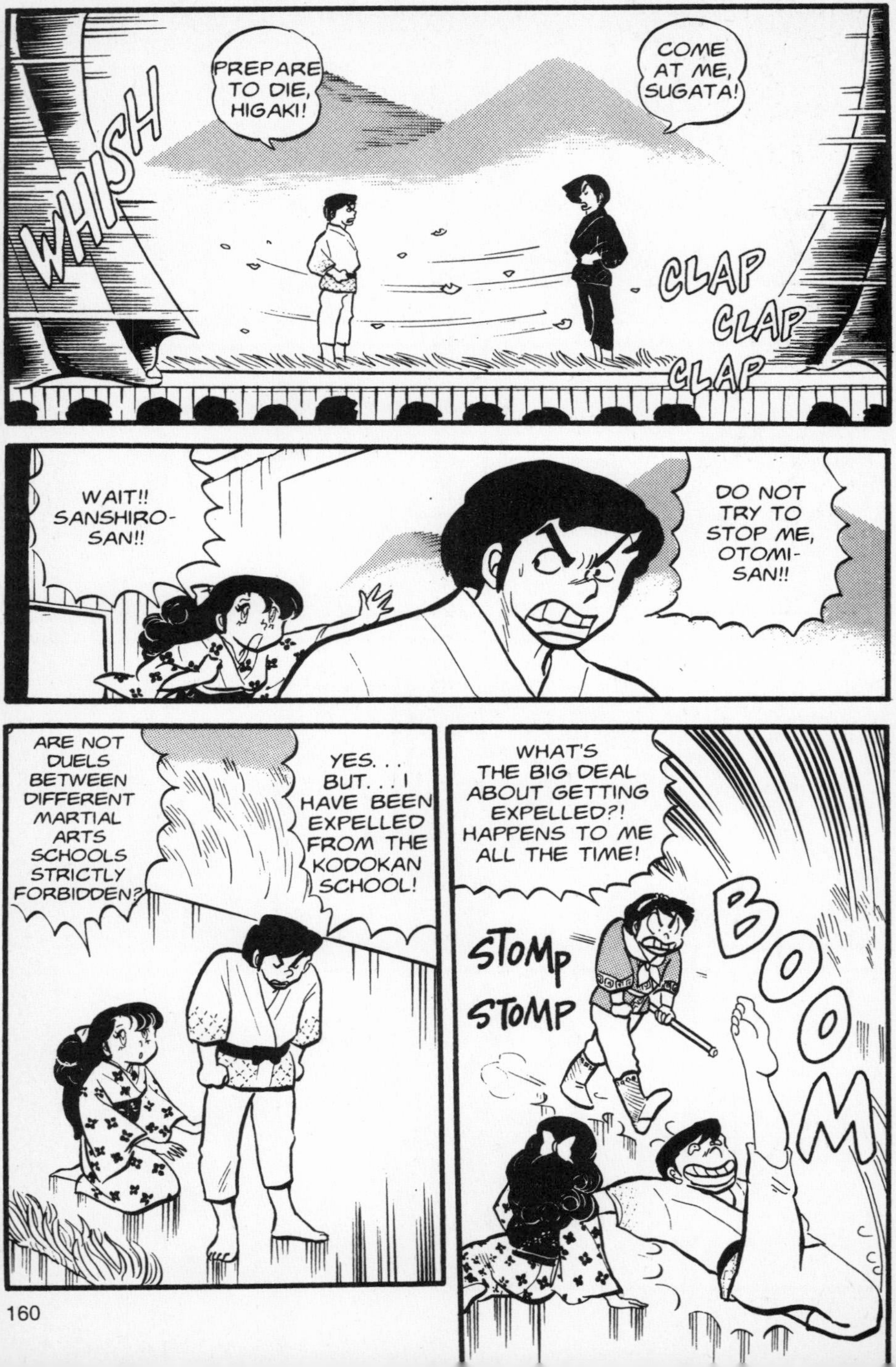
PREPARE TO DIE, HIGAKI!
COME AT ME, SUGATA!
WHISH
CLAP
CLAP
CLAP
WAIT!! SANSHIRO-SAN!!
DO NOT TRY TO STOP ME, OTOMI-SAN!!
ARE NOT DUELS BETWEEN DIFFERENT MARTIAL ARTS SCHOOLS STRICTLY FORBIDDEN?
YES. . . BUT. . . I HAVE BEEN EXPELLED FROM THE KODOKAN SCHOOL!
WHAT'S THE BIG DEAL ABOUT GETTING EXPELLED?! HAPPENS TO ME ALL THE TIME!
STOMP
STOMP
BOOOM

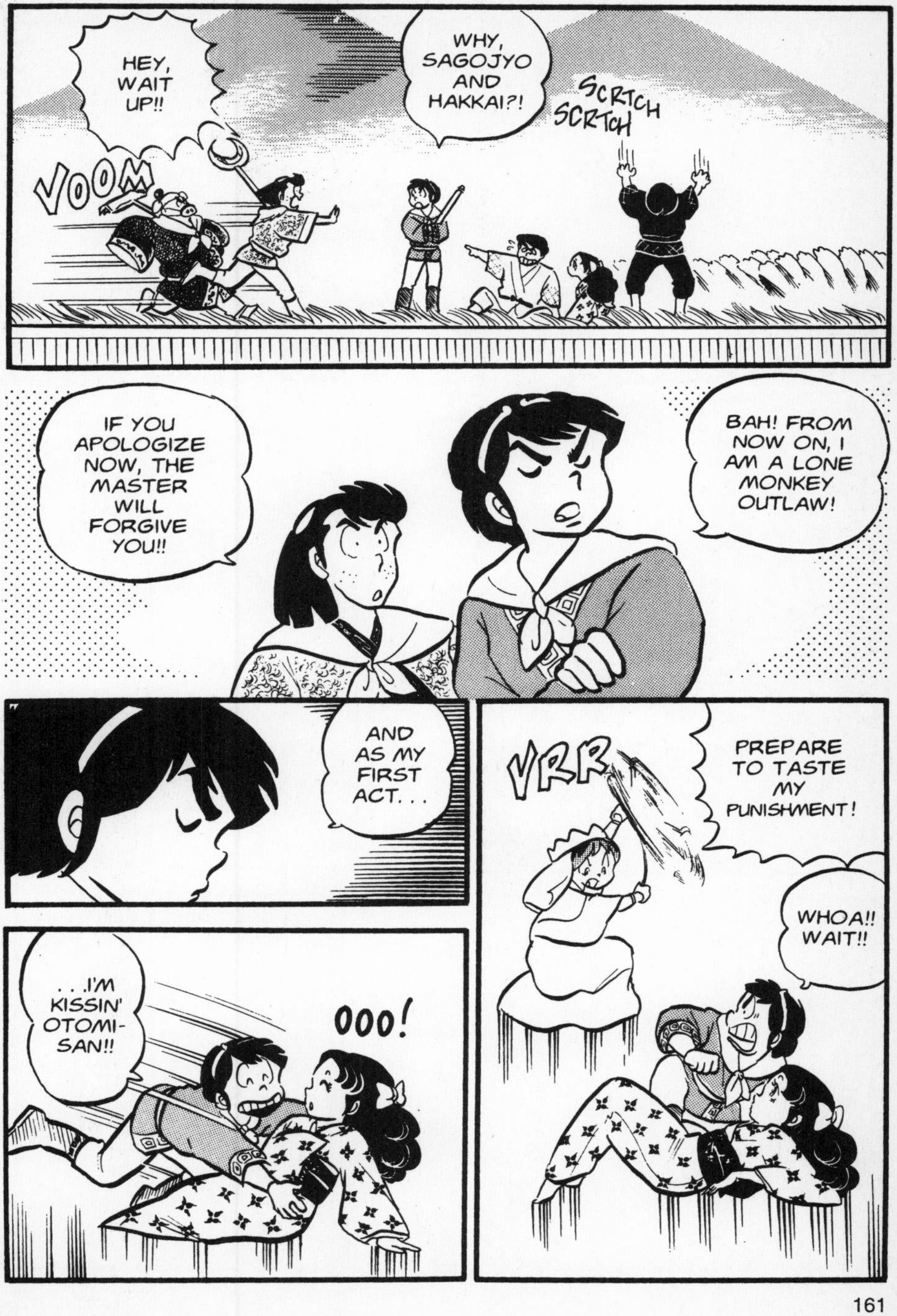

HEY, WAIT UP!!
WHY, SAGOJYO AND HAKKAI?!
SCRTCH SCRTCH
VOOM
IF YOU APOLOGIZE NOW, THE MASTER WILL FORGIVE YOU!!
BAH! FROM NOW ON, I AM A LONE MONKEY OUTLAW!
AND AS MY FIRST ACT. . .
VRR
PREPARE TO TASTE MY PUNISHMENT!
WHOA!! WAIT!!
. . .I'M KISSIN' OTOMI-SAN!!
OOO!

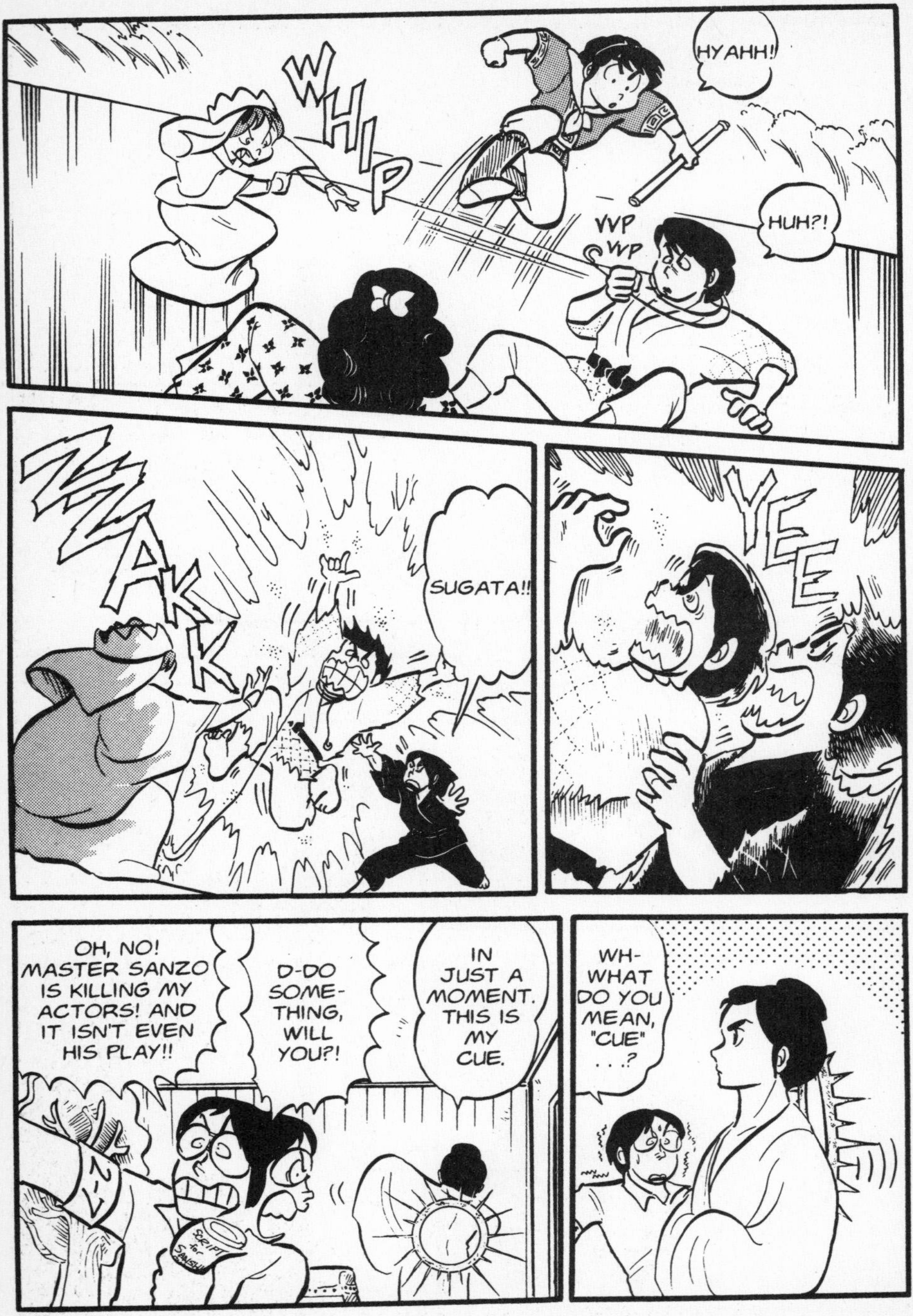
WHIP
HYAHH!
VVP VVP
HUH?!
NNAKK
SUGATA!!
YEEE
OH, NO! MASTER SANZO IS KILLING MY ACTORS! AND IT ISN'T EVEN HIS PLAY!!
D-DO SOME-THING, WILL YOU?!
IN JUST A MOMENT. THIS IS MY CUE.
WH-WHAT DO YOU MEAN, "CUE" . . .?

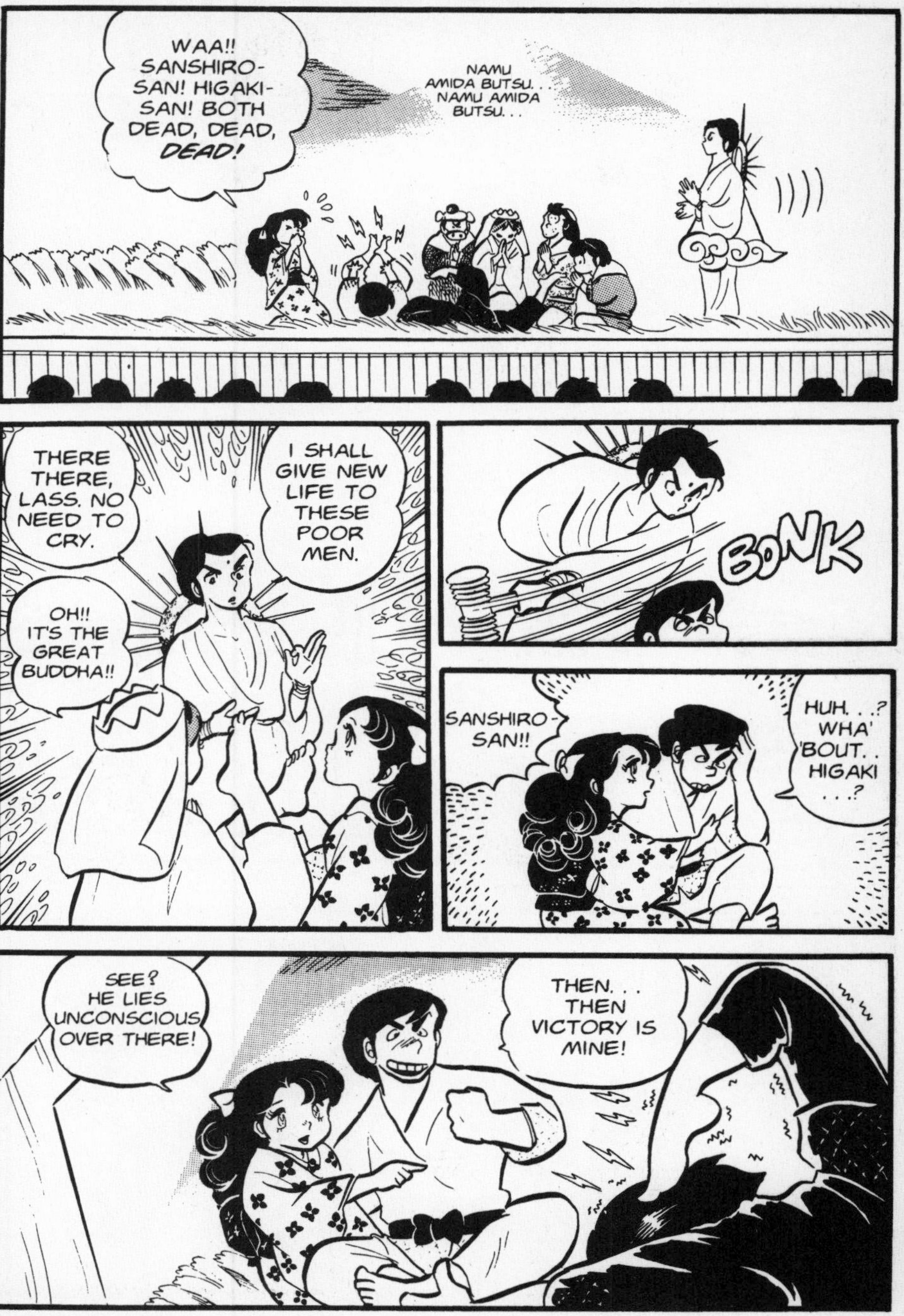
WAA!! SANSHIRO-SAN! HIGAKI-SAN! BOTH DEAD, DEAD, DEAD!
NAMU AMIDA BUTSU. . . NAMU AMIDA BUTSU. . .
THERE THERE, LASS. NO NEED TO CRY.
I SHALL GIVE NEW LIFE TO THESE POOR MEN.
OH!! IT'S THE GREAT BUDDHA!!
BONK
SANSHIRO-SAN!!
HUH. . .? WHA' 'BOUT. . HIGAKI . . .?
SEE? HE LIES UNCONSCIOUS OVER THERE!
THEN. . . THEN VICTORY IS MINE!

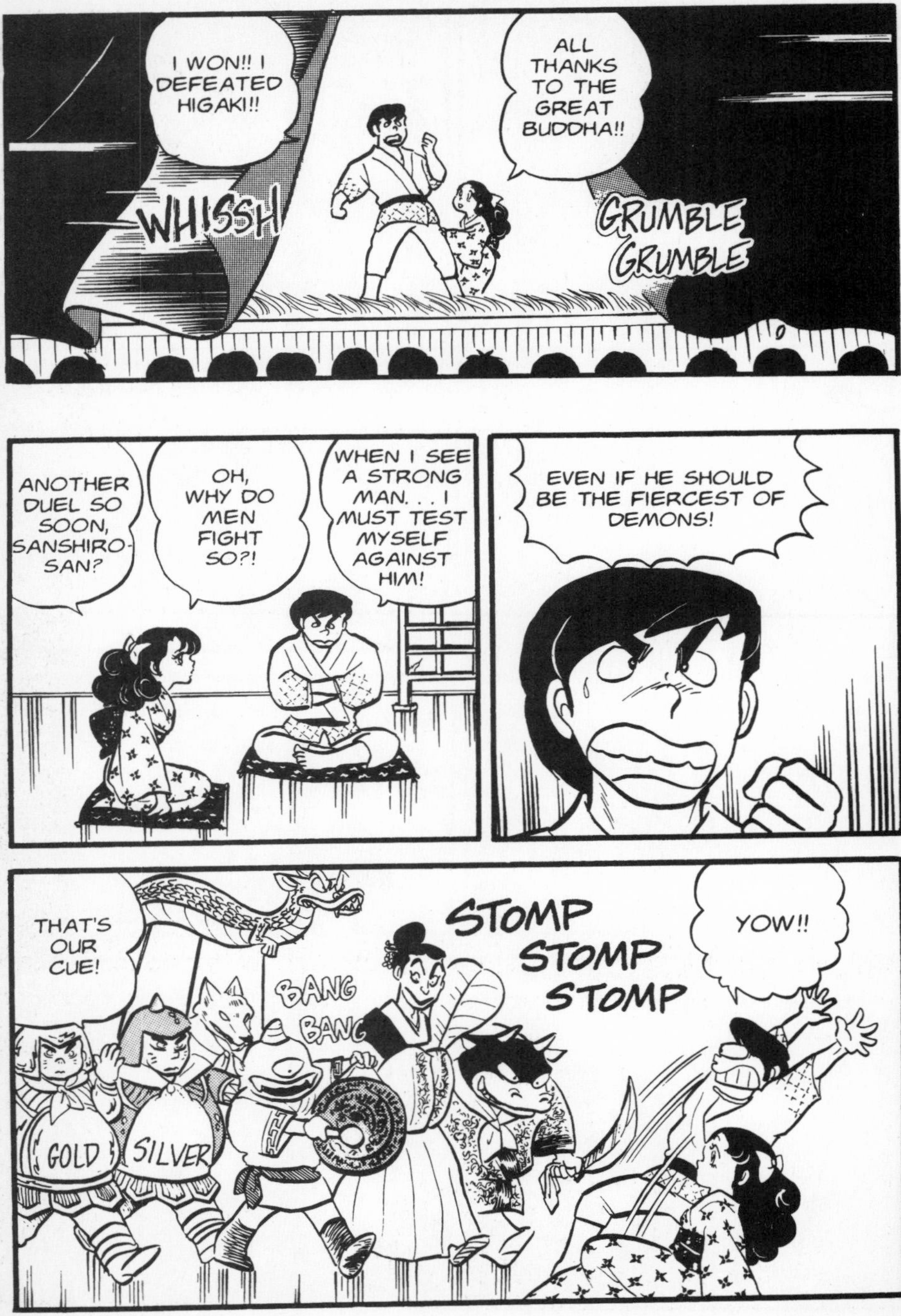
I WON!! I DEFEATED HIGAKI!!
WHISSH
ALL THANKS TO THE GREAT BUDDHA!!
GRUMBLE GRUMBLE
ANOTHER DUEL SO SOON, SANSHIRO-SAN?
OH, WHY DO MEN FIGHT SO?!
WHEN I SEE A STRONG MAN. . . I MUST TEST MYSELF AGAINST HIM!
EVEN IF HE SHOULD BE THE FIERCEST OF DEMONS!
THAT'S OUR CUE!
BANG BANG
GOLD
SILVER
STOMP STOMP STOMP
YOW!!

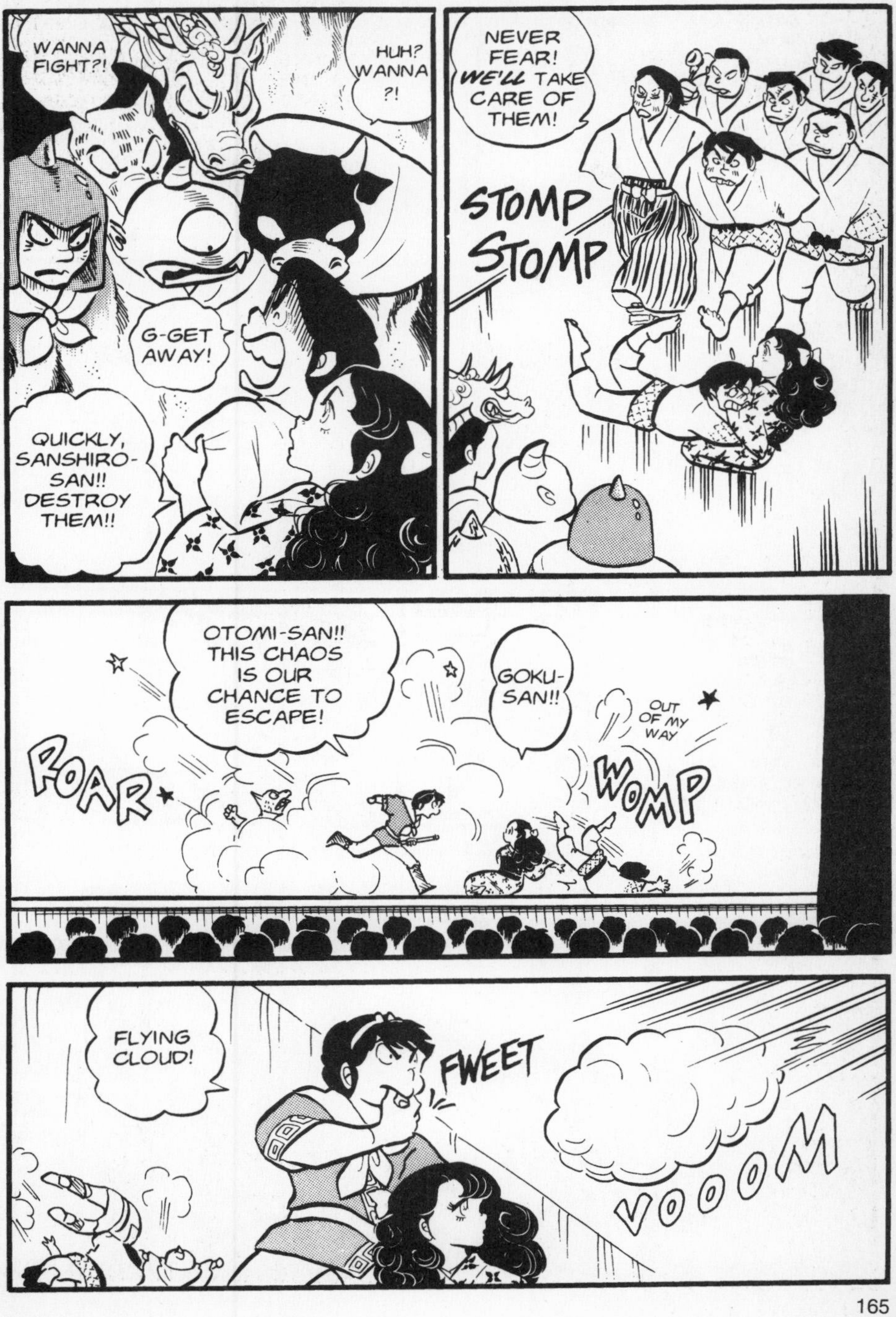
WANNA FIGHT?!
HUH? WANNA ?!
G-GET AWAY!
QUICKLY, SANSHIRO-SAN!! DESTROY THEM!!
NEVER FEAR! WE'LL TAKE CARE OF THEM!
STOMP STOMP
OTOMI-SAN!! THIS CHAOS IS OUR CHANCE TO ESCAPE!
GOKU-SAN!!
OUT OF MY WAY
ROAR
WOMP
FLYING CLOUD!
FWEET
VOOOOM

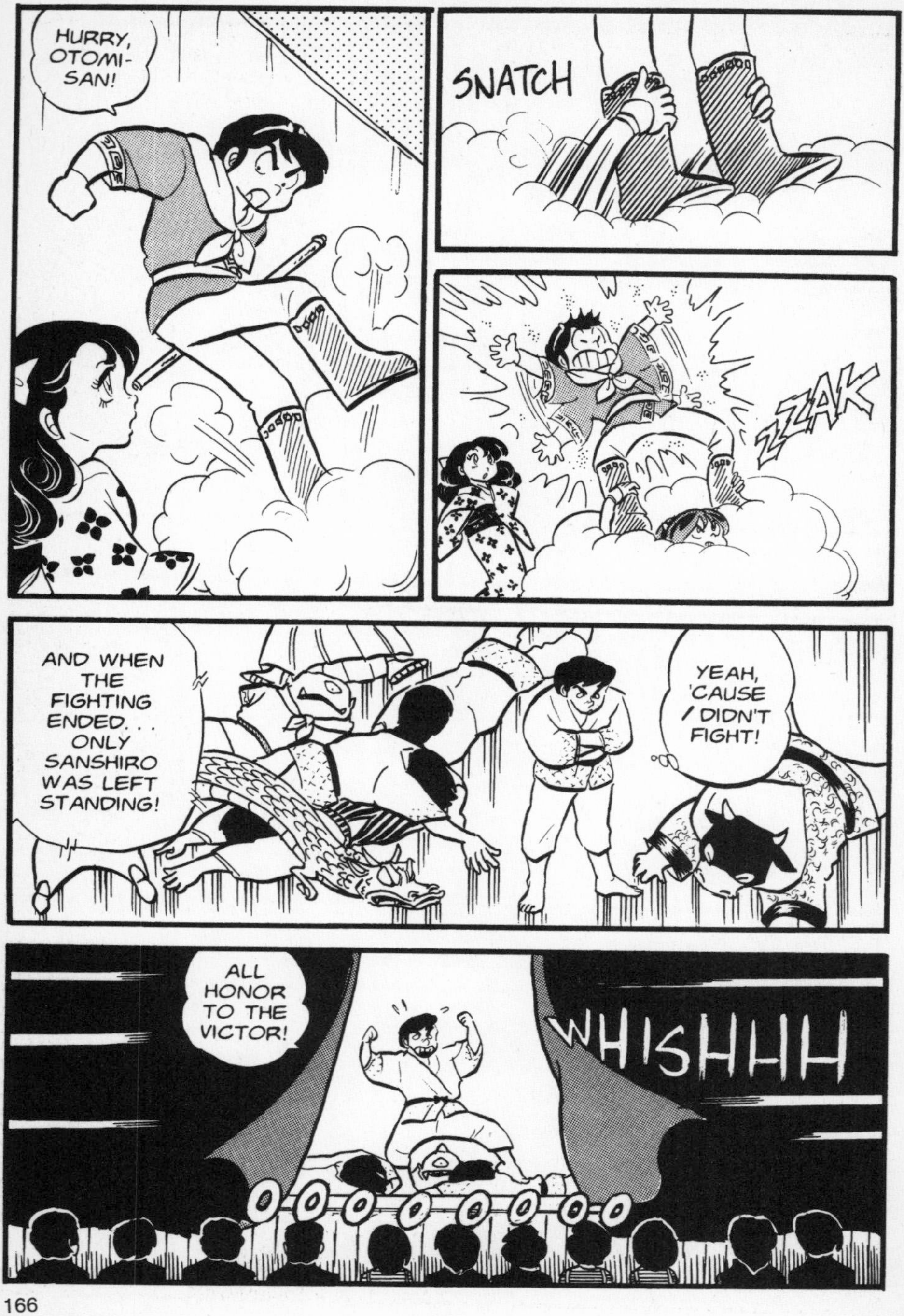
HURRY, OTOMI-SAN!
SNATCH
ZZZAK
AND WHEN THE FIGHTING ENDED. . . ONLY SANSHIRO WAS LEFT STANDING!
YEAH, 'CAUSE I DIDN'T FIGHT!
ALL HONOR TO THE VICTOR!
WHISHHH

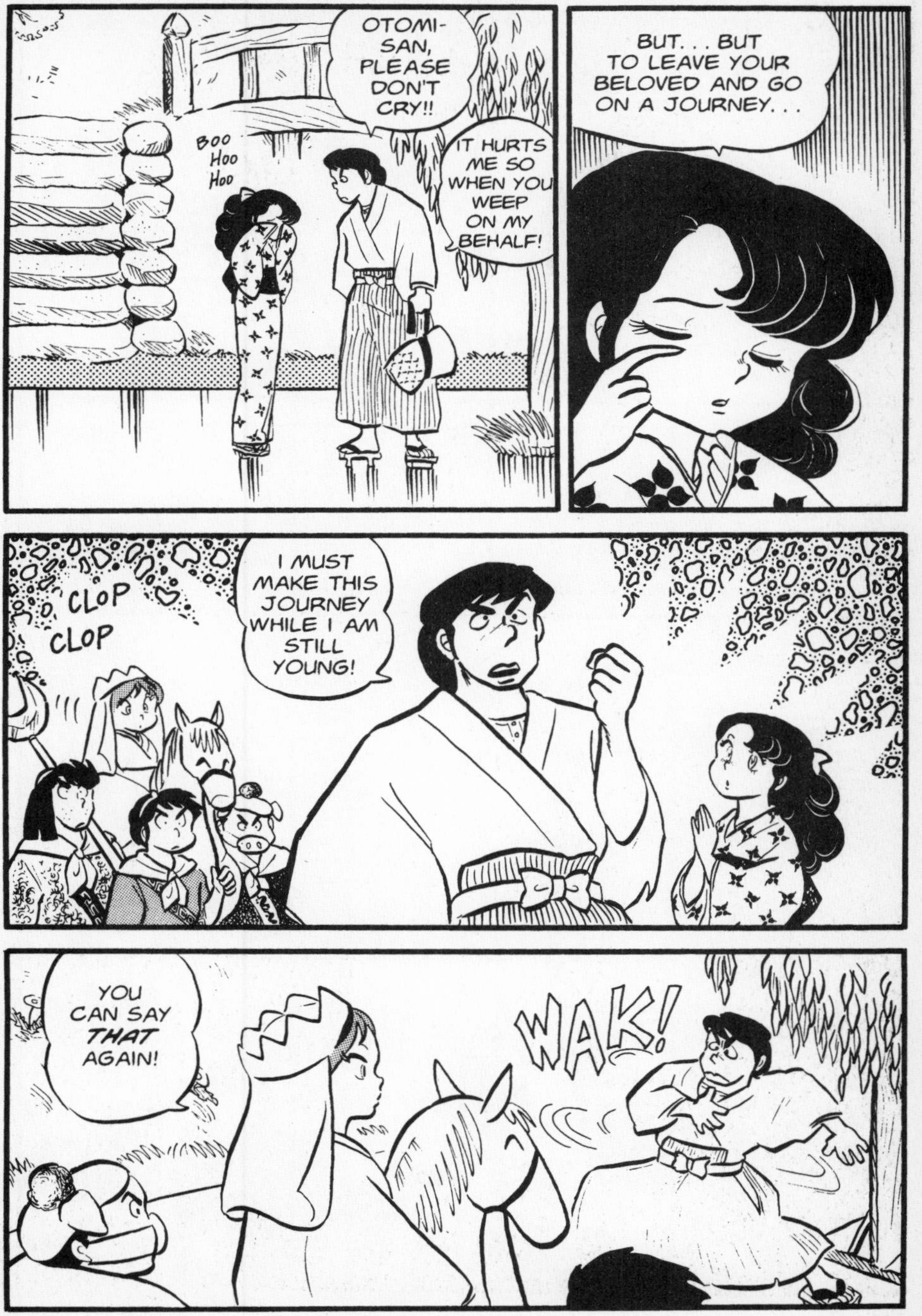
OTOMI-SAN, PLEASE DON'T CRY!!
BOO HOO HOO
IT HURTS ME SO WHEN YOU WEEP ON MY BEHALF!
BUT. . . BUT TO LEAVE YOUR BELOVED AND GO ON A JOURNEY. . .
CLOP CLOP
I MUST MAKE THIS JOURNEY WHILE I AM STILL YOUNG!
YOU CAN SAY *THAT* AGAIN!
WAK!

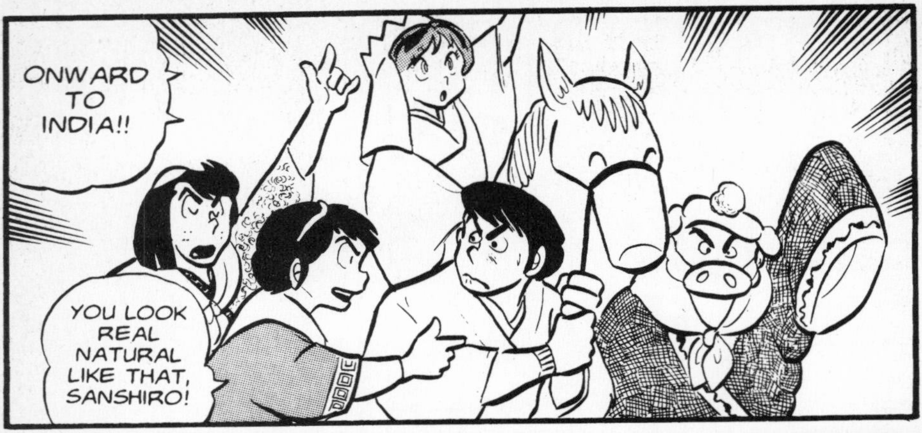
ONWARD TO INDIA!!
YOU LOOK REAL NATURAL LIKE THAT, SANSHIRO!

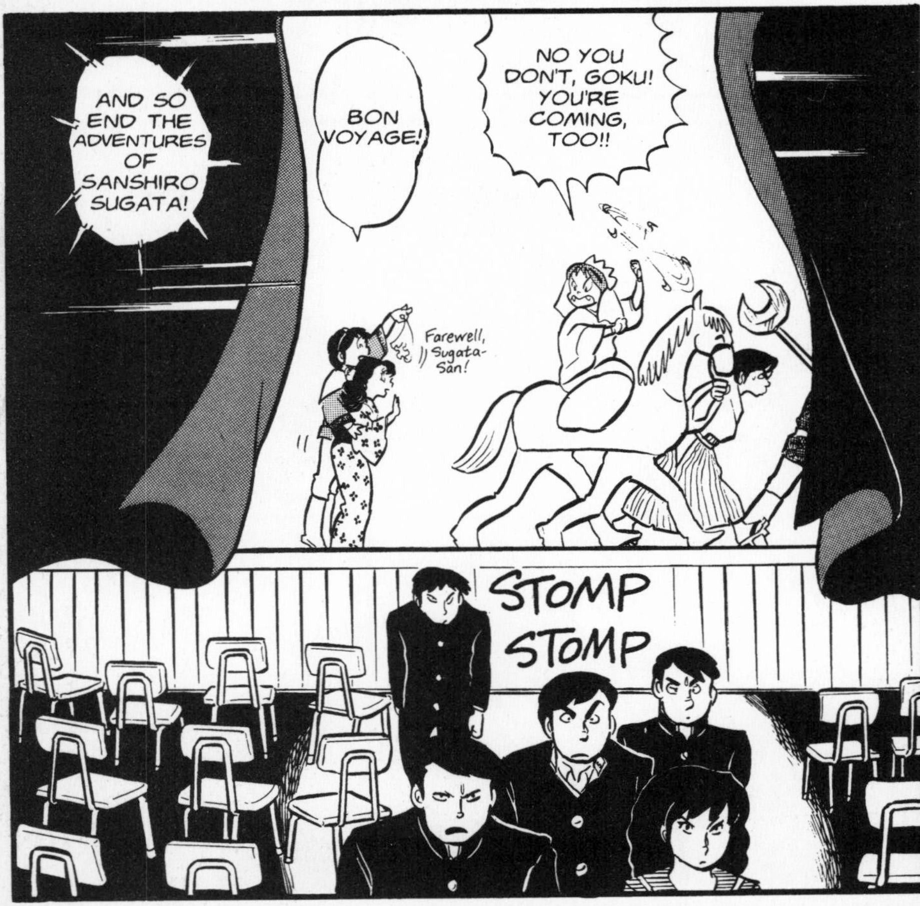
AND SO END THE ADVENTURES OF SANSHIRO SUGATA!
BON VOYAGE!
NO YOU DON'T, GOKU! YOU'RE COMING, TOO!!
Farewell, Sugata-San!
STOMP
STOMP

PART ELEVEN

HAVE YOUR CAKE AND...

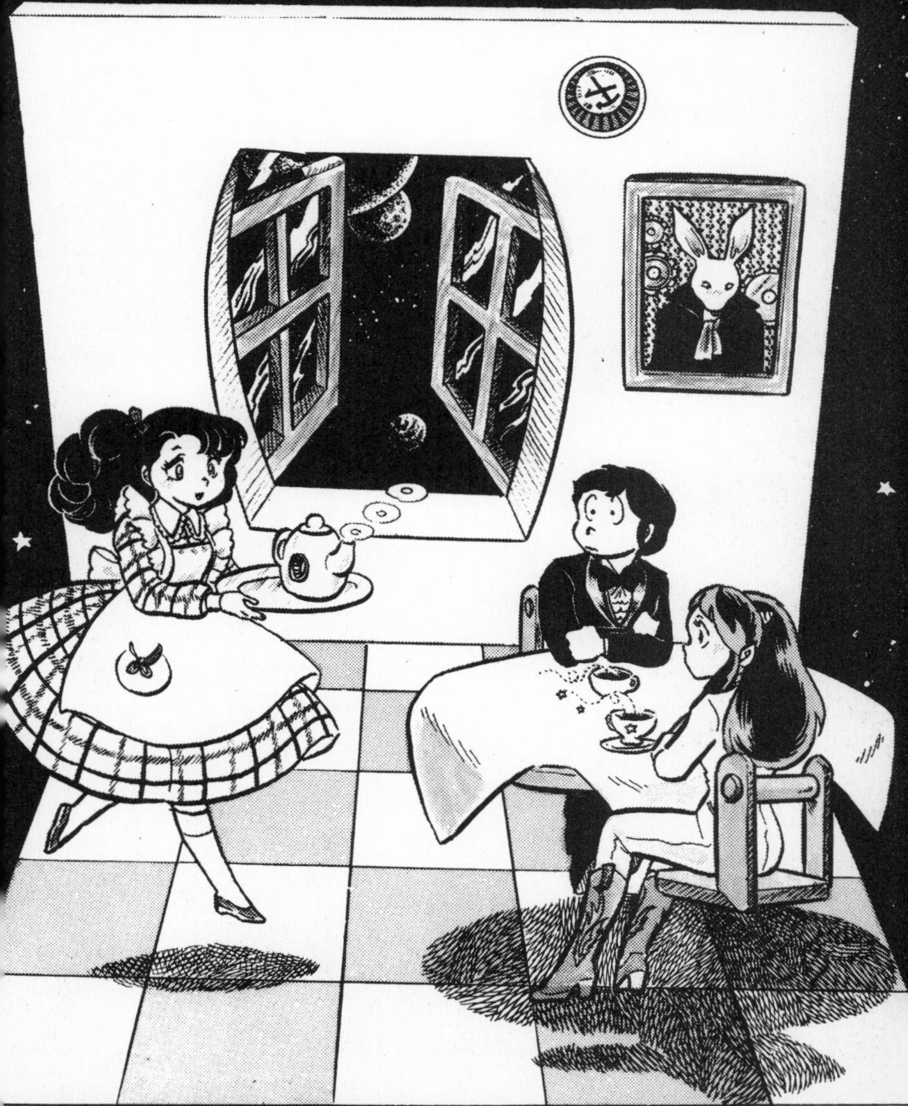

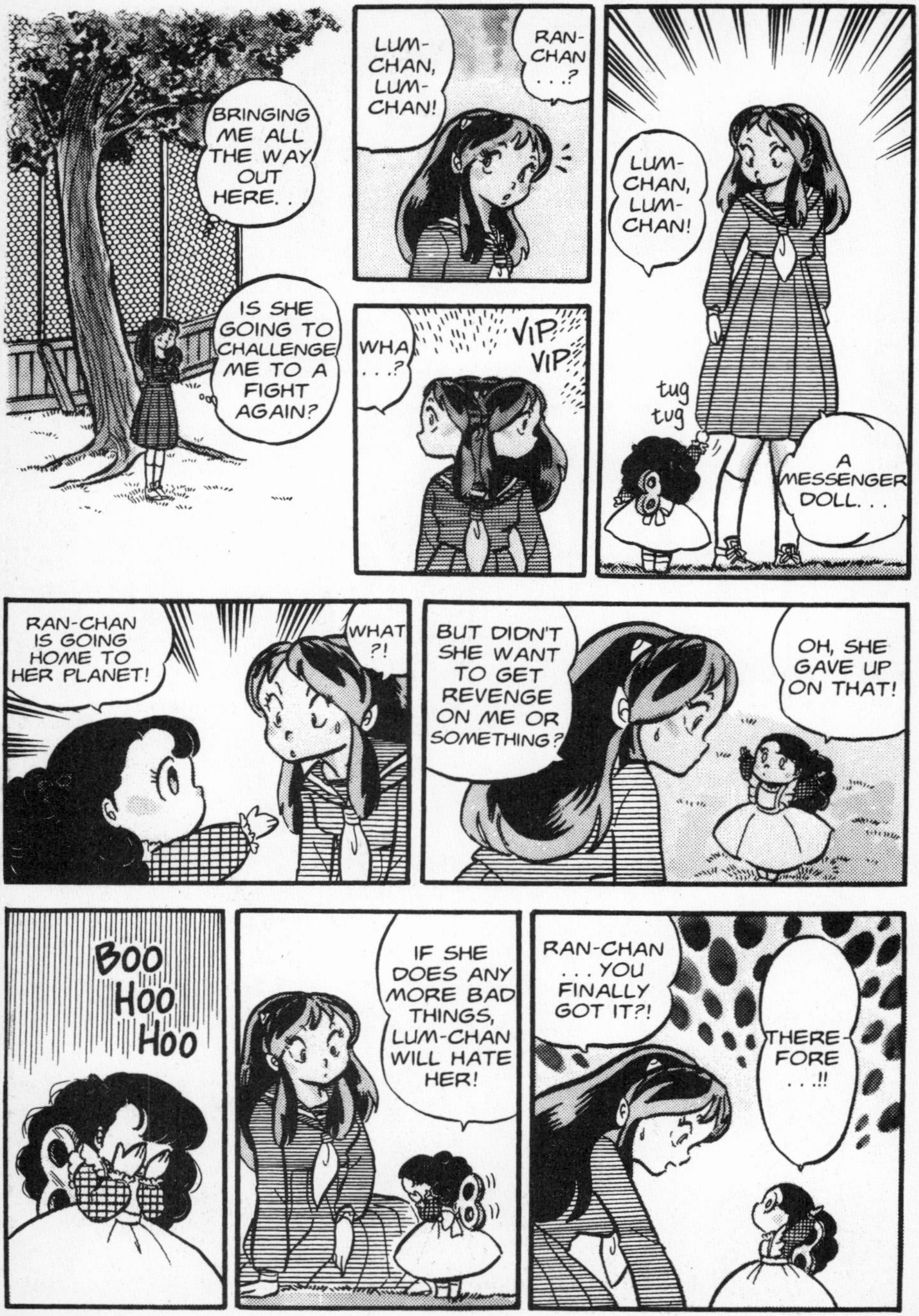
BRINGING ME ALL THE WAY OUT HERE. .
IS SHE GOING TO CHALLENGE ME TO A FIGHT AGAIN?
LUM-CHAN, LUM-CHAN!
RAN-CHAN . . .?
WHA . . .?
VIP VIP
LUM-CHAN, LUM-CHAN!
tug tug
A MESSENGER DOLL. . .
RAN-CHAN IS GOING HOME TO HER PLANET!
WHAT ?!
BUT DIDN'T SHE WANT TO GET REVENGE ON ME OR SOMETHING?
OH, SHE GAVE UP ON THAT!
BOO HOO HOO
IF SHE DOES ANY MORE BAD THINGS, LUM-CHAN WILL HATE HER!
RAN-CHAN . . . YOU FINALLY GOT IT?!
THERE-FORE . . .!!

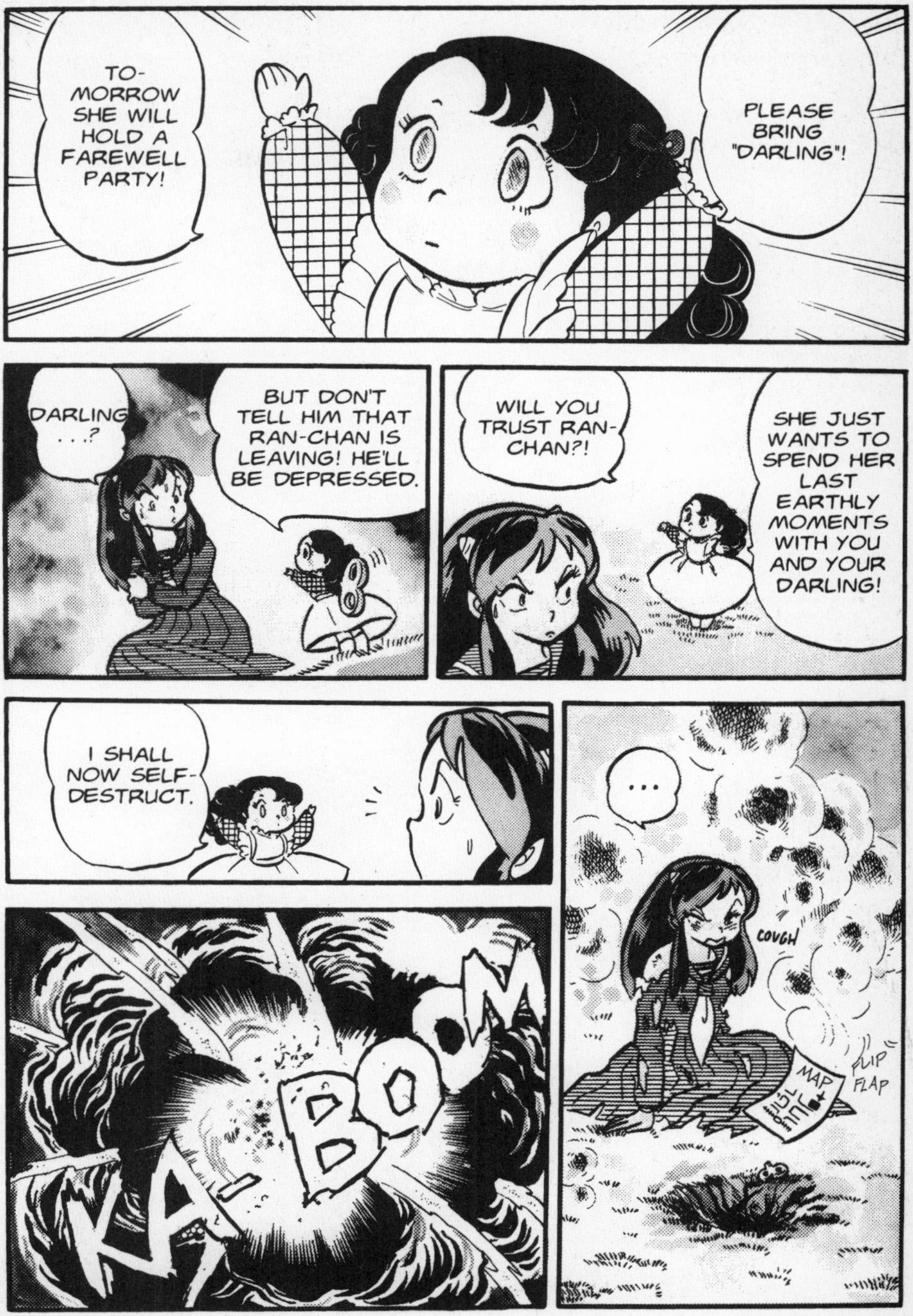
TO-MORROW SHE WILL HOLD A FAREWELL PARTY!
PLEASE BRING "DARLING"!
DARLING . . .?
BUT DON'T TELL HIM THAT RAN-CHAN IS LEAVING! HE'LL BE DEPRESSED.
WILL YOU TRUST RAN-CHAN?!
SHE JUST WANTS TO SPEND HER LAST EARTHLY MOMENTS WITH YOU AND YOUR DARLING!
I SHALL NOW SELF-DESTRUCT.
KA-BOOM
...
COUGH
MAP
FLIP FLAP

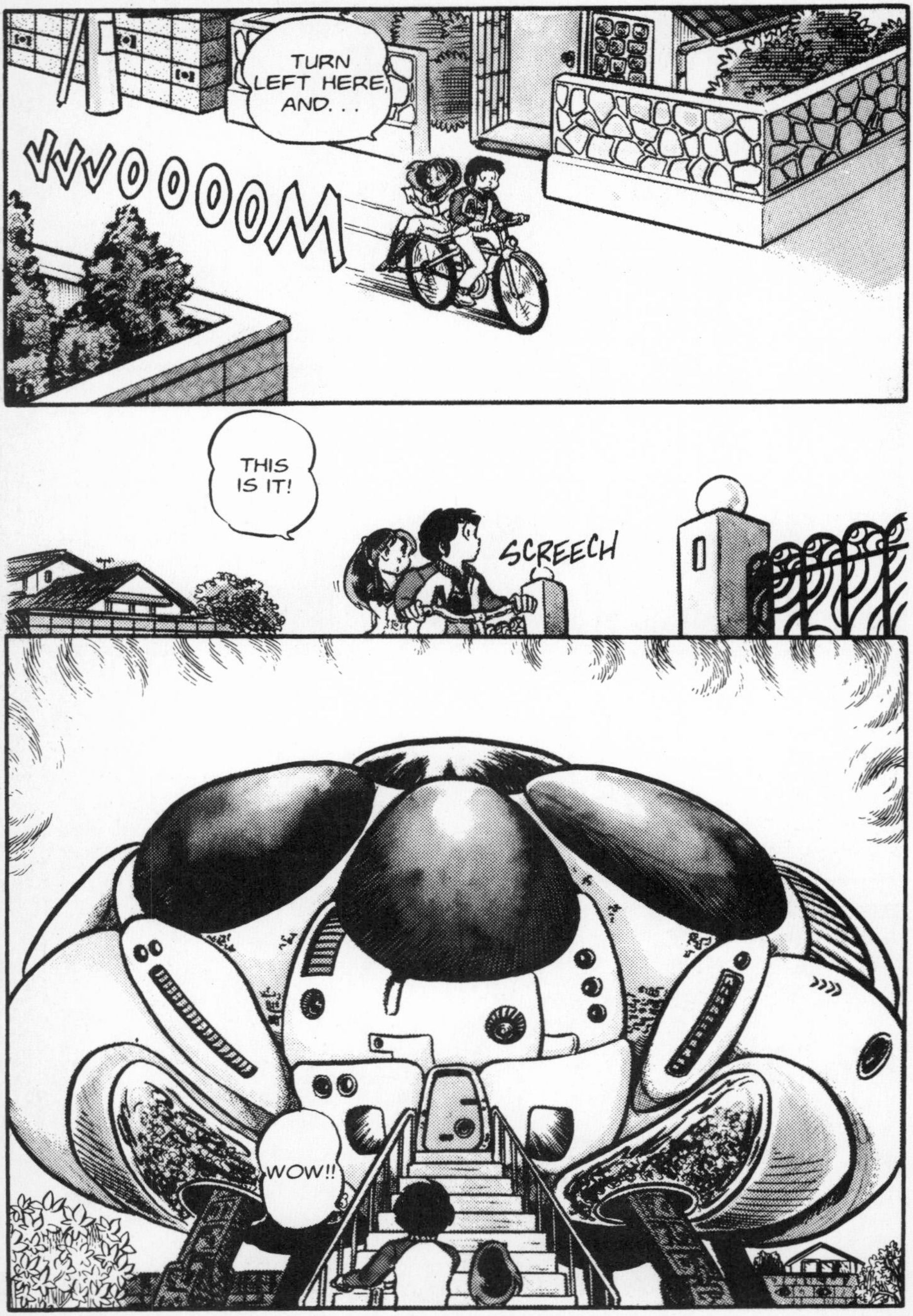
TURN LEFT HERE, AND. . .
VVVOOOOM
THIS IS IT!
SCREECH
WOW!!

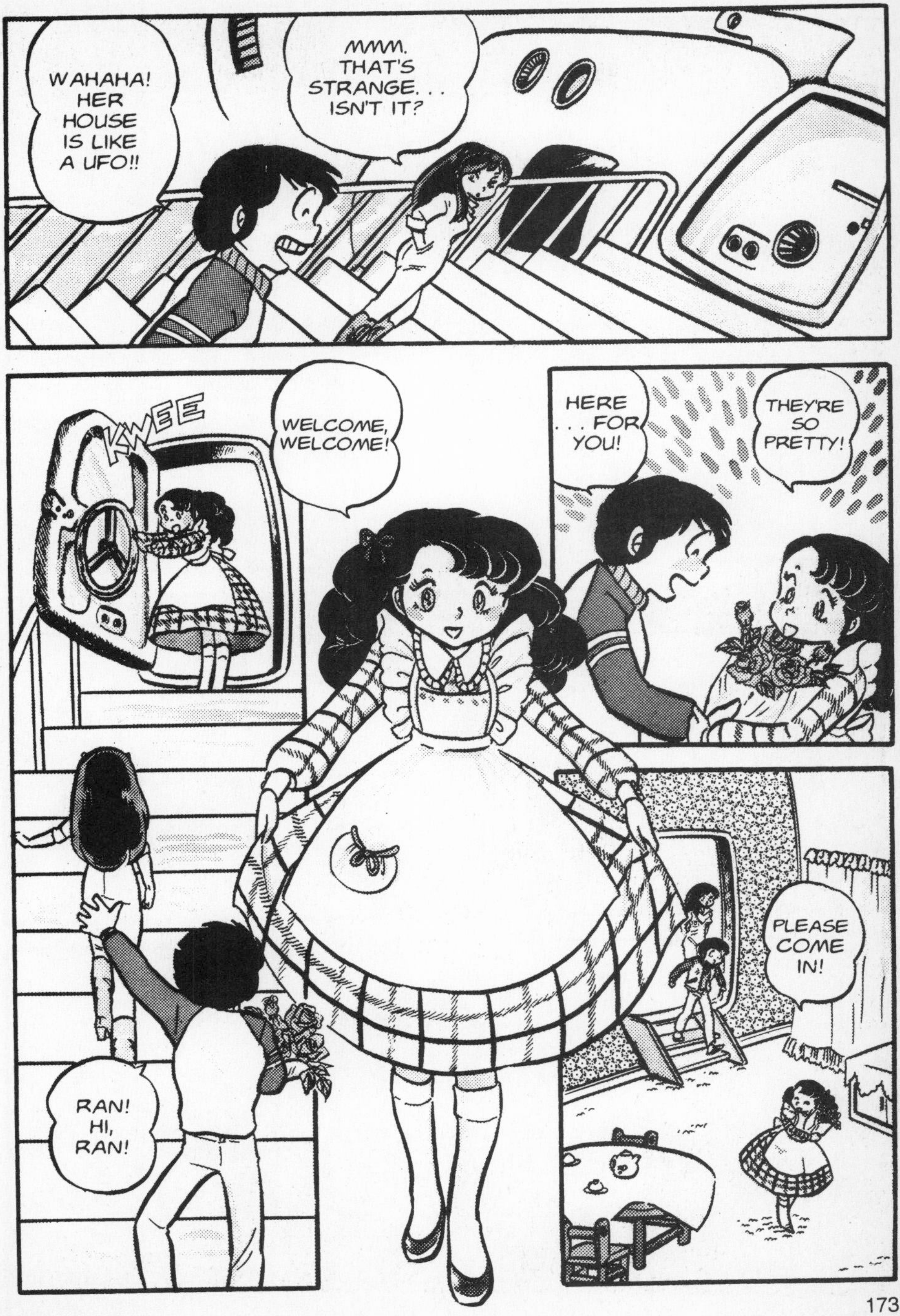
WAHAHA! HER HOUSE IS LIKE A UFO!!
MMM. THAT'S STRANGE. . . ISN'T IT?
KWEE
WELCOME, WELCOME!
RAN! HI, RAN!
HERE . . . FOR YOU!
THEY'RE SO PRETTY!
PLEASE COME IN!

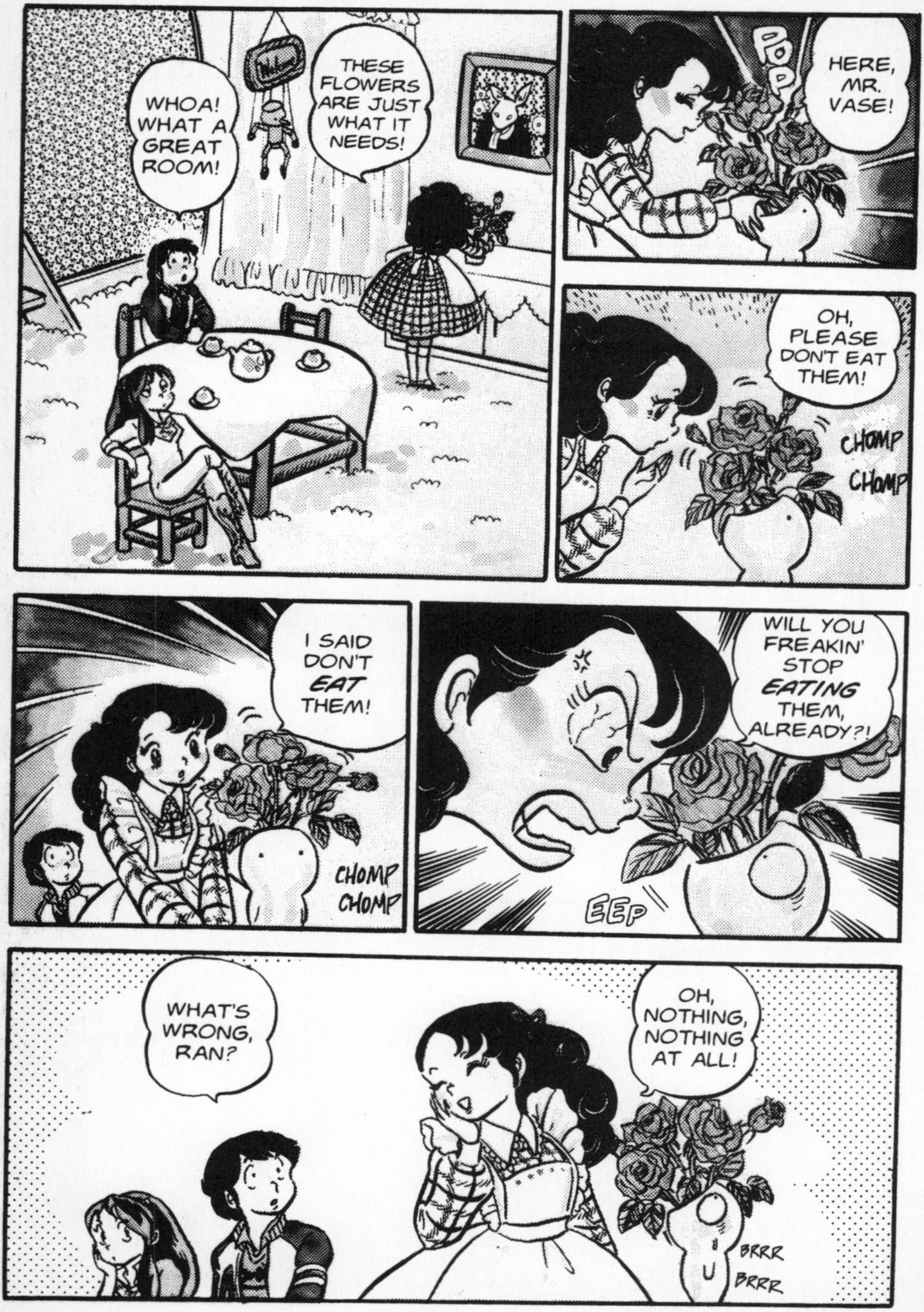
WHOA! WHAT A GREAT ROOM!
THESE FLOWERS ARE JUST WHAT IT NEEDS!
POP
HERE, MR. VASE!
OH, PLEASE DON'T EAT THEM!
CHOMP
CHOMP
I SAID DON'T EAT THEM!
CHOMP
CHOMP
WILL YOU FREAKIN' STOP EATING THEM, ALREADY?!
EEP
WHAT'S WRONG, RAN?
OH, NOTHING, NOTHING AT ALL!
BRRR
BRRR

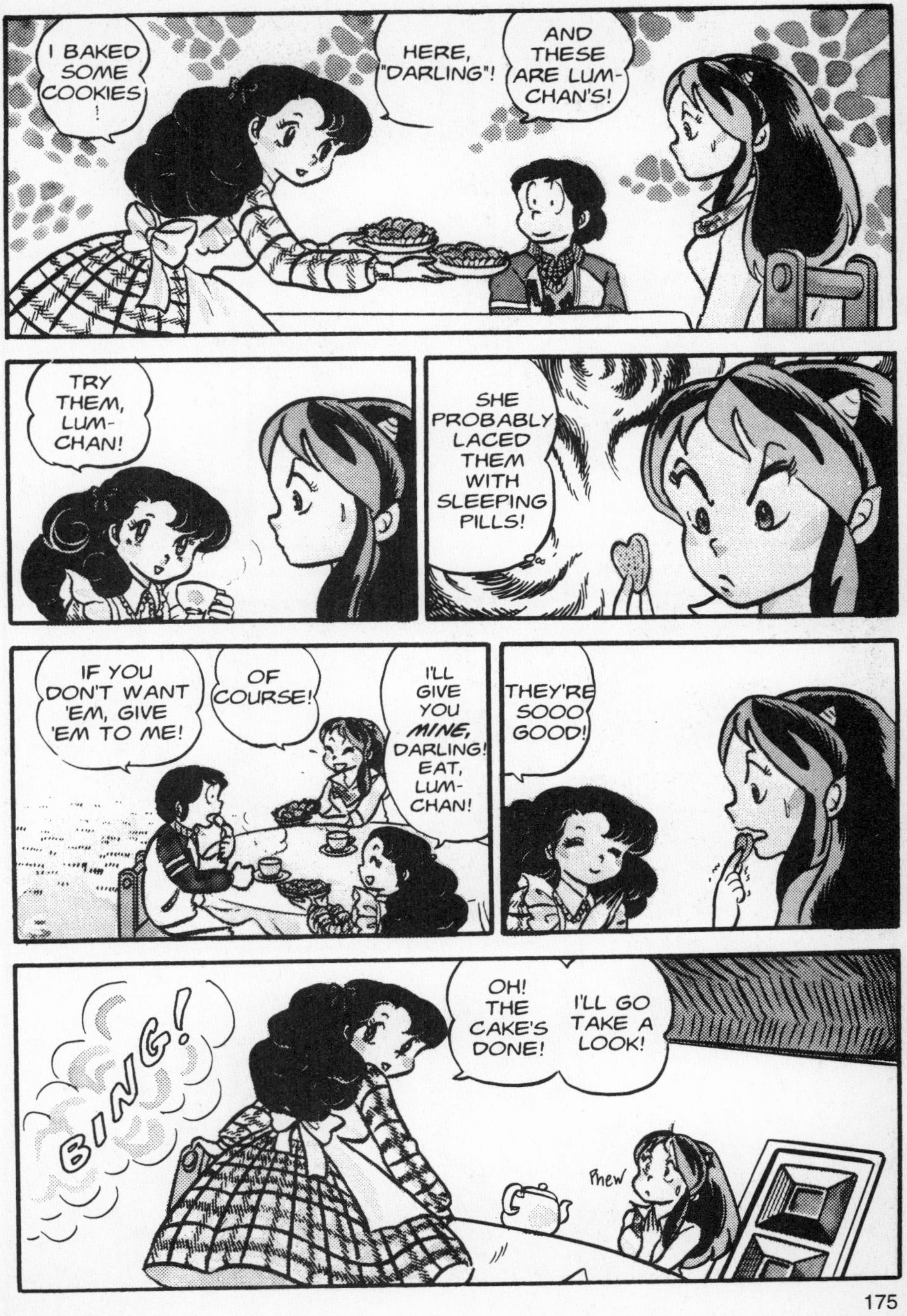
I BAKED SOME COOKIES!
HERE, "DARLING"!
AND THESE ARE LUM-CHAN'S!
TRY THEM, LUM-CHAN!
SHE PROBABLY LACED THEM WITH SLEEPING PILLS!
IF YOU DON'T WANT 'EM, GIVE 'EM TO ME!
OF COURSE!
I'LL GIVE YOU *MINE,* DARLING! EAT, LUM-CHAN!
THEY'RE SOOO GOOD!
BING!
OH! THE CAKE'S DONE!
I'LL GO TAKE A LOOK!
Phew

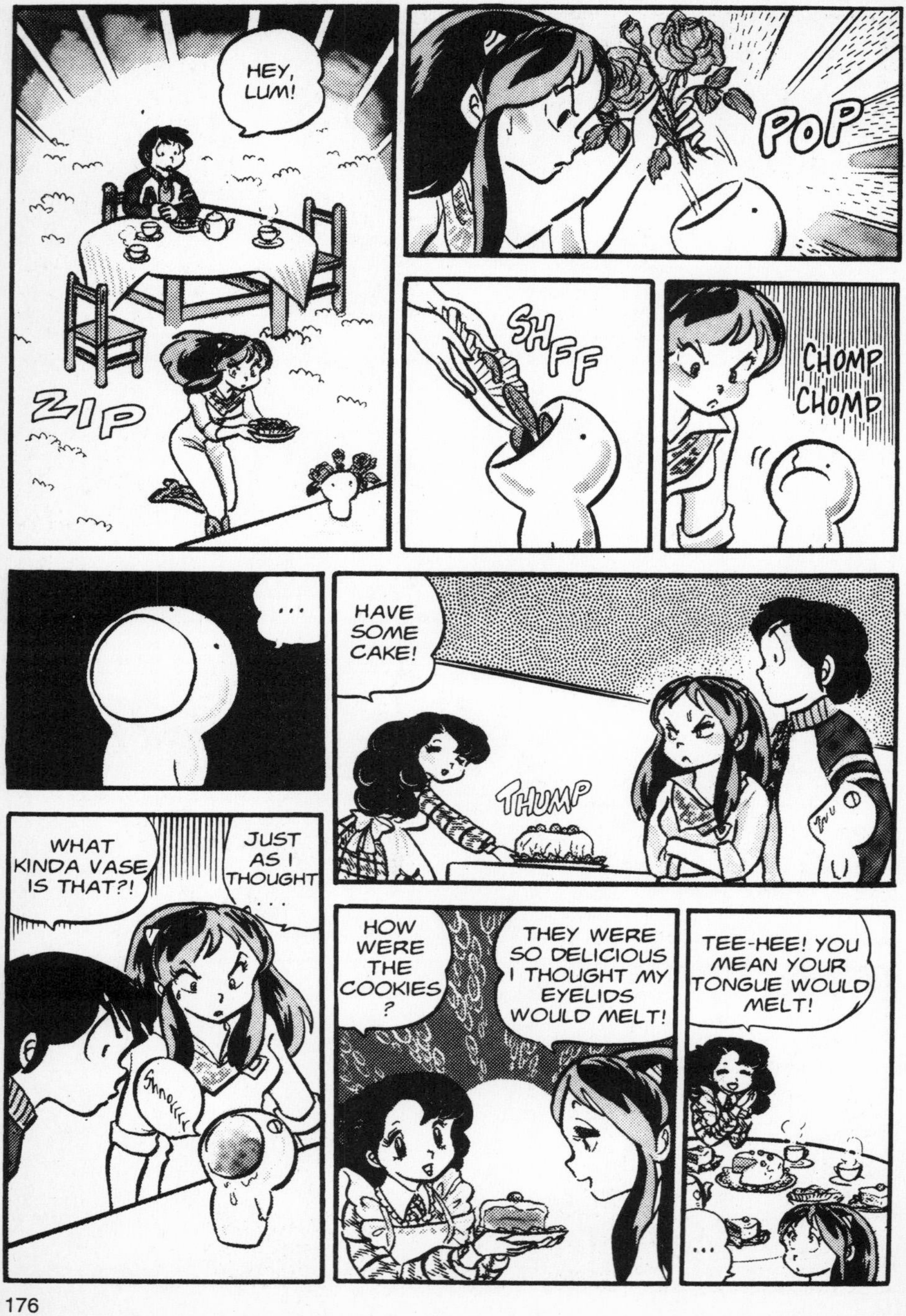

HEY, LUM!
ZIP
POP
SHFF
CHOMP CHOMP
...
HAVE SOME CAKE!
THUMP
WHAT KINDA VASE IS THAT?!
JUST AS I THOUGHT . . .
HOW WERE THE COOKIES?
THEY WERE SO DELICIOUS I THOUGHT MY EYELIDS WOULD MELT!
TEE-HEE! YOU MEAN YOUR TONGUE WOULD MELT!
...

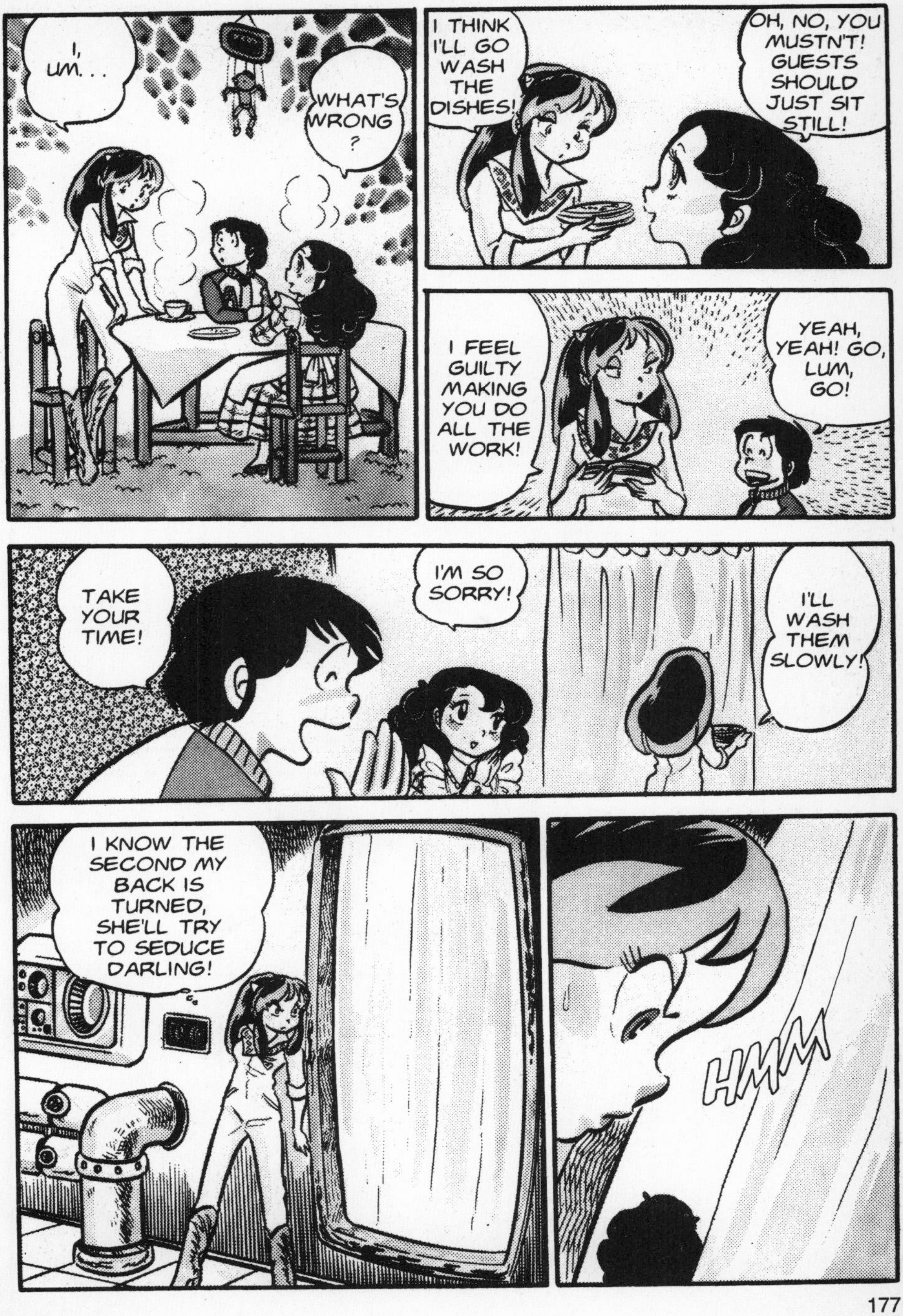
I, UM. . .
WHAT'S WRONG ?
I THINK I'LL GO WASH THE DISHES!
OH, NO, YOU MUSTN'T! GUESTS SHOULD JUST SIT STILL!
I FEEL GUILTY MAKING YOU DO ALL THE WORK!
YEAH, YEAH! GO, LUM, GO!
TAKE YOUR TIME!
I'M SO SORRY!
I'LL WASH THEM SLOWLY!
I KNOW THE SECOND MY BACK IS TURNED, SHE'LL TRY TO SEDUCE DARLING!
HMM

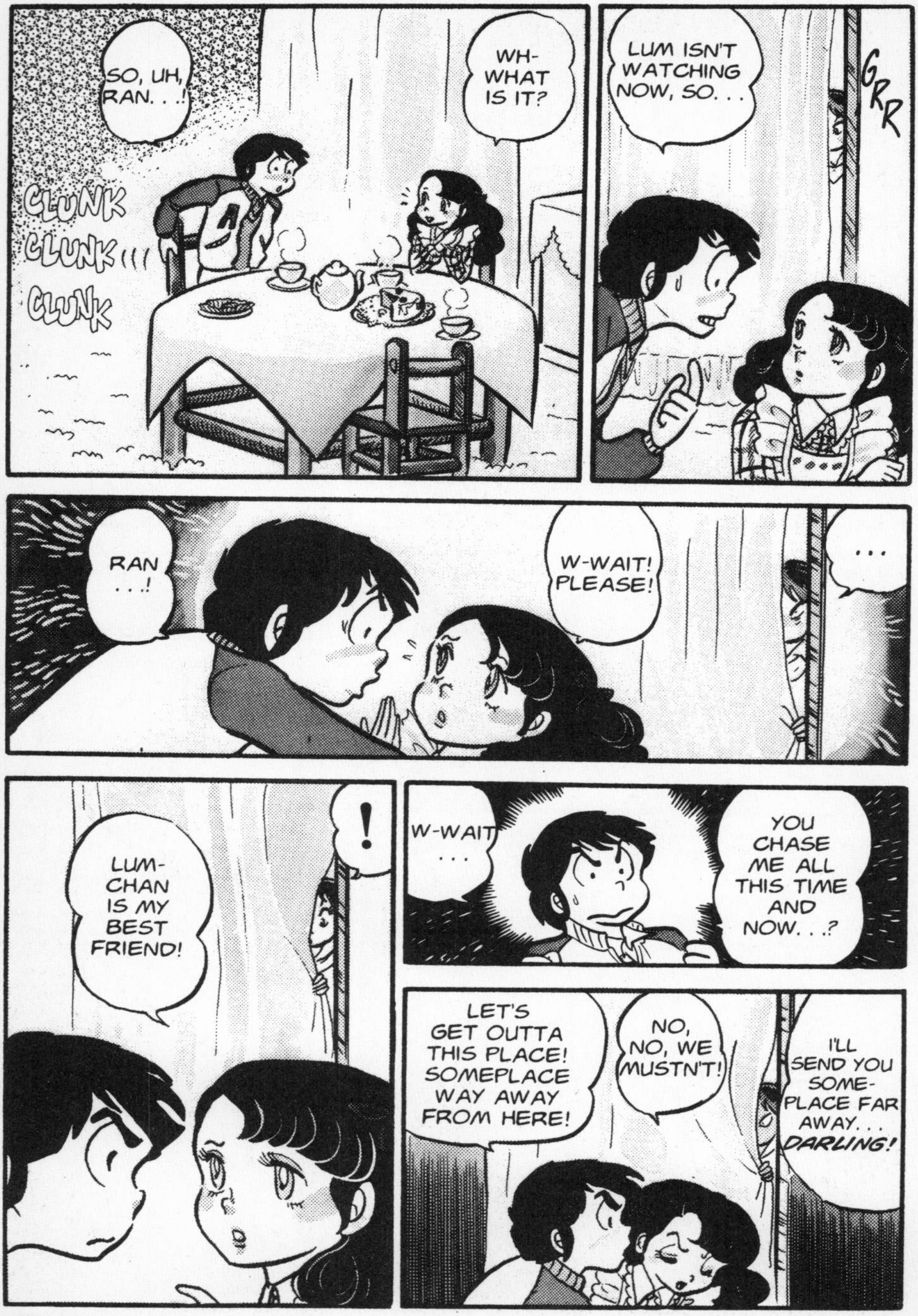
SO, UH, RAN. . .!
WH- WHAT IS IT?
CLUNK
CLUNK
CLUNK
LUM ISN'T WATCHING NOW, SO. . .
GRR
RAN . . .!
W-WAIT! PLEASE!
. . .
LUM- CHAN IS MY BEST FRIEND!
!
W-WAIT . . .
YOU CHASE ME ALL THIS TIME AND NOW. . .?
LET'S GET OUTTA THIS PLACE! SOMEPLACE WAY AWAY FROM HERE!
NO, NO, WE MUSTN'T!
I'LL SEND YOU SOME- PLACE FAR AWAY. . . DARLING!

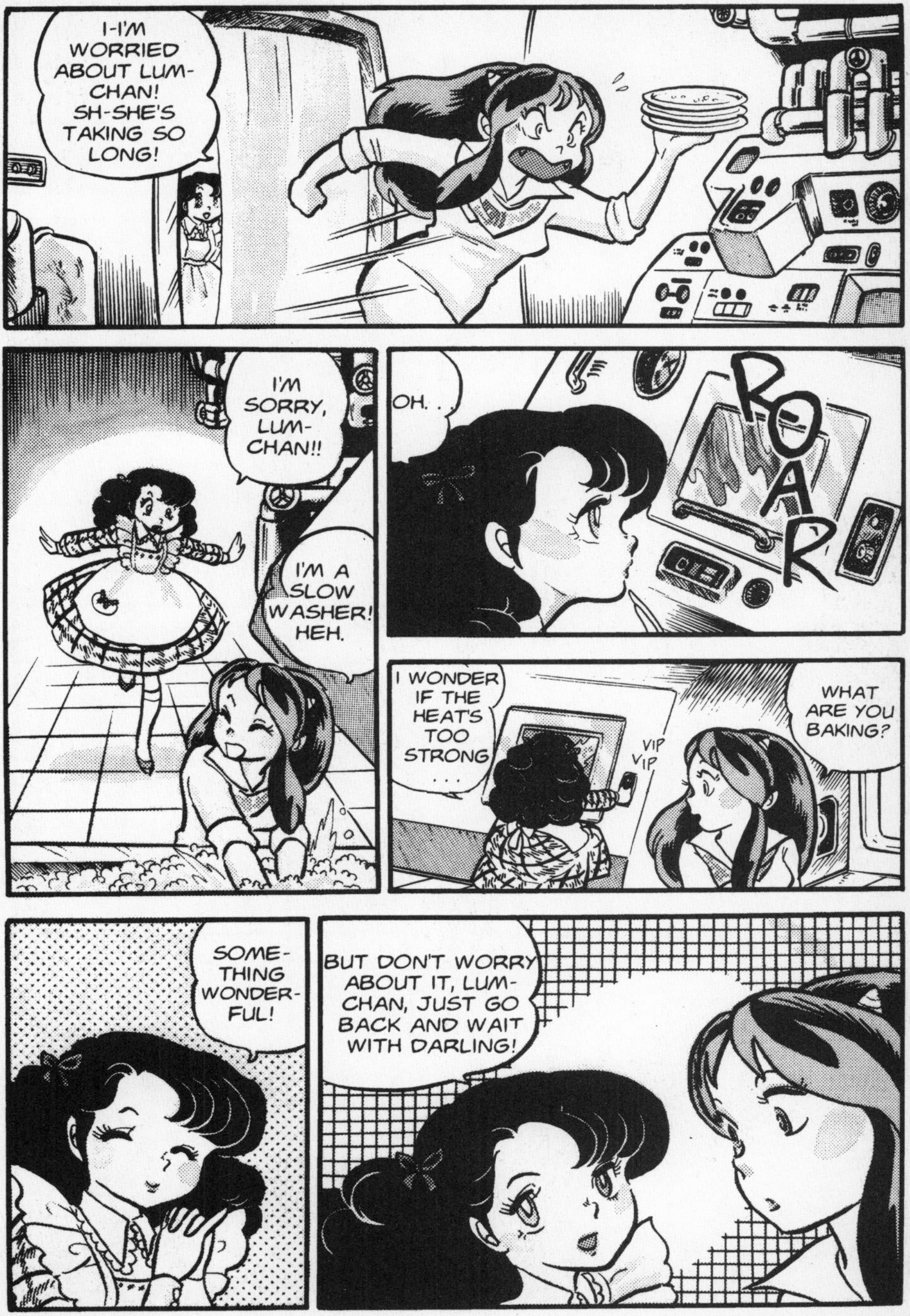
I-I'M WORRIED ABOUT LUM-CHAN! SH-SHE'S TAKING SO LONG!
I'M SORRY, LUM-CHAN!!
I'M A SLOW WASHER! HEH.
OH. . .
ROAR
I WONDER IF THE HEAT'S TOO STRONG . . .
VIP VIP
WHAT ARE YOU BAKING?
SOME-THING WONDER-FUL!
BUT DON'T WORRY ABOUT IT, LUM-CHAN, JUST GO BACK AND WAIT WITH DARLING!

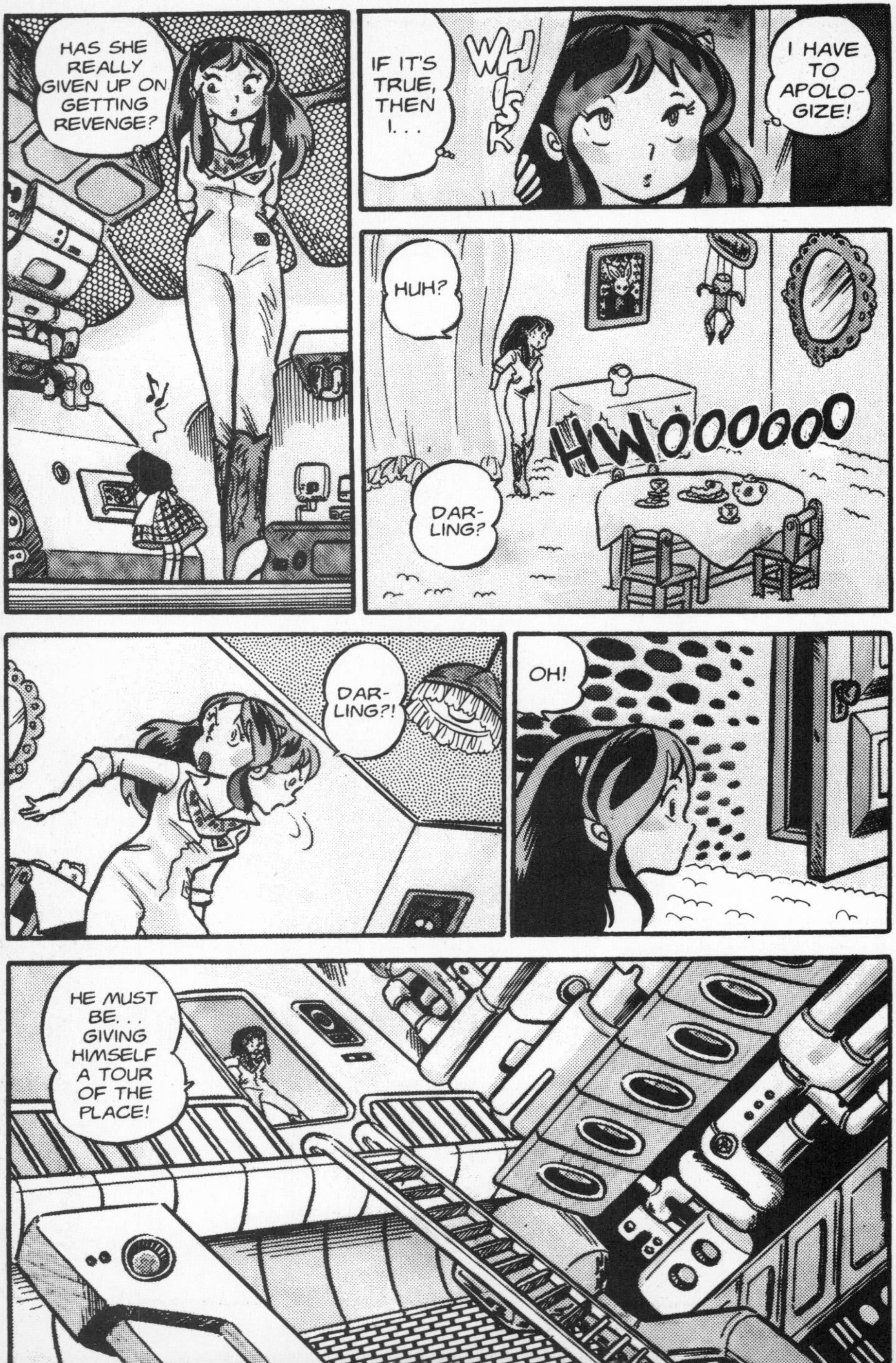
HAS SHE REALLY GIVEN UP ON GETTING REVENGE?
IF IT'S TRUE, THEN I. . .
WHISK
I HAVE TO APOLO-GIZE!
HUH?
HWOOOOOO
DAR-LING?
DAR-LING?!
OH!
HE MUST BE. . . GIVING HIMSELF A TOUR OF THE PLACE!

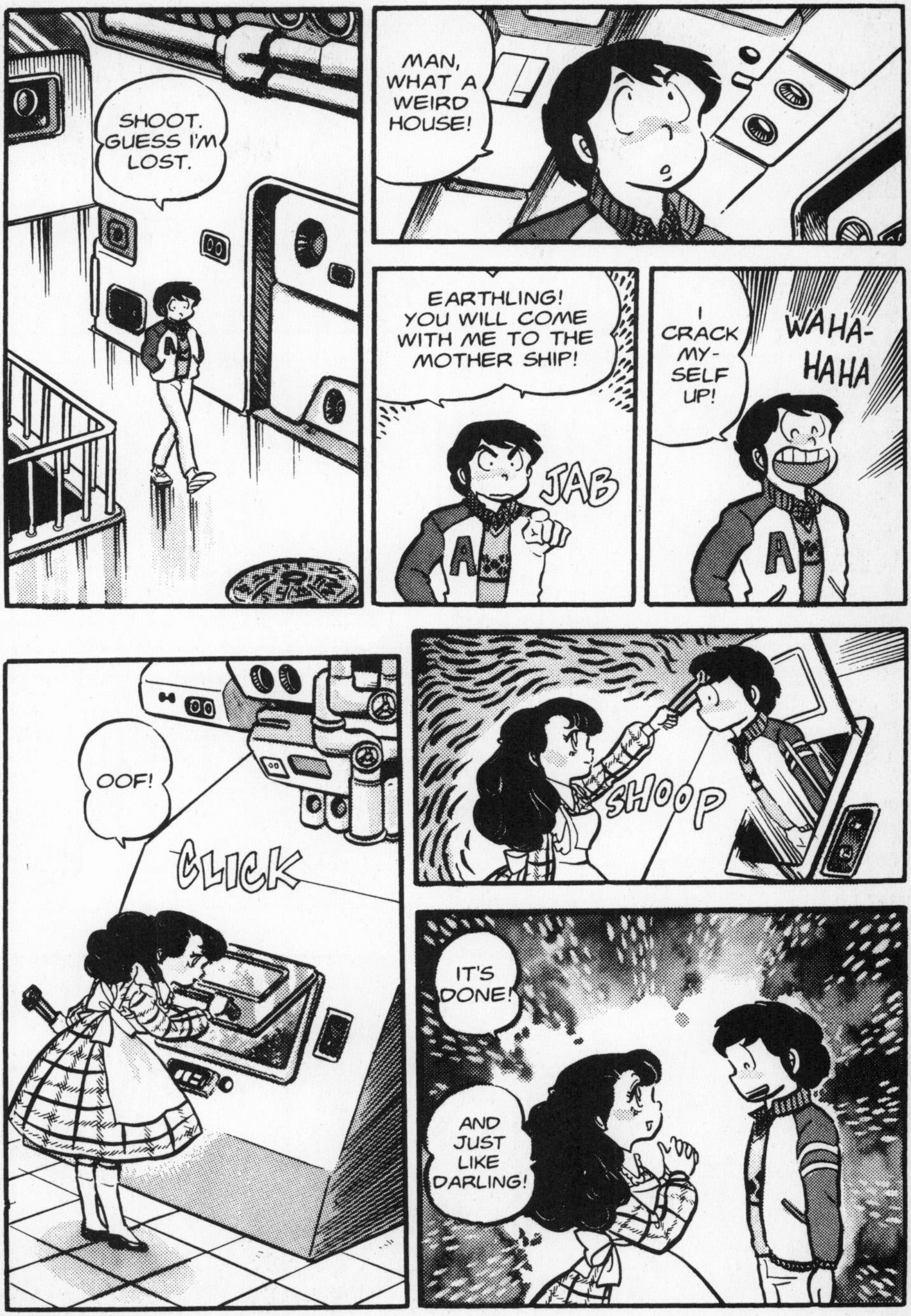
SHOOT. GUESS I'M LOST.
MAN, WHAT A WEIRD HOUSE!
EARTHLING! YOU WILL COME WITH ME TO THE MOTHER SHIP!
JAB
I CRACK MY-SELF UP!
WAHA-HAHA
OOF!
CLICK
SHOOP
IT'S DONE!
AND JUST LIKE DARLING!

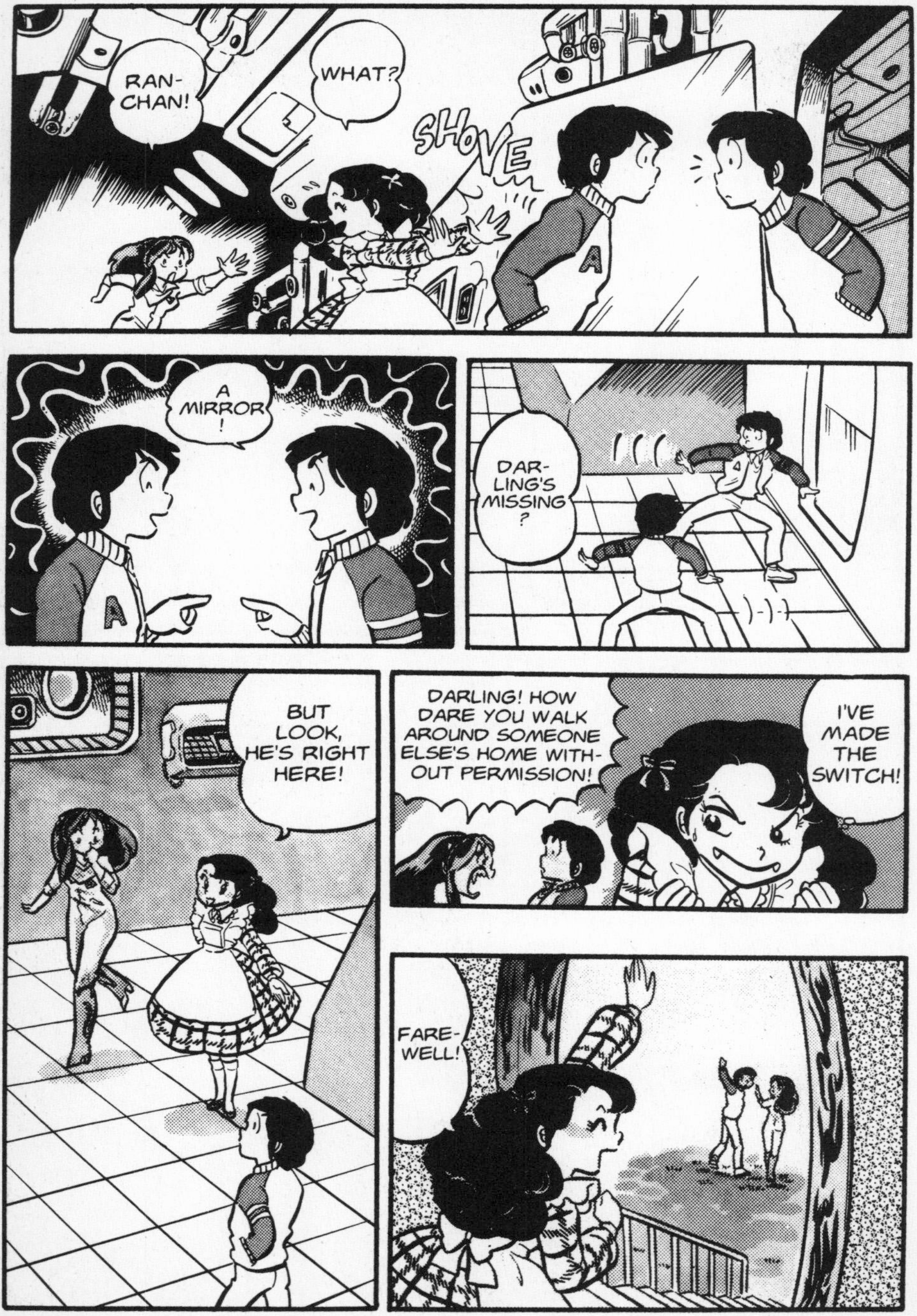
RAN-CHAN!
WHAT?
SHOVE
A MIRROR!
DAR-LING'S MISSING?
BUT LOOK, HE'S RIGHT HERE!
DARLING! HOW DARE YOU WALK AROUND SOMEONE ELSE'S HOME WITH-OUT PERMISSION!
I'VE MADE THE SWITCH!
FARE-WELL!

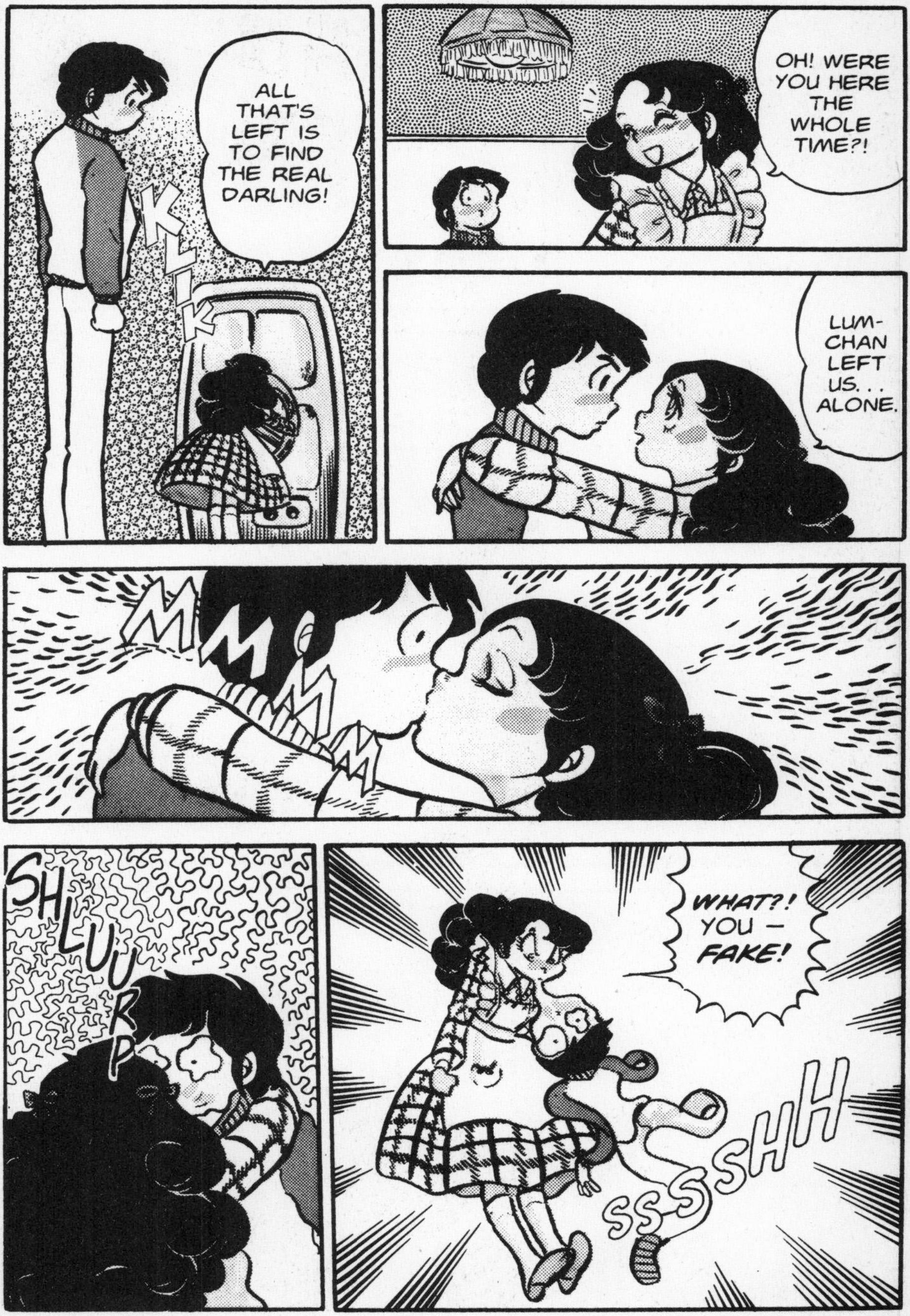
ALL THAT'S LEFT IS TO FIND THE REAL DARLING!
KLIK
OH! WERE YOU HERE THE WHOLE TIME?!
LUM-CHAN LEFT US. . . ALONE.
MMMM
SHLUURP
WHAT?! YOU - FAKE!
SSSSHH

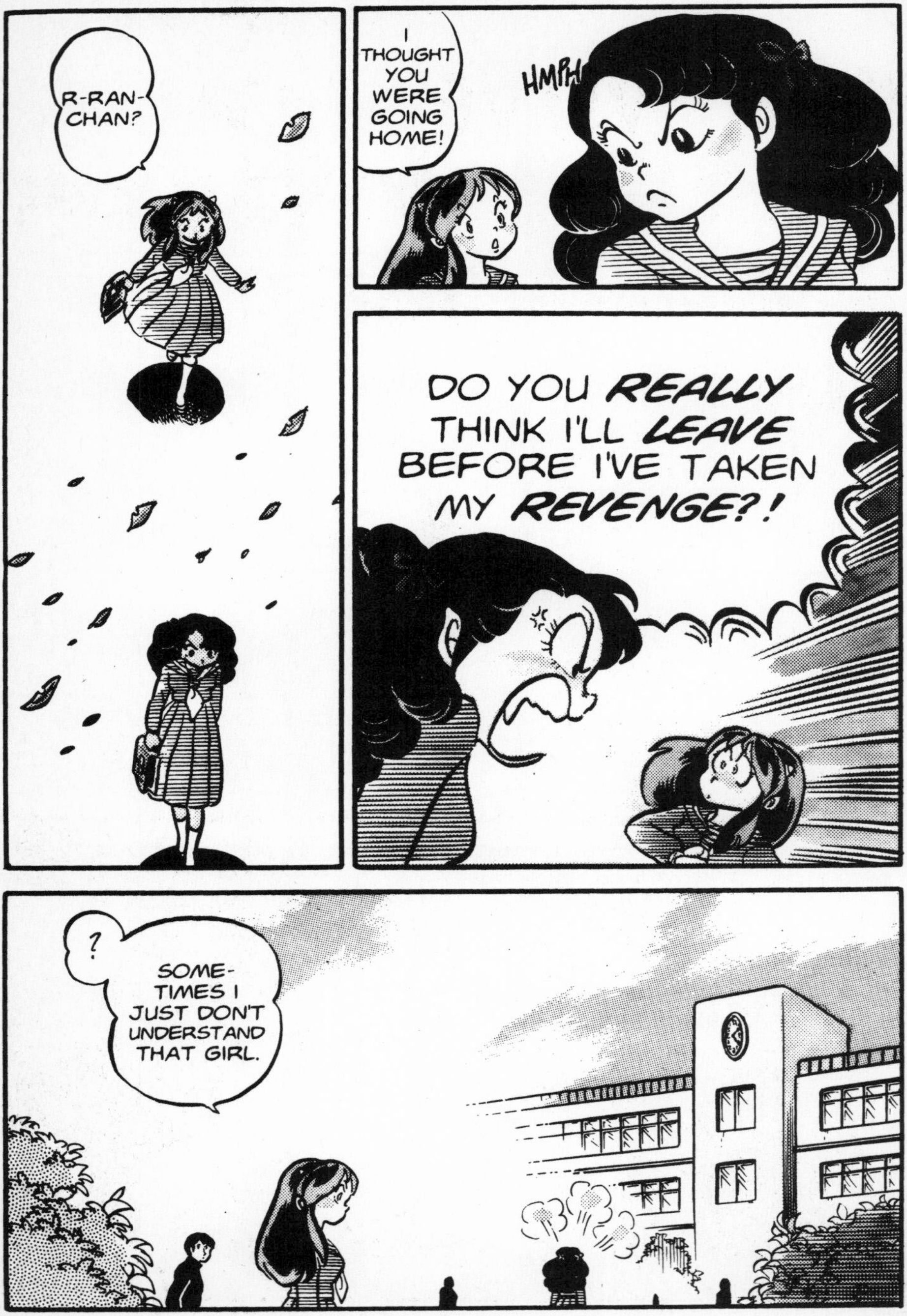
R-RAN-CHAN?
I THOUGHT YOU WERE GOING HOME!
HMPH
DO YOU REALLY THINK I'LL LEAVE BEFORE I'VE TAKEN MY REVENGE?!
?
SOME-TIMES I JUST DON'T UNDERSTAND THAT GIRL.

PART TWELVE
A NARROW ESCAPE FROM MEMORY LANE

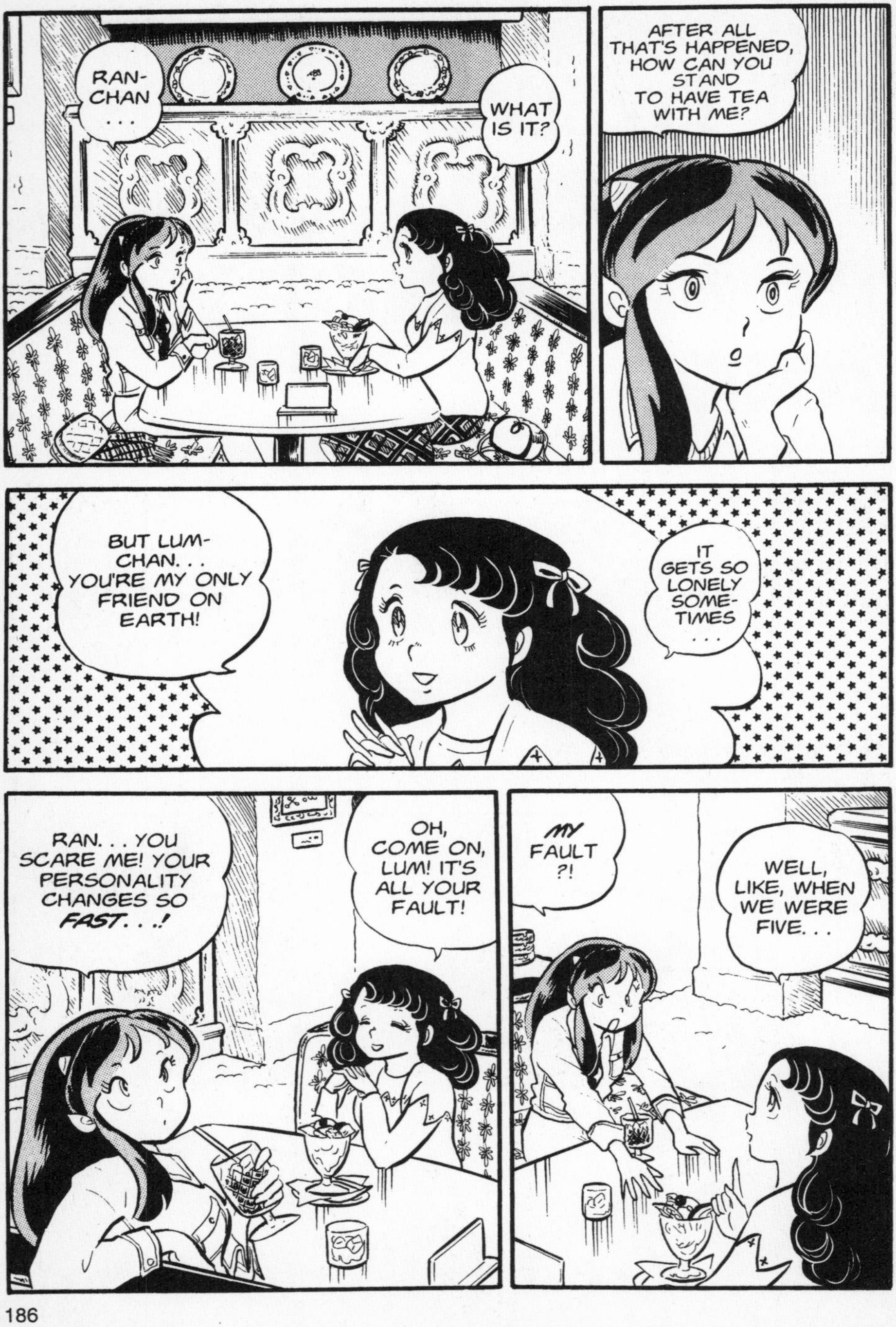
RAN-CHAN . . .
WHAT IS IT?
AFTER ALL THAT'S HAPPENED, HOW CAN YOU STAND TO HAVE TEA WITH ME?
BUT LUM-CHAN. . . YOU'RE MY ONLY FRIEND ON EARTH!
IT GETS SO LONELY SOME-TIMES . . .
RAN. . . YOU SCARE ME! YOUR PERSONALITY CHANGES SO FAST. . .!
OH, COME ON, LUM! IT'S ALL YOUR FAULT!
MY FAULT ?!
WELL, LIKE, WHEN WE WERE FIVE. . .

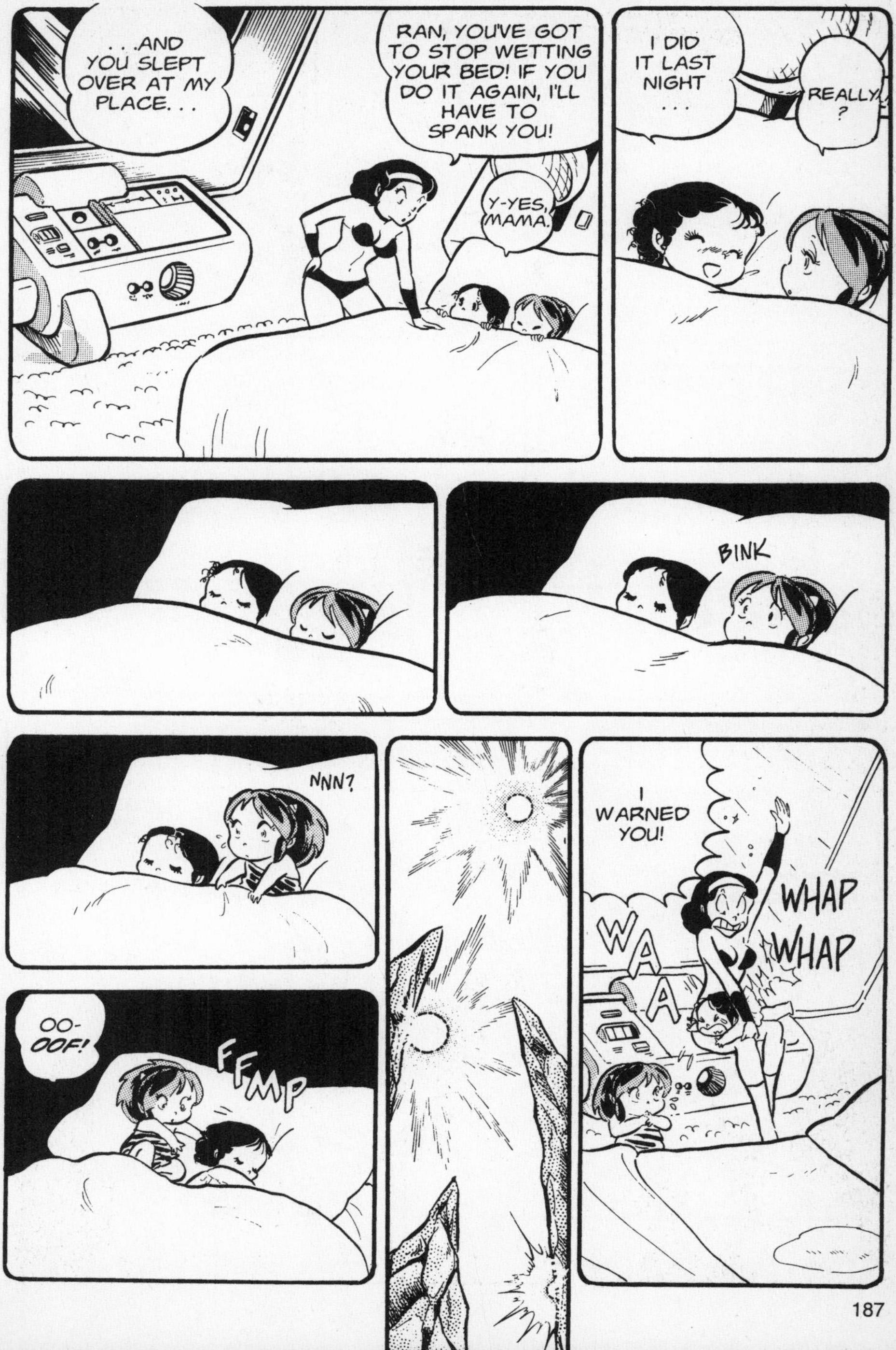

. . .AND YOU SLEPT OVER AT MY PLACE. . .
RAN, YOU'VE GOT TO STOP WETTING YOUR BED! IF YOU DO IT AGAIN, I'LL HAVE TO SPANK YOU!
Y-YES, MAMA.
I DID IT LAST NIGHT . . .
REALLY ?
BINK
NNN?
OO-OOF!
FFMP
I WARNED YOU!
WHAP
WHAP
WAA

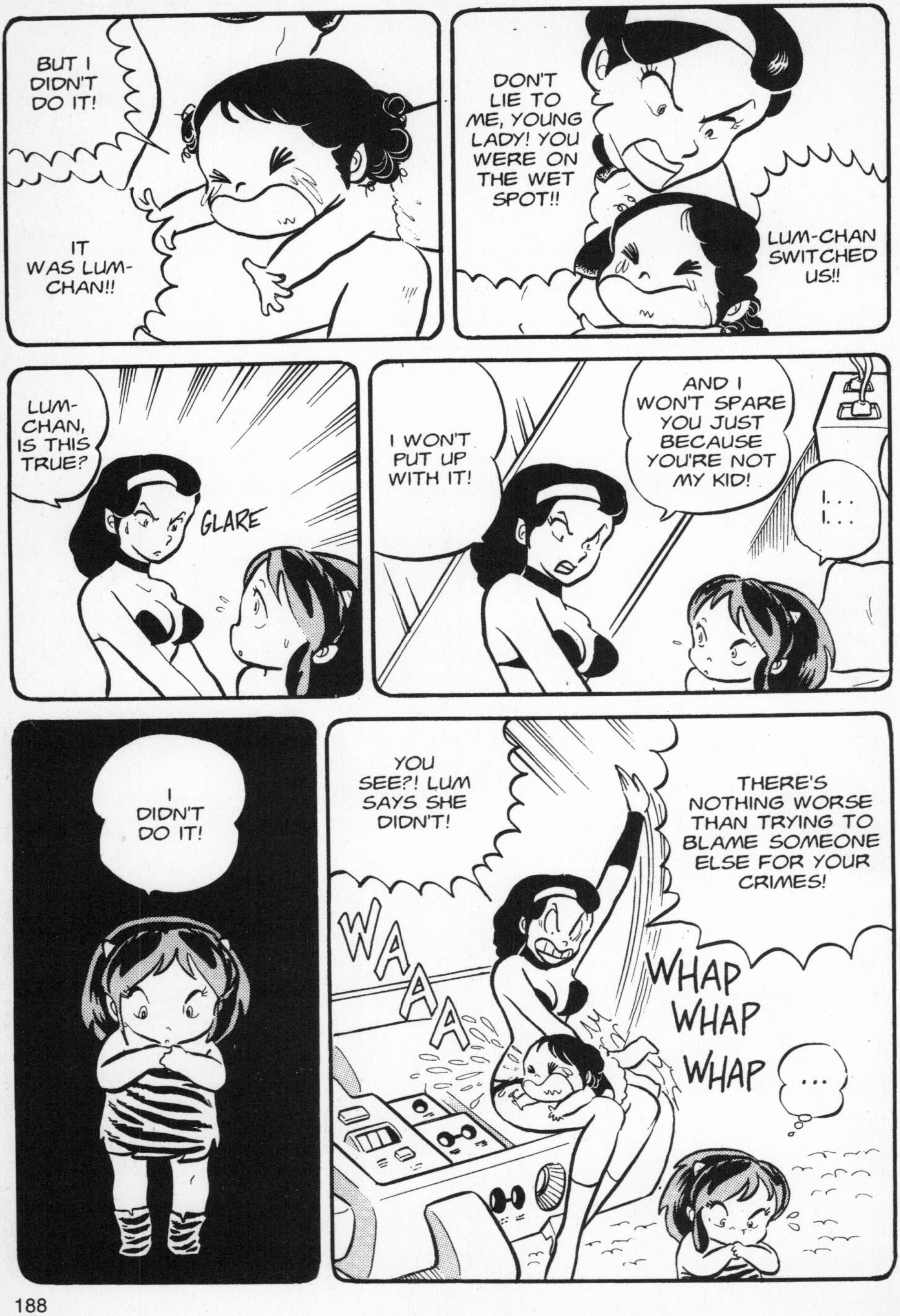

BUT I DIDN'T DO IT!
IT WAS LUM-CHAN!!
DON'T LIE TO ME, YOUNG LADY! YOU WERE ON THE WET SPOT!!
LUM-CHAN SWITCHED US!!
LUM-CHAN, IS THIS TRUE?
GLARE
I WON'T PUT UP WITH IT!
AND I WON'T SPARE YOU JUST BECAUSE YOU'RE NOT MY KID!
I... I...
I DIDN'T DO IT!
YOU SEE?! LUM SAYS SHE DIDN'T!
THERE'S NOTHING WORSE THAN TRYING TO BLAME SOMEONE ELSE FOR YOUR CRIMES!
WAAAA
WHAP WHAP WHAP
...

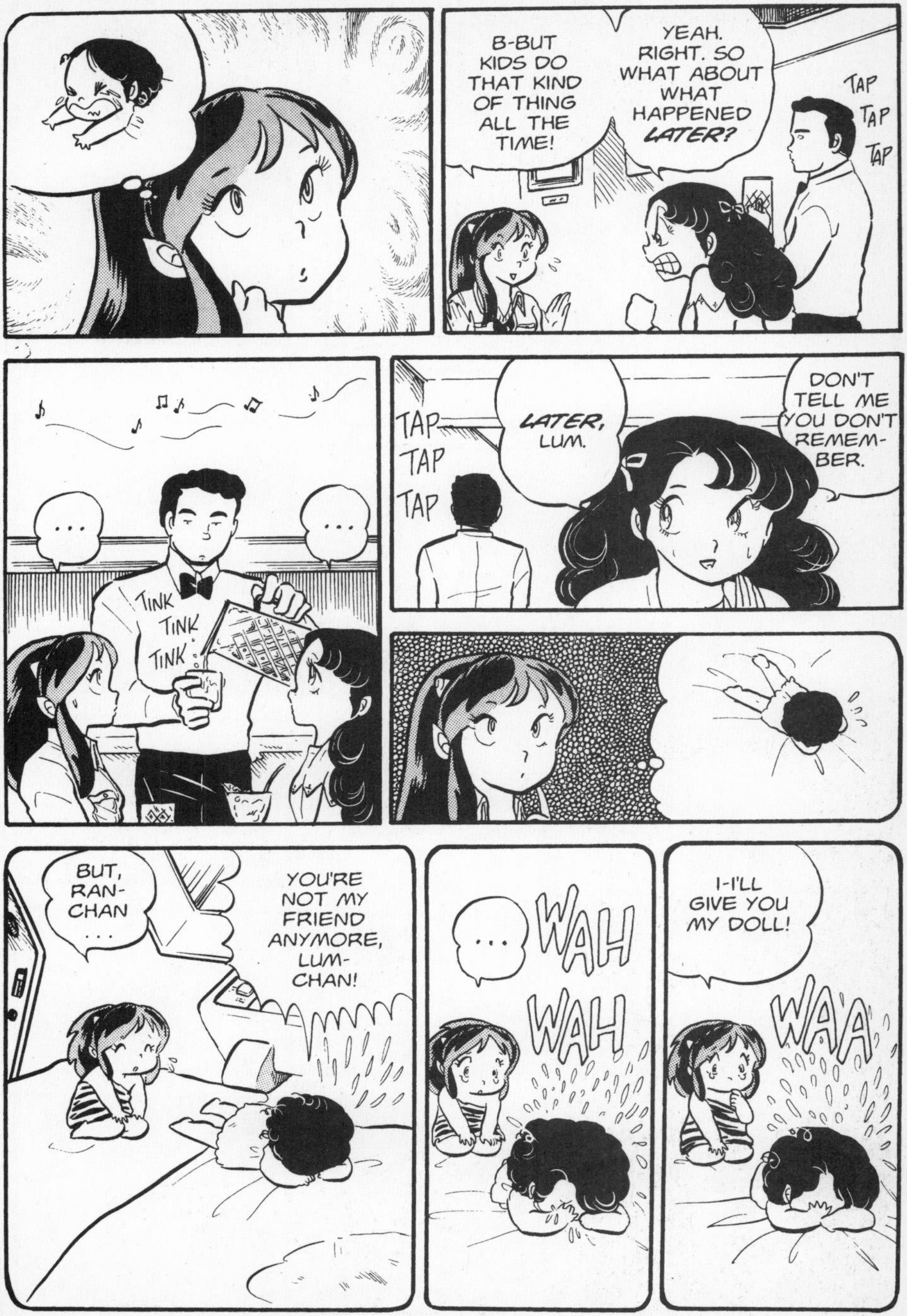

B-BUT KIDS DO THAT KIND OF THING ALL THE TIME!
YEAH. RIGHT. SO WHAT ABOUT WHAT HAPPENED *LATER?*
TAP TAP TAP
♪ ♫ ♪ ♫ ♪ ♪
...
...
TINK TINK TINK
TAP TAP TAP
LATER, LUM.
DON'T TELL ME YOU DON'T REMEMBER.
BUT, RAN-CHAN ...
YOU'RE NOT MY FRIEND ANYMORE, LUM-CHAN!
...
WAH WAH
I-I'LL GIVE YOU MY DOLL!
WAA

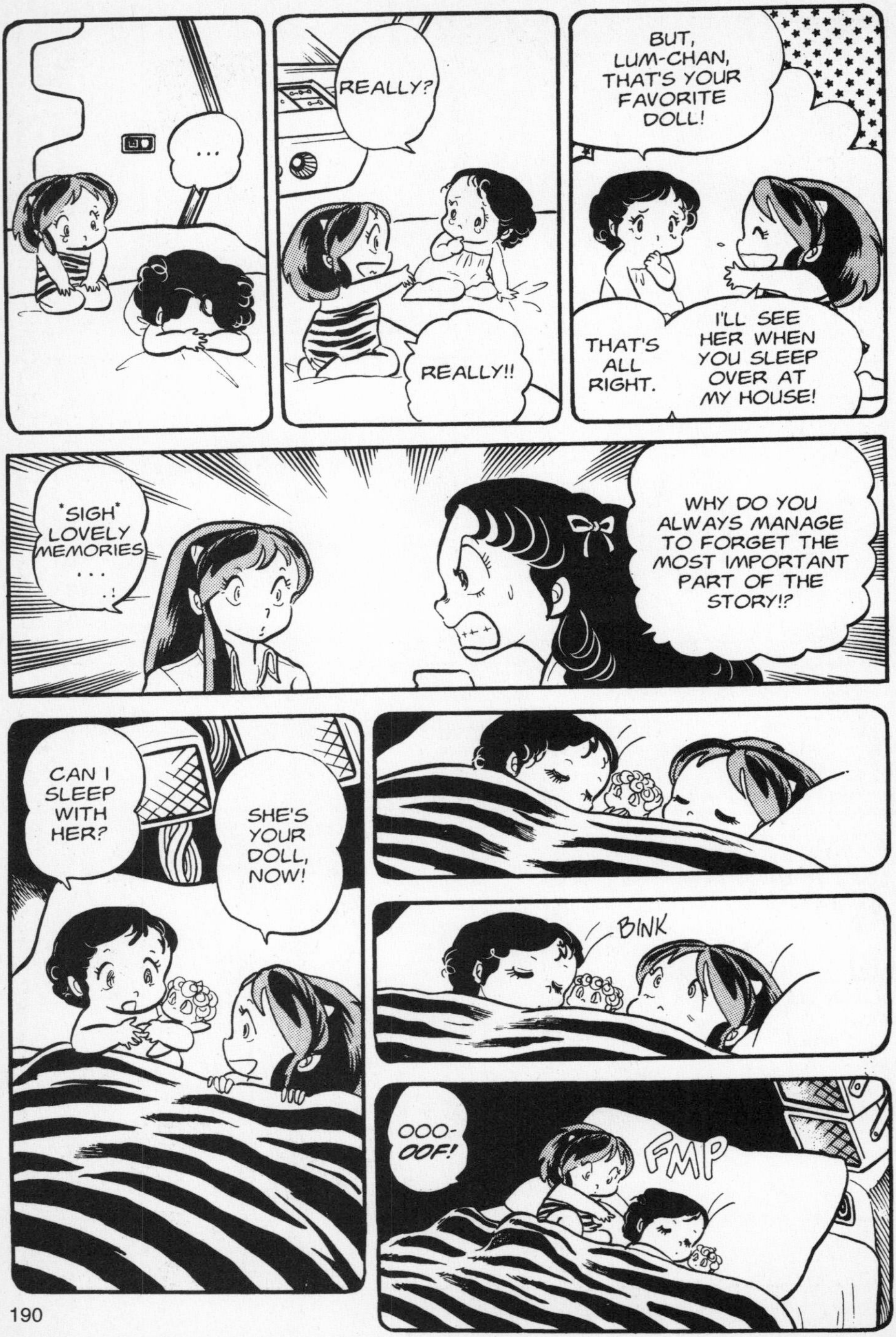
...
REALLY?
REALLY!!
BUT, LUM-CHAN, THAT'S YOUR FAVORITE DOLL!
THAT'S ALL RIGHT.
I'LL SEE HER WHEN YOU SLEEP OVER AT MY HOUSE!
SIGH LOVELY MEMORIES . . .
. !
WHY DO YOU ALWAYS MANAGE TO FORGET THE MOST IMPORTANT PART OF THE STORY!?
CAN I SLEEP WITH HER?
SHE'S YOUR DOLL, NOW!
BINK
OOO-OOF!
FMP

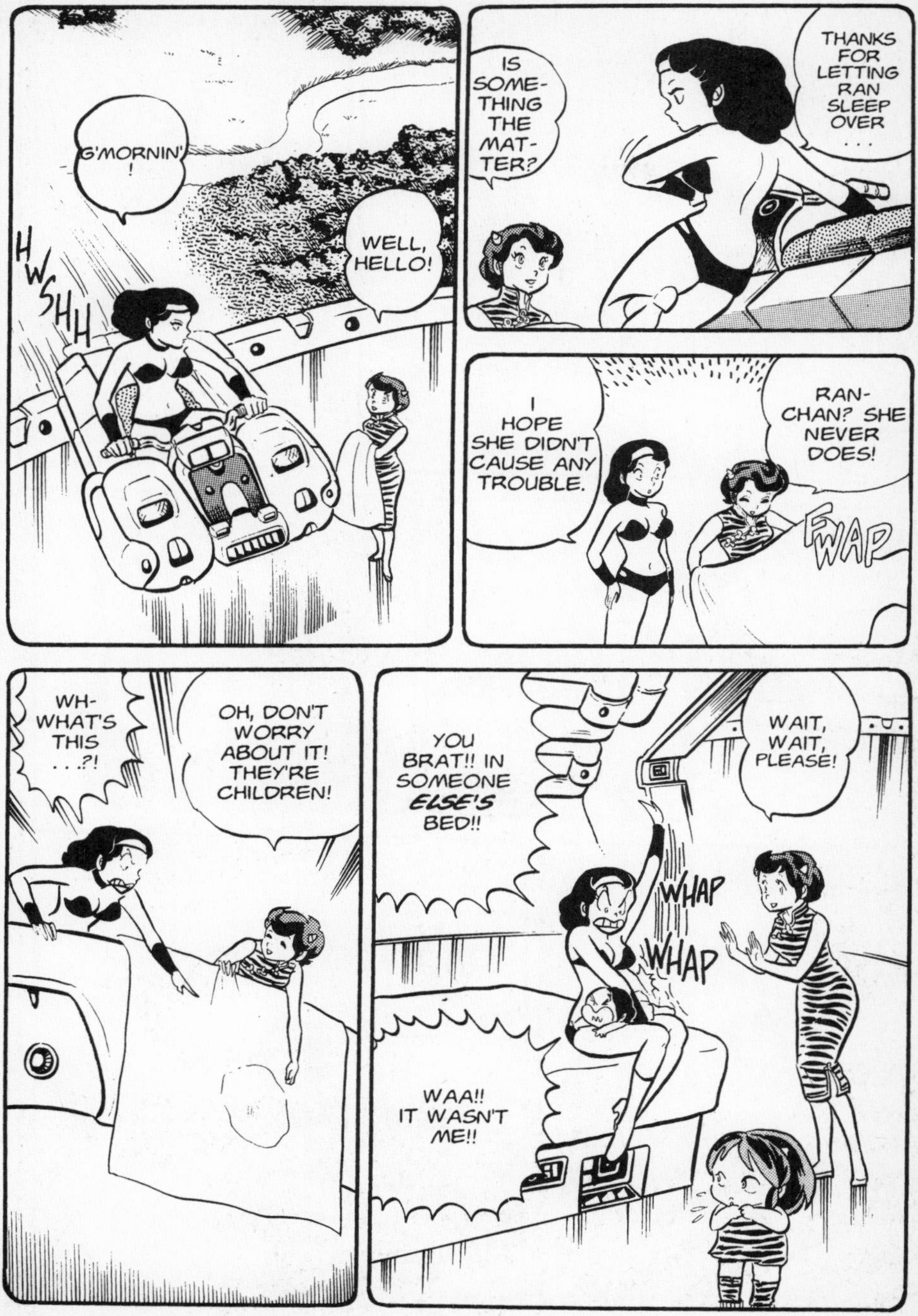
G'MORNIN'!
WELL, HELLO!
HWSHH
IS SOMETHING THE MATTER?
THANKS FOR LETTING RAN SLEEP OVER . . .
I HOPE SHE DIDN'T CAUSE ANY TROUBLE.
RAN-CHAN? SHE NEVER DOES!
FWAP
WH-WHAT'S THIS . . .?!
OH, DON'T WORRY ABOUT IT! THEY'RE CHILDREN!
YOU BRAT!! IN SOMEONE *ELSE'S* BED!!
WAIT, WAIT, PLEASE!
WHAP
WHAP
WAA!! IT WASN'T ME!!

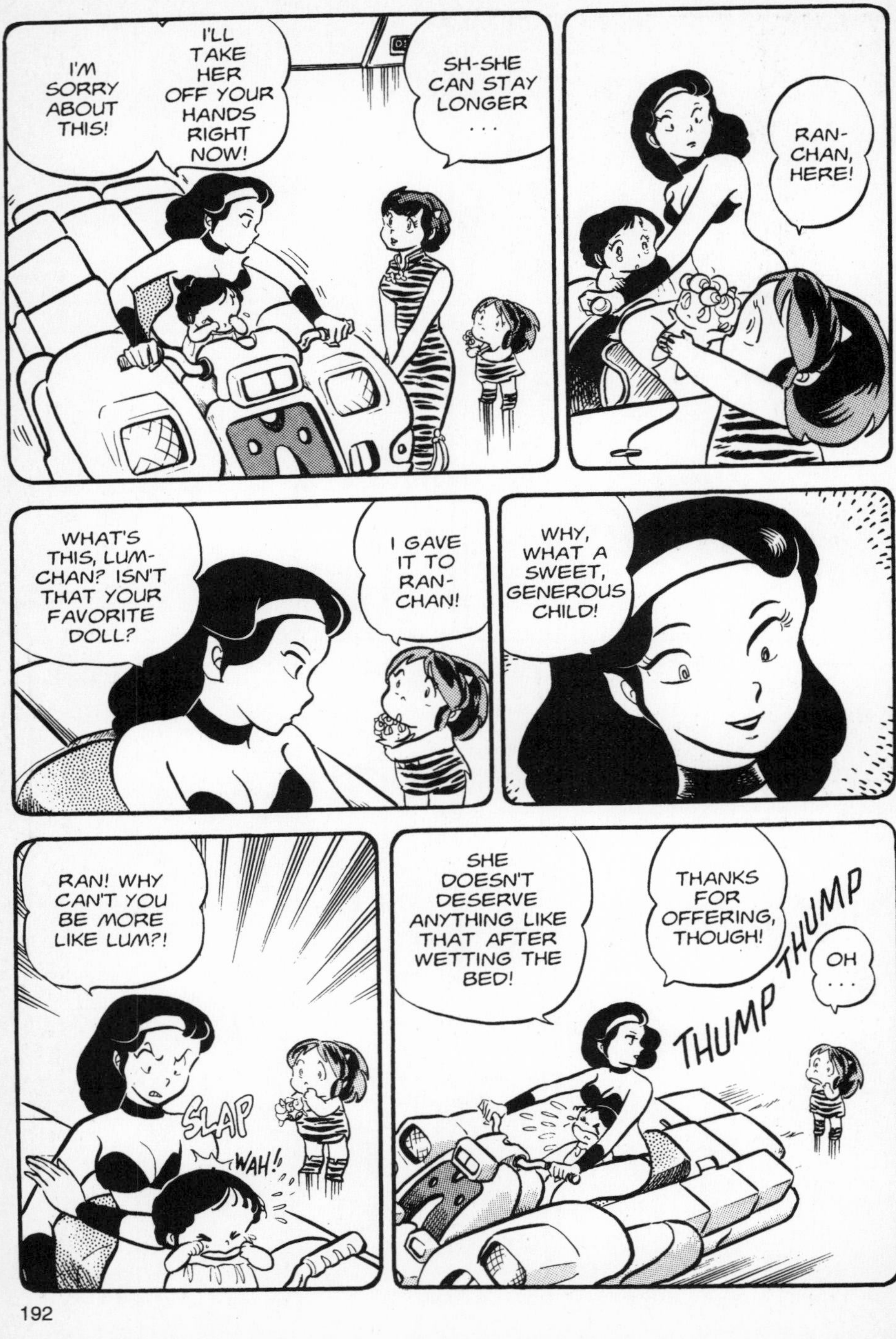
I'M SORRY ABOUT THIS!
I'LL TAKE HER OFF YOUR HANDS RIGHT NOW!
SH-SHE CAN STAY LONGER . . .
RAN-CHAN, HERE!
WHAT'S THIS, LUM-CHAN? ISN'T THAT YOUR FAVORITE DOLL?
I GAVE IT TO RAN-CHAN!
WHY, WHAT A SWEET, GENEROUS CHILD!
RAN! WHY CAN'T YOU BE MORE LIKE LUM?!
SLAP
WAH!!
SHE DOESN'T DESERVE ANYTHING LIKE THAT AFTER WETTING THE BED!
THANKS FOR OFFERING, THOUGH!
THUMP THUMP
OH . . .

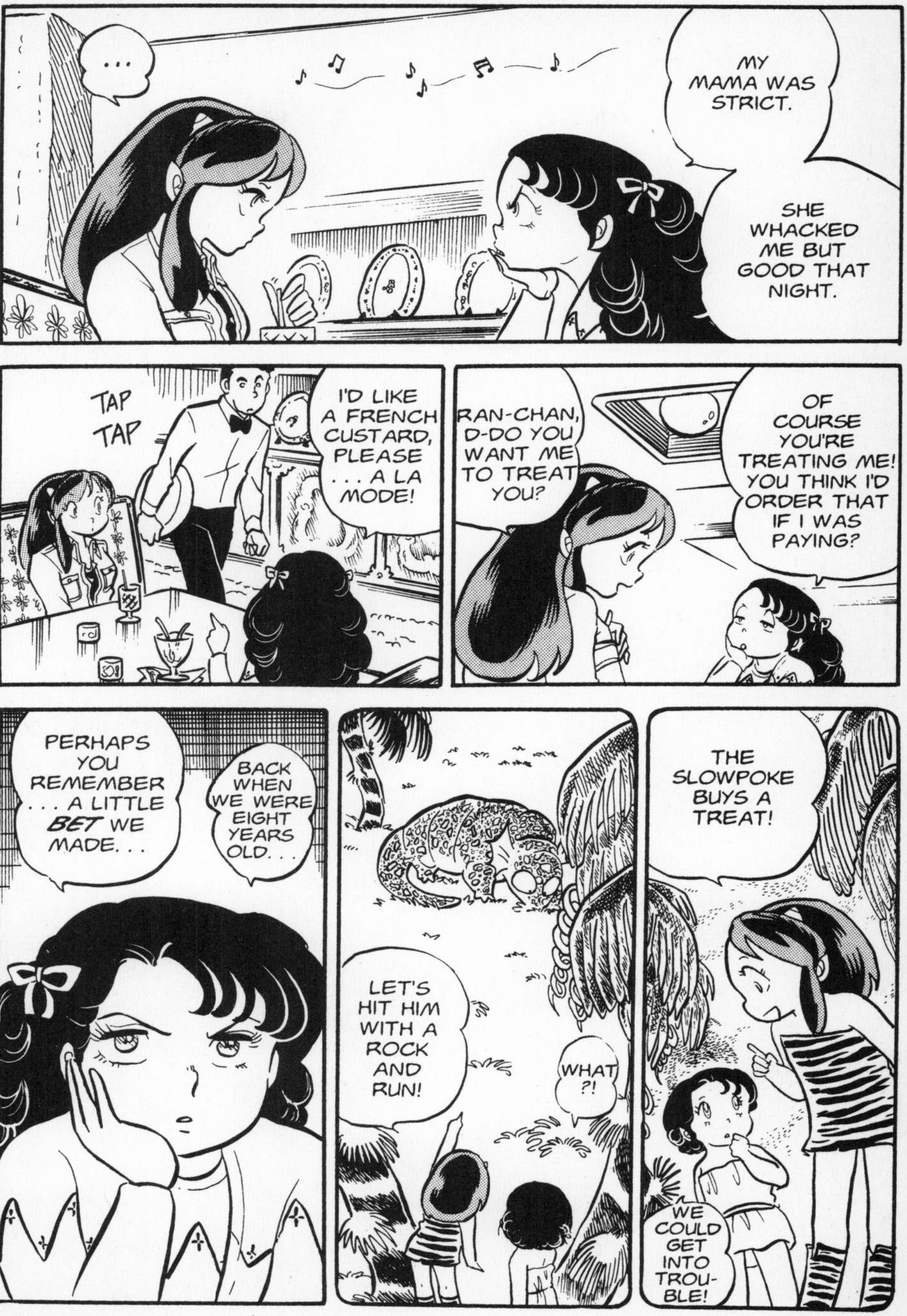
...
MY MAMA WAS STRICT.
SHE WHACKED ME BUT GOOD THAT NIGHT.
TAP TAP
I'D LIKE A FRENCH CUSTARD, PLEASE . . . A LA MODE!
RAN-CHAN, D-DO YOU WANT ME TO TREAT YOU?
OF COURSE YOU'RE TREATING ME! YOU THINK I'D ORDER THAT IF I WAS PAYING?
PERHAPS YOU REMEMBER . . . A LITTLE BET WE MADE. . .
BACK WHEN WE WERE EIGHT YEARS OLD. . .
LET'S HIT HIM WITH A ROCK AND RUN!
WHAT ?!
THE SLOWPOKE BUYS A TREAT!
WE COULD GET INTO TROU-BLE!

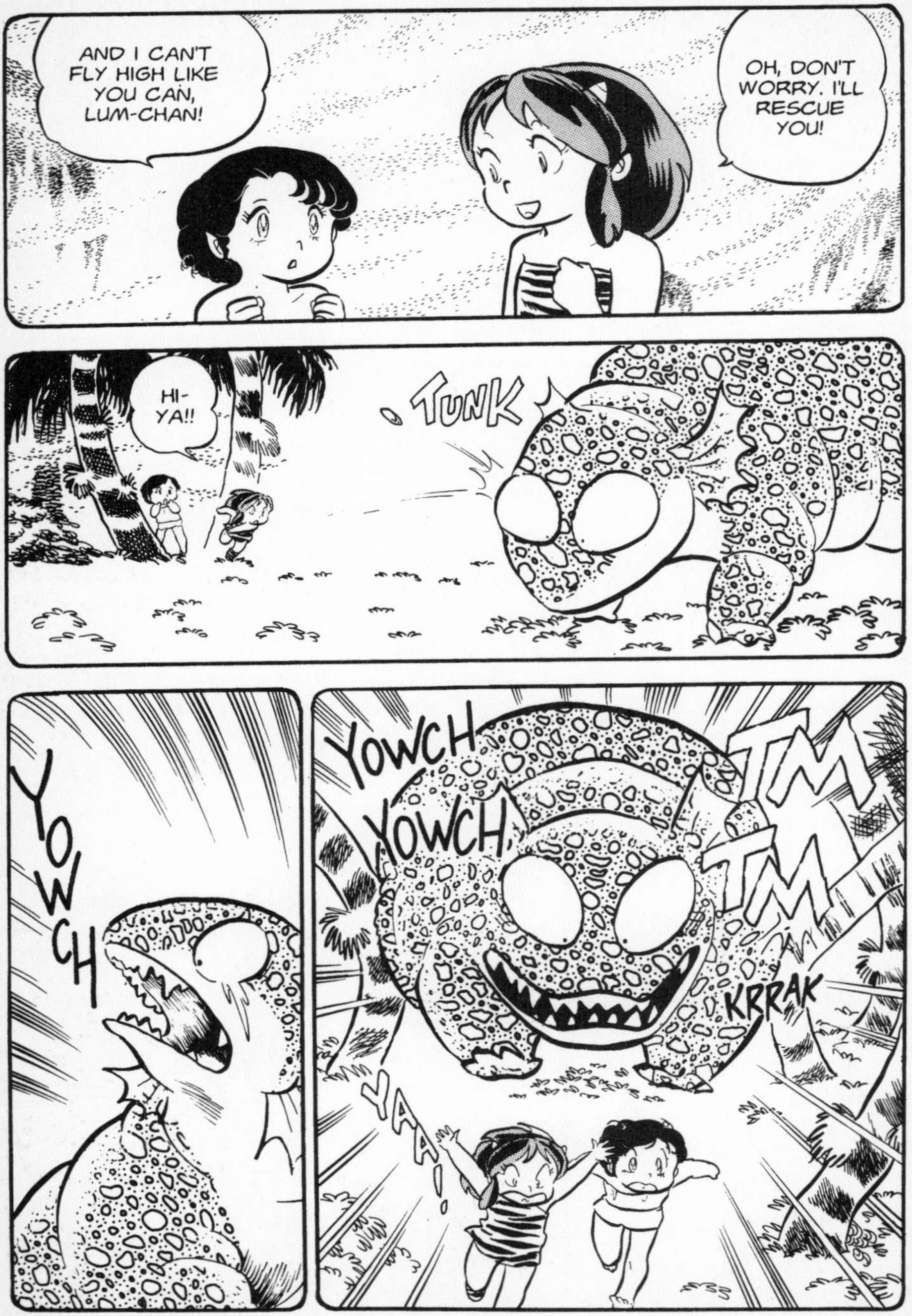
AND I CAN'T FLY HIGH LIKE YOU CAN, LUM-CHAN!
OH, DON'T WORRY. I'LL RESCUE YOU!
HI-YA!!
TUNK
YOWCH
YOWCH
YOWCH,
TM
TM
KRRAK
YAA!

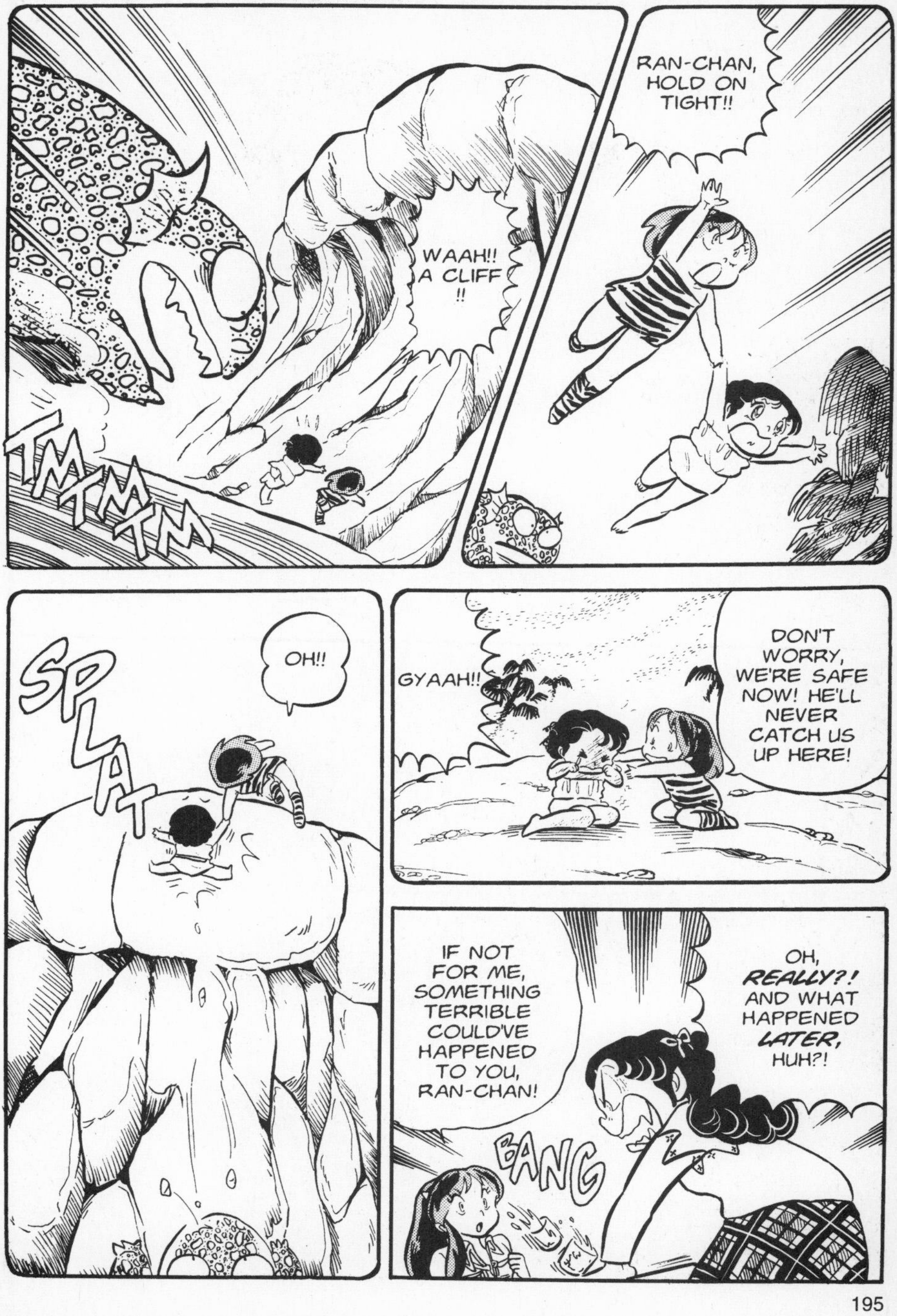
WAAH!! A CLIFF !!
TMTMTM
RAN-CHAN, HOLD ON TIGHT!!
SPLAT
OH!!
GYAAH!!
DON'T WORRY, WE'RE SAFE NOW! HE'LL NEVER CATCH US UP HERE!
IF NOT FOR ME, SOMETHING TERRIBLE COULD'VE HAPPENED TO YOU, RAN-CHAN!
OH, REALLY?! AND WHAT HAPPENED LATER, HUH?!
BANG

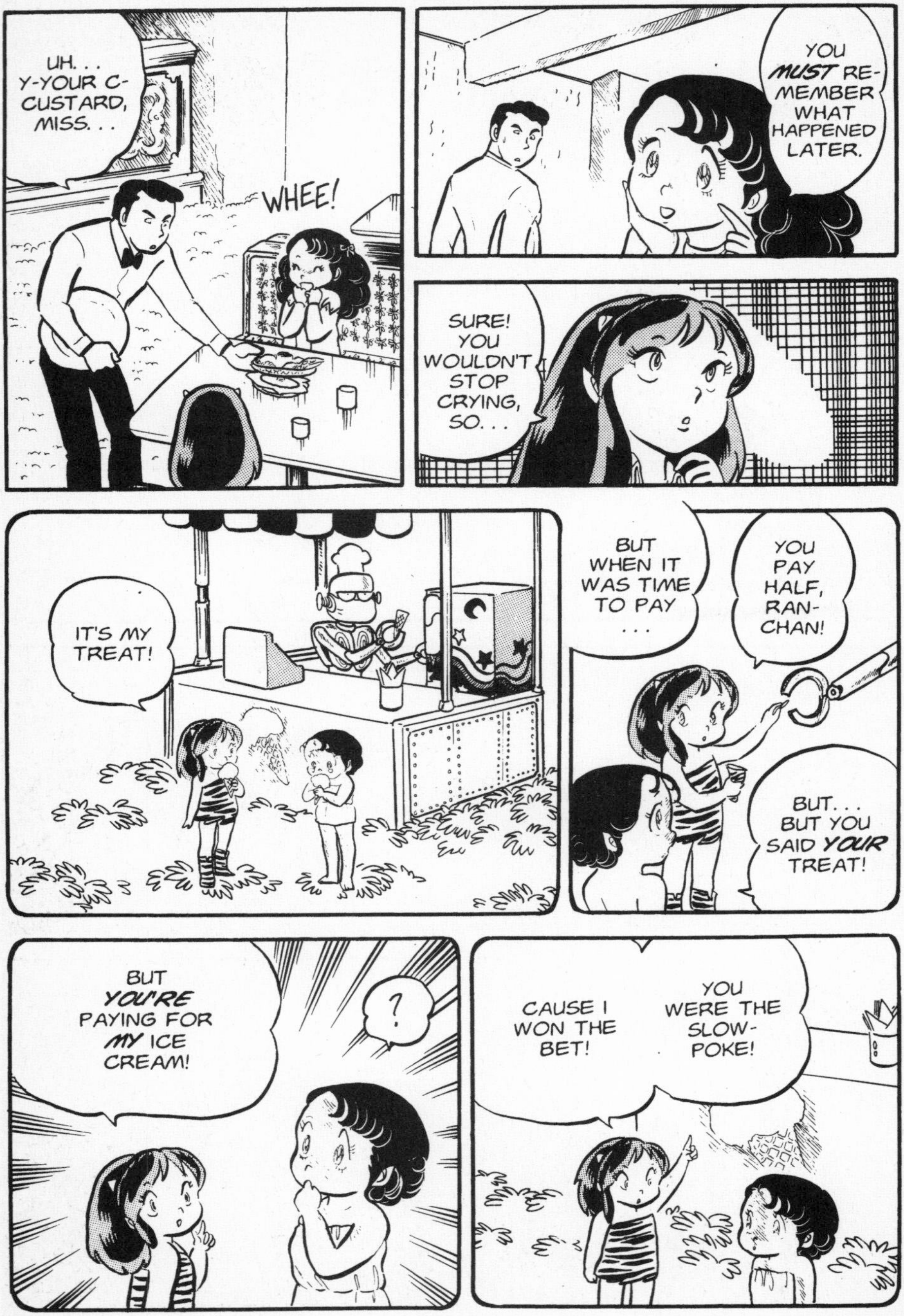
UH. . . Y-YOUR C-CUSTARD, MISS. . .
WHEE!
YOU MUST REMEMBER WHAT HAPPENED LATER.
SURE! YOU WOULDN'T STOP CRYING, SO. . .
IT'S MY TREAT!
BUT WHEN IT WAS TIME TO PAY . . .
YOU PAY HALF, RAN-CHAN!
BUT. . . BUT YOU SAID YOUR TREAT!
BUT YOU'RE PAYING FOR MY ICE CREAM!
?
CAUSE I WON THE BET!
YOU WERE THE SLOW-POKE!

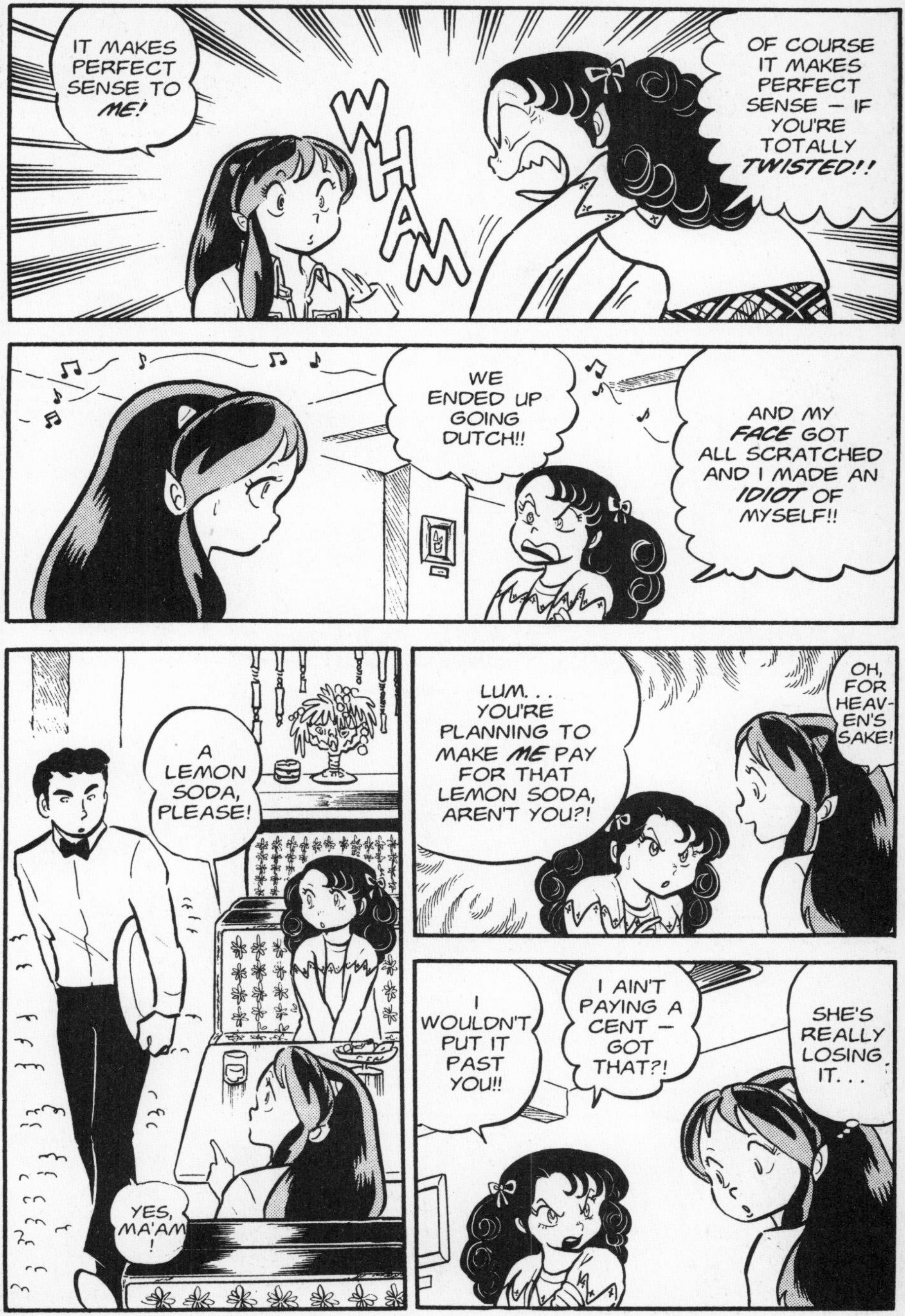
IT MAKES PERFECT SENSE TO ME!
WHAM
OF COURSE IT MAKES PERFECT SENSE — IF YOU'RE TOTALLY TWISTED!!
WE ENDED UP GOING DUTCH!!
AND MY FACE GOT ALL SCRATCHED AND I MADE AN IDIOT OF MYSELF!!
A LEMON SODA, PLEASE!
YES, MA'AM!
LUM. . . YOU'RE PLANNING TO MAKE ME PAY FOR THAT LEMON SODA, AREN'T YOU?!
OH, FOR HEAV-EN'S SAKE!
I WOULDN'T PUT IT PAST YOU!!
I AIN'T PAYING A CENT — GOT THAT?!
SHE'S REALLY LOSING IT. . .

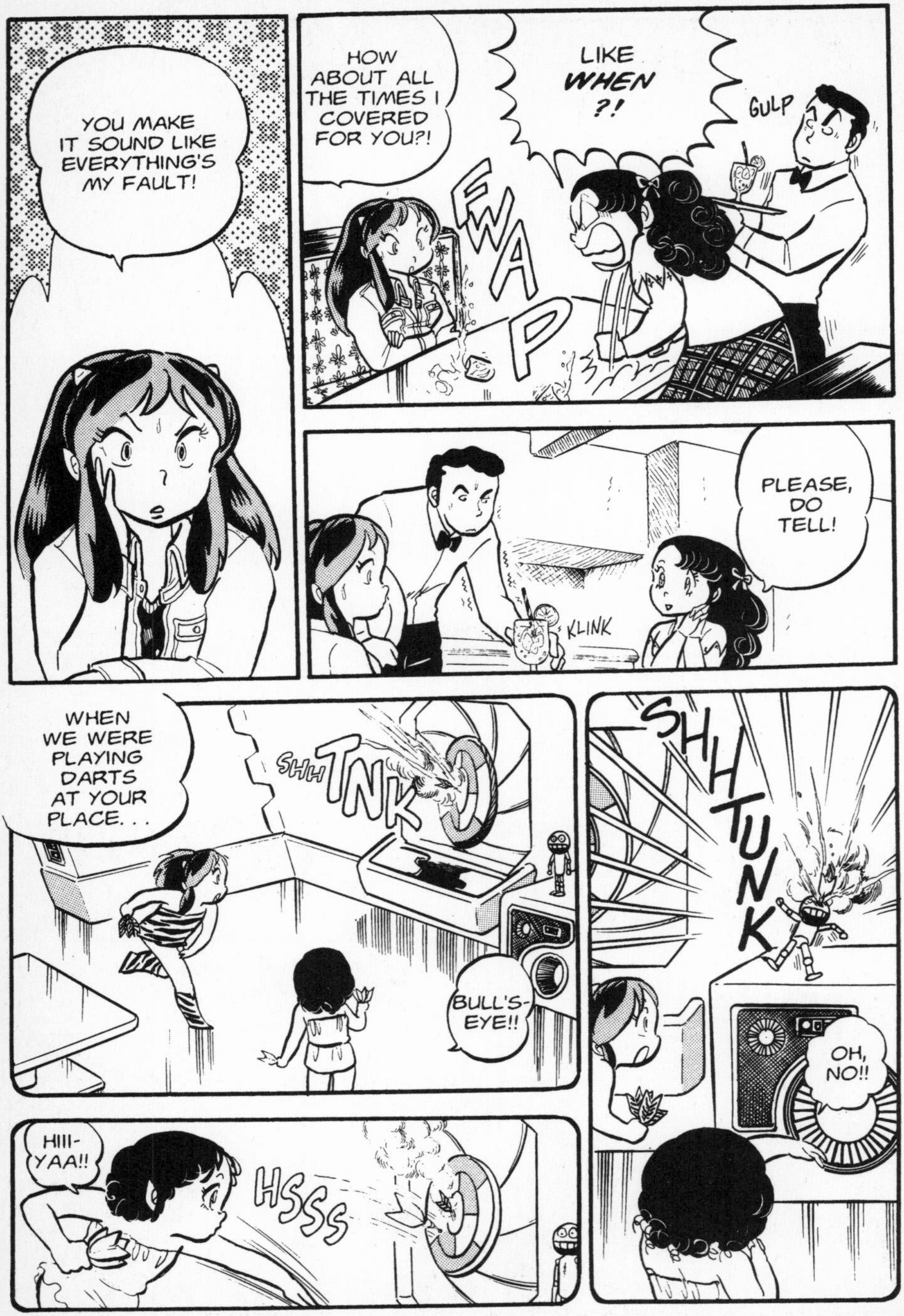
YOU MAKE IT SOUND LIKE EVERYTHING'S MY FAULT!
HOW ABOUT ALL THE TIMES I COVERED FOR YOU?!
LIKE WHEN ?!
GULP
FWAP
PLEASE, DO TELL!
KLINK
WHEN WE WERE PLAYING DARTS AT YOUR PLACE. . .
SHH TNK
BULL'S-EYE!!
SHHTUNK
OH, NO!!
HIII-YAA!!
HSSS

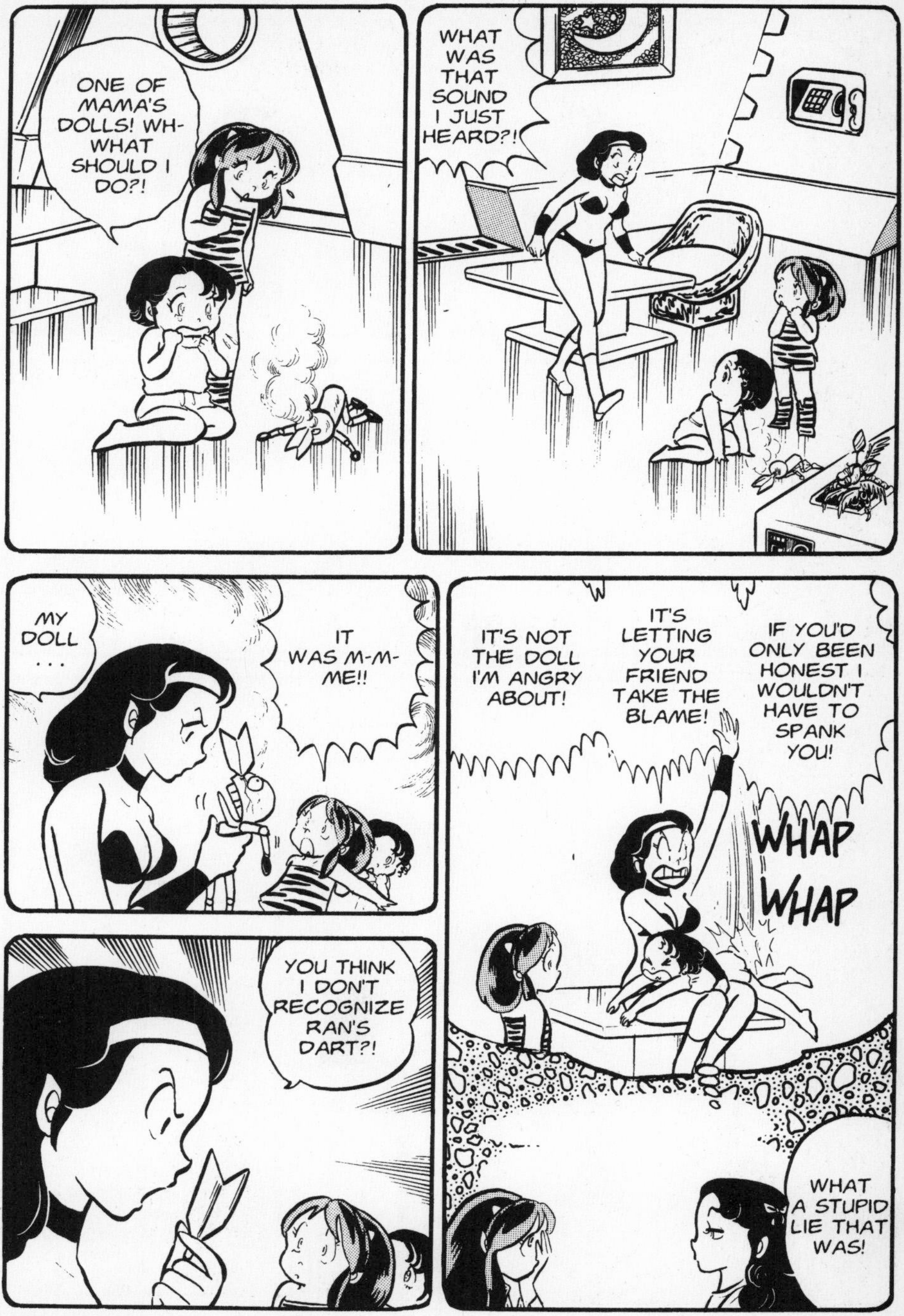
ONE OF MAMA'S DOLLS! WH-WHAT SHOULD I DO?!
WHAT WAS THAT SOUND I JUST HEARD?!
MY DOLL . . .
IT WAS M-M-ME!!
YOU THINK I DON'T RECOGNIZE RAN'S DART?!
IT'S NOT THE DOLL I'M ANGRY ABOUT!
IT'S LETTING YOUR FRIEND TAKE THE BLAME!
IF YOU'D ONLY BEEN HONEST I WOULDN'T HAVE TO SPANK YOU!
WHAP
WHAP
WHAT A STUPID LIE THAT WAS!

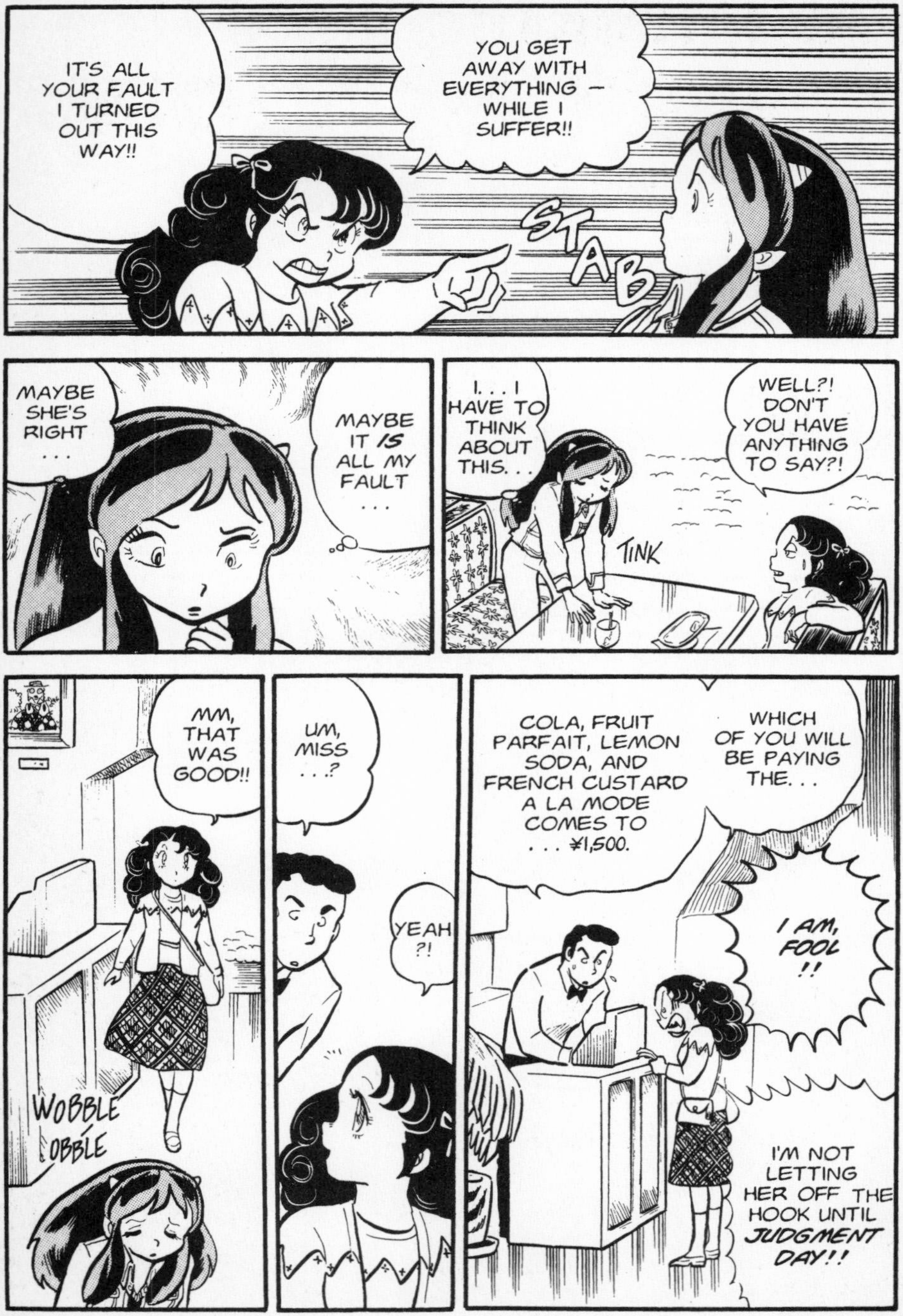
IT'S ALL YOUR FAULT I TURNED OUT THIS WAY!!
YOU GET AWAY WITH EVERYTHING — WHILE I SUFFER!!
STAB
MAYBE SHE'S RIGHT . . .
MAYBE IT *IS* ALL MY FAULT . . .
I. . . I HAVE TO THINK ABOUT THIS. . .
WELL?! DON'T YOU HAVE ANYTHING TO SAY?!
TINK
MM, THAT WAS GOOD!!
WOBBLE OBBLE
UM, MISS . . .?
YEAH ?!
COLA, FRUIT PARFAIT, LEMON SODA, AND FRENCH CUSTARD A LA MODE COMES TO . . . ¥1,500.
WHICH OF YOU WILL BE PAYING THE. . .
I AM, FOOL !!
I'M NOT LETTING HER OFF THE HOOK UNTIL JUDGMENT DAY!!

PART THIRTEEN
A VERY NARROW ESCAPE

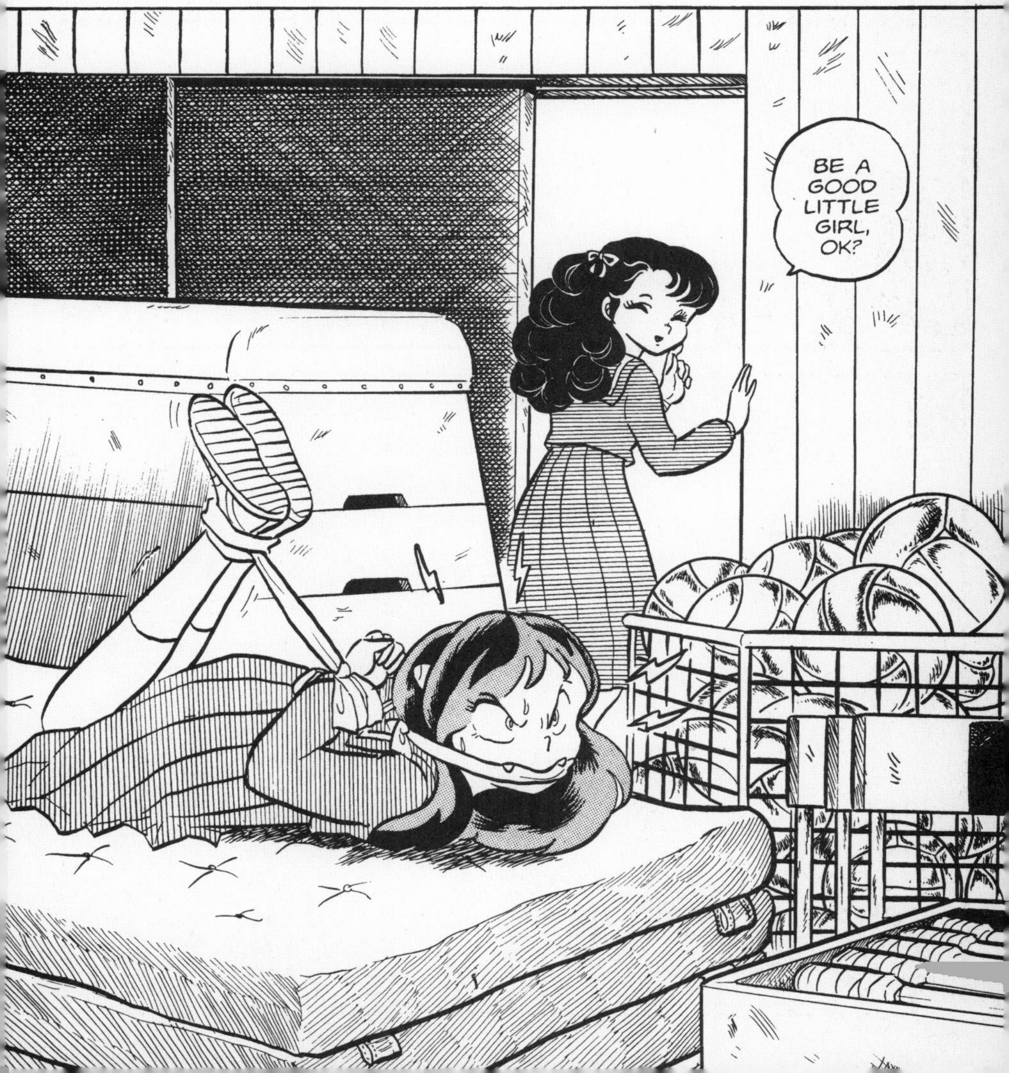
BE A GOOD LITTLE GIRL, OK?

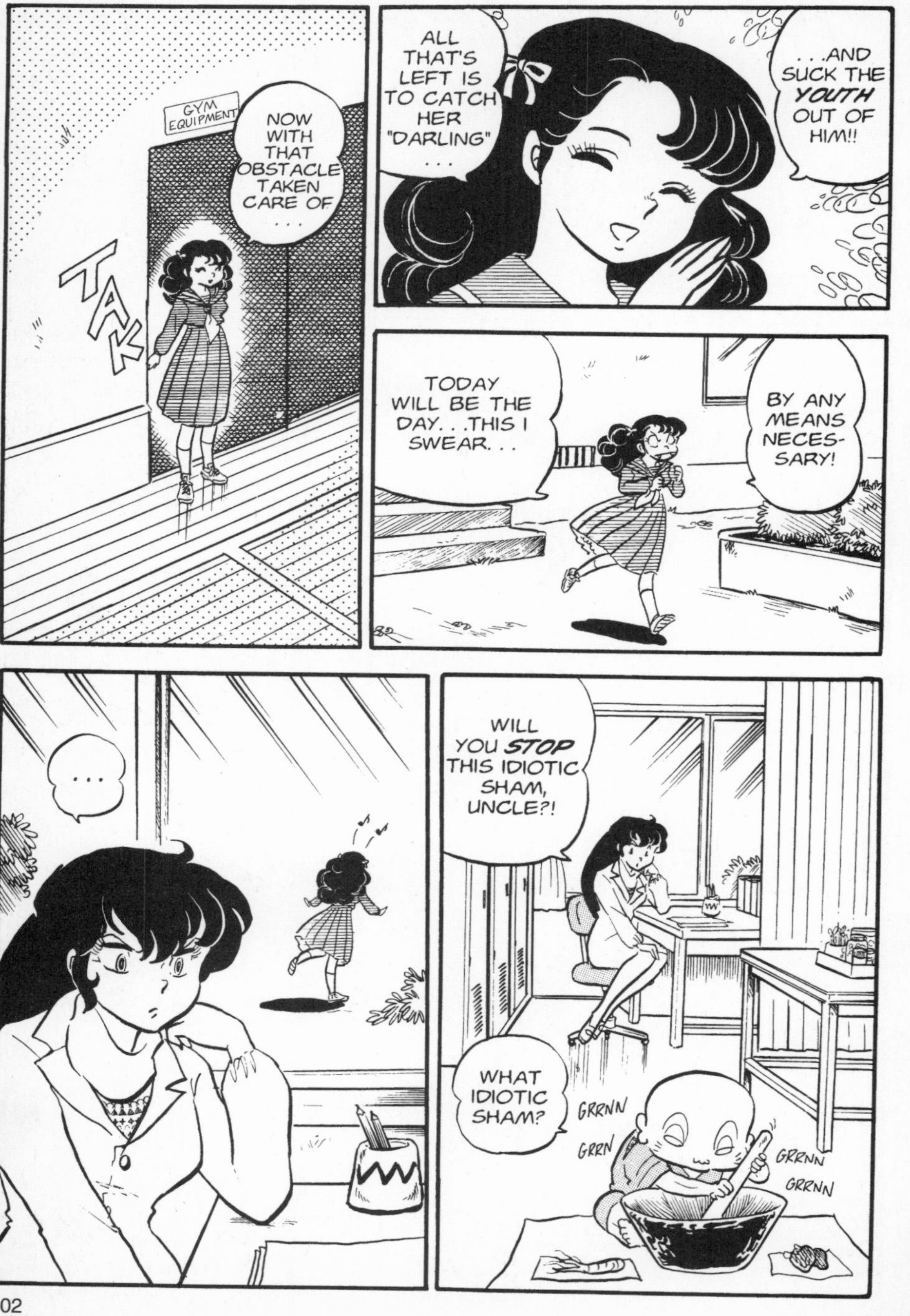
GYM EQUIPMENT
NOW WITH THAT OBSTACLE TAKEN CARE OF . . .
TAK
ALL THAT'S LEFT IS TO CATCH HER "DARLING" . . .
. . .AND SUCK THE YOUTH OUT OF HIM!!
TODAY WILL BE THE DAY. . .THIS I SWEAR. . .
BY ANY MEANS NECES-SARY!
. . .
WILL YOU STOP THIS IDIOTIC SHAM, UNCLE?!
WHAT IDIOTIC SHAM?
GRRNN
GRRN
GRRNN
GRRNN

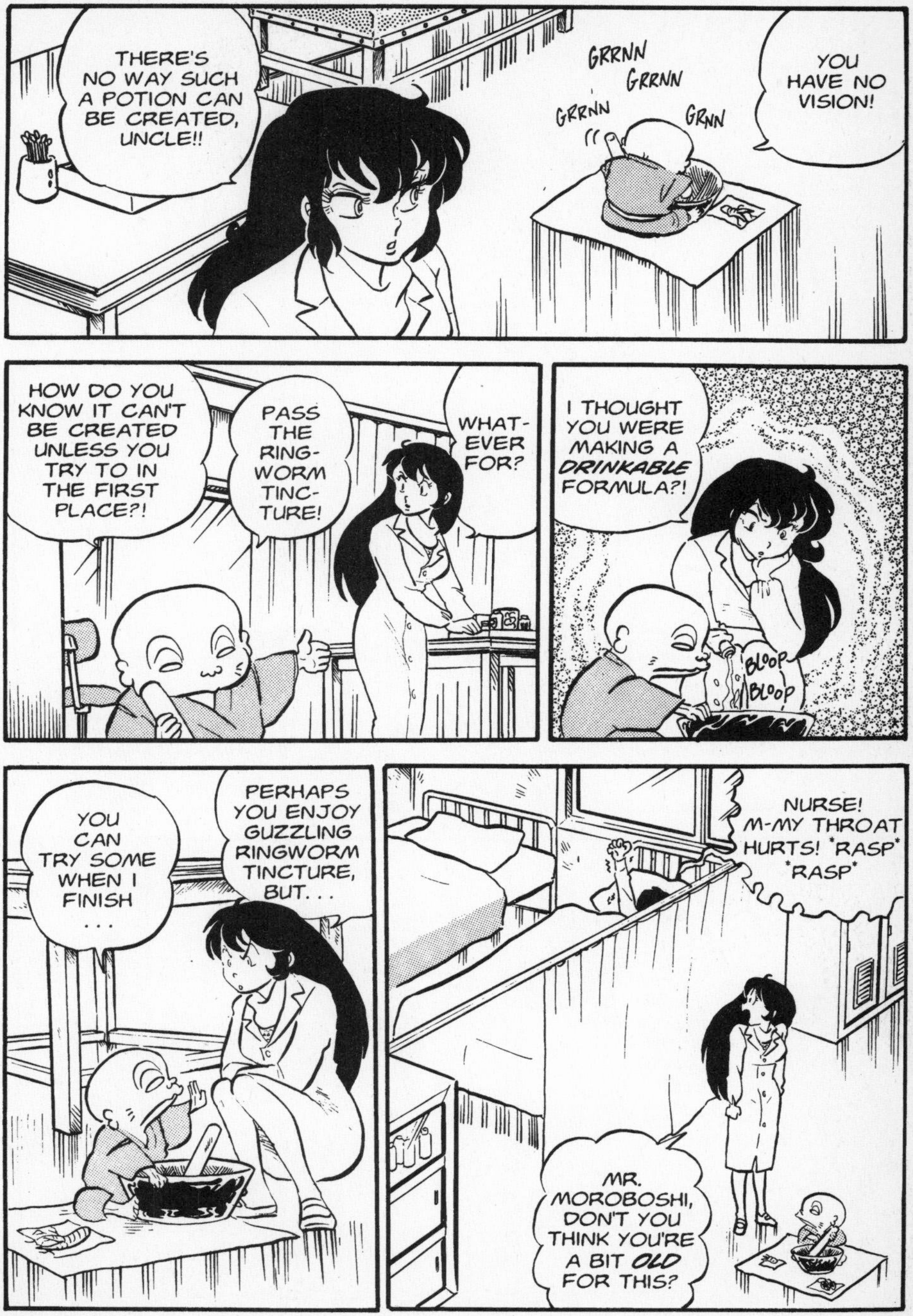
THERE'S NO WAY SUCH A POTION CAN BE CREATED, UNCLE!!
GRRNN
GRRNN
GRRNN
GRNN
YOU HAVE NO VISION!
HOW DO YOU KNOW IT CAN'T BE CREATED UNLESS YOU TRY TO IN THE FIRST PLACE?!
PASS THE RING-WORM TINC-TURE!
WHAT-EVER FOR?
I THOUGHT YOU WERE MAKING A DRINKABLE FORMULA?!
BLOOP
BLOOP
YOU CAN TRY SOME WHEN I FINISH . . .
PERHAPS YOU ENJOY GUZZLING RINGWORM TINCTURE, BUT. . .
NURSE! M-MY THROAT HURTS! *RASP* *RASP*
MR. MOROBOSHI, DON'T YOU THINK YOU'RE A BIT OLD FOR THIS?

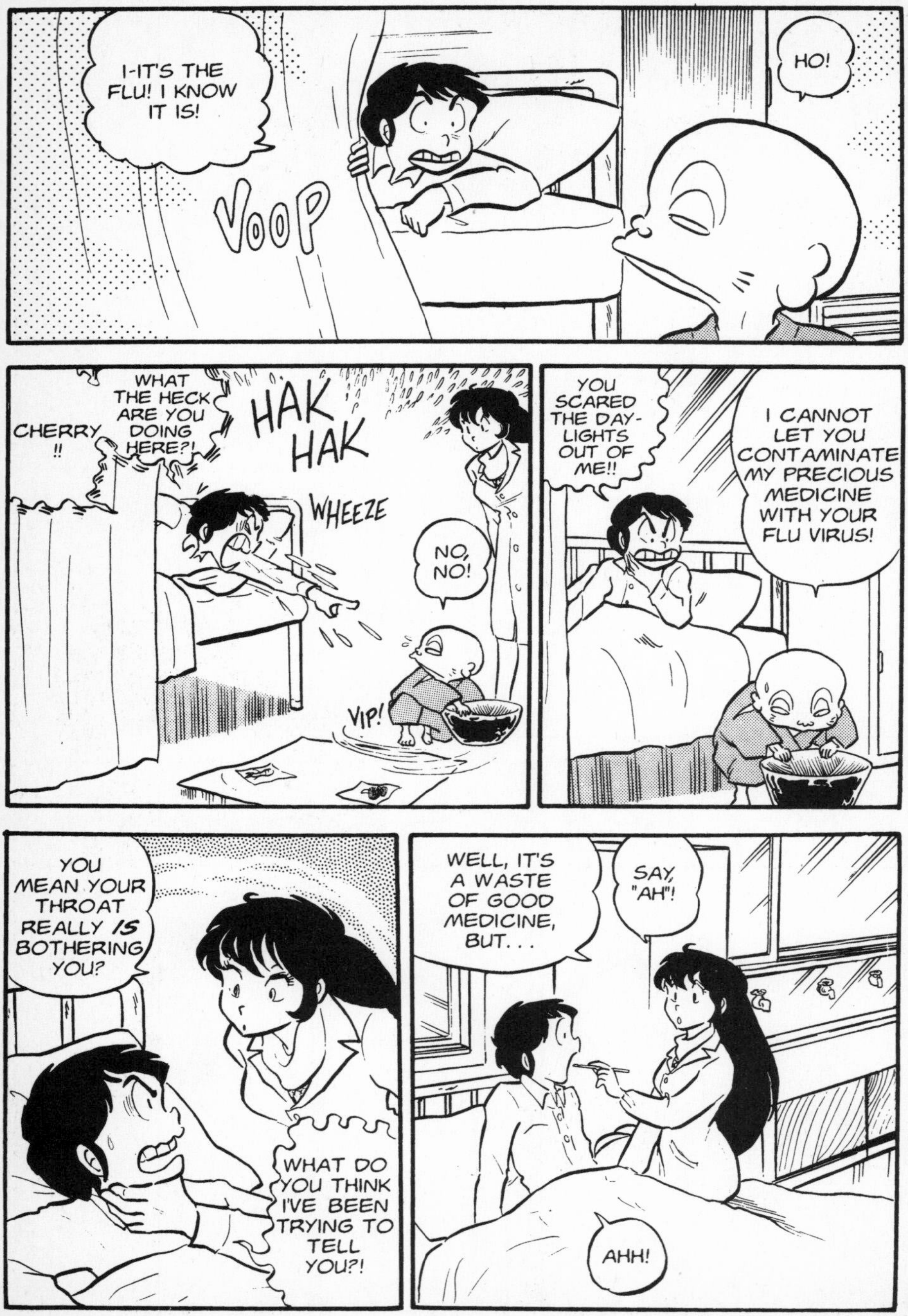
I-IT'S THE FLU! I KNOW IT IS!
VOOP
HO!
CHERRY !!
WHAT THE HECK ARE YOU DOING HERE?!
HAK HAK
WHEEZE
NO, NO!
VIP!
YOU SCARED THE DAY-LIGHTS OUT OF ME!!
I CANNOT LET YOU CONTAMINATE MY PRECIOUS MEDICINE WITH YOUR FLU VIRUS!
YOU MEAN YOUR THROAT REALLY *IS* BOTHERING YOU?
WHAT DO YOU THINK I'VE BEEN TRYING TO TELL YOU?!
WELL, IT'S A WASTE OF GOOD MEDICINE, BUT. . .
SAY, "AH"!
AHH!

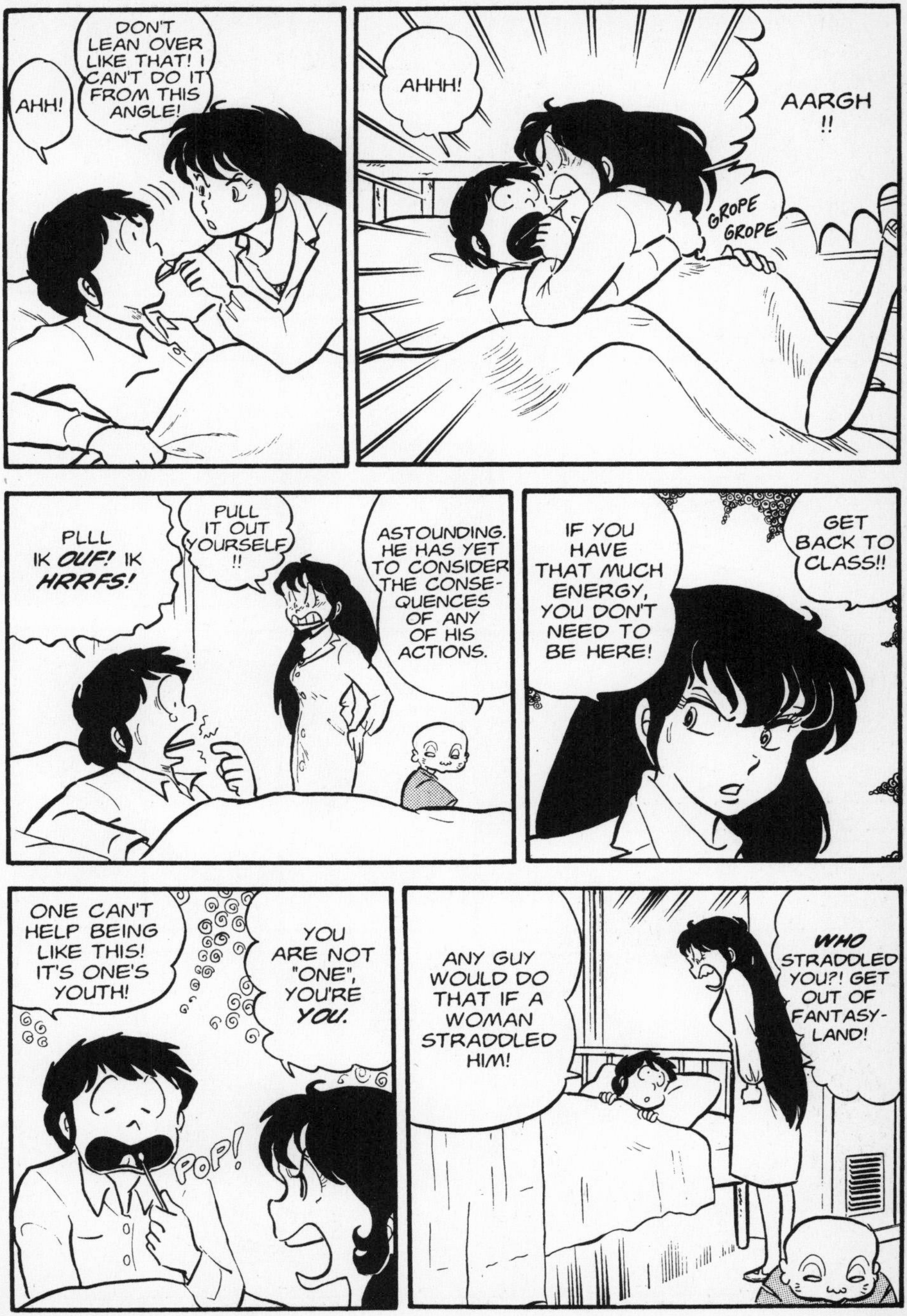
AHH!
DON'T LEAN OVER LIKE THAT! I CAN'T DO IT FROM THIS ANGLE!
AHHH!
AARGH !!
GROPE GROPE
PLLL IK OUF! IK HRRFS!
PULL IT OUT YOURSELF !!
ASTOUNDING. HE HAS YET TO CONSIDER THE CONSE-QUENCES OF ANY OF HIS ACTIONS.
IF YOU HAVE THAT MUCH ENERGY, YOU DON'T NEED TO BE HERE!
GET BACK TO CLASS!!
ONE CAN'T HELP BEING LIKE THIS! IT'S ONE'S YOUTH!
YOU ARE NOT "ONE", YOU'RE YOU.
POP!
ANY GUY WOULD DO THAT IF A WOMAN STRADDLED HIM!
WHO STRADDLED YOU?! GET OUT OF FANTASY-LAND!

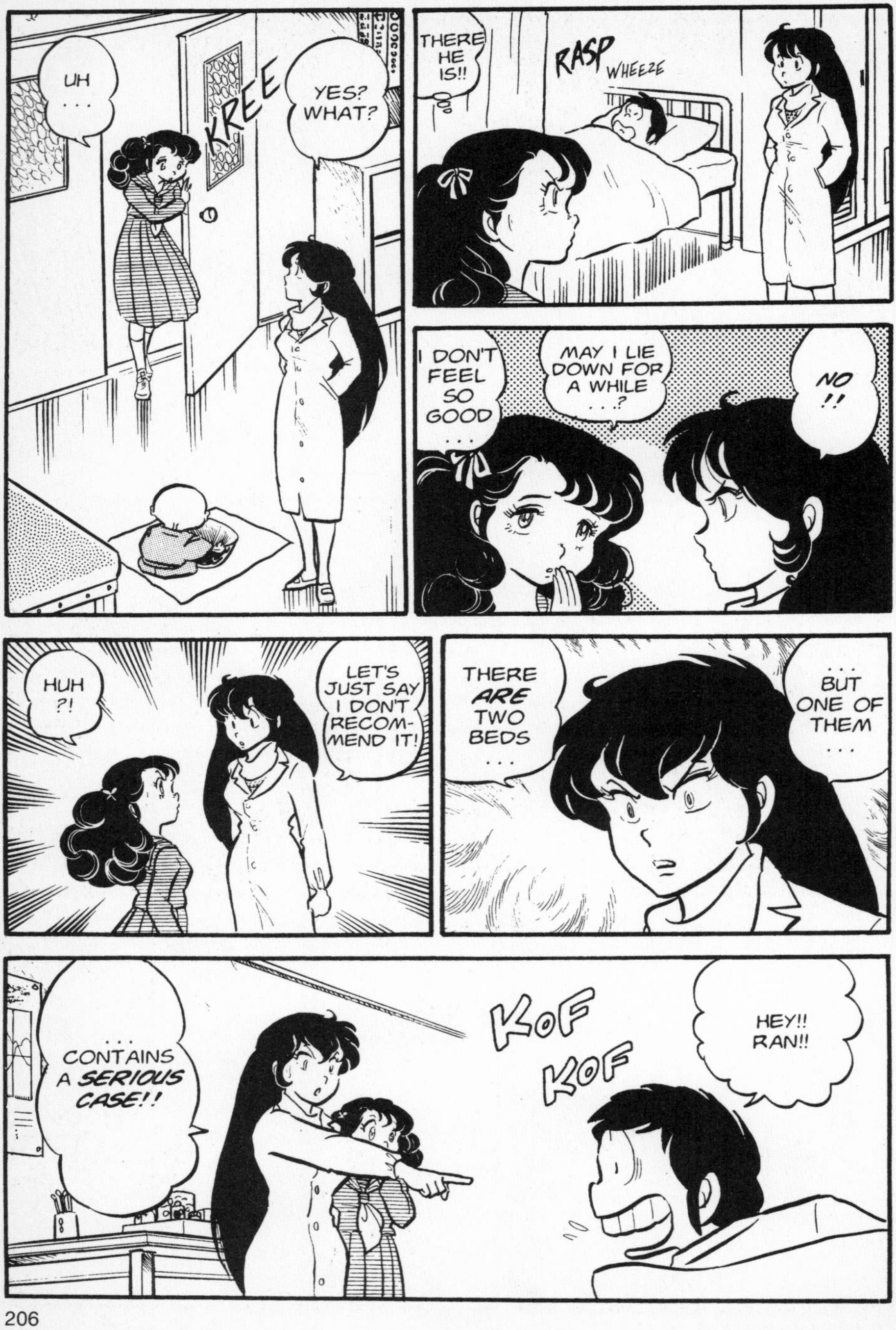
UH . . .
KREE
YES? WHAT?
THERE HE IS!!
RASP WHEEZE
I DON'T FEEL SO GOOD . . .
MAY I LIE DOWN FOR A WHILE . . .?
NO !!
HUH ?!
LET'S JUST SAY I DON'T RECOMMEND IT!
THERE ARE TWO BEDS . . .
. . . BUT ONE OF THEM . . .
. . . CONTAINS A SERIOUS CASE!!
KOF KOF
HEY!! RAN!!

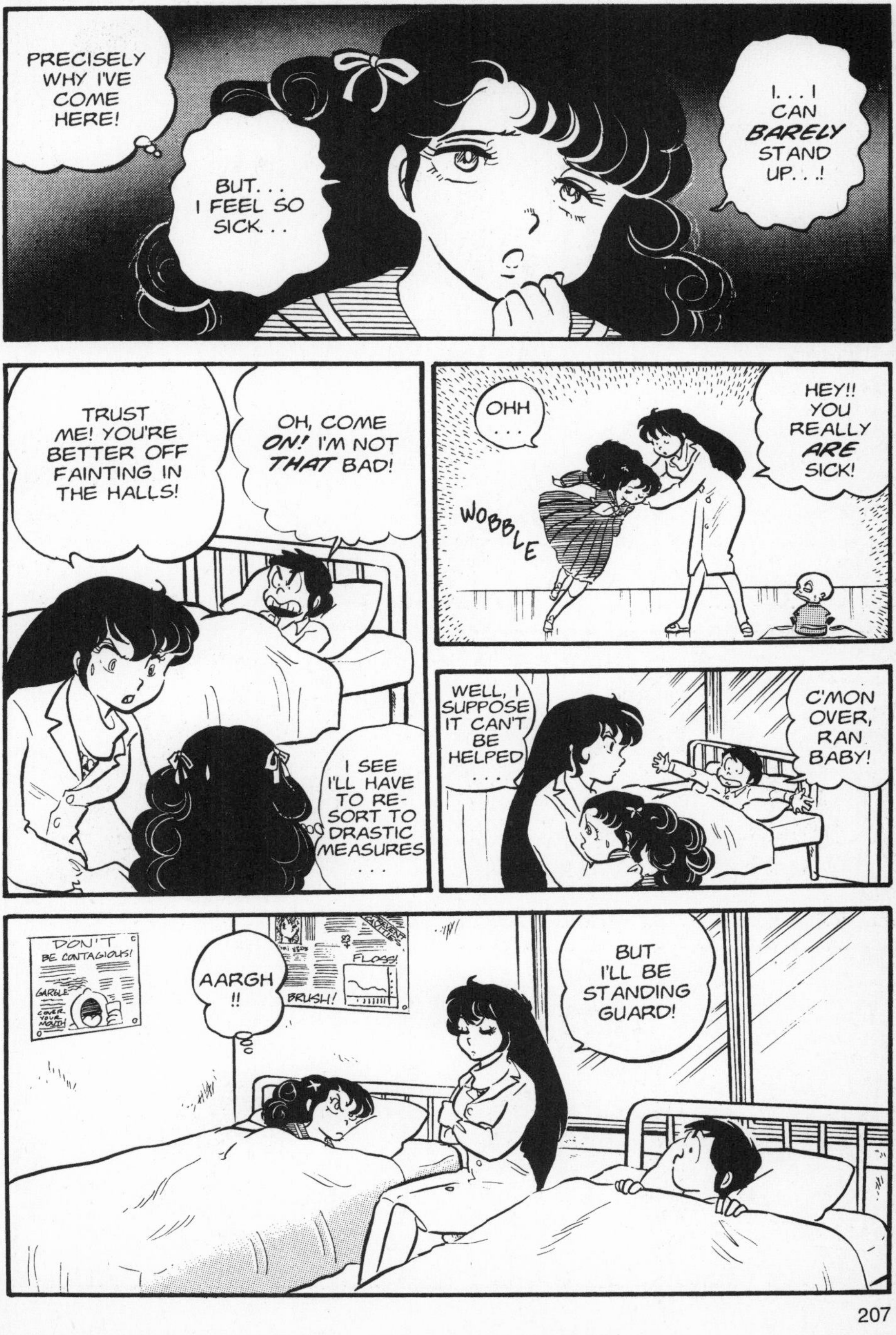
PRECISELY WHY I'VE COME HERE!
BUT... I FEEL SO SICK...
I... I CAN *BARELY* STAND UP...!
TRUST ME! YOU'RE BETTER OFF FAINTING IN THE HALLS!
OH, COME *ON!* I'M NOT *THAT* BAD!
I SEE I'LL HAVE TO RE-SORT TO DRASTIC MEASURES...
OHH...
WOBBLE
HEY!! YOU REALLY *ARE* SICK!
WELL, I SUPPOSE IT CAN'T BE HELPED...
C'MON OVER, RAN BABY!
DON'T BE CONTAGIOUS!
GARGLE
COVER YOUR MOUTH
FLOSS!
BRUSH!
AARGH!!
BUT I'LL BE STANDING GUARD!

DO YOU REALLY THINK I'M *THAT* SLEAZY?!

TAKE A GUESS.

OH, GREAT! NOT ONLY AM I SICK, I'M BEING TREATED LIKE SOME LECHEROUS PERVERT!

RASP WHEEZE

OH, YES, *SO* SICK.

GET YOUR *HANDS* OFF THERE!

YOW!

IT'S JUST MY *YOUTH!*

I CAN'T TAKE MY EYES OFF YOU FOR EVEN A SECOND!!

RRG RRG

...

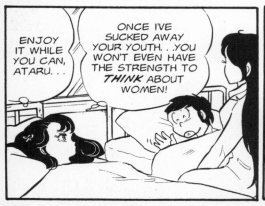

ENJOY IT WHILE YOU CAN, ATARU...

ONCE I'VE SUCKED AWAY YOUR YOUTH...YOU WON'T EVEN HAVE THE STRENGTH TO *THINK* ABOUT WOMEN!

BUT FIRST ...I HAVE TO GET HER OUT OF THE WAY!!

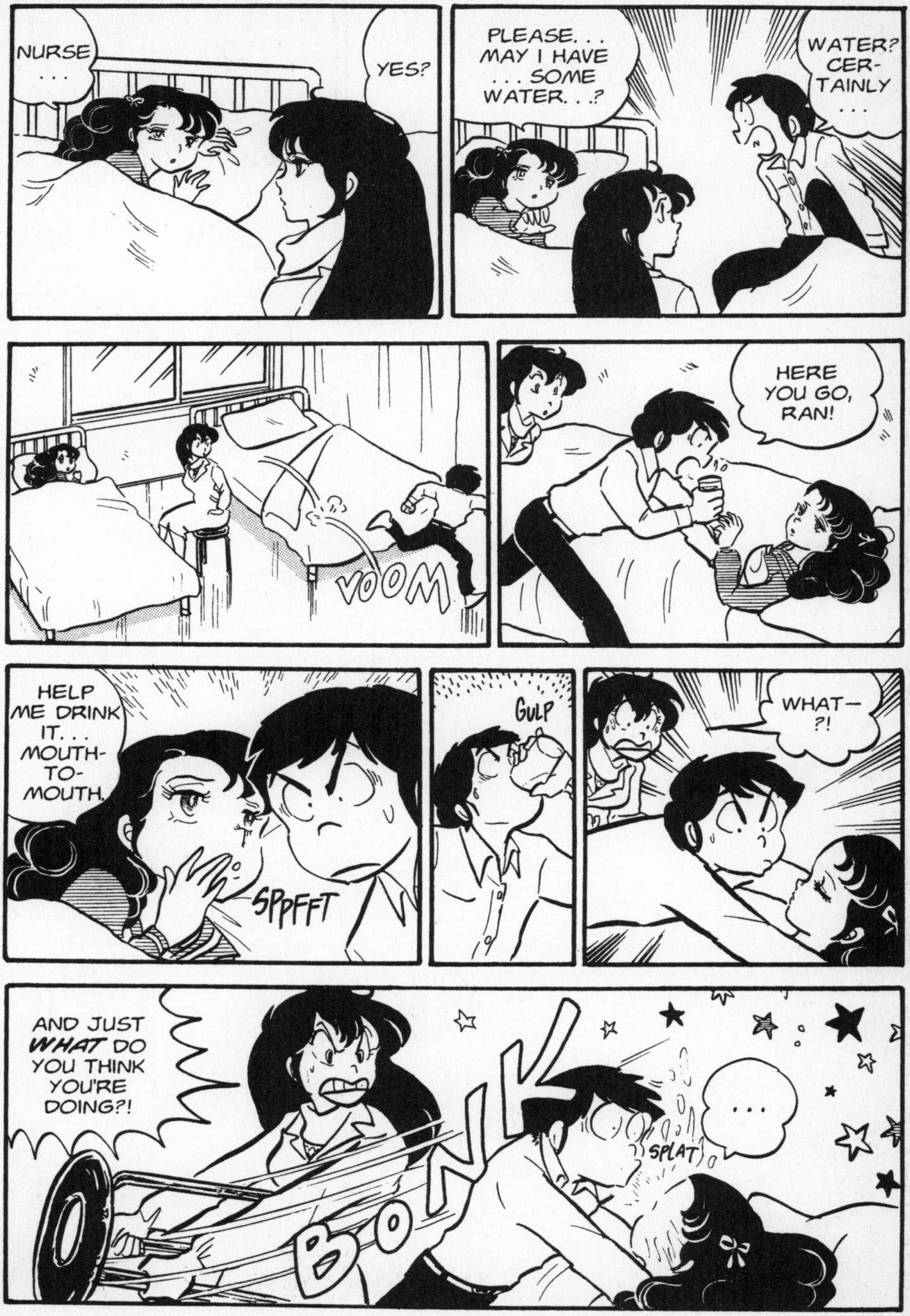
NURSE . . .
YES?
PLEASE. . . MAY I HAVE . . . SOME WATER. . .?
WATER? CER-TAINLY . . .
VOOM
HERE YOU GO, RAN!
HELP ME DRINK IT. . . MOUTH-TO-MOUTH.
SPPFFT
GULP
WHAT—?!
AND JUST WHAT DO YOU THINK YOU'RE DOING?!
BONK
SPLAT
. . .

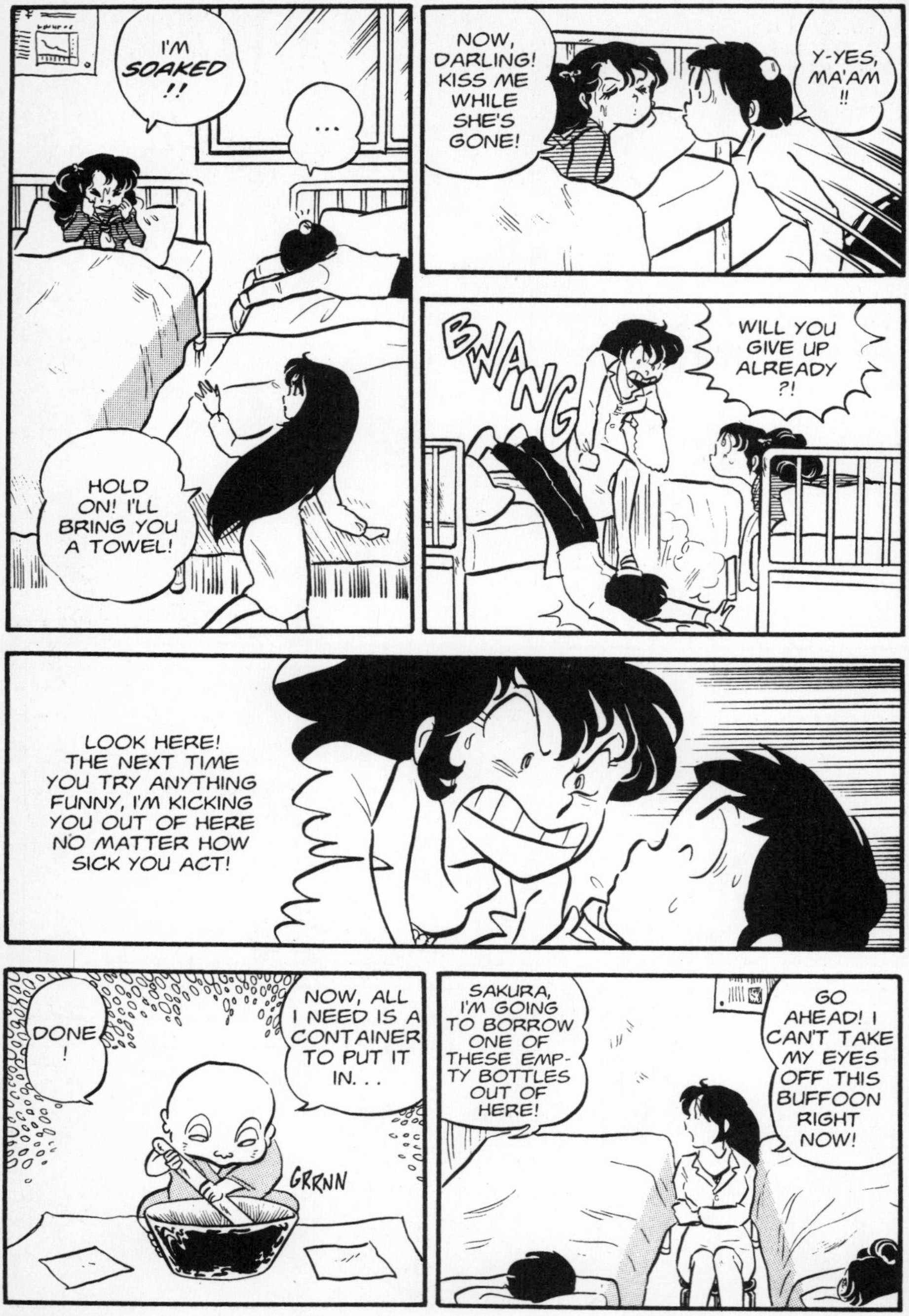
I'M SOAKED !!
...
HOLD ON! I'LL BRING YOU A TOWEL!
NOW, DARLING! KISS ME WHILE SHE'S GONE!
Y-YES, MA'AM !!
BWANG
WILL YOU GIVE UP ALREADY ?!
LOOK HERE! THE NEXT TIME YOU TRY ANYTHING FUNNY, I'M KICKING YOU OUT OF HERE NO MATTER HOW SICK YOU ACT!
DONE !
NOW, ALL I NEED IS A CONTAINER TO PUT IT IN. . .
GRRNN
SAKURA, I'M GOING TO BORROW ONE OF THESE EMP-TY BOTTLES OUT OF HERE!
GO AHEAD! I CAN'T TAKE MY EYES OFF THIS BUFFOON RIGHT NOW!

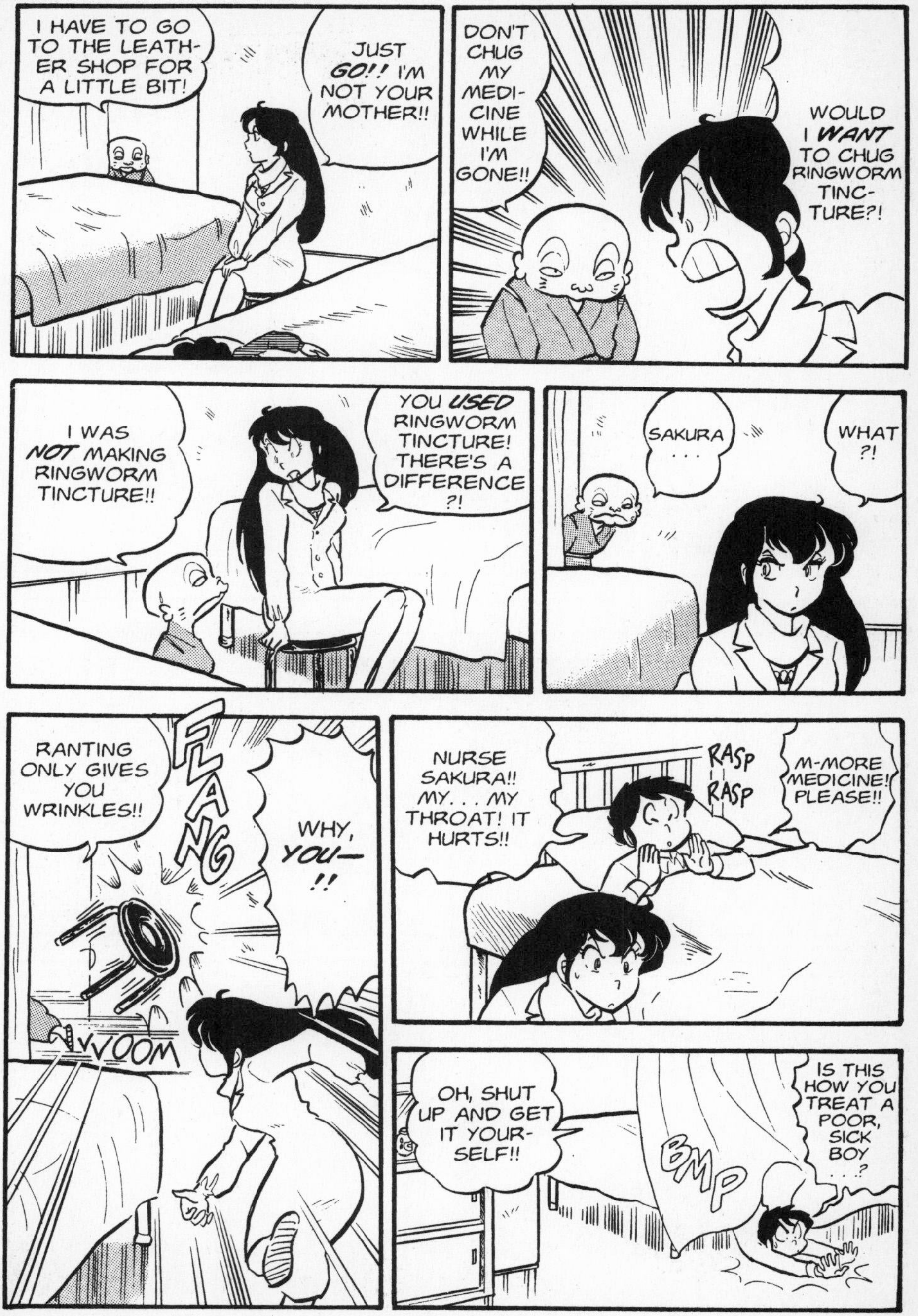
I HAVE TO GO TO THE LEATHER SHOP FOR A LITTLE BIT!
JUST GO!! I'M NOT YOUR MOTHER!!
DON'T CHUG MY MEDICINE WHILE I'M GONE!!
WOULD I WANT TO CHUG RINGWORM TINCTURE?!
I WAS NOT MAKING RINGWORM TINCTURE!!
YOU USED RINGWORM TINCTURE! THERE'S A DIFFERENCE ?!
SAKURA . . .
WHAT ?!
RANTING ONLY GIVES YOU WRINKLES!!
FLANG
WHY, YOU— !!
VVOOM
NURSE SAKURA!! MY. . . MY THROAT! IT HURTS!!
RASP RASP
M-MORE MEDICINE! PLEASE!!
OH, SHUT UP AND GET IT YOURSELF!!
BMP
IS THIS HOW YOU TREAT A POOR, SICK BOY . . .?

WHICH ONE IS IT?

THE ONE LABELED "THROAT MEDICINE," DOLT!

THIS MUST BE IT...

I'LL JUST CHUG THE WHOLE THING!!

GLMP
GLMP
GLMP
GLMP

GAG

BLEAH! BLEAH! BLEAH!

G-G-GONNA... HURRRL...!

?

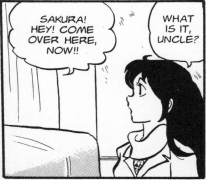

SAKURA! HEY! COME OVER HERE, NOW!!

WHAT IS IT, UNCLE?

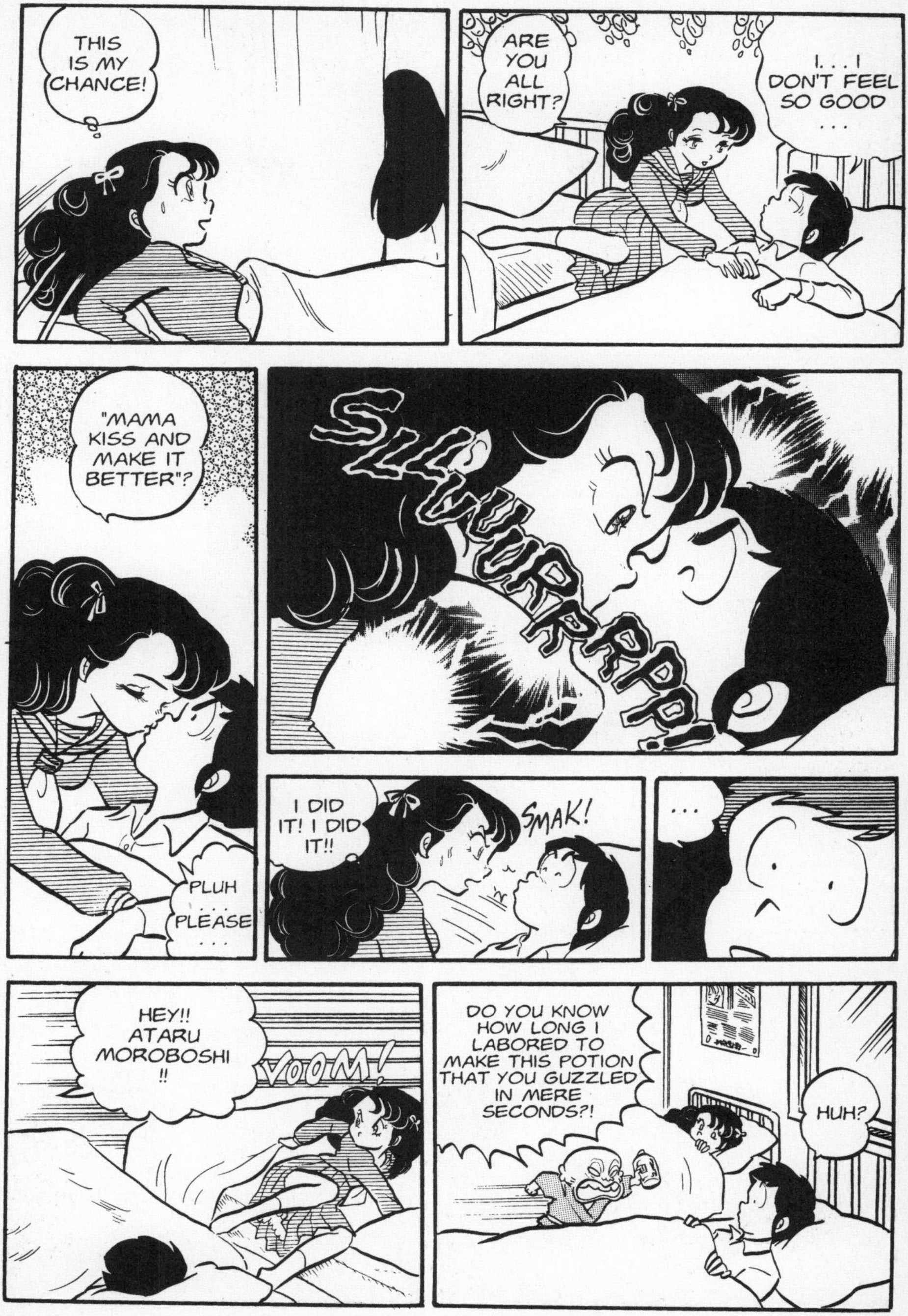
THIS IS MY CHANCE!
ARE YOU ALL RIGHT?
I. . . I DON'T FEEL SO GOOD . . .
"MAMA KISS AND MAKE IT BETTER"?
PLUH . . . PLEASE . . .
SLLLUURRPPP!
I DID IT! I DID IT!!
SMAK!
. . .
HEY!! ATARU MOROBOSHI !!
VOOM!
DO YOU KNOW HOW LONG I LABORED TO MAKE THIS POTION THAT YOU GUZZLED IN MERE SECONDS?!
HUH?

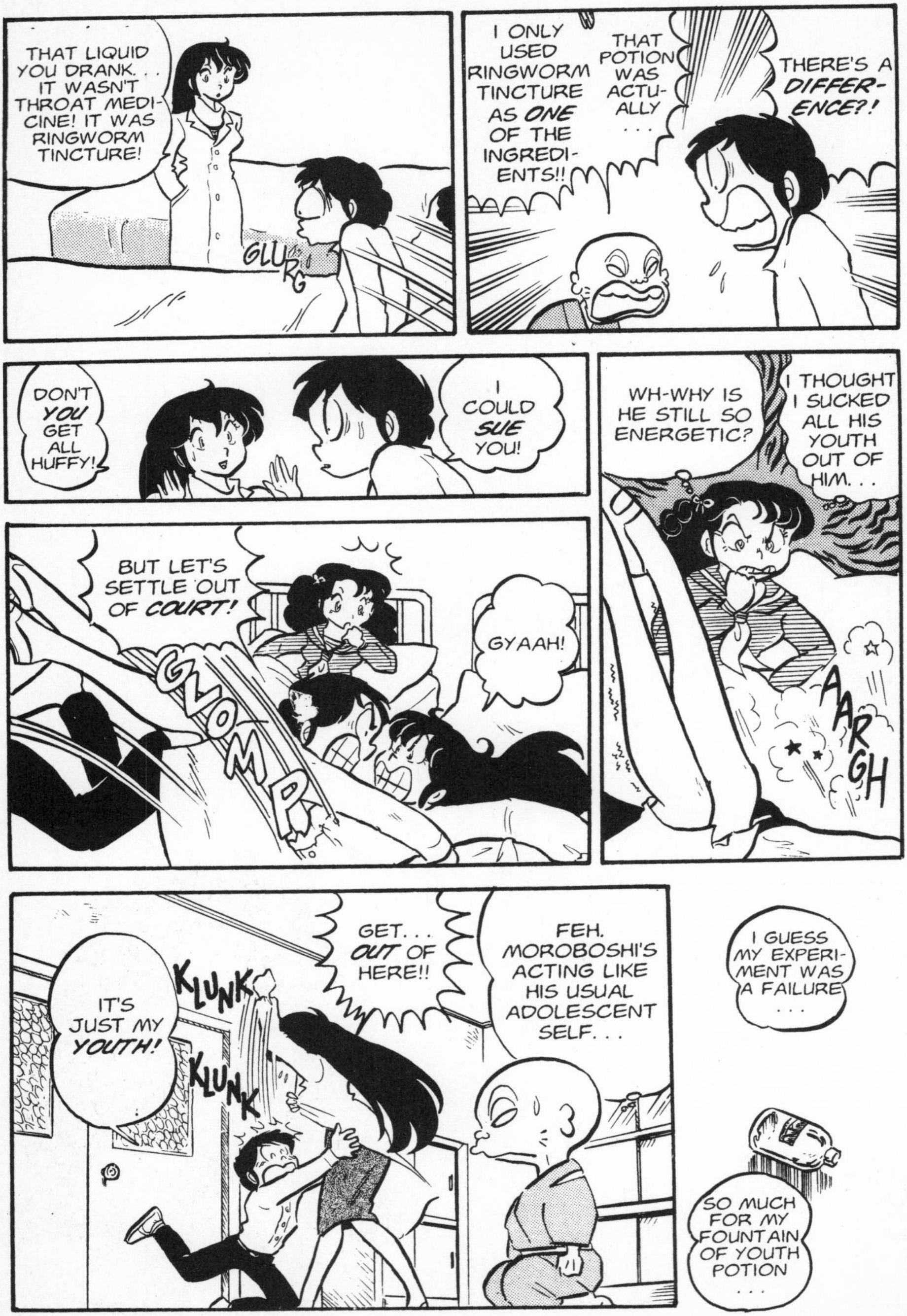
THAT LIQUID YOU DRANK. . . IT WASN'T THROAT MEDICINE! IT WAS RINGWORM TINCTURE!
GLURG
I ONLY USED RINGWORM TINCTURE AS ONE OF THE INGREDIENTS!!
THAT POTION WAS ACTUALLY . . .
THERE'S A DIFFERENCE?!
DON'T YOU GET ALL HUFFY!
I COULD SUE YOU!
BUT LET'S SETTLE OUT OF COURT!
GVOMP
GYAAH!
WH-WHY IS HE STILL SO ENERGETIC?
I THOUGHT I SUCKED ALL HIS YOUTH OUT OF HIM. . .
AARGH
IT'S JUST MY YOUTH!
KLUNK
KLUNK
GET. . . OUT OF HERE!!
FEH. MOROBOSHI'S ACTING LIKE HIS USUAL ADOLESCENT SELF. . .
I GUESS MY EXPERIMENT WAS A FAILURE . . .
SO MUCH FOR MY FOUNTAIN OF YOUTH POTION . . .

TO BE CONTINUED!